A Society without Fathers or Husbands

A Society without Fathers or Husbands

The Na of China

Cai Hua

Translated by Asti Hustvedt

ZONE BOOKS · NEW YORK

2001

The publisher would like to thank both the Centre National du Livre at the French Ministry of Culture for its assistance and the author for his careful review of the translation.

© 2001 Urzone, Inc.
611 Broadway, Suite 608
New York, NY 10012

Originally published in France as *Une Société sans père ni mari: Les Na de Chine* © 1997 Presses Universitaires de France.

Printed in the United States of America.

Distributed by The MIT Press,
Cambridge, Massachusetts, and London, England

Library of Congress Cataloging-in-Publication Data

Hua, Cai.
    [Une société sans père ni mari. English]
    A society without fathers or husbands : the Na of China / Cai Hua: translated by Asti Hustvedt.
       p.   cm.
    Includes bibliographical references.
    ISBN 1-890951-12-9.
    1. Naxi, (Chinese people). 2. Matriliny — China — Yunnan Province. 3. Ethnology — China — Yunnan Province. I. Hustvedt, Asti. II. Title.
DS731.N39H8313 2001
306.8'089'951—dc21   99–10528

                                              CIP

For my parents and Wenjin

Contents

Acknowledgments

The French Ministries of Foreign Affairs and Cultural Affairs, the Fyssen Foundation, and CISS/UNESCO have all financed my research during different stages of this project. The Laboratory of Ethnology and Comparative Sociology at the University of Paris X, Nanterre, directed successively by Annie Lebeuf, Roberte Hamayon, and Raymond Jamous, and the Laboratory of Social Anthropology at the Collège de France, directed by Françoise Héritier and Elisabeth Copet-Rougier, welcomed me and supported me throughout my years of work.

Thanks to the support of Alexander W. Macdonald and Eric de Dampierre, I was able to pursue my studies in ethnology at the University of Paris X, Nanterre. During my first year in France, on Friday afternoons, Eric de Dampierre kindly gave me a private class that introduced me to anthropology. Alexander W. Macdonald directed my master's thesis and my DEA. Kristofer Schipper directed my doctoral dissertation. His understanding and patience were valuable to me. Françoise Héritier and Olivier Herrenschmidt guided me during the second year of my master's program and helped me, with sustained attention, to prepare my research. I am grateful to Olivier Herrenschmidt for his written remarks and systematic advice on various points in my thesis. My long stay in the field was conducted under their supervision. I obtained a position as an assistant at the Collège de France on the recommendation of Françoise Héritier, and this allowed me to carry out my fieldwork on the Na. While writing this book, I continually benefited from her advice and encouragement. Olivier Herrenschmidt followed my work very closely and spent much time reading the manuscript, discussing each chapter with me.

Chen Lufan and Ning Chao were of great help while I was in Kunming researching this book.

My stays in Yongning were greatly facilitated by Yang Biao, Luzo Anibima, and A Pitsodgema and the hospitality of the Anibima, Ago, and Imain *lignées*, who opened up their homes to me. While writing my master's thesis, I benefited from the advice of Patrick Menget, Lucie Rault, and Anne Vergati.

I received support, in various forms, from Georges Augustin, Laurent Barry, Marie-Florence Bennes, Pascal Bouchery, Laurence Caillet, Jean Chiocchetti, Clare Cléret, Marie-Andrée Couillard, Roland Goeldner, Jacqueline Gougenheim, Philippe Guilleman, Jean-Pierre Hassoun, Jean Hirigoyen, Colette Kouchner, Solange Lefebvre, Ouiza Loutis, Li Yanmei, Rémi Mathieu, Joseph Parais, Christine Peuteuil, Frank Pieke, Marie-Claire Quiquemelle, Philippe Ramirez, Philippe Roche, Guy Sinelle, Joël Thoraval, Priscille Touraille, Françoise de Valence, and Francis Zimmermann.

I thank all of these institutions, professors, colleagues, and friends from the bottom of my heart.

Finally, I must express my gratitude to Claude Lévi-Strauss for reading my master's thesis and my doctoral dissertation and for the advice and encouragement he gave me.

A Note on the Transcription

of Na and Chinese Words

The language spoken by the Na has not yet been studied systematically. In *Naxi yu jianzhi* (The handbook of the Naxi language), the only linguistic publication that mentions Na, the authors understand it to be one of the six dialects of the Naxi language and cite only a few Na phonemes in passing, while comparing it with other dialects.[1]

While in the field, I gathered and recorded, using the international phonetic alphabet, thirteen vowels, two semi-consonants, and thirty-one consonants. In the present study, I use the following transcription:

The thirteen vowels are transcribed as follows:
ä   a   unrounded open back vowel as in *father*
o   o   rounded half close back vowel as in *close*
i   i   unrounded close central vowel as in *bead*
a   é   rounded half open front vowel as in *hay*
ɛ   ai   unrounded half open front vowel as in *air*
ɨ   ï   unrounded close central vowel as in *she*
ə   e   rounded half close front vowel as in *egg*
u   u   rounded close back vowel as in *room*
ɔ   ao   rounded half close back vowel as in *awe*

ɛ̃   in nasalized unrounded half open front vowel as in *matin* in
    French

ĩ   ing nasalized unrounded close central vowel as in *sing*

õ   on nasalized rounded half close back vowel as in *on* in French

ɔ̃   ong nasalized half close back vowel as in *song*

The two semi-consonants:

w   w voiced bilabial continuant as in *way*

j   i, when *i* is placed between a consonant and a vowel or in
    front of a vowel. In kinship terminology and village names,
    j is transcribed with *y*.

The thirty-one consonants:

p   p voiceless bilabial stop as in *put*

t   t voiceless alveolar or dental stop as in *tot*

k   k voiceless velar stop as in *kit*

b   b voiced bilabial stop as in *bat*

d   d voiced alveolar or dental stop as in *dot*

g   g voiced velar stop as in *got*

f   f voiceless labiodental fricative as in *fop*

s   s voiceless alveolar fricative (hisser) as in *sap*

ʃ   sh voiceless alveolar fricative (husser) as in *shut*

z   z voiced alveolar fricative as in *zap*

ʒ   j voiced alveolar fricative as in *jour* in French

l   l dental or aveolar non-fricative lateral as in *lull*

m   m bilabial nasal as in *mom*

n   n alveolar nasal as in *not*

ɲ   ng velar nasal as in *rang*

h   h voiceless pharyngeal fricative as in guttural *h* in pinyin

t   th voiceless retroflex stop

d   dh voiced retroflex stop

ɭ   lh retroflex non-fricative lateral

dʒ   dg voiced alveolar or dental fricative as in *judge*

tʃ ch voiceless dental stop + voiceless alveolar fricative as in *church*

dz dz voiced dental stop + voiced alveolar fricative as in *z* in pinyin

ts ts voiceless dental stop + voiceless alveolar fricative as in *c* in pinyin

dZ dZ voiced dental stop + voiced palatal fricative as in *j* in pinyin

tç tç voiceless dental stop + voiceless palatal fricative as in *q* in pinyin

ç   ç voiceless palatal fricative as in *x* in pinyin

z   Z voiced palatal fricative

r   r voiced uvular fricative as in *r* in French

R   R alveolar lateral flap as in *run*

ŋ   ng velar nasal

ȼ   hl voiceless dental or alveolar lateral fricative as in *hlamba* in Kafiri

For the Chinese transcription, I follow the pinyin.

In figures throughout the book, I use the following symbols:

△	male
⚠	deceased male
○	female
∅	deceased female
	male or female
— or ⊔	visit relationship
=	cohabitation relationship
⠿ or ⊔	marriage relationship
⊓	sibling link
|	link between generations
⋮	adoption relationship

Introduction

When reading ancient Chinese texts, known for their richness as well as their age, one sometimes comes across notes that at first seem indecipherable. In *Dian lue*, for example, under the subtitle "The Cuan,"[1] Xie Zhaozhe, an author from the Ming dynasty, writes: "In this day and age, the various groups of the Cuan have spread out to the various prefectures of the Dian and live there in steep mountainous regions." There, he continues, "custom has it that husband and wife do not see each other during the day but share the same bed at night. The children do not see their father until they are ten years old. The wives and the concubines are not jealous of each other."[2] What a strange way of life! If the husband and the wife do not see each other during the day, where do they eat? Where do they work? How do they spend their days? And where do they sleep? Apparently, they spend the night together in the husband's house, for if they did not do so, it would be hard to imagine how the children, who must live with their mother, would not see their father until the age of ten. If this is the case, why does the father not feel the desire to see his children? If jealousy is a fundamental human emotion, how is it that the wife and the concubines are not jealous of each other? All of this remains extremely enigmatic!

To what ethnic group do the Cuan belong? A comment made by Xie Zhaozhe later might serve as a clue: "The Cuan who lived in Lijiang and in the region bordering Sichuan were called Mo-so."

Among the diverse groups that the Han (the ethnic majority of China) refer to as Mo-so, those that live in Yongning and its surrounding areas refer to themselves as Na.[3] They are mountain farmers and have a population of approximately 30 thousand. Even today, women and men from this ethnic group freely engage in sexual relations with several partners and change them whenever they so desire. The man visits the woman at night in her house, where she lives with her sisters and brothers from the different generations of her *lignée*,[4] and in the morning, he returns to his own *lignée*'s house, the habitat that constitutes the exclusive economic center of his work, production, and consumption.

There is no economic bond between the partners. The children born of this sexual commerce will be a part, invariably, of the mother's *lignée*, whose members see to their upbringing without any intervention whatsoever from the genitor. He is only "identified" by his resemblance to the child. Sometimes, since a woman has different sexual partners, he is not even known. Moreover, I have not found any term that would cover the notion of father in the Na language. Their terminology for kinship is strictly consanguineal and matrilineal. The transmission of inheritance is carried out, from one generation to the next, collectively.

The visits, as modalities of sexual life, are of two types: the furtive and the conspicuous. In addition to these two modalities, cohabitation (or concubinage in the traditional sense) and marriage are also present in this society. However, the majority of the population lives exclusively according to the modality of the visit, and those that follow the modalities of cohabitation and marriage engage in furtive visits at the same time.

Xie Zhaozhe must have heard about or read accounts of the

customs of the Mo-so, which were interpreted according to the values of the narrators. The same can be said about other authors from various eras. Fan Ye, for example, in a chapter titled "The Ethnic Groups of the Southwest" in *Houhan shu*, the Chinese annals of the years A.D. 25–220, relates the following: in Wen-jiang, north of Sichuan, "women are superior, the group of relatives is constituted of those of maternal lineage. When someone dies, they burn the corpse."[5] In *Yunnan zhilue* (Monographic account of the Yunnan), Li Jing, an author from the Yuan dynasty (1279–1368), reports: "The Mo-so ethnic group lives north of Dali at the Tibetan border and on the banks of the Jingsha River.... The women wear their hair shorn to the level of their eyebrows and wear woolen threads instead of skirts. They are not ashamed to leave their sexual parts exposed. Once married, they no longer have any sexual taboos."[6]

Yanyuan xianzhi (Account of the Yanyuan District) notes: "The licentious customs of the Yanyuan are such that the women are usually not given in marriage."[7] *Yanyuan gaikuan* (Records of Yan-yuan) states: "None of the inhabitants of Zuo-suo (the region neighboring Yongning, in the Yanyuan District) have formal marriages. They recognize the mother but do not know of the existence of the father. Given that such customs have been with them since ancient times, they do not find them bizarre. They are joyous and have the habit of dancing together in a large group of men and women. Many merchants from far away, when passing through the region, become attached to them and spend their entire fortune there. They remain with them until old age and fall sick and die there."[8]

In his 1936 investigative report, "Yongning jianwen lu" (Notes on Yongning), the linguist Zhou Rucheng writes, in a section entitled "The Marriage of *açia*":

The ethnic group "Luhin" [the Na] from Yongning are a traditional matrilineal society. The people do not marry. In their familial organization, there is only a mother, not a father. The economic authority of the family is in the hands of the women. They alone have the right of inheritance.

The matrimonial style in Yongning is called *açia*. The male and female *açia* can be sexually active together, and their parents and neighbors consider this legitimate. At night, the men go off to the women's homes and return to their own houses the next morning. They are not allowed to bring their *adhu* (girlfriend) to their house to be with their wife. The children born from this type of relationship do not belong to the man. He has no kinship relationship to them and does not oversee their upbringing.

The relationship between *açia* is innocent, pure, and entirely free. Once they make the decision, by themselves, to love, they delight only in spiritual pleasure, not in material pleasure. In this way, a great number of conflicts are avoided. The family is very united and happy, since there is no fighting between husband and wife, no quarrels between father and son, no hatred between sisters-in-law (the wives of the brothers) or between mother-in-law and daughter-in-law. The love between a mother and a daughter in their own home is everlasting.

Açia have the freedom to stay together if they get along well and to separate when they are no longer happy with each other without this posing any problem.

The Lamaist monks also have the right to *açia* relationships. This is not forbidden by religious law.[9]

Two westerners, an Italian and an American, have also vaguely noted the customs of the Na.

In *Devisement du monde (The Travels of Marco Polo)*, Marco Polo relates:

They do not consider it objectionable for a foreigner, or any other man, to have his way with their wives, daughters, sisters, or any other women in their home. They consider it a great benefit, in fact, saying that their gods and idols will be disposed in their favor and offer them material goods in great abundance. This is why they are so generous with their women toward foreigners. When a man of this region sees a foreigner come to his house to find lodging or anything else, he happily and joyously welcomes him. He swiftly goes to fetch his wife and orders her scrupulously to fulfill the foreigner's wishes. And then he goes off to the fields or his vineyards and does not return as long as the foreigner remains in the house. Many times, a foreigner has wallowed in bed for three or four days with a poor sap's wife. As soon as the master of the house has left, the foreigner indicates that he is there by hanging his hat or some other article in the window or on the courtyard door; this is a sign that he is inside. As long as the husband sees this sign on his home, he dares not return, for fear of interrupting their pleasures. All women — wives, daughters, sisters, the whole lot — give themselves freely, with the idea that, in exchange for the favors provided this stranger, their gods and idols will give them eight times as much in herds and the fruits of the earth. When the foreigner has left, the master returns to find his entire household given to rejoicing and hope; he delights in their accounts of their escapades with the foreigner, and all of them offer prayers to their gods! This is done in the entire province of Gaindu, and they see no shame in it. The Great Khan forbids this custom, but it continues to be practiced, for all do so, and none will accuse another.[10]

Later Polo writes, "In this kingdom (Iaci), *the natives do not consider themselves injured when others have connection with their wives* [emphasis mine], provided the act be voluntary on the woman's part; in this case, it is not considered a misfortune but a jackpot."[11]

Joseph F. Rock denounces: "The moral state of the Hli-khin

population is certainly a peculiar one. The word father is unknown, and it is next to an insult to inquire of a Hli-khin boy as to the whereabouts of his father. They all say they have no father. They all possess an *A-gv* (maternal uncle); this may be the brother of their mother or their actual father, without their being certain who their father is. They know and acknowledge only an *A-gv*.... Furthermore, the reverse of Chinese marital relations prevails among the lay population. In Yung-ning it is the woman who remains in the home, and she takes unto herself a man as husband whom she keeps as long as he works, and as long as she enjoys his presence. She can send him away at any time, and take unto herself another husband. Her brother, if she has one, may remain with her and he takes the place of the father, and it is he who is addressed as *A-gv*. The result of this promiscuous sexual intercourse is an enormous amount of syphilis and other venereal diseases. The moral standard of Yung-ning is thus anything but high."[12]

These authors each report, from various perspectives, fragments of the Na customs from this region. Of course, not all of the information cited above is ethnological, far from it! Value judgments abound, and the authors' interpretations, when they appear, are often wrong. The authors almost always confuse the various categories of women. For example, Li Jing and Marco Polo, who both wrote during the Yuan dynasty, believed that the married Na, both husband and wife, had no sexual taboos. But were the visited females actually the wives of the visiting males?

However, in spite of their shortcomings, these accounts serve as certain proof that this form of life dates from long ago and that it is not a narrowly specialized social phenomenon, as is the case of the Nayar of South India who belittled the roles of husband and father. On the whole, these historical recordings seem to show that in ancient times the Na were not the only ethnic group in the region to practice this kind of life.

Even if these studies contain a certain amount of ethnographic value, they have not inspired further research by ethnologists. Zhou Rucheng's work might have prompted further scientific study. However, because of the Second World War and events that took place in China, he was not able to publish his findings until 1986. Serious studies of the Na were simply not available until the 1960s.

Between 1956 and 1963, the permanent committee of the popular National Assembly of China conducted investigations into all of the ethnic minorities in Yunnan in order to draw up a historical survey and a monographic summary for each one. The first systematic fieldwork on the Na was conducted by three Chinese researchers in 1960: Song Enchang, Zhu Baotian, and Wu Guanghu. The kinship that this first exploration uncovered was so interesting that a second team of ten or so ethnologists was sent to the region between the Winter of 1962 and the Spring of 1963.[13] They were divided into several small groups, and each one was assigned one or two cantons in the People's Commune of Yongning.[14] When their research was completed, they published a four-volume report of their findings under the title *Yunnan shen Ninglang Yizu zizhixian Yongning Naxizu Shehui ji qi muquanzhi de diaocha paogao* (Investigative report on the society and matriarchy of the Naxi of Yongning in the autonomous district of the Yi of Ninglang in Yunnan; 1963, 1964, 1977, 1978).

Two studies, one in 1980 and one in 1983, were published as a direct result of these investigations: *Yongning Naxi zu de azhu huyin he muxi jiating* (The *azhu* marriage and the matrilineal family of the Naxi of Yongning) and *Yongning Naxi zu de muxi zhi* (The matrilineal system of the Naxi of Yongning).[15] Their methodology, their analyses, and their conclusions are well represented by the following extract:

From the perspective of historical materialism and dialectical materialism, Engels has shown that the evolution of marriage in man passes through the stages of consanguineal marriage, group marriage, conjugal marriage, until it reaches monogamy. Before the democratic reforms [of 1956], the state of marriage and the family for the Naxi makes one think that they were in the process of passing through, or were about to pass through, this evolution and also makes one think that the origin of the *adhu* (friendship) marriage, foreshadowing the stage of conjugal marriage, can be found, most certainly, in group marriage. Therefore, it is completely natural that there is, in their matrimonial relationships, remnants of group marriage and traces of the matrilineal clan community.[16]

Since the 1970s, in addition to these two books, dozens of discussions and complementary reports have surfaced on the subject. But on the whole, these publications do not significantly differ in their presuppositions.

Because these studies were guided by evolutionism, two inadequacies repeatedly turn up. On the one hand, the researchers did not learn the Na language and therefore missed essential concepts, since the testimonies were filtered through a translator. On the other hand, they failed to treat the realm of kinship exhaustively. Indeed, most of the essential concepts of Na kinship were completely overlooked; even the distinction between the two types of visits went unnoticed. Consequently, while this material represents great progress in comparison with previous work, it remains incomplete and therefore is difficult to use when conducting scientific research.

I discovered the Na in a publication by my colleagues at the Institute of History of the Province of Yunnan, where I worked as a researcher. At the beginning of my studies in the Department of Ethnology and Comparative Sociology at the University of

Paris X, Nanterre, I realized that the concepts of kinship in French and English anthropology were not sufficient to treat this case. I presented these concerns to Professor Eric de Dampierre, and he expressed the first specific scientific interest in this population. With his encouragement, I chose this society as a subject for research.

My first visit to the field was in the summer of 1985. I toured the villages of two provinces in order to understand this ethnic group as it lived in different places. While working on the constitutive elements of kinship, I verified the findings of my predecessors. During the summer of 1986, I returned to the field to examine the questions raised by my research.

At this stage of my work, my hypothesis was the one I had advanced in 1986 and then in 1994, and went as follows: given that cohabitation can only be practiced when a given generation within a *lignée* has no girls, the Na mode of sexual life, represented for the most part by the visit, cannot be considered a marriage, under any definition.[17] Moreover, their kinship terminology, when compared with others', lacks half of the terms for known relations. In other words, no terminology for affines exists. The Na *matrilignée* is made up exclusively of consanguineal relations and is therefore fundamentally different from what we usually refer to as a family.

How can a society function with neither husbands nor fathers? This first hypothesis raised a series of questions. First of all, ethnographic questions: What are the norms of the visit and of cohabitation? How do the Na conceptualize the relationship between the visitor and the visited and the relationship between the cohabitants? Chinese ethnologists believed that it was probably the Na chief who inaugurated the first marriage and that this practice then spread to the aristocrats and the wealthy. The rule of descent for the Na chief is patrilineal. If throughout history the majority of the population has followed the mode of the visit, why and how did the chief adopt marriage rather than continuing to live according to tradition? Is the rule of descent that he follows truly patrilineal? If marriage is the result of the diffusion of another culture, rather than something that was generated from within, did this society once exist without marriage altogether? In other words, if cohabitation is a traditional practice, should it be considered a type of marriage? Given that incest is prohibited in this society, and that most of the *lignées* do not exchange women or men, where and how does reciprocity take place? Finally, how can a society be established only on consanguineal *matrilignées* and not on families?

Next, questions concerning certain anthropological concepts arose. Given that the mode of the visit differs in its essential aspects from the mode of marriage and that the *pater* is lacking, the structure of the purely matrilineal *lignée* differs from that of the limited family. Is it possible to conceive of a more rigid definition for marriage and for the family? Why is it that, according to all available anthropological knowledge, only the Na live without marriage? Are they the exception that confirms the rule? If the answer is yes, which rule are they confirming?

The Na, who are proud of their customs, spoke freely about them to researchers in the 1960s. The publications that resulted from this research created all sorts of problems for the Na, in particular the monogamy campaigns during the Cultural Revolution, which set out to normalize the Na by force. As they say, "once bitten, twice shy." Since then, the Na have carefully avoided revealing anything about their traditions to outsiders.

The people of Yongning keep an eye on strangers, especially researchers. Each time someone comes to the area to gather information about their customs, the villagers immediately inform those in charge. My first trip there was no exception. When I met with a Na official, he warned me straightaway: "The researchers from the 1960s published lies about our customs, they bent the truth." He added: "The people here have already vowed that if they ever set foot in Yongning again, they will kill them. And if that ever happens, we can do nothing to stop them." I tried to explain that the theory that had guided those first researchers was called evolutionism and that my point of view was entirely different, that previous researchers had not understood the Na traditions, and this was only another reason to undertake a new study, in order to make the truth known. After a long discussion, I finally managed to convince him and colleagues.

My third stay in Yongning lasted one year, 1988–1989. According to the investigative reports of my predecessors, the villages belonging to the administrative village of Wenquan, to the northeast of the Yongning basin, have the highest percentage of inhabitants who practice the mode of the visit.[18] My first investigation had confirmed this. I therefore chose as the parameters of my research five villages in this area, which, in November 1989, included 474 people living in sixty-five households.

Thanks to letters of introduction from a vice secretary (a Na) of the Communist Party of China Committee of the Ninglang District, I was taken into the home of a *lignée* whose mistress practiced cohabitation with a retired Na cadre. This *lignée* was made up of two generations. After about four and a half months, the retired cadre expressed his anxiety to me: "You have come to study us. We want to support you. But if you ever publish your study and trouble comes from it, as it did after the study in the sixties, we alone will be compromised. People will say that you lived with our *lignée*, and will accuse us of telling you everything. We cannot take that risk. It would be better for us if you changed houses now. Then we would not be held responsible all by ourselves." This argument was expressed in such a way that it was clear I had no choice. Since I was already familiar with the other villagers, I chose as my second *lignée* a household that spanned four generations. Then, three months later, I took the initiative to go and live with yet another *lignée*, one that had three generations. Moving from household to household, while psychologically difficult, especially in the beginning, was a good experience in the end. It allowed me to observe a diversity of *lignées* in their everyday life and therefore to have a more thorough knowledge of them.

In this way, through live testimony and direct participation, I set up a genealogy of each *lignée*, using the methods proposed by Françoise Héritier.[19] Then, according to this genealogical data, I drew up a list of the partners of each sexually active individual. This list also included information on the genitor of each individual (including any genitors of the deceased that the villagers could remember) and on the sexual modality practiced by Ego and each of his partners. Finally, I came to understand their concepts of kinship and their four modalities of sexual life.

I gathered information on social stratification, political and economic regimes, and religion from people who had belonged, before 1956, to the three social strata: *sïpi* (aristocracy), *dzéka* (commoner class), and *we* (serfs).

By July 1992, I had completed part of the description and part of the analysis of their kinship system. While I was writing, however, certain pertinent questions arose, as did the need to include the aristocratic *lignées* in my genealogical data. These *lignées* were dispersed in villages that fell outside my initial parameters of research; but during a fourth trip, I was able to collect the genealogies of ten of these *lignées*. Before 1956, marriage was almost always practiced by patricians, so to find out who among the aristocrats had married, why they had married, and how many of them had married, it was necessary to obtain the genealogies of the entire aristocratic stratum. Therefore, during the summer of 1992 I undertook my fourth field trip.

My field data and the historical material I uncovered in the ancient Chinese texts provided the main sources for this present work. Some of my statistics and certain information about the political and agrarian systems before 1956, as well as some examples concerning people who live in villages outside the parameters of my investigation, were culled from the reports mentioned above.

The present work concerns, above all, the Na kinship system. It is divided into three parts. In part 1, after a general presentation, I examine Na social stratification, the political and economic regimes from the Qing dynasty until the era of the Guomindang, religion to the present day, and the different ethnic groups that live near the Na in order to give some context for this system of kinship. In part 2, I present and analyze the foundation of Na kinship and the four existing modalities of their current sexual life. I will also attempt to show the connection between their conception of kinship and their mode of sexual life. In relation to other societies, Na matrimonial phenomena reveal specific traits that I will examine from both an ethnological and a historical perspective. I will also attempt to reveal the origins and characteristics of Na marriage. This section concludes with an account of the attitudes held by the local governments since 1956 toward Na customs and the measures they adopted during various periods in response to them. In part 3, I first compare the modalities of Na sexual life with marriage in its general sense, from an anthropological point of view; then I compare the basic unit of Na kinship and economy with the family. Finally, I attempt to analyze, yet once again, the definitions of marriage and of the family.

In view of the absence of anything like it in ethnographic information, and consequently of adequate anthropological concepts, the system of Na kinship and especially their modalities of sexual life necessitate meticulous and detailed attention to both description and analysis. Moreover, while in other societies there is only one formal modality of sexual life, in Na society there are four. It follows that my work includes chapters of unequal length, depending on the importance and complexity of their diverse themes.

international border
province border
railroad
road
○ province capital
● prefecture headquarters
• district headquarters
· canton headquarters

Map 1. Distribution of the Mo-so.
Source: *Map of the People's Republic of China* (Beijing: Cartographic Press, 1985).

CHAPTER ONE

General Presentation

Identity

Before the 1950s, four groups living in the Yunnan and Sichuan provinces were referred to as the Mo-so (摩梭) by the Han, the ethnic majority of China.[1] Each of these groups went by its own name and continues to do so. One group, the Naxi (with an approximate population of 210,000), resides in Lijiang and the surrounding areas in Yunnan. A second group, the Na (with an approximate population of 30,000), lives in the Yongning basin[2] and the surrounding areas to the north of the Ninglang District in Yunnan and to the west of the Yanyuan District in Sichuan. The third group, the NaRu (with an approximate population of 7,000), inhabits the Muli and Yanbian Districts in Sichuan. A fourth group, the Nahing (with an approximate population of 3,000), lives to the south of the Ninglang District and in the village of Zhanzidang in the Yongshen District in Yunnan.

Originally, the Mo-so came from branches of the Qiang, an ancient population from the Tibeto-qin plateau in northwestern China. Since the end of the second century A.D., the Mo-so have lived in the Yanyuan region. During the fifth century, they also appeared in the Lijiang region, and in the early eighth century, they could be found farther south, in the Bingchuan region, east

35

of Er Lake (Erhai), where they established Yuexi *Zhao* (also called Mo-so *Zhao*), one of the six famous principalities.[3] In 738, the Nan Zhao principality conquered the five others and thereby formed a kingdom. Following this event, the Mo-so disappeared from the region of Erhai, leaving no traces in the Chinese texts or in reality; they can only be found in the regions where they live today.[4]

According to their own designations, the names of these four groups all share the syllable *na*, whose meaning — as a proper name — is unknown. In their spoken language, *na* as a general term is always used as a qualitative adjective that means black. *Xi*, *Ru*, and *hing* all signify people or human beings.

Linguistic Classification

The Jingsha River, upriver from the Yangzi, cuts the region in two. The groups on the east side of the river, the NaRu, the Na, and the Nahing, understand one another. They do not, however, understand the Naxi, who live on the west side of the river. Chinese (in its spoken and written forms) serves as their common language. Chinese linguists believe these groups use two dialects of the same language.[5] Their languages all belong to the Yi branch of the Tibeto-Burmese family. The western group uses *donba* writing, pictography, and another written form called *geba*, which is phonetic. But only the shamans know how to use these two written forms. The eastern groups are without the written word.

Official Identification

In 1958, the central government organized investigations to identify the various ethnic groups. The provincial authorities were in charge of identifying their local inhabitants. In Yunnan, since the Naxi constituted the largest group, the central government authorized their name as that of the three groups in Yunnan. All of the Na, Naxi, and Nahing living in Yunnan Province are, consequently, listed as Naxi. On the other hand, the NaRu and the Na living in Sichuan are identified by the provincial government of Sichuan and confirmed by the central government as part of the Mongolian ethnic group. This designation is justified by their claiming to be descendants of those left behind in the region by the army of Kublai Khan. Ever since this official identification was applied, villages of the same ethnic group but on different sides of the province's border have been identified as two distinct ethnicities. For example, to the north of the Yongning basin, certain villages are now considered Naxi, and others, less than one kilometer away, are Mongolian. However, these "Mongols" have nothing in common with the Mongols in Mongolia: not one among them even knows how to pronounce a single word in Mongolian.[6]

The Claiming of Identity

For more than a decade, the Na from Yongning have requested that the government, on every level from local to central, officially recognize them as an ethnic group distinct from the Naxi of Lijiang. The People's Assembly of Yunnan Province has agreed to call the Na of Yongning Mo-so *ren* (Mo-so people) but not Mo-so *zu* (Mo-so ethnic group).[7] To be considered an ethnic group, ratification by the central government is necessary.

Geography of the Yongning Region

Before 1956, the territory over which the Na chief reigned roughly corresponded to the northern half of the Ninglang District. In this work, I refer to this area as Yongning Region. For the most part, this region has four types of relief: mountains that reach an altitude of 3,800 to 4,500 meters, the Yongning basin (2,670 meters in altitude), the shores of Lake Lugu (2,700 meters), and the terraces (about 1,600 meters) of the Jingsha River valley.

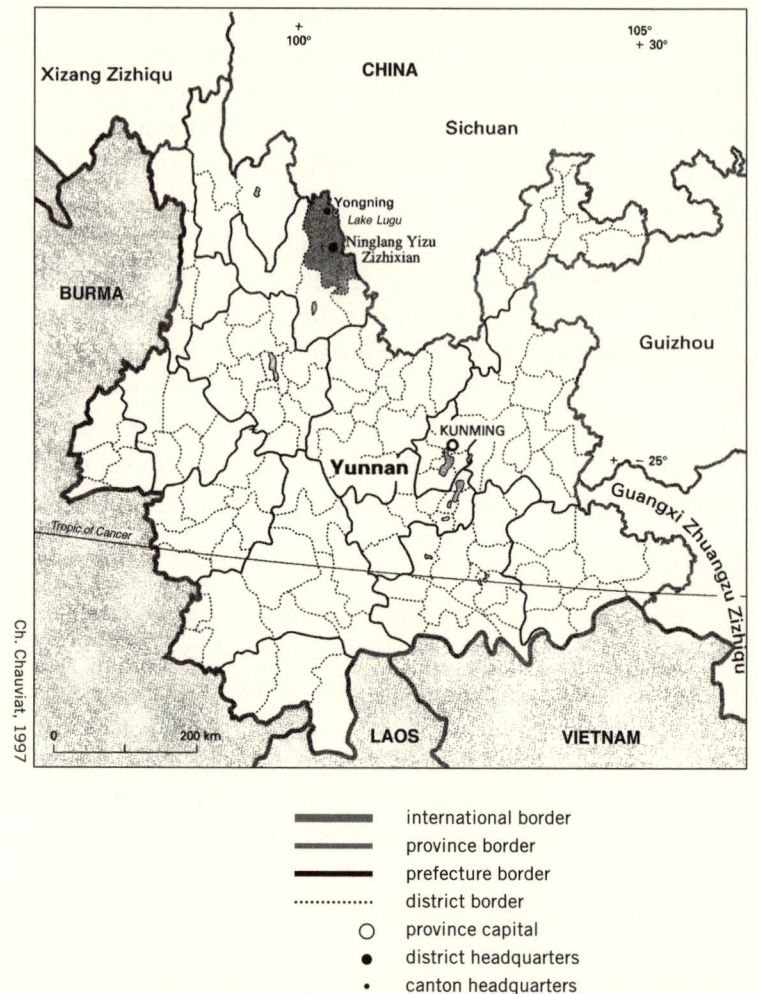

▓▓▓▓▓▓	international border
▬▬▬▬	province border
▬▬▬▬	prefecture border
············	district border
○	province capital
●	district headquarters
·	canton headquarters

Map 2. Location of the autonomous district of the Yi of Ninglang.
Source: *The Accounts of the Autonomous District of the Yi of Ninglang* (Kunming: The Ethnic Minorities of Yunnan Press, 1993).

Covered mostly with pine trees, firs, and chestnut trees, the mountains are rich in animal and plant life, some of which is used in precious Chinese remedies. In the Jingsha River valley, which has a subtropical climate, there are two harvests of rice per year. Corn, sorghum, wheat, and several varieties of fruit, such as oranges, clementines, and pears, are also grown there.

Because the Na I am focusing on are distributed throughout the Yongning basin and along the shores of Lake Lugu, I will examine the geography of this area more closely. Located between 100° 67'–100° 69' longitude east and 27° 75'–27° 77' latitude north, the Yongning basin is surrounded by tall mountains. With an area of 70 square kilometers, it is traversed, from the southwest to the east, by the Kaitçi River and, in the northwest, by the Wenquan River. In the south is a mountain that the Na call Gemu (mountain goddess) and the Chinese call Lion Mountain, because of its shape. In the northwest, there is a hot spring.

In the basin and along the shores of the lake, the annual cold season lasts from 150 to 170 days, and the average annual temperature is between 10 and 11 degrees Celsius. The rainy season falls between June and September, and the annual rainfall is between 1,000 and 1,500 millimeters.

The Lines of Communication

At present, Yongning has two roads. The first leads south and connects to the city of Ninglang. It was not constructed until 1971. Today, there is a bus that runs daily between Yongning and the city of Ninglang. There is usually not even one truck a day on this road. Another road, built seven years ago, connects Yongning to the town of Yanyuan. To the north, there is only a rugged path that leads to Wujué in the Muli District, and to the west, a road is under construction that will eventually reach the shores of the Jingsha River. Before the 1970s, transportation was even more difficult. For example, the trip between Yongning and Lijiang took at least ten days, since one could only get there on foot.

The postal service, set up in 1970, barely functions. Stamps are not always available. When you make a telephone call from Yongning to the city of Ninglang, it is almost impossible to hear the person you are calling, who, in turn, understands next to nothing of what you are saying. Communication is even more difficult between Yongning and the town of Kunming, the county seat of Yunnan Province.

The Economy

Cultivated Plants

In 1960, in the Yongning basin, the Na population was 6,222, whereas today it is estimated to be approximately 12,000. The Na are farmers, and traditionally they have cultivated oats, buckwheat, *manqing* (*Brassica rapa*), and flax only.[8] However, since the end of the nineteenth century, under the influence of Han immigrants, they have cultivated Dekkan wheat (*Echinochloa crus-galli*), corn, wheat, potatoes, sunflowers, soybeans, and other vegetables, such as beans, pumpkins, and milkweed. Before 1956, Dekkan wheat was approximately 35 percent of the crop, oats 25 percent, wheat 19 percent, and corn 16.5 percent. Only after the 1950s did they begin to grow rice. Today, it is the main crop and takes up approximately 70 percent of the cultivated fields. The irrigation system of the paddy fields is presently undergoing improvements initiated by the local government. Several decades ago, peach, apple, and wild-pear trees were introduced to the region.

Agricultural Techniques and Tools

The basin territory was once divided into several sectors, depending on where the villages were located. Each sector was divided into several parcels of land, whose crops were rotated on an annual basis. The soil in the middle of the basin was more easily irrigated than that in the outer areas. Therefore, the order in which the grains were cultivated was fixed: the first year was Dekkan wheat, the second year was wheat, the third year was oats. Each parcel was planted with the grain chosen for that year to facilitate irrigation and grazing in the fields. The land that the Na felt was too difficult to irrigate and drain was left fallow for one or two years.

On the non-irrigable land, usually that on the slopes, they planted corn, potatoes, and *manqing*. In their gardens, they grew flax, potatoes, beans, pumpkins, and milkweed. With the exception of *manqing*, the Na rarely grew legumes.

Hydraulic systems were sorely lacking or, if they existed, had serious shortcomings. There was only one canal, which was poorly maintained, making drainage and irrigation difficult. When it came time for sowing, arguments concerning the water towers frequently arose.

As they continue to do today, each household regularly dried a bed of leaves in the stable, and this produced a mixed manure, the only fertilizer traditionally used. Human excrement is not used, since there are no latrines.[9]

Metal agricultural tools, such as plows, hoes, sickles, axes, and knives, are bought in the neighboring Han regions. Tools made out of wood, such as plow frames, wooden hoes, and flails, are fabricated by the Na.

The villagers work, on average, seven hours a day and seven months a year. One adult is responsible for a half hectare of land and receives about 500 kilos of grain in return. With the surplus, he can feed one other person.

Livestock

The Na have raised buffalo, cows, horses, and mules since the 1920s. The buffalo and cows come from the Han regions and the horses from Tibetan territory. At first, each time someone bought a buffalo or a cow, he would ask a Lamaist monk to pray for the animal's good health. However, as the numbers of livestock purchased grew larger, these blessings became more and more rare and eventually stopped altogether. The villagers use horses and mules to fetch wood for the household and to transport crops and manure. Straw from rice, wheat, and Dekkan wheat, as well as corn stalks, is used as fodder for the winter.

Raising goats is rare, since a grass that grows in the basin is hazardous to their health. Just as rare is the raising of yaks, which can only be done at high altitudes 1,000 meters above the Yongning basin. Only a few Tibetan households raise yaks.

Each household generally keeps ten, twenty, or even thirty chickens and several pigs. Today, on average, two people consume the pork from one pig, approximately 60 kilos, per year. Pork is extremely important. In November, each household slaughters one or two pigs and another one or two at the New Year. Once the entrails and hooves are removed, the pig is boned, and the meat is abundantly salted, then sewn up with linen thread. Pork treated in this way can be preserved for a long time. It is the only protein that the Na stock for regular consumption. This kind of pork (*bo cha* in Na) is the only food considered of quality: it is served by households to guests, it is the standard and obligatory offering at funerals, and it is used as payment to religious officials and as reimbursement for acts of kindness. The Na used to trade it for grain, salt, tea, cotton, and such, and they would also use it to pay back interest on a loan. In fact, salted pork functioned as a kind of currency and is even today considered a symbol of wealth. For example, to indicate a household's wealth, the villagers point to the amount of *bo cha* it has. In 1956, 30 percent of the households did not own any cows, horses, or mules, and more than 60 percent had no buffalo. Today, each *lignée* possesses at least one buffalo and one or more horses.

Crafts

Spinning and weaving flax are tasks that every woman is capable of doing. Each household plants flax in its garden and sometimes in the fields as well. During the winter months, women spend much of their time spinning and weaving. The loom is of the most simple kind, merely a wooden frame. It takes fifty to sixty warps to make one skirt, thirty to forty to make one pair of pants, and twenty to make a sack. Some households produce a modest surplus that they trade for grain, tea, salt, brown sugar, and such. They generally make their own clothing.

Most households also know how to brew beer. This skill was introduced to the Na by the Han and the Naxi. The villagers know how to extract oil from *qingciguo*, a wild fruit that grows in the region. This fruit is so rare that it is served only at funerals and for the New Year. In each village, there are still several men who know how to weave baskets, fences, and sieves out of bamboo. Carpenters are not a professional group as such but rather are those who have more building experience than others. They help build houses, cupboards, benches, and chests, which are always very basic. In general, the villagers repair their own houses.

All of the cooking utensils used by the Na originated with other ethnic groups. For example, their wooden bowls and iron or bronze pots are Han, while their vases and teapots are Tibetan. Their wooden mortars and pestles and small stone mills are also fabricated by the Han.

While the villagers who live along the shores of Lake Lugu

subsist mainly by agriculture, they also fish and make their own nets and canoes for this purpose.

Caravan Transportation

The Na began raising horses and mules in the 1920s and organized caravans inspired by the Tibetan caravanners. At that time, they were only involved in transporting merchandise for Han, Bai, and Naxi merchants and were not directly invested in the business. The caravans' itinerary in the western part of Yunnan included Xiaguan, Dali, and Lijiang; in the southwestern part of Sichuan, it included Muli, Kangding, and Xichang, going as far as Tibet and India. Yongning, which had very little to offer to the caravan commerce, was only a stop on the way. Given the high cost of transportation during the 1930s and 1940s, one day of transport by horse was worth 3 *bankai* (a unit of silver money issued by the Yunnan government), the equivalent of 15 kilos of rice. Because of this, more and more households wanted horses, and some went so far as to pawn their land to get them. During the Second World War, traffic along this route increased greatly. Because other regions were occupied by the Japanese, the Na caravan business rapidly expanded.

A household that owned many horses would send two of its members to transport the caravan, or it might hire villagers to do so. Those who did not own enough horses would join with other households and group their animals together. Most households only used their livestock for the caravans during the slow agricultural season, and only a few engaged in caravan transportation full-time.

Since there was no postal service, the villagers would entrust their money to the caravanners and send it where it was needed: to children, for example, studying in monasteries in Lhasa.

Between 1950 and 1958, the Na caravans again developed rapidly. However, they completely disappeared during the campaign by the People's Commune.

Commerce and Manufacturing

The Na used to go barefoot. Only after the arrival of a Naxi leather currier at the beginning of the twentieth century did they begin to wear leather shoes. The demand for shoes grew quickly, and five other Naxi curriers immigrated to Yongning. Because they set up their workshops and stores in Batsïgu, the village designated a new street name, Currier Street, which, until the end of the 1940s, was home to thirty businesses: curriers, blacksmiths, restaurants, shops, silversmiths, hair salons, casinos, and opium dens.[10] Because of this, the town became the center of the region. The shoppers on Currier Street were usually people passing through, Tibetans for the most part. Among all of the merchants on Currier Street, not one was Na.

Until the 1960s, the Na would only wear shoes for the New Year and during the harsh winters. Before 1956, the following articles, which came from neighboring regions and ethnic groups, were scarce: matches, paper, pottery, porcelain, tea, salt, cotton, brown sugar, straw hats, iron, bronze, and shoes. And while several forms of silver money, as well as bills from the Nationalist Republic, were in circulation, business was mainly conducted through bartering.

The Administration of Yongning

From the Yuan dynasty until 1956, the Mo-so and neighboring ethnic groups in the Yongning region were ruled by Mo-so chiefs. During the Ming dynasty, when they were most divided, they lived under ten chiefs. Yunnan Province incorporated Yongning, Langqu and Lijiang, and Sichuan included Guabie, Gouboshu, Zhongsuo, Zuo-suo, Yousuo, Qiansuo, and Housuo. The central

45

government called the indigenous chiefs *tusi*. The first character in the word, *tu*, means indigenous, and the second, *si*, means chief.

In 1956, the headquarters of the Na *tusi* was in the Yongning basin. His territory extended from the middle of Lake Lugu to the Jingsha River and spanned a distance of approximately 70 kilometers from west to east. The Wujué monastery and the village of Kaxipo marked the northern and southern borders of his territory respectively, a distance of approximately 130 kilometers. This territory roughly corresponds to two-fifths of what is now the Ninglang District in Yunnan Province.

Under the Han dynasty, the region of Yongning was dependent on the Yuexi *jun* (the prefecture of Yuexi):[11]

- From 618 to 1279, during the Tang and Song dynasties, it was joined with the kingdoms of Nanzhao and Dali.

- In 1279, the Yuan established Yongning *zhou* (sub-prefecture of Yongning), managed by Lijiang *lu* (the prefecture of Lijiang).

- Under the Ming dynasty, in 1382, it was placed under the authority of Beishen *zhou* (the prefecture of Beishen). In 1384, it was passed over to the command of Heqing *junmin fu* (the military and administrative prefecture of Heqing). In 1396, it became dependent on Langcang *wei junmin zhihui shisi* (the military and administrative prefecture of Langcang). In 1406, the court promoted Yongning *zhou* to the level of *fu* (prefecture) and placed it under the direct authority of the Yunnan government.

- Under the Qing dynasty (1698–1911), the Yongning region was placed under the Yongbei *fu* (the prefecture of Yongbei).

- Under the Guomindang Republic, from 1911 to 1949, the provincial government reunited the region of Yongning with that of Langqiu to form one district, whose name, Ninglang, is made up of two characters from Yongning and two characters from Langqiu. This name is still in use.

During the Ming and Qing dynasties, the leader of a *fu* held the title *zhifu*. In Chinese, in this context, *zhi* signifies governor, director, or president. *Zhifu* means governor of the *fu*.

The Na *tusi* was appointed in 1406 by the central government as *zhifu*. Since then, he has been called *sïpi zhifu* by the Na. The first half of this name, *sïpi*, is a Na term that means head, chief, director, or president.[12] The expression *sïpi zhifu* basically consists of a repetition that I translate as governor. In the present work, I use the term *zhifu* to designate the Na *tusi*, the highest chief in the Yongning region, because it is the official title.

Having abolished the local government of the Guomindang in the Ninglang District, the Chinese Communist Party formally installed its own government in 1956. At the same time, it put an end to the *tusi* regime in the Yongning region. Thus, Na history can be broken down, more or less, into two periods: the one before 1956, under the regime of the *tusi*, and the one after 1956, under communism. If we start counting at the beginning of the Qing dynasty (the Manchurians), the first period lasted 305 years (1644–1949). In the following pages, I will examine the social stratification, the political regime, and the landownership system in place during the first period, to contexualize the Na kinship system historically. I will examine the period after 1956 when I discuss the attitudes of local governments toward Na customs.

CHAPTER TWO

Social Stratification until 1956

Rules of Conduct

In 1956, the Na were divided into three strata: *sïpi, dzéka,* and *we.* The *zhifu* of Yongning set up the following rules for the conduct of each stratum:

Only the *sïpi* were entitled to wear wool and silk fabric, the colors yellow, red, blue, and black, clothing with edges embroidered in gold thread, and gold jewelry. Only *sïpi lignées* had the right to use round pillars as the central supports of their main houses and tile shingles on their roofs.

The *dzéka* and *we* had to live in traditional houses with two square central pillars and wear linen clothing and white or linen-colored skirts.[1] The following is an example of an infraction. A woman who earned her living from a Tibetan caravan wore clothing embroidered with gold thread during a fair organized by a Buddhist monastery. The *zhifu*'s wife noticed her, and the offender was punished. The jackets worn by the *we* had to be colorless. It was forbidden for the *we* working as servants in the *zhifu*'s residence to sit or smoke next to the *zhifu* or to use kitchen utensils that belonged to his family.

Any *sïpi, dzéka,* or *we* who visited the *zhifu*'s office had to prostrate himself before him. After having been received, it was customary for the visitor to leave by backing away while bowing very low. Everyone who passed in front of the official residence had to remove his or her head covering, hat if it was a man and scarf if it was a woman, and had to keep silent, with head bowed. If on horseback, he or she was required to dismount. If a *sïpi, dzéka,* or *we* encountered the *zhifu* or another chief, such as the *guanren,* or general administrator, while walking, he or she had to withdraw to the side of the road, head bowed, and give him the right-of-way.

Each fall, the *zhifu* began the harvest season in his own fields. Everyone else had to wait three days before harvesting. When villagers hunted, which was rare, they gave a portion, or even all, of the game to the *zhifu.* If they killed a stag, only the thighs, skin, and antlers were offered. When they trapped an otter or slew a leopard, the skins alone were offered.

Sïpi

The term *sïpi* literally means chief, but it is used figuratively to refer to the highest social stratum. The *sïpi* stratum was made up of *lignées* descended from the *zhifu*'s family throughout the eras.[2] In 1956, it included thirty-two households.[3] I translate *sïpi* as aristocracy to designate it as a social stratum.

In cases of marriage among the *sïpi,*[4] which always involved virilocal residence, the rule of transmission of social status was male-lineal.[5] For example, the children of a married *sïpi* man always belonged to the *sïpi* stratum, no matter what the social status of his wife. The children of a married *sïpi* woman belonged to her husband's stratum. There has been only one case, however, in which a *sïpi* woman married a commoner. If cohabitation took place in a virilocal residence, which was always the case, the rule was also male-lineal. For example, the children born to an aristocratic man belonged to the *sïpi* stratum, regardless of their mother's status. In cases of the visit, the children always inherited their mother's status, no matter what the stratum of her visitors.

Other combinations that could be logically surmised did not exist in practice for the men and women of the *sïpi* stratum. This can be explained by the simple fact that *sïpi lignées* always controlled the modality of sexual life practiced by their members, with the result that their descendants did not become *dzéka* or *we*.

The Na used the term *ong* (bone) to refer to the carrier that transmitted social status among members of the *sïpi*. But in this context, *ong* was figurative. This subtle notion is of great importance. This rule of transmission of status has led certain researchers to believe that the rule of descent, in respect to aristocrats, is patrilineal.

Dzéka

The word *dzéka* means the people. This social stratum included the majority of Na households. I use the term *commoners* to designate the members of this stratum.

In 1956, the commoners were distributed throughout 646 households. Certain commoner households originally belonged to the *sïpi* stratum, but because of a conflict or an estrangement with the *zhifu*'s family, they had been demoted to the rank of *dzéka*. For example, there were twelve households that the Na referred to as *shaRen*, a term whose meaning is unknown. According to my sources, these households were originally descendants of the *zhifu*'s family and were therefore part of the *sïpi* stratum. Following a struggle for power with the *zhifu*, which the *shaRen* lost, the *zhifu* employed the *shaRen* as wardens in the prison. Every New Year's Day, when the *shaRen* brought gifts to the *zhifu* to wish him a happy New Year, he would throw the gifts on the ground in front of them, a ritual gesture that expressed the bad memory of an event long ago.

Another example of households that originally descended from the *zhifu*'s family can be found in the Azo *lignées* from the village of Azo, which is within the parameters of my investigation. However, they were separated from the *zhifu* a long time ago and are now in the same social position as the commoners. The only trace of their former status as *sïpi* can be found in the round central pillars in their main house. No one knows the exact date of this shift in status.

On the other hand, the *bashi lignées* of Han origin never had a consanguineal relationship to the *zhifu*'s family and belonged to the commoner stratum. However, thanks to their high position in the *zhifu*'s regime, they enjoyed the privileges of the aristocratic stratum.

Most commoners lived exclusively according to the modality of the visit. The Na of this stratum said that the transmission of status occurred through the maternal line.

I have already mentioned the rule of status transmission in a marriage or cohabitation between a *dzéka* and a *sïpi*. Marriage has never occurs between a *dzéka* man and a *we* woman or the other way around. Cohabitation between a *dzéka* and a *we* will be discussed in the following section.

We

The *we* belonged to their master and worked as servants, either inside his home or in his fields. I translate the name of this stratum as serfdom.

The *we* could be transferred. For example, the *zhifu*'s children were always given several *we* when they moved out of the *zhifu*'s residence. The *we* could be sold one by one or by a household if it was exclusively made up of *we* people. For example:

1. The Lafu *lignée* is *we*. It once belonged to the *sïpi lignée* of Bodzi but had been sold several generations earlier to the general administrator's family for the price of 2 *dou* of corn.[6]

2. The Luzo *lignée* (aristocratic) in the village of Zhoshi sold, at various points, three *we*. Among these sales, a person from the Gezo *lignée* was sold for 3 *dou* of corn, a person from the Eche *lignée* was sold for 60 pounds of salt, and a person from the Dadzu *lignée* was sold for a horse, 20 *bankai,* and 30 pounds of salt.[7]

The *we* could be traded by their masters, which often served to bring the serfs closer to their master's residence.

The stratum was for the most part made up of two categories of people: those who had lost their means of subsistence and criminals. The following is a detailed classification of the serfs:

1. The servants of the *zhifu*'s family since the time of Yamaa.[8]

2. The perpetrators of serious crimes who, after being released from prison, were demoted by the *zhifu* and became his servants.

3. Those who did not respect the customs. For example: (a) Tuji found herself confronted by two aristocrats engaged in a fight and did nothing to stop them. She was demoted to the rank of *we* by the *zhifu*. (b) The Pota *lignée* had many sons. When their mother died, instead of carrying her casket out the door as was customary, they lifted it out through the roof, which was a transgression. The *zhifu* demoted the entire *lignée* to the rank of serf.

4. Those sent by their ascendants to the *zhifu* because of disobedience.

5. Descendants from other ethnic groups who went to Yongning and, unable to find other employment, worked in the *zhifu*'s home as servants in order to survive.

6. Those who, unable to pay a debt, were brought to work in the home of their creditor or of the *zhifu*. For example: (a) The Shadga *lignée* from the village of Ago was indebted to a *lignée* from Dzébo. Because it was unable to pay off the debt, Samu, one of the daughters, was taken away as a serf. Later, Samu had a

daughter, who was sold by her master to the Tsie *lignée*. (b) The Shudu *lignée* was ruined because of its debts. It had twenty members, all of whom were handed over to the *zhifu* to become serfs.

7. People who were ruined who gave themselves up voluntarily to the *zhifu* to become serfs in order to survive or turned up on the doorstep of aristocratic *lignées* or wealthy commoners or even wealthy serfs. The latter two cases, however, were rare. For example: (a) The commoner Tsaita *lignée* in the village of Little Loshu owned two serfs. (b) Latse, a serf, became rich during the 1930s and then owned several serfs.

8. Those who became increasingly poor and sold members of their *lignée* as serfs. For example: the impoverished *lignée* of Shadami from the village of Jiabu sold Hlamu as a *we* to the *mkhan-po*, a religious leader, for the price of one cow and 1 *dou* of beans.

In the first half of the twentieth century, some serf *lignées* became wealthy through commerce, the caravan trade in particular. They acquired significant amounts of land and livestock. There were even some poor individuals who, instead of turning themselves over to the chiefs, became serfs in these newly rich *lignées*. For example:

1. The male members of the Lather *lignée* were serfs. At the beginning of the century, the *lignée* was very poor. However, over the course of three decades, through the caravan transports, trading in other regions, and Yongning usury, it became very rich and ended up owning fifty horses and mules and 30,000 *bankai*. During the 1940s, it acquired, through purchase and pawning, almost 100 *dZia* of land and hired four farmhands annually.[9] It even bought a house with a tile roof from an aristocrat in Dzébo and kept several people as serfs.

2. In Loshu, the Sozha *lignée* owned two serfs.

Apart from the two *bashi lignées*, Chen and Shen, commoner and serf *lignées* owning *we* is a phenomenon exclusive to the twentieth century.

In 1956, 280 households had serfs, and approximately ten serfs, without homes, worked in the *zhifu*'s residence. These 280 households were of two types: those in which only the members of one sex were serfs and those in which members of both sexes were serfs. Of the first type, those in which only the male members were serfs were by far the majority.[10]

The servitude of these *lignées* is more or less ancient. For example, in the villages of Batsi, Abu, Hlijigu, Yumi, Zhoke, and Zhoshi, there were sixty-seven households in which the members of one sex or both sexes were serfs. Among these households, three claimed to have been *we* as far back as Yamaa, five claimed to have been so for nine generations, two for seven generations, twelve for five generations, seven for four generations, nine for three generations, one for two generations, and one for one generation. Twenty-seven households knew that their history began after Yamaa's era, but they did not know the exact date.

The number of serfs owned by the *zhifu* continually grew, for new serfs were always joining his residence. Other influential and rich *lignées* would also receive serfs from ruined *lignées*, but this was rare.

The majority of serfs were originally commoners. There is only one case of serfs who were originally aristocrats: the Risi *lignée* in Zhongshi. The rest of the serfs came from *lignée* that had been serfs since the era of Yamaa and from other ethnic groups.

A change in status could only occur by downgrading, that is, by moving from high to low, from the aristocratic to the commoner stratum or from the commoner to the serf stratum. If a person committed a crime and was demoted to a *we* by the *zhifu*, he could be redeemed by his *lignée* or could redeem himself, as long as he lived alone. But once he set up a household, the restoration of his status through payment for his crime was no longer possible.

A household in which the male members or the members of both sexes were serfs, and which had two or more boys, could buy back one or two of its male children so they could become Lamaist monks, but it could never buy back the oldest son. The *zhifu* set the price of the purchase, which could range from 50 to 100 pounds of boned pork.

While rare, it sometimes happened that a newly rich household, after much pleading to the *zhifu*, was granted permission to pay a sum, instead of working. But even if it paid regularly, its status did not change. Once it stopped paying, it had to begin working again.

The *zhifu* installed new serfs in his home or close to his home, so that they would be near their place of work. Those who became serfs inside the household lived there. When a single serf who came to live in the *zhifu*'s residence wanted to set up his own home, his or her only choice was cohabitation, which had to be officially declared to the *zhifu*.

In cases of cohabitation, transmission of status was parallel. For example, when a male commoner cohabited with a female serf, their sons were commoners, and their daughters were serfs. Similarly, when a female commoner cohabited with a male serf, their daughters were commoners, and their sons were serfs. The children born from two serfs were always serfs.

Generally, cohabitation between a male serf and a female aristocrat was not practiced by the *sïpi* stratum but there are some exceptions (see p. 347 below). Moreover, marriage between a male commoner and a female serf is unheard-of. In general, when a commoner *lignée* considered a marriage or a cohabitation for one of its sons, or indeed an adoption, it looked to someone from a commoner *lignée*.

Cohabitation was not an option for the descendants of a *lignée* in which the members of both sexes, or one of the sexes, were serfs. When the new generation included both a girl and a boy, they practiced the mode of the visit exclusively. In the case of the visit, the male descendants of a *lignée* in which only the male members were serfs would always be serfs. The female descendants of a *lignée* in which only the female members were serfs would also always be serfs. As for *lignées* in which both sexes were serfs, their descendants would be serfs forever.

I do not have any information about the rules for determining the status of the children of a female serf who lived by herself.

The transmission of status for the children born from cohabitation, even if the cohabitants also practiced the modality of the visit, was always parallel. It passed down from mothers to daughters and from maternal uncles to nephews. Under this rule, a commoner woman could bring commoner daughters into the world and non-commoner sons (serfs); a serf woman could bear serf daughters and non-serf sons (commoners). This is an unusual phenomenon!

I use the word *parallel* here literally, since this application of status transmission has nothing to do with the Na rule of descent. If we dissect this parallel rule, we find that it does not equal patrilineal plus matrilineal but results in another equation altogether, one that may be articulated as follows: male-lineal plus female-lineal.

A *lignée* that had an only child who was a girl, or that had only boys, could profit from this parallel rule, since, if the members of both sexes were serfs, it could change the status of the members of one of the sexes in the next generation through cohabitation or adoption. Conversely, a *lignée* in which only the members of one sex were serfs could become a *lignée* in which both sexes were serfs. For example:

1. Five generations ago, in the Ran *azi lignée* in Zhoshi, only the men were serfs. Since they had no descendants, this *lignée* adopted a serf woman from the Siuba *lignée* in Zébo. In the next generation, the members of both sexes were serfs.

2. The Nadgobizu *lignée* in Zhoke was exclusively serf on the male side. Because this *lignée* had only boys, one of them had to cohabit virilocally with a commoner woman. Therefore, in the next generation, only the male descendants were serfs.

3. Both sexes of the Gezo *lignée*, also in Zhoke, were serfs. Gezo (male) cohabited with Dgima (female), in whose *lignée* only the men were serfs. The Gezo *lignée* therefore became half serf (the male members) and half commoner (the female members.)

Given these rules, a *lignée* in which the members of only one sex were serfs could technically become, through adoption or cohabitation, a non-serf *lignée*. However, I was unable to find anyone who could give me information about whether or not this had been forbidden by the *zhifu* and if any attempts of this nature had occurred. In fact, it was not in the best interest of the masters for exclusively serf *lignées* to become half serf, and commoner *lignées* were reluctant to let one of their members cohabit with a serf.

To maintain the serf population, the *zhifu*, from time to time, gave a female serf to a *lignée* that was lacking female descendants and therefore was at risk of disappearing, or he set up two serfs together so that they could establish a new household.

A female or male serf and her or his descendants always belonged to the same master. Sometimes cohabiting serfs belonged to two masters, the woman to one and the man to another.

As a general rule, in *lignées* in which the members of one sex were serfs, the males for example, only the eldest son had to work for the master. The other sons usually worked at home, but their master could call for them when he was in need of extra help. A *lignée* could send the eldest son, or a younger son, for the permanent work. The rule simply stated that one man had to work for the master. *Lignées* in which both sexes were serfs had to provide one man and one woman for the master. Serfs began working for the master at the age of thirteen and continued until they were forty-seven if they were women and fifty-seven if they were men. To circumvent this rule, some households tried to put off the puberty ritual for their children.

All *lignées* in which the members of one sex or both sexes were serfs maintained economic independence. Their masters could not take away their property, such as land, livestock, and grain.

Some serfs who were close to the *zhifu* were given administrative positions, which were often quite lucrative. Some even became intimates of the *zhifu* and therefore enjoyed a much more elevated rank in society. Consequently, there were commoners who, coveting such a position, voluntarily became serfs in the *zhifu*'s home. However, it was not guaranteed that they would succeed in getting what they were after. For example: the Goa *lignée* belonged to the commoner social stratum, as did the Lumei *lignée*. Both were descended from the aristocratic stratum. The ascendants of these two *lignées*, having seen that certain members of households in their lineages had been given positions by the *zhifu*, became serfs in the *zhifu*'s home, hoping that they, too, would get a good position. But, judging them incapable, the *zhifu* gave one of them the job of raising pigs and the other one that of stablehand.

Because there were always criminals, impoverished *lignées*, and poor individuals, and because serfs remained serfs, the serf stratum had a natural tendency to grow. Sources from various villages unanimously dated the first appearance of this stratum in the era of Yamaa. As for what existed before, I can say for certain that the formation of the aristocracy came about through a more or less close kinship relationship to the *zhifu*'s family. But although the term *sïpi* means chief, not all of the *lignées* that made up the stratum were dominant in this society. The commoner stratum consisted of *lignées* that maintained their legal independence. The serf stratum was characterized by servitude and a partial loss of legal independence for both individuals and *lignées*. That is, every serf had the duty to work for his master. This distinguished their stratum from the other two social strata, whose members were free.

We have seen that there are three rules for the transmission of status: paternal, maternal, and parallel. Married or cohabiting aristocrats followed the paternal rule, while female aristocrats living according to the modality of the visit followed the maternal rule. For cohabiting serfs and for serfs born from a cohabitation who practiced the modality of the visit, the rule was parallel. For a commoner male married to an aristocratic woman, the rule was paternal. On the other hand, according to my sources, the rule for commoners practicing the modality of the visit was maternal. However, this did not appear to me quite so obvious. It is true that the children of a commoner woman who received visits remained commoners, no matter what the status of the genitor. However, if we take into consideration all of the possibilities for the transmission of status that applied to commoners, this in and of itself is not enough to claim that the rule was maternal. In a cohabitation between a female commoner and a male serf or between a male commoner and a female serf, the commoner woman could only give birth to commoner girls, while the commoner man transmitted his status only to the sons of his female cohabitant. This shows that for a commoner *lignée*, if all of its members practiced the modality of the visit, the rule for the transmission of status would be not maternal but parallel.

We can therefore see that since the *zhifu* stipulated that the parallel rule apply to the status of children born from a cohabitation between a female commoner and a male serf (or the other way around), the logic of this parallel rule extended to purely commoner households as well. But because only the modality of the visit was practiced from generation to generation in most commoner households, the rule of status transmission applied in theory only. Moreover, since the society is matrilineal, the parallel rule, at least in appearance, is the same as the maternal rule. Matriliny, then, becomes the point of reference, and the parallel rule is completely overshadowed and buried. (This parallel rule in no way applies to aristocratic men who were married or cohabiting.)

The following question arises: why did the *zhifu* establish this parallel rule instead of a paternal rule, as existed for aristocratic men, or a maternal rule, as existed for aristocratic women? I believe that this state of affairs was the result of a practical concern. In the case of cohabitation between a female serf and a male commoner, if the paternal rule applied, there would no longer be any male serfs after one generation. In the opposite situation, that of cohabitation between a male serf and a female commoner, the consequences were far more serious. This rule posed no problem with the male children of this couple, since they would be serfs. However, once these children embarked on a life of the visit, there would no longer be a point of reference. If the *zhifu* ordered them included in the feminine line, the situation would be even worse. In cohabitation between a female serf and a male commoner, there were always serfs at the *zhifu*'s disposal, but the consequences of this arrangement made finding a cohabitant too difficult. In the opposite situation, cohabitation between a male serf and a female commoner, the *zhifu* would run out of serfs beginning with the next generation. Moreover, many more men than women had become serfs on an individual basis. In both

CHAPTER THREE

The Political Regime until 1956

To give a better understanding of the political regime of the *tusi* in Yongning, I will first briefly describe the policies of the various dynasties and of the Nationalist Republic in regard to the ethnic minorities in China.

An Overview of the **Tusi** System in China

Prior to 1956, the government policy on ethnic minorities can be divided into two periods: the first begins in 221 B.C. and ends in A.D. 1253, and the second spans the period from 1253 until 1956.

The First Period

During the first period, which lasted for 1,474 years, the central government of each dynasty continuously implemented a policy called *ji mi zhi zhi*. The word *ji* means halter, *mi* means bit, *zhi* means of, and *zhi* means policy. With this metaphoric phrase, the government expressed its mastery over the ethnic minorities through its chief, just as one controls horses and cows by the head, using a halter and a bit.

In practice, under all of the dynasties, once a territory was conquered and its indigenous chiefs had submitted to the court and recognized it as sovereign, the central government would bestow on them a hereditary title. It would then leave these indigenous chiefs to rule their territories and to reign over their people as they saw fit, without interfering with their social organization or intervening in their internal affairs. In this way, the central government's domination over these people was only exercised through the intermediary of the indigenous chiefs.

Under the Qin dynasty (221–206 B.C.), the indigenous chiefs kept their own titles. However, under later dynasties, the court sometimes handed out supplementary Han administrative titles to the particularly faithful and obedient, without, however, conferring any real power on them, as they did for the Han chiefs who held the same titles.

Under the Tang dynasty (A.D. 618–907), the emperor Li Shimin maintained: "Since ancient times, the entire world has believed that the Zhonghua (the Han) are superior and the *yidi* (ethnic minorities) are inferior. I love them all the same."[1] He decreed the establishment of the prefectures and sub-prefectures of Jimi, in the regions of the ethnic minorities, to function as formal administrative regions in which the chiefs were all natives and their positions passed down through heredity.

In 1253, the court of the Song dynasty (A.D. 960–1279), influenced by the Tang, instituted a regulation on the transfer of power. When an aging *tusi* considered stepping down, the minor chiefs of his ethnic group, together with the chiefs of neighboring ethnic groups, were now required to present their request for an heir unanimously to the court, which would then give the imperial order to grant the request. This marks the beginning of the central government's seizure of power.

The Second Period
Unlike in the first period, when ethnic minorities were governed exclusively by their own chiefs, in the second period (1253–1956),

the central government sent mandarins into the regions to rule them jointly with the native chiefs.

Founded by the Mongols, an ethnic minority, the Yuan dynasty (1279–1368) conquered more territory than its predecessors had. It adopted a policy called *meng, yi can zhi* (the joint participation of Mongolian mandarins and other ethnic groups' chiefs in the government). Because of this, Mongolian as well as non-Mongolian chiefs were appointed at every level of local government in the Han regions. However, in the ethnic-minority regions, they existed only on the prefectural to provincial levels; below the prefecture, a native chief always administered by himself.[2]

This dynasty also implemented a policy of not only appointing native chiefs, as the preceding dynasties had done, but also formally conferring on them an official mandate, a seal, and other papers. Thus two types of mandarins appeared: *liuguan* and *tuguan* (or *tusi*). *Liu* literally means moving or mobile and figuratively means mutable; *guan* means mandarin. The term *liuguan* referred to mandarins who were likely to be moved from one post to another by the government that appointed them. Their position was not a right of inheritance. I translate *liuguan* as magistrate. *Tu* means native. The term *tuguan* designated native mandarins whose position was hereditary. They could not be transferred to other posts. I translate *tuguan* as native chiefs.

The Yuan dynasty promulgated an entire series of decrees concerning the native chiefs. For the first time in Chinese history, the nomination, promotion, punishment, and transmission of a *tusi*'s power had to conform to these regulations. Moreover, the central government began to take censuses of ethnic minorities in areas near the Han regions in order to impose taxes and form a native army. As mandarins of the court, the native chiefs were required to pay tribute. This is how the institution of the *tusi* began to take form. However, the government's policies were not always applied in the same way in different regions. The policies rapidly affected central China whereas they were less rigorously implemented or simply ineffectual in remote and isolated areas.

After seeing the Mongols frequently resort to force to conquer ethnic-minority regions, the Ming dynasty (1368–1644) tried a different tack. Basing its policies on favors to the native chiefs and governing by deterrence, it was able to subjugate the ethnic minorities peacefully. Once it had pacified the ethnic minorities, it instigated a series of new regulations. For example, it appointed only the leaders of the ethnic groups as chiefs and gave them salaries. These chiefs could be promoted to a higher position, all the way up to minister, if they excelled in carrying out their responsibilities. They therefore had the opportunity to become magistrates. To rule more effectively, the Ming dynasty applied strict rules. For example, if a native chief transgressed court regulations, he was punished in the same manner as a Han mandarin: demotion or suspension of his position, deportation, and condemnation to death. The rules under the Yuan, in the same circumstances, had been less strict: when a native chief had committed a crime, he was punished, but maintained his position.

In the middle of this dynastic period, the court initiated a new policy called *gaituguiliu* (the replacement of a native chief by a magistrate) for when a native chief committed the crimes of usurpation, launching an attack on a neighboring ethnic group, or failing to provide an heir. This policy created repeated rebellions among the ethnic minorities when it was applied. For example, the governor of the two Guang (Guangdong and Guangxi) stated: "The installation of magistrates [in the regions of ethnic minorities] is merely a nominal and empty gesture. Before, the natives gave us 3 thousand soldiers every year to have at our disposal. Since the implementation of this policy, the provincial government has had to provide several thousand soldiers every year, in order to protect itself from native revolts."[3]

As a result of the severe consequences of this policy, the court had to reinstall native chiefs in certain regions and to take another measure called *zhongjian zhuman* (the multiplication of native chiefs). Under this policy, more minor native chiefs were named in regions controlled by powerful *tusi* in an effort to weaken their power. In other words, it was a policy of divide and conquer.

The Qing dynasty (1644–1911) was founded by an ethnic minority, the Manchurians. To control the other ethnic groups and protect itself from them, it instituted an extreme policy, according to which it was no longer possible for a native chief to become a magistrate. The salary system was replaced by official land for the native chief, also referred to as the "land accompanying the seal." To curb the native chiefs' power, the new dynasty took severe measures:

1. It reconfigured borders to obstruct the expansion of native chiefs.

2. It set up surveillance posts at points of passage and forbade native chiefs and members of their ethnic groups from leaving their region without permission from the authorities. A native chief who transgressed this rule would be stripped of his power; a common native in the same situation would receive eighty blows from a club on the buttocks.

3. In certain regions, it named sons other than the eldest to succeed the *tusi* so as to weaken the power of this position.

4. It named magistrates in certain regions where a *tusi* already existed.

In other respects, the Qing dynasty more or less maintained the Ming dynasty regulations.

In 1726, the Qing court launched a massive national campaign aimed at replacing native chiefs with magistrates. Only the *tusi* in border regions or in very remote and isolated regions, or those who had accomplished certain feats and had never rebelled, were untouched.

Under the Guomindang government (1911–1949), the *tusi* regulations underwent few changes. The transmission of the *tusi*'s power, for example, took place according to the same procedures as it had during the Qing dynasty, with one small difference: it could now be officially ratified by the provincial government authorities, instead of requiring the central government. The administrative system was modified, but the government in ethnic-minority regions did not drastically change.

From this brief overview, we see that during each era, the central government, by officially naming the native chiefs, invested each of them with the power to run a local government that constituted, for the court, an administrative institutional base. So, while they remained under the authority of various superior governmental institutions, the *tusi* enjoyed some degree of autonomy.

The Political Regime of the Na Tusi

The position of *zhifu* was inherited. Each succession had to be ratified by the court.[4] The last *zhifu* was named A Minzhu in Han and Tsïepitso in Na.[5]

Under the Guomindang, the central government replaced the bronze seal given to the Na *zhifu* by the preceding government with a wooden seal and an official mandate. However, until 1956, each New Year's Day, the *zhifu* would make a tour through several villages surrounding his residence, accompanied by two people who would carry, on a frame, the mandarin costume that had been conferred on him by the court of the Qing dynasty. The *zhifu* would also have certain religious rituals performed annually in his residence by Lamaist monks.

Under the Qing dynasty and until the Guomindang era, the tasks that the central government assigned to the *zhifu* included controlling the ethnic groups of the region, collecting taxes and transporting them to the authorities, arresting thieves and bandits, and sending the local army on expeditions ordered by the higher government.

The *zhifu* was endowed with political power. He had at his disposal an administration whose hierarchy was as follows: *zhifu*, highest Na governor in the Yongning region; *zongguan*, general administrator;[6] *bashi*, assistant to the general administrator; and *shiye*, secretaries.

The architecture of the *zhifu*'s residence was typically Han and included a house for the *zhifu*'s family and servants, the *zhifu*'s office, two storehouses for grain, a stable, and a prison. According to oral tradition, the *zhifu*'s residence moved throughout history and has been located successively in the following villages: Kaitçi, Azo, Tozhi, Ago, Bodzi, and Zhoshi. In 1956, it was in Zhoshi. I do not know the reasons for these changes in location nor how long it was in Zhoshi. Even today, there are traces of these moves in the aristocratic and serf *lignées* in all of these villages and their surroundings, with the exception of the village of Ago. For example, all of the Azo *lignées* in Azo originated with the *zhifu*'s family, while in the neighboring village, the six Ragi *lignées* are all serfs.

Detailed information about the military organization of the Yongning region does not exist. During the Guomindang era, the *zhifu* had approximately ten young serf men as bodyguards. In the 1920s, an army of 170 soldiers recruited from the commoners was formed. The soldiers furnished their own provisions, while their arms were issued by the government of the Yongbei District. Under the direct command of the *zhifu*, the main part of the army was stationed in Yongning, and a smaller brigade was in Baerqiao to guard the storehouses of grain. This force was disbanded in 1928.

Then, in 1942, following a directive from the Ninglang District government, another army of one hundred soldiers was formed, in the same manner as before. In 1948, it, too, was disbanded.

As supreme chief of the region, the *zhifu* had legal power. If someone inflicted bodily harm on another person, in a brawl for example, he would order that the offender be beaten with a wooden board, in the Chinese manner. He also judged criminals. Generally, he would first incarcerate those who committed serious crimes, such as murder, placing them under surveillance by unarmed guards. After being sentenced, the criminals were placed in stocks and paraded through the villages. Then if their *lignées* were unable to redeem them, the *zhifu* would demote them to the status of serfs and put them to work for his family. The right to sentence a criminal to death did not come under his jurisdiction, however. A victim's family could lodge a complaint against the murderer with the higher governments, which did have the power to impose the death penalty. Several requests of this nature were presented, but the families lodging the complaints were always outsiders. In general, the Na are unaware that, according to Han law, they are entitled to lodge such a complaint.

The central government arbitrated conflicts between the Na in the Yongning region and their neighbors. For example, according to Han texts and Chinese genealogy of the *zhifu*, the Yongning region underwent a period of unrest between 1417 and 1438 that was provoked by the Na *tusi* living in Sichuan Province. Pusan, the third chief in the genealogical list of the *zhifu*'s family, was assassinated by the Na chief of Zuo-suo. In 1423, Pusan's brother Nanba succeeded him, while the region continued to be invaded by these neighbors. In 1438, with the approval of the emperor, a magistrate was installed in Yongshen to control the entire region. Ever since, the situation between Na groups has been calm.

Under the Ming dynasty, the *zhifu* was not affected by the reforms that aimed to replace the native chiefs with magistrates, nor was he affected by a similar campaign under the Qing dynasty, which touched far more regions than that of the Ming. This can be explained, according to the genealogy of the *zhifu*'s family, by two facts: the Yongning region is not in itself very important, being both remote and sparsely populated; and when the Qing army arrived in Yunnan, the Na chief voluntarily submitted to the court, serving as an example for all of the other chiefs of ethnic minorities in Yunnan, and so was well appreciated.

The *zhifu* appointed the officials in his administration. In general, he chose someone of great ability from among the aristocrats and appointed him general administrator. This position was the *zhifu*'s assistant. A Duoqi and A Shaoyun were the last two general administrators. They successfully encroached on the *zhifu*'s political power through subtle manipulation. From the beginning of the century until 1956, they settled all affairs of any importance. Although the *zhifu* nominated the general administrator during this era, this was merely a formality. We will examine all of this in more detail in chapter 12.

The *bashi* were also appointed by the *zhifu* as assistants to the general administrator. They were in charge of all correspondence between the *zhifu* and the local or central government, taxes, and the inventory of grain harvested in the *zhifu*'s territory. These positions were always filled by members of the same three families, all of Han origin: the Chen, the He, and the Shen. They immigrated approximately ten generations ago and became integrated. Among them, the Chen held the position the longest and enjoyed great prestige in this society.

For *shiye*, the *zhifu* always employed well-read Han from the neighboring Han regions, such as the Heqing and Yongshen Districts. As secretaries, their job was to prepare the *zhifu*'s papers in

Chinese for the local or central government, to teach Chinese to the *zhifu*'s sons, and to serve as interpreter for the *zhifu* and government officials.

The *zhifu* also assigned other positions, such as the steward, who managed the administration's daily spending and the inventory control of crops from the administration's land as well as from the *zhifu*'s private property,[7] and the irrigation supervisor, who was in charge of water distribution during the sowing period.

The Division of the Yongning Region into Two Zones

The *zhifu* divided the Yongning region into two parts: the central zone, which covered almost the entire Yongning basin except for the villages located beyond Walabié to the northeast, and the outlying zone, which was connected with the rest of the region.

In the central zone, under the authority of the general administrator and his assistants, there were nine *raimi*. This post also had a Han name, *huotou*, which means head of the group. Each *raimi* was in charge of the villages surrounding his own residence. (I refer to this kind of ensemble of villages as a village grouping.) For example:

1. The *raimi* of the five border villages within my parameters of research was a member of the Raimi *lignée* living in the village of Raimi.[8]

2. A member of the Aisha *lignée* who lived in the village of Hliwalo was given the position of *raimi* and was in charge of six villages: Lalo, Ami, Amilo, Hliwalo, Jabu, and Ga-sa.

The *raimi*'s job was to collect taxes, including various taxes from the *lignées* of his village grouping, and to serve as an arbitrator and reconciler during conflicts between villagers. The position was inherited. When the *lignée* of a *raimi* did not have a male adult, one of its female members could take over. Each *raimi* received a parcel of land (approximately 5 *dZia*) as payment for his services. Most of the *raimi* were commoners, with the exception of a few who were serfs.

The outlying zone was much larger than the central zone. Its population, however, was less dense and very dispersed. Unlike the central zone, the outlying zone was divided into twenty-four jurisdictions, each of which was directly governed by a *guanren*. This Han term can be translated as the chief of the jurisdiction. Each *guanren* had an assistant called a *zhazi*.

The *zhifu*, the general administrator, and A Zicai each managed two jurisdictions. There were therefore twenty-one *guanren* in all at the head of these twenty-four jurisdictions. Among them were twelve aristocrats (two of them women), seven commoners, and two serfs.

Under the *guanren*, the *zhifu* also placed nine *raimi*, as well as one *hadzi* (a village chief), in each village, with the exception of those that already had a *raimi* living there. The *raimi* in the outlying zone had the same responsibilities and enjoyed the same privileges as those in the central zone.

In 1912, the *zhifu* installed three *zonghuotou* in the central zone, in positions that were superior to the *raimi*, and three in the outlying zone. *Zonghoutou*, a Chinese term, means the head of a group of heads. Each *zonghuotou* was in charge of two, three, or four village groupings. They served as intermediaries between the general administrator and the *raimi*. I translate *zonghuotou* as chief of the regrouping of villages. When a *zonghuotou* did not perform his job satisfactorily, the *zhifu* relieved him of his command and replaced him.

In the outlying zone, it was up to the *guanren*, accompanied by the *bashi*, to collect taxes and bring them to the *zhifu*. They also served as arbitrators in disputes that the *raimi* had been unable to settle. They were paid in grain and other goods in their jurisdiction. To increase their privileges, the *zhifu* decreased the amount of tributes they were required to pay.

In the outlying zone, some of the villages only had households of other ethnic backgrounds. In these cases, the *zhifu* would appoint an influential person as the *kezhang*, a Han term that means chief of inhabitants of foreign origins. Like the *raimi*, they were each in charge of several villages. With the exception of the villages in which a *kezhang* resided, the *zhifu* would install a chief called a *paishou* (meaning head of a small group in Han) in each village.

Figure 3.1 illustrates the administrative and political hierarchy within the *zhifu*'s administration, in both the central and outlying zones.

one *zhifu*

one *zongguan* and one *bashi*

administration of the *zhifu*	central zone		outlying zone
			twenty-one *guanren* and twenty-one *zhazi*
two *shiye*	three *zonghuotou*		three *zonghuotou*
	(Na villages)	(Na villages)	(villages of foreigners)
	nine *raimi*	nine *raimi*	*kezhang*
		hadzi	*paishou*

Figure 3.1. Yongning *fu*: Political organization under the *zhifu*.

The Traditional Rights of Commoners

When the behavior of the *zhifu*, the general administrator, or the *guanren* did not conform to custom, the commoners had the right to revolt. Traditionally, however, only the Pumi commoners had the right to start a rebellion.[9] The person who launched the revolt would pass out small wooden boards to the villagers; on each board was attached a woolen cord whose end branched out into several threads. Each thread contained a knot that represented one day. For example, three knots meant that anyone who received a board had to assemble in three days at the usual spot, a place southwest of the village of Batsïgu. The rebellion could be led by one or several villages.

Following the assembly, the rebels would head for the house of the *raimi* they were fighting against. They would seize his belongings and kill his livestock. Often, once he heard the news, the *raimi* and members of his *lignée* would flee. When the *zhifu* came to arbitrate between the two sides, in an attempt to reconcile them, he was required to arrive on foot, without a hat or shoes. After the arbitration, the guilty individual was required to ask the rebels for forgiveness. If the man in question was the *zhifu* himself, he had to make the request. But there is no record of that ever occurring. The following two examples involved chiefs:

1. In 1921, the employees of the Chen *bashi* led a herd of yaks to graze in the Muding valley. On more than one occasion, they let them enter the Pumi's fields and trample their plants, without ever apologizing. Moreover, they visited the Pumi women and never took care of the children that resulted from these relations.[10] All of this incited anger among the Pumi villagers, who mobilized a force of about a thousand Pumi and Na people who lived in the same village grouping. They then headed toward the home of the Chen *bashi* and killed twelve cows. As a result of the negotiations that followed, led by the *zhifu* and the general administrator, the Chen *bashi* asked the rebels for forgiveness and prepared a feast for them, with seven cows and 250 liters of alcohol.

2. Kaitçi *sïpi*, the *guanren* of Pujio, was not a good leader of the villagers in his jurisdiction. Each year, he raised taxes and demanded more grain. In 1939, the commoners of Pujio rose up against him. Thanks to the intervention of several Lamaist monks, some of his belongings were saved.

These examples emphasize the following point: as the holders of political power, the *zhifu*, the general administrator, and the other *guanren* made up the dominant group in this society. The other minor chiefs, with the exception of the *raimi*, served only as intermediaries between the group of governors and their subjects and had no power to make political decisions.

The *zhifu*, appointed governor by the central government, was granted supreme power in the region. Using insignia and rituals, he regularly reinforced his legitimacy and the sacredness of his power and played the role of representative and guarantor of the entire society. However, inside the group of governors, the general administrator was an adversary who competed with the *zhifu* for power. The possibility to do so arose from the nature of his position: serving as a go-between for the *zhifu* and the rest of society, he had the opportunity skillfully to manipulate the relationships between individuals, on the one hand, and between ethnic groups, on the other. He therefore played a dynamic role in political life. While the general administrator was able to encroach on the executive power of the *zhifu*, he was not in any way able to usurp his title or his judiciary power.

In contrast to the group of governors were the commoners. In accordance with social consensus, they usually submitted to the *zhifu* and other *guanren*. But if they felt that a governor was abusing his power, even if he was the *zhifu*, they would rebel by destroying that governor's belongings. Events of this nature reveal, first of all, that the *zhifu* was expected to react to conflict in a prescribed way: instead of suppressing a rebellion by force, he was required to intervene peacefully. Similarly, his manner of participation in the negotiations was ruled by tradition: he had to arrive on foot, without his horse, hat, or shoes. All of this was part of his duty toward his subjects. When the negotiations came to a close, he had to ask the rebels for forgiveness. Through these actions, he was symbolically reduced to the rank of the common man, and the society seemed, at least temporarily, egalitarian.

What is more, the resolution process was always the same, no matter which governor was subjected to the rebellion. This custom suggests that a governor's abuse of power challenged not the relationship between himself and a group of commoners but the entire social order. In other words, when a governor did not follow social consensus, recourse to force by the commoners was legitimate, and because of this, the *zhifu* did not have a monopoly on the use of force. This right of the commoners served to overcome a crisis, to reinstate social consensus, and to get society running again. It maintained equilibrium in the society.

Between the governors and the commoners was a third social group, the *raimi*. With the exception of the *zhifu*, the *raimi* was the only position in the entire political hierarchy that had both a Na name and a Han name (*huotou*); other positions had only a Han name. Second, except for the *zhifu*, only the *raimi* received land as payment for their job. Third, as is the case for the *zhifu*, this position was hereditary.

The most important part of the *raimi*'s role was its double aspect: he represented the *zhifu* in times of peace and represented the commoners during a rebellion. The *raimi* was the leader of his village grouping and the interlocutor between villages. He focused dissension, organized the rebellion, and negotiated with the *zhifu*. No matter what happened, the *zhifu* could take no action against him, since his position was hereditary. Thus he oscillated between two social roles: the dominator and the dominated. The duality of this position joined together the governing group and the common people in Na society. The *zhifu* would appear during a crisis as an arbitrator with authority rather than power. Therefore, he was not customarily endowed with absolute power over his subjects.

This social structure was very effective and the solution for rebellion highly ritualized. The double nature of the *raimi*'s position and the arbitrating role of the *zhifu* reveal a mechanism that differs greatly from that of the despotic central government. This raises the following question: Is this the remnant of an ancient procedure that the Na have managed to retain from the days before the ascendancy of the imperial court of China?

An answer to this question might lie in the two types of laws that coexisted in their political life: laws established by the central government and laws originating from custom. While implementing the central government's laws, the *zhifu* also followed laws based on custom. On the level of judiciary power, the situation was analogous. Take a murderer, for example. The governmental court of the district would undoubtedly condemn him to death, while the *zhifu*, even in the worst case imaginable, would only demote him to the rank of a serf.

We have seen that political life in this society was conditioned by three social groups: the governors, the commoners, and the *raimi*. It was based on a conception of equality when it came to the use of force between dominators and dominated; the legitimacy of the *zhifu*'s power rested jointly on his nomination by the court (or the death of a predecessor, when it was a matter of succession) and social consent, two opposing institutions in that one is despotic and the other egalitarian. Since the *zhifu*, as the holder of executive power, observed both governmental and customary laws, the political structure only truly revealed itself in times of transition between peace and crisis and therefore can only be grasped in this dynamism.

This analysis leads to the conclusion that by applying its legislation to Na society, the central Chinese government transmitted its despotic conceptions to the Na. But, rather than replacing the Na's traditional political ideas, these conceptions combined with them. In the political realm, the Na retained a certain degree of autonomy. In other words, they did not transform into a completely despotic society, the way the Han did.

Finally, on the issue of political organization, several questions remain: When did the ascendancy of the central government of China reach Na society? Was the *zhifu* imitating the ways of the court when he gave land to the *raimi* as a salary and made their position hereditary, or was this directly stipulated by the central government? In fact, it would be interesting to know what kind of political regime the Na had before the ascendancy of the central government. However, about this I have not to date found any information, either in the field or in the Chinese texts.

CHAPTER FOUR

Landownership: The System until 1956

By 1956, in the Yongning region, the fields, moors, fallow lands, and prairies had been completely partitioned among the inhabitants. The land was divided into two types: that belonging to the administration of the *zhifu* and that belonging to each *lignée*. As a deed to the property, each owner received a paper *hongzhao*, issued by the Guomindang government, and an engraved wooden plaque, issued by the *zhifu*.

Public Land

I will first examine the property of the *zhifu*'s administration.

The property assigned by the central government to the administration of the *zhifu* was called *elu* by the *zhifu*. The letter *e* means external, and *lu* means the land: in other words, the administration's land (*guanzhuan*) or the land that accompanies the seal (*suiyintian*). In 1956, this land consisted of 226 *dZia*, divided into twenty lots, all of them in the Yongning basin. The revenue generated by this property paid the *zhifu*'s salary as well as other public-service expenses, for example, wages for the secretaries and receptions given in honor of the government officials sent for inspections to Yongning. Given the way in which this land was used, I translate *elu* as public property. This piece of property was inalienable: the central government strictly forbade the sale of administration land in ethnic-minority regions.

Using a rotation and a fallowing system, the *zhifu* cultivated Dekkan wheat, corn, wheat, and oats. Every year, the Dekkan wheat fields needed to be plowed four times, the cornfields twice, and the wheat and oat fields once. Each *lignée* that owned taxable land in the Yongning basin was obligated to plow these fields. This duty applied to all three social strata, including the family of the administrator. Only the *zhifu*'s family, and the few *lignées* that had separated from it two generations earlier or less were exempt from this obligation.

Each household was assigned a lot, whose location and surface area were fixed, to plow on the public property. To fulfill this task, the rich *sïpi lignées* sent their serfs. Households without cattle or those living too far from the field could pay others, or exchange services with them, to do the work. But paying the *zhifu* directly, to escape this service, was not allowed.

Once the plowing was finished, the responsibility of cultivating these fields fell on the internal *dzéka* (those living in the Yongning basin), who were divided into three groups. The first group was made up of thirty households, which were required to work for ninety days. The second group included nineteen households, which worked less than forty days. The third group, of twenty-seven households, worked less than ten days. Oral tradition has it that the differentiation between the first two groups was established according to the surface area of land that they originally held. The third group was mostly made up of *lignées* that had originated in the family of the *zhifu* but were now considered commoners. The Azo *lignées* in Azo and the Ata *lignées* in Hliwalo are examples of this. According to one tradition, these *lignées* estranged from the *zhifu*'s family were initially not required to work in the fields. At some point, however, the *zhifu* decided to cultivate rice in a *çilu* (rice field). Since he did not have enough laborers, he asked the Azo and the Ata *lignées* to lend a hand. From that time on, it became customary for them to work the public land.

Among the *lignées* in the first category, five households were exempt from this obligation. They paid the *zhifu* either with money or goods or with a farm animal, for example. In the second category, thirteen *lignées* were exempt, four of them for the following reasons: the Nata and the Ina because the great-uncles on their maternal sides carried the *zhifu*'s mail three times a year to Kunming, the capital of the province; the Awumi because a Lamaist monk from their *lignée*, a very talented painter, had decorated the Lamaist room in the *zhifu*'s residence; and the Wagwa because one of its members, a very good tailor, had sewn clothing for the *zhifu*. In addition, some commoner households were exempt from the task of cultivation because one of their members held a position in the political organization, such as that of *bashi*, the household's steward, *raimi*, or craftsman.

Commoners who lived outside the central zone were called outlying commoners. Instead of working the public land, as the commoner *lignées* living in the Yongning basin did, they gave a specified amount of grain or money to the *zhifu* each year, depending on the surface area of their property. Certain outlying commoner *lignées* who lived in villages to the north of Walabiai, however, were required to work during the plowing and harvest seasons. This service also initially began as a favor to the *zhifu*, but then became an obligation.

The *zhifu* appointed managers to preside over the *elu*: one *hoe*, four *kwahei*, and one *gemao*. The *hoe* was in charge of setting up the schedule and organizing the work. Under the direction of the *hoe*, each of the four *kwahei* was in charge of several parcels of land. Their job was to inform the households of their workload and schedule and to supervise them in the fields. The job of the *gemao* was to assure the quality of the work and oversee the entire process from the *hoe* down to the workers in the field. This position was held by a member of the Azo *lignée*. All three positions were hereditary.

The *zhifu* also set up twenty *laowuma* jobs; seventeen of them were held by serfs and three by commoners. As payment, the *zhifu* gave each of them a plot of land, ranging in size from 1 *dZia* to 3 *dZia*. They were each assigned one parcel of the *elu*, and their task was to manage its irrigation and to watch over its plants. During plowing, the *laowuma* were also responsible for preparing tea and serving lunch, provided by the *zhifu*, to the *hoe*, *gemao*, *kwahei,* and laborers.

The job of transporting the harvested crops to the *zhifu*'s residence was assigned to commoner and serf households that owned horses or mules.

Plowing of the *elu* always began on January 15.[1] On this date, the *zhifu* slaughtered a pig provided by the aristocratic *lignée* whose turn it was to do so, to prepare a feast for the field managers and the Lamaist monks who came to the *zhifu*'s house to pray for a healthy crop.

The Shifts in Landownership

Before examining privately owned land and the property rights of the three social strata, I will look at the rules concerning the sale, pawning, and renting of land.

Selling land was only allowed in the aristocratic stratum. Pawning land, however, was authorized on all three levels and was frequently practiced among the Na. It was carried out in two forms: the dead pawn and the living pawn.

For a dead pawn, the *lignée* that borrowed against its property was obligated to provide the lending *lignée* with land deeds. The borrower was also required to draw up a contract that had his fingerprints on it. To protect themselves from the borrower's retracting, the lending *lignée* would also ask the *zhifu* to draw up a new engraved wooden plaque. Once he had pawned his property, the borrower could not repurchase it, and all government taxes and services on the *elu* became the responsibility of the lending *lignée*. Because of this, a dead pawn was the equivalent of a sale. This type of pawn developed in the Han regions as a way around the central government's rule forbidding the sale of land and was adopted by the Na, but it rarely took place.

The price of a living pawn was approximately 50 *bankai* or 50 pounds of boned pork per *dZia*. The government taxes and *elu* service remained the responsibility of the *lignée* that was borrowing against its land. The contract was drawn up in Tibetan and handed over to the lending *lignée*. The borrower reserved the right to repurchase his property. Moreover, when he was short of money and an emergency arose, he could ask the lender to add to the sum for the land already pawned. If both sides agreed, the borrower added a note to the contract, and the lender paid the additional sum. This might even be repeated several times, until the lending *lignée* refused. In some cases, there were as many as nine additions, and the final price ended up being so high that the borrower was no longer in a position to buy back his land. In this way, a living pawn became a dead pawn. By 1956, a good number of *lignées* had had their land in hock for several decades, indeed for several generations, without being able to buy it back. The wealthy lending *lignées* often preferred to pay additional sums, to ensure that they could keep the land indefinitely. The lending *lignée* would sometimes cultivate the land obtained in the pawn itself, but it could also rent the land out to others or, with the consent of the borrower, repawn it to other *lignées*.

Land was pawned for the following reasons: to pay for a funeral, to redeem a criminal, to pay off a debt, to compensate for a year of scarcity, to pay taxes or tributes, or to buy farm animals. In most cases, a *lignée*'s desire to have a proper funeral brought about the pawning of land.

Lignées that obtained land through pawning can be divided into two categories: wealthy aristocratic *lignées* and upstart *lignées*; and serf and commoner *lignées,* which, lacking land, attempted to acquire a means to make a living. Prior to 1956, the living pawn was common; at least half of the Na population had resorted to it.

There were two forms of renting land: sharecropping and tenant farming. With sharecropping, the most common rental arrangement among the Na, the landowner took one-third of the harvest when it was corn or Dekkan wheat and two-fifths when it was wheat or oats, which required less work. The sharecropper made three or five piles of the harvested grain in the fields, and the owner chose his first. Sometimes, *lignées* paid their rent with commodities other than grain: chickens, butter, or alcohol, for example. However, this occurred mostly between aristocratic *lignées* and their serfs. Sometimes they paid with work; however, this only took place between commoners and serfs. Some share-croppers paid their rent with grain and with ten to fifteen days of work.

In general, the sharecroppers were commoners or serfs. Among those who rented out their land, most were wealthy aristocrats, but there were also some rich commoners and serfs. A sharecrop-per, no matter what his status, had the right to break the lease. When the lease was between a commoner and a serf, the share-cropper was not required to give the owner anything during the negotiations. On the other hand, if he rented the land from a chief or a Lamaist monastery, he was obligated to give them presents.

Tenant farming took place, for the most part, between the Na and other ethnic groups. Usually, the two sides agreed on a set amount for the rent and recorded it on the lease. The families of other ethnic groups felt that once the lease was concluded, they would be able to harvest more, since their share of the crops would depend solely on their efforts. Na aristocrats insisted on a security deposit from recently immigrated *lignées* of other ethnic groups. If they were unable to pay the security deposit, their rent would be raised to an amount approximately equivalent to 50 percent of the harvest. The rent was usually paid in grain. Only the merchants and craftsmen who rented small patches of land to plant vegetables paid with money. Their leases were much more expensive.

I will now look at the property of the three social strata and the means of production.

Land Owned by Aristocratic Lignées

The land owned by the *zhifu*'s family was called *krulu*. As opposed to *elu*, *kru* means internal (*lu* means land). I translate this word as private land. In 1956, the *krulu*, also in the Yongning basin, was 113 *dZia*, divided into twenty-one plots.

The *zhifu* put ten serf *lignées* in charge of plowing this land. He allocated tools and one buffalo to each of them, as well as 1 *dZia* of land with which to feed the buffalo. When a buffalo became too weak to work, the *zhifu* would replace it. Once a *lignée* gave the buffalo's hide to the *zhifu*, it was entitled to keep the meat. An *ikwa* (the person in charge of the buffalo) was appointed to oversee the animals' conditions.

In 1956, the cultivation of the *krulu*, with the exception of the plowing, was assigned to forty-two serfs (thirty-five men and seven women) who came from thirty-six *lignées*. The men worked in the fields, and the women ground the grain, prepared the meals, and fabricated large linen sacks. These serfs were permitted to return home to work only one day out of four.

The plowing of the *krulu* was managed by the steward of the *zhifu*'s family. Under his direction, two *kwahei* and ten *laowuma* were appointed. The cultivation of this land was much more elaborate than that of the *elu*. The manure was furnished by the *zhifu*'s residence, and if there was not enough, the steward would send serf women to fetch more from the villagers, who were not allowed to refuse. The production generated by the *krulu* greatly exceeded that of the *elu*, even though its surface area was less than half the size of the *elu*. In 1956, for example, the grain harvest from the *elu* weighed 80.5 *dan,* while that of the *krulu* weighed 96 *dan.*[2]

Two storehouses on the *zhifu*'s property stored the harvested grain from the *elu* and the *krulu* separately. The *zhifu* sold grain to other ethnic groups, other regions, and to the caravans.

The *zhifu*'s oldest son, as the official heir, inherited the bulk of the *krulu*. His brothers and sisters each received a part of this land, as well as several serfs, when they left home. A Mingzhu was named the last *zhifu* when he had already left the *zhifu*'s residence and had received 41.5 *dZia* of land as the third son. Designated the successor of his older brother, he continued to manage this parcel of land separately, renting out 29.5 *dZia* of it. The total production of this land, in 1956, was 62 *dan*.

The *zhifu* also owned property in the outlying zone from which he collected, in 1956, 350 *dan* in rent. Moreover, as a *guanren*, the *zhifu* benefited from other revenue.

When an aristocratic *lignée* expired or was without a workforce, the *zhifu* had the right to seize its land. For example, the *zhifu* took Dashi, the only surviving member of the Adgi *lignée*, into his home and took her land (about 40 *dZia*). When Dashi reached adulthood and left the *zhifu*'s residence, she received only 6 *dZia* of land.

Aristocratic *lignées* that had recently separated from the *zhifu*'s family and had a member who held a position in the political organization owned more land and more serfs. For example:

1. A Zhangshen was the paternal uncle of the last *zhifu*, as well as his predecessor's younger brother. Strengthened by his position as uncle, he occupied, once he left the *zhifu*'s residence, a group of buildings in Tozhi and took half of the family's property: land, livestock, and serfs.

2. The administrator's *lignée* had once been a part of the *zhifu*'s family. At the beginning of the century, this *lignée* owned no more than several dozen *dZia* of land. After A Duoqi encroached on the *zhifu*'s power, his *lignée* managed to acquire, through purchases and pawns, much more land. In 1956, it had 229 *dZia* of land in the basin and serfs from thirty-seven *lignées*. Twenty of these serfs (sixteen men and four women) worked on 131 *dZia* of the land. The production from this property was 131 *dan*. The administrator organized the working of these fields in the same manner as the *zhifu* did, with one *kwahei* and thirteen *laowuma*. The rest of his land, 98 *dZia*, was rented to commoners and brought in 39 *dan* in rent. From the outlying zone, he received another 350 *dan* of grain.

3. The *lignée* of A Zicai also separated from the *zhifu*'s family a long time ago. A Zicai had the reputation of being a competent man in the aristocratic stratum. He entered the army of the Guomindang and became a colonel. As a benefit of his position, his *lignée* elevated its status and repurchased the land it had pawned. In 1956, it owned 115 *dZia* of land in the basin, 50 *dZia* in the outlying zone, fifteen serfs, and a large quantity of livestock.

On the other hand, *lignées* that had split from the *zhifu*'s family even earlier and did not have a member in a political position owned less land and fewer serfs and sometimes had lost everything. For example:

1. The aristocratic *lignées* in Bodzi were once, a long time ago, part of the *lignée* of Sonla, the *zhifu*'s younger brother. Sonla received several hundred *dZia* of land when he left home. During Getso's generation, the *lignée* was split into three households, and its land was divided into three parts. Later, other separations occurred and therefore more dividing up of the land. In just five generations, the three *lignées*, Dashi, Gézo, and Luzo, had sold their land, piece by piece, either to other aristocratic *lignées* or to the Lamaist monastery. At the same time, they were also selling their serfs. It was from one of these *lignées* that the *zhifu* purchased Dindgu, one of his family's serfs.

In the beginning of 1950, among the thirteen aristocratic *lignées* in Bodzi that had descended from Sonla, only the Naji owned a serf, and the Tamu bought a serf from another ethnic group. Most of these *lignées* were ruined. In fact, so much so that the Na gave them the nickname "poor *sïpi*." Nonetheless, they continued to enjoy certain privileges. For example, in spite of the *lignées'* decline, the common folk were still required to dismount from their horses when they passed in front of their houses.

2. In Zhongshi, the Jishi *lignée* had only 6.5 *dZia* of land, and the Dzuma *lignée* had only 3. However, in that same village, the Gézo *lignée* had no property at all and became sharecroppers.

3. The Risi *lignée* in Zhongshi sold off its land, piece by piece, to the Chen *bashi*. Three generations ago, it finally sold off its last piece of land. Without a means of subsistence, the entire *lignée* went to the *zhifu*'s residence and offered themselves as serfs.

For *lignées* that had only a few or no serfs, the work in the fields was done, in part or completely, by their own members.

If an aristocrat committed a crime, his *lignée*'s land and serfs could be taken away by the *zhifu*. For example, Naji from Batçi killed a villager in a fight. The *zhifu* confiscated his land and serfs.

Land Owned by Commoner Lignées

Each commoner *lignée* owned a plot of land, which could be given away, rented, or pawned; selling it was forbidden, however. In general, commoners cultivated their land themselves. Sometimes, households with a great deal of property rented out part of it or hired farmworkers annually, or day workers for those periods in which much work was required in the fields.

When a household was in great need of land, it could rent from wealthy aristocratic *lignées*. For example, when Ami, a *baolu* (a woman who has left her original *lignée* because of internal dissension), had children, she rented a small plot of land from an aristocratic *lignée* in Loshu. In general, when land was needed temporarily, for example for a year, as a result of crop rotation, a household would rent from another commoner *lignée*.

In the outlying zone, the land of certain commoner *lignées* was taken away by the *zhifu* or another *guanren* when they were unable to pay their taxes. For example, at the end of the eighteenth century, the inhabitants of Jiachu were unable to pay their taxes three years in a row and therefore the *zhifu* seized all of their land.

When a commoner *lignée* died out or was without a labor force to cultivate its land, or if someone living alone committed a crime, the *zhifu* had the right to seize the land. Part of the property seized in this manner would be added to the *krulu*, and the rest would be distributed among *lignées* who requested it from the *zhifu*. *Lignées* that wanted to obtain land in this manner had to prostrate themselves before the *zhifu* and bring him money or gifts. The Na refer to this as bringing prostration money.[3] The following examples can be cited:

1. Because the Diubu *lignée* in Naha was without descendants, its property (9 *dZia*) was seized by the *zhifu*, who distributed it to the following three *lignées*: Sonnami Ishi, Lather Dindgu, and Waguan Gezo.

2. Four generations ago, there was only one woman left in the Sola *lignée* in Batçi. The *zhifu* confiscated her land (8 *dZia*) and gave it to the Ondzé *lignée* (commoner) in Hliwalo, who, in exchange, offered the *zhifu* two mules and one of its daughters as a serf.

Land Owned by Serfs

Landownership in the serf strata has extremely diversified origins:

1. It was customary for the *zhifu* to give a piece of land, ranging in size from 1 to 3 *dZia*, to a serf when he set up a household. This land was not taxed and would always belong to the serf and his descendants, but it could never be given away, sold, pawned, or rented.

2. The *zhifu* had the custom of giving a piece of land to *lignées* that had a member who held a position in his administration, such as the mail carrier or the manager of the buffalo and the fields. This sort of land was not taxed, but once the person no longer held his job, it had to be returned to the *zhifu*.

3. Certain commoner *lignées* held on to their land even after they had been demoted to the rank of serf. They were therefore required to continue paying taxes. They had, however, the right to pawn or rent their land but not to sell it or give it away.

4. After seizing the land of a *lignée* that had died out, the *zhifu* could give it to a *lignée* in which some or all of the members were serfs. In this case, the *lignée* was required to pay the taxes on the land. Its rights concerning this land were identical to those listed in number 3.

5. Sometimes a *lignée* received land from a *lignée* to which it was related. In this case, the donor continued to pay the taxes.

When households in which one or more members were serfs lacked property, they acquired most of the land they cultivated through pawning and sharecropping.

Land Owned by the Village

In the outlying zone, some of the land was collectively owned. For example, the members of two villages in Loshu owned a piece of land that had been given to them by the *zhifu* because of its proximity to their villages. At one time, the villagers rented it to immigrant Han families. The rent was shared among them. There were two other kinds of collective land. The first was property that had been cleared by several *lignées* who, after farming it themselves for some time, rented it out to others and shared the rent. The second kind of collective land was most often seen in villages far from the Yongning basin in which there were only a few households. When one of the households died out, the *zhifu* would not seize their land. Instead, the other households would take care of it together and rent it out.

Before 1956, in the Yongning basin, almost a third of the land was uncultivated, and it was customary for several Na *lignées* to clear it together.

Taxes and Tributes

The Na had to pay two kinds of taxes. The first was a national tax that was paid to the central government. The *zhifu* collected it from the households, and then turned it over to the district government. The second was a local tax that the *zhifu* also collected. When he was paid in cash, he sent it to the provincial government. When he was paid in kind, he turned over these supplies to the district government or the government army stationed in the region. Payment in kind covered the needs of the permanent and local armies stationed in Yongning. All *lignées* that owned land were required to pay taxes, including the aristocratic *lignées*. Only the *zhifu*'s family and the *lignées* that had split off from his family within the past two generations were exempt. It sometimes happened that the *zhifu* granted extremely impoverished *lignées* permission not to pay the second tax.

According to oral tradition, the amount of taxes each household was required to pay was determined by the amount of land it owned: 1 *liang* of money per each *gu* of land.[4] However, given the large amount of property that was pawned and the amount of property obtained through clearing, the taxes that each *lignée* paid in 1956 were not in proportion to the land they used. For example, the Ago *gnao lignée* paid 0.75 *bankai* for 25 *dZia,* while the Ago *apo lignée* paid 1.5 *bankai* for 15 *dZia,* and the Miindge *lignée* paid 1.5 *bankai* for 35 *dZia.*

Moreover, each commoner household was required to bring the *zhifu* tributes on an annual basis: one basket of zucchini, one basket of *manqing,* one bale of linen (2 pounds) and two large linen bags, one basket and two sieves for each *gu* of land they possessed, one pig every nine years, and several dozen pounds of wheat and oats.[5] During the construction or renovation of the house and enclosing walls of the *zhifu*'s residence, each household was required to provide one man to work for anywhere from several days to one month. *Lignées* that owned a mare had to lend it, as well as a man, for one day to transport the harvested crops from the outlying zone to the *zhifu*'s storehouses. During inspections by government authorities, each household had to provide, when its turn came up, one chicken and ten bowls of alcohol (about 42 liters).

Each time a member of the *zhifu*'s family had a puberty ritual, a marriage, or a funeral, every household was required to give the *zhifu* several pounds of boned pork, and each village grouping was required to offer a cow, linen fabric, and 1 *liang.*

In addition to this, certain households were required to pay special tributes to the *zhifu.* For example, depending on whose turn it was, one of the five *lignées* in the village of Gahla had to give ten iron arrowheads on the first day of the year, even though these arrows no longer served any purpose and had not done so for a long time. Tradition also demanded that the villages of Shuzhi and Yumi offer the *zhifu* five large fish every year, because, according to legend, the *zhifu* had once passed through these villages and had eaten fish. Later, when the *zhifu* no longer found this fish to his liking, he asked the villagers to replace it with ham.

In all of the villages, the older people said that, like the three strata, taxes and tributes did not exist before Yamaa. When did the central government begin to collect taxes from the Na, and when did the *zhifu* begin to offer a tribute to the emperor?

Han texts to offer answers to these questions.

Yunnan tongzhi (The general report of Yunnan), from 1576, states that official and civil land in the regions was governed by the *tusi* of Yunnan, but it does not mention anything about the Yongning *tusi*'s jurisdiction.[6] *Dian zhi* (The report of the Dian), from 1652, however, explicitly mentions that the inhabitants of Yongning *fu* "were people from other ethnic groups (non-Han) who lived under a *tusi*. The government has no representation there and has not asked them to pay taxes or required any service from them." "They only pay a tribute of 27 *liang* and five horses."[7] It was not until 1765, according to *Yongbei fu zhi* (The account of the prefecture of Yongbei), that the central government "actually collected 190 *liang* 4 *qian* 1 *fen* 6 *li* of money" in taxes from the Yongning *tusi*'s jurisdiction.[8] These taxes were paid annually.

This information shows that under the Ming dynasty the *zhifu* of Yongning paid a tribute to the central government but not taxes and that under the Qing dynasty the original Na landowning system underwent a change. But what was the Na landowning system before the central government imposed its laws? And how did these laws modify it? Due to a lack of available sources, it is impossible, at least for the time being, to answer these two questions.

After the Republic of China was established in 1911, the Guomindang government continued to apply the same policies to ethnic minorities as the Qing dynasty had. The new government simply conducted a rational cadastral survey. Yongning was surveyed in 1938.

In accordance with Han society, which is patrilineal, only an adult male, the head of the household, had the right to represent a family and therefore to sign any papers concerning landownership. Only when there was no adult male in the household could an adult female put her signature on such documents. The Na followed the same convention, as can be seen in the signed contract for land exchanged in 1897 between the *zhifu* and Chen *bashi* under the Qing dynasty. Likewise, in "The Inventory of Rentals in the [Yongning] Basin," drawn up in 1919 by the administrator, and on land leases issued after the 1938 cadastral survey by the district government, the signature is that of an adult male in the majority of cases.

I found no mention in the Han texts of any tributes that the Na were required to pay to the *zhifu*.

From the above description, we can see that every *lignée* that owned land had to pay taxes and that practically every aristocratic and commoner household was required either to work the public land or to transport grain for the *zhifu*. These obligations relating to public land were a tax in kind paid to the *zhifu*'s administration. Therefore, until 1956, the Na had two kinds of taxes to pay: one to the central government and one to the local government.

We have seen that the Na did not begin to pay taxes to the central government until the Qing dynasty. Since the taxes they paid to the *zhifu* were connected to the government tax, they most certainly date from this same era. We know that the Na were already paying tributes to the central government during the Ming dynasty, and, if it is true that tributes paid by the Na to the *zhifu* date back only as far as the era of Yamaa, a question, already raised, comes up again: Who was Yamaa, and what occurred during his era?

Under the landownership system followed by the Na until 1956, in spite of the ban on commoners' selling their land, the dead and living pawns of land parcels by aristocrats and commoners were the equivalents of sales. In fact, when the owner was unable to buy back the land he had pawned, either in a living or a dead pawn, the situation became identical to that of a sale.

The dynamic aspect of the concession of land could have consequences for one's social status. Aristocrats who lost their land could be demoted to the rank of commoners or even the rank of serfs (such a demotion could also have a political cause, a struggle for power, for example).[9] Most commoners, excluding those who became serfs because they had committed a crime, were demoted due to the concession of their land. Therefore, the loss of land constituted the most significant threat to their status.

As governor, the *zhifu* benefited from several advantages. Throughout history, he continued to obtain new land by seizing the property of *lignées* that had died out and to enjoy a never-ending supply of serfs thanks to his judiciary role. These two privileges, among others, allowed the *zhifu* to give land as well as serfs to each of his children in each generation and thereby maintain the economic equilibrium of his family.

I have already mentioned that at the beginning of the century, the *zhifu*'s real power fell into the hands of the administrator. However, this in no way affected his judicial privileges. The *zhifu* still benefited from all of the privileges associated with his title. This demonstrates the effectiveness of the central government's control over the regions in which the native chiefs ruled.

Finally, several remaining points need to be mentioned:

1. Part of the land seized by the *zhifu* would be added to his private property rather than ceded to the public land or to commoners in need of land. This fact suggests that the *zhifu* was able to act, according to his own strategies, on his own behalf.

2. That a household that had fallen to the rank of serf was able to keep its nontaxable land testifies to the flexibility of the *zhifu*'s management and to the flexibility of the system of social stratification.

3. In this society, no matter what their status, the *lignées* all owned material goods. Serf *lignées*, even while they could be sold by their master, enjoyed economic independence. Thus all of the households, with the exception of the *zhifu*'s, had the possibility to become rich as well as poor. Certain aristocratic *lignées* lost a part, indeed sometimes all, of their means of production and serfs. On the other hand, certain commoner and serf *lignées* became rich and owned not only a great deal of land but also serfs. We can see by this that the status of a *lignée* neither guaranteed its economic circumstances nor prevented it from degradation. Therefore, each household's economic level can be disassociated from its status. This suggests that on an economic and judicial level this society maintained an aspect of equality.

As this section comes to a close, I will simply state that until the Ming dynasty, on issues of landownership, the administrative rules of the central Chinese government were not fully implemented in the Yongning region. Only later, with the Qing dynasty, did the influence of the central government reach the Na. The institution of public and private property and of taxes marked the central government's increased control of the Na.

CHAPTER FIVE

Religions

Na religious life is guided by coexisting beliefs: those of their own religion, in which the priests are called *daba*, and those of Tibetan Buddhism. These two religions have influenced each other. Because the subject of this book is social structure, I have focused primarily on the study of kinship in my fieldwork. Moreover, since the available data make a complete study in this domain impossible, I will merely present certain facts here that give some sense of the connection between the religious life, on the one hand, and kinship and political life, on the other.

The Daba

The Na use the word *daba* to refer to their religious specialists. The majority of *daba* are men; however, before the 1940s, several women were *daba*. When they are not engaged in religious activities, they spend most of their time working the land. They have no organization and conduct their rituals individually.

Without a scripture, the *daba* practice their rites using oral accounts only. Because the language of these accounts is ancient Na, the *daba* of today can only understand the sections that they frequently use. The villagers told us me following anecdote about the scriptures of the *daba:* "At one time, the *daba* had their canons written on pigskin. One day, while traveling, the masters were hungry. Since they had nothing to eat, they cooked and ate their books. Ever since then, they have had no scripture."

During their rituals, the *daba* use a hat and hold a small square staff, approximately 30 centimeters long and 2.5 centimeters wide. On the four surfaces of the staff are engraved drawings of a man, a woman, a steer, a horse, a goat, a pig, a dog, a tiger, a leopard, a lion, a deer, a fish, a flower, some grass, and a tree.

The *daba* recite prayers for the following rituals:[1]

1. *bu sï nin*, the annual ritual of offerings to the ancestors. During this ritual, a *daba* familiar with the ancestors of a lineage recites their names so that they will come back and share in the Na New Year's Day feast. This ritual was abolished in 1958, the first year of the People's Commune period. Today it is only practiced in some very remote villages.

2. *dZI do*, the ritual for sending the souls of the dead to the place where their ancestors reside.

3. *na dgu bu*, the annual ritual for chasing away impurities. This ritual only took place in the *zhifu*'s residence. It was conducted in the place where waste was discarded, in November of the lunar calendar, to wish the *zhifu*'s family a good and happy year.

4. *dza bu*, the annual ritual of making a sacrifice to the spirit of the mountains.

5. *na tié bu*, the ritual of making a sacrifice to *na tié*, the female spirit who takes care of gynecological diseases.

6. *dZi kru bu*, the ritual of making a sacrifice to the spirit of the wells who watches over diseases of the eyes.

7. *ge shu bu*, the ritual for calling out to the soul of a person who was frightened by an accident or a bad dream.

8. *wai grai*, the ritual for making the soul of a dying person return so that he can live for a few more days.

9. *do na tçi*, the ritual of exorcising the dark demon from the sick.

10. *za bu*, the ritual used for chasing away the demon *za*.

11. *hai krai*, the prayers addressed to *za* so that he will let the dead pass through on the path that leads to their ancestors.

12. *si bu tu*, the ritual conducted so that newlyweds would stay together for life. This ritual was only performed for the *zhifu*'s family.

13. *cho do cho*, the prayers said during the service of offerings to the ancestors.[2]

One of the *daba*'s instruments, called a *dga*, represents the male sex on one side and the female sex on the other. This wooden sculpture symbolizes the supreme power of the *daba*. Currently, in the Yongning basin, it is in the possession of the *daba* in Dapo. Others can be found in neighboring regions, in Labo, for example.

Only the *daba* who possesses this statuette can take on three disciples. These disciples first learn to recite the prayers and to serve as assistants to their master during rituals. When the *daba* becomes too old to continue his practice, he conducts a ritual during which the three disciples, who are seated with their eyes closed, must recite the prayers. The one who sees the *dga* while praying inherits all of his master's abilities. The *daba* then hands over the *dga*, as well as a leather armor, to him. From that day on, he can officiate at the rites and instruct disciples. After this ritual, the other disciples can also preside over rites, but they are not entitled to take on disciples. However, they are entitled to pass on their knowledge to their uterine niece or nephew (although this is extremely rare). If a *daba* is married, he sometimes passes his knowledge on to a son.

According to the *daba* in Dapo, on the day that a disciple receives the *dga*, the master orders the disciple's brother to slaughter a red bull and a black chicken for a ceremony, during which a feast is prepared. Representatives from each *lignée* in the surrounding villages are invited.

In another version of this, according to a *daba* who also lives in the Yongning basin, a black chicken is slaughtered because the *dga* originated from a white eagle.

A third version comes from a *daba* in Labo. According to him, on the day chosen by the master to hand over his power to the disciple, the disciple is asked to undergo a complicated ritual in front of the senior members of the villages and the *daba*. Once this examination is over, a black bull is sacrificed. Finally, the master leads his disciple to the snow-covered slopes of the mountains where he secretly transmits his power. This is how knowledge is transmitted from one generation to the next.

The *daba* participates in all of the farmwork. When he conducts a ritual, he is very poorly paid.

Daba and Lamaist monks share certain rituals, for example, those of divination, of calling forth the soul of someone who is scared, of healing, of offering services to the spirit of the mountains, and of funerals. When a *daba* becomes sick, he sometimes calls in a Lamaist monk and vice versa. However, because the two religions do not send their dead to the same place, only a *daba* can perform rituals that have anything to do with ancestors and recite the prayers aimed at sending the soul of a dead one to join his ancestors in Sibuanawa. Traditional religion treats the dead as members of a social group, whereas Buddhism treats the dead as individuals.

Between 1956 and 1980, religion was more and more discouraged in China. After 1980, the practice of major religions, such as Taoism, Buddhism, Christianity, and Islam, was authorized once again by the government. But other religions were still considered superstitions, and therefore forbidden. Three decades of repression took their toll. On the one hand, many villagers no longer remember the rituals of the *daba* very well, and on the other hand, the *daba* themselves are quite old or gone altogether.[3] This is why the *daba* spoke to me somewhat timidly and why the cadres were extremely cautious when in need of a ritual carried out by a *daba*. For example, during my last stay in 1992, I interviewed three *daba*. One of them told me that in six days he would be conducting rituals for a *lignée* and invited me to attend. The day arrived, and I began by looking for the chief of the *lignée*, a cadre in the district government whom I had met during my third visit. When he saw me, he warmly invited me into his home for a meal and started talking with me. However, he canceled all of the planned rituals to be conducted by the *daba*.

The Lamaist Monks

The Na piously believe in Tibetan Buddhism. Before the 1960s, two sects existed in Yongning, the white and the yellow (*gelugpa*, or virtuous), who had arrived there through Muli, a neighboring district to the north, in Sichuan Province. In 1956, the white sect included 220 Lamaist monks, of whom 188 were Na and the rest were Pumi. Eighty of them had received their religious training in Batan, in Sichuan. Their monastery was in Dgebo and had been built in 1356. The yellow sect included 511 Lamaist monks, of whom 441 were Na, 56 were Pumi, and 3 were Tibetan. Their Dgamége monasteries, to the west of the Yongning basin, were constructed in 1556.[4] The monastery in Dgebo and two of the three buildings in Dgamége were destroyed during the Cultural Revolution. Today, only the yellow sect remains, and in 1989 it included 172 Lamaist monks.

At first, the position of *mkhan-po*, the leader of the order, was conferred on Lamaist monks who had successfully completed their studies in Lhasa, usually Tibetans. However, in the twentieth century, the second son of the *zhifu* was given this role in the monastery of Dgamége. Until 1956, both A Shaofu and A Minqi, from two successive generations of the *zhifu*'s family, held this position. But before 1954, the two monasteries had only Tibetan living Buddhas.

Every Na household is devoted to Buddhism and sets up a room for Buddhist activities. The Lamaist monk in a *lignée* usually lives at home, where he reads the sacred texts, and only goes to the monastery once in a while. In each Na household that has two or more sons, at least one of them, usually the youngest, would become a Lamaist monk. In the past, when a household had three sons, two of them might become Lamaist monks. Therefore, before 1956, almost one-third of the adults were Lamaist monks. This extremely high percentage led Joseph F. Rock to think that this society practiced the modality of the visit because there was a shortage of men.[5] In reality, most of the Lamaist monks in Yongning, as members of *matrilignées*, were practicing then, and are practicing now, the mode of the visit, just like the other villagers.

Prior to 1956, young Lamaist monks, on the eve of their departure for Tibet, would set up a tent on the banks of the Kaitçi River in Riyuehe and spend the night there with a lover. Those who did not have a lover would pay a woman for this night, for they believed that if they did not have sex, not only would an accident occur on their trip to Lhasa but they would not succeed in getting a high-level diploma.

Even those who had already pronounced their vows did not observe chastity. A Shaofu knew many women while he was the *mkan po*. After his nephew succeeded him, he began to cohabit with a serf in a house that belonged to the monastery. Some Tibetan Lamaist monks from the Zhongdian District (a Tibetan region northwest of Yunnan) were forced, after their stay in the Na monastery, to remain in Yongning for the rest of their lives because the monasteries in Zhongdian absolutely refused Lamaist monks who did not respect their vow of chastity.

Children who become Lamaist monks begin their studies at about seven years old. Before 1956, each child had to pay 1 *liang*, the load of wood one horse could carry eighteen times over, and 20 pounds of grain as tuition. The Lamaist monks who studied only in Yongning did little manual labor, while those who were trained in Lhasa devoted themselves exclusively to religious practice. On the other hand, almost half of all Lamaist monks traded with the caravans between Lijiang and Tibet because their status facilitated travel and contact with other ethnic groups, especially with Tibetans.

Lamaist monks are well respected and enjoy a privileged status, both inside and outside the home. Those educated in Tibet for a long time rise to an even more prestigious level. Even their ascendants are required to look up to them. For example, when a Lamaist monk comes to sit near the hearth of the main room, he takes the seat usually reserved for the eldest member of the *lignée*.

In 1956, the Dgamége monastery owned 278 *dZia* of land, most of which was obtained through pawning. While A Shaofu was the *mkan po*, 257 *dZia* of this land were rented out. In addition, the monastery had a fund of 20,516 *bankai* that it lent out with interest, and this was its main source of income.

When a Lamaist monk commits a crime, the *mkan po* punishes him. In general, the punishment is more severe than the *zhifu*'s punishment for the same crime committed by a layman. For example, Ishi (a Lamaist monk) from the Gefu *lignée* in Ami, along with Tsie from the neighboring village, robbed a Han merchant from the Heqing District. All of his land (15 *dZia*) was confiscated by A Shaofu, the *mkan po*, to the benefit of the Dgamége monastery. Ishi was demoted to the rank of serf.

Prior to 1956, the Lamaist monks of the Dgamége monastery organized nine fairs every year, which were attended by Na from all of the villages.

The Political Role of the Buddhist Organization

In contrast to the *daba*, who, with no organization and being few in number, have no influence on political life, the Buddhists are the second most important organization in Na society in all of the region. Only their power is a match for secular power. Several historical events illustrate the influence of Buddhist power on the political life of this society:

1. A Shaofu had great political importance. When he was *mkan po*, he would not countenance the general administrator's encroachments on his older brother's power. In one way or another, he repeatedly tried to defy him. Relations between the two powers were therefore very tense.

In 1935, A Shaoyun, the general administrator, was behind a plot to have the monastery pillaged by a group of Tibetans. One night, these Tibetans destroyed the belongings of the monastery and killed the livestock in the villages that surrounded it. The next day, a cow returned to Yongning and was claimed by a Lamaist monk from Totçi. But a Pumi from Bitçi also insisted that the cow belonged to him. The monk therefore complained to the *mkan po*, and the Pumi complained to the administrator general, who decided to confiscate the cow. This decision outraged both the villagers and the Lamaist monks. Therefore Ala, the *raimi* of Bitçi, sent out the knotted cords and succeeded in assembling more than a thousand villagers and Lamaist monks. They ravaged the property of the administrator general, who fled to an island in Lake Lugu, and then to Baijiaoba. Since Mishawa, a Yi chief, was an accomplice to the administrator, the rebels massacred his livestock as well.

A Shaoyun sought the help of the Pumi chiefs in Muli and of the Yi. Together, they gathered several thousand Pumi and Yi and, under the command of Mishawa, returned to attack the Dgamége monastery. They killed several dozen Lamaist monks and destroyed many houses. As they were leaving, they set fire to the monastery and to the villages along their return route.

This is the most significant event of the first half of the century, one that many of the older Na remember well. Following this incident, the Guomindang government sent two officials to Yongning, who had two *raimi* — the organizers of the rebellion — shot. During this rebellion and its aftermath, the *zhifu* was merely a puppet of the general administrator.

2. In 1931, the leader of Lhasa declared that Losan, A Shaoyun's half brother, was the reincarnation of a living Buddha in the monastery of Delimin (in Sichuan). After his studies in Lhasa, under normal circumstances, Losan would have gone to Delimin. But in order to monopolize both political and religious powers, A Shaoyun succeeded, through corruption, in getting him to return to Yongning in 1954. That year, Losan became the first Na religious leader to be a living Buddha.

3. After 1956, the government promoted atheism. Little by little, it went from propaganda to an all-out ban on religion. During the Cultural Revolution, Losan was forced to leave Yongning and go to Ninglang. But this did not lessen the hold that he had on the Na. In 1985, with a change in policy regarding religion, Losan was able to return to Yongning for the first time in almost two decades, to participate in the feast of the goddess. The Na people came to greet him.

The unification of political and religious power that, from the beginning of the century, had been in the hands of the *zhifu*'s family, followed by the desire of the administrator general to unite these two powers in himself, shows the enormous influence of Buddhism. The holder of secular power could not truly rule in this society without mastering religious power at the same time.

Under Tibetan influence, the secular leader often tried to unite, and thereby monopolize, secular and religious powers in his family by having one of its members be a religious leader. But he could not succeed in unifying these powers in the hands of one person, as is the case in Tibet, for they did not come from the same source. Not only did they not share the same legitimacy, but they originated in different cultures and represented two hetero-geneous conceptions. Because of this, once these two powers were separated and fell into the hands of two people who not only were from different families but opposed each other, their structural heterogeneity unbalanced society and threatened to create turmoil. The possibility of the separation and the opposi-tion of these powers constitutes a dynamic factor of political life. Clearly, Tibetan Buddhism has influenced Na political structure.

CHAPTER SIX

Neighboring Ethnic Groups

In the preceding chapters, I have sometimes referred to the different ethnic groups that live near the Na. In this chapter, I present a general survey of all of the neighboring ethnic groups in order to examine the ruling Na's attitudes toward them and relations with them. Today, in the Yongning region, the neighbors of the Na include ten ethnic groups: the Pumi, the Han, the Zhuang, the Yi, the Li-su, the Miao, the Tibetans, the Naxi, the Bai, and the Hui (Muslim). In relation to the Na, these groups are minorities and are less powerful, both economically and politically.

Characteristics of the Neighboring Ethnic Groups

The Pumi

The Pumi are farmers and number approximately 30 thousand. They are spread out in the districts of Langping (which has approximately 15 thousand of them) and Ninglang (which has approximately 75 hundred). The rest can be found sporadically in the districts of Lijiang, Yongshen, Wi-xi, Zhongdian, Muli, and Yanyuan.

Long ago, the Pumi lived east of Sichuan. In the middle of the thirteenth century, subjugated by the Yuan dynasty, they entered

Yunnan with the Mongolian army, which was heading south with the aim of conquering the kingdom of Dali.[1] At that time, they were hunters and farmed on burned land.

Pumi society is patrilineal, and they practice monogamy. Marriages are arranged by parents. Only the sons are entitled to inherit their parents' property; the house is always bequeathed to the eldest son. The Pumi language, which has no written form, belongs to the Qiang branch of the Tibeto-Burmese family. Except for the *hangui*, their priests, the Pumi believe in Tibetan Buddhism.

From the time they first arrived in Yunnan Province until 1956, the Pumi were ruled by the Na and the Naxi of Lijiang. Therefore, there were two types of social organization in this ethnic group: those living in Langping and its surrounding areas were under the Han regime, without social stratification, while those in the Yongning region were stratified during the era of Yamaa. Among the latter, the majority were *dzéka*, a few were *we*, and none were *sïpi*. They were required to respect the customary rights of the *zhifu* of Yongning. The Pumi were the Na's only neighboring ethnic group implicated in their social-stratification system. They are the second-oldest ethnic group in the Yongning region. Most of the other ethnic groups immigrated to Yongning much more recently.

The Han

Only a few Han families immigrated around 1800. They are now almost completely assimilated and are taken for Na by the Na. For example, the family of the Chen *bashi* in Kaitçi came from the Yanyuan District in Sichuan nine generations ago. The most significant Han immigration from the south to the Yongning region did not occur until the 1930s or later. For the most part, these later immigrants came with their families and kept up their own customs. Currently, they number approximately 2 thousand people.

The Zhuang

The Zhuang from the Guangxi arrived five generations ago, during the second half of the nineteenth century, through Guizhou Province.[2] Today, there are approximately 1 thousand of them.

The Yi

For the most part, Yi immigration to Yongning occurred at two different times, in 1920 and in 1935. Because they were accustomed to living high in the mountains and surviving by growing potatoes and corn and raising goats, the *zhifu* gave them the mountains southwest and northeast of the Yongning basin.[3]

The Li-su

The Li-su, who now live on the banks of the Jingsha River, arrived approximately 130 years ago. In 1956, they numbered only 1 hundred. Today, there are about 7 thousand of them because of recent immigration. They are mainly farmers, but during the slow seasons in the fields, they mine for gold in the river.

The Miao

The Miao are farmers who immigrated to Yongning at the end of the nineteenth century. There are about 5 hundred of them there today.

The Tibetans

Since the 1930s, Tibetan immigration to Yongning has been sporadic. Currently, there are approximately 1 hundred Tibetans in Yongning from the districts of Zhongdian and western Sichuan. They speak a very different dialect from that spoken in Tibet. Before 1956, some of them took care of raising yaks in aristocratic households. Today, about ten Tibetan families tend to yaks; the others are farmers.

The Naxi, the Bai, and the Hui

Currently, the Naxi, the Bai, and the Hui each has a population of approximately 1 hundred. They moved to Yongning during the Second World War and worked as leather-shoe makers, carpenters, tailors, and shopkeepers.

The Zhifu's Attitude toward Immigration

Beginning with the *gaituguiliu* campaigns of the Qing dynasty, the Na rulers strongly tried to curb the massive immigration of other ethnic groups into the Yongning region, in particular, that of the Han. They strictly forbade the Na people to learn Chinese and to grow rice and people of other ethnic groups to open shops in the town of Yongning. For example:

1. On assignment in Yongning, an inspector from the Yongbei District government under the Guomindang proposed to the *zhifu* that he cultivate rice. Instead of preparing rice plants right there in Yongning, the administrator had them brought back from the banks of the Jinsha River by several of his valets. With more than 1,000 meters' difference in altitude between Yongning and the banks of the river, where the climate is very hot, the plants died quickly.

2. In 1923, a Han farmer tried to grow rice on land he was renting in the Yongning basin. After the planting, the *zhifu*, who had been informed, reprimanded Ishi, the Na owner of the land, and ordered the farmer immediately to uproot the plants.

The Na rulers believed that if rice grew in Yongning, the Han would arrive in droves, because in their eyes, the Han lived off rice. If this were to happen, the central government would be able to install a Han magistrate in Yongning, which might weaken the Na's power or, if he replaced the Na *zhifu*, overturn it altogether. The ban on rice growing was, consequently, a preventive measure against Han immigration and therefore against administrative intervention by the central government.

However, the Na rulers never attempted to forbid Na Lamaist monks from going to Tibet to pursue their religious studies. At that time, one out of ten Na Lamaist monks did so, and the number continued to grow.

This contrast in the Na chiefs' attitudes toward Han culture and Tibetan culture is revealing. It shows that the Na rulers considered Han immigration to and the introduction of Han culture in Yongning direct threats to their administrative authority, which depended on a Han government. Tibetan influence, on the other hand, represented no real threat. Tibetan culture, notably its religion, was, as we have seen, capable of setting religious power in opposition to secular power and therefore of upsetting the balance of Na political life. However, this potential was completely latent, because such an opposition could only come about when secular and religious power was not controlled by the same family.

Another event that illustrates the Na rulers' attitudes occurred during the Guomindang era in the 1920s. When merchants and craftsmen from various ethnic groups arrived in Batsïgu to set up shops, government officials in charge of taxation came to the town. A Duoqi, the administrator at the time, prevented the opening of these shops: "In Yongning, under my authority, opening a store or conducting business is not permitted. If the existence of the stores brings a Han administrator to Yongning, the store owners will be responsible for any consequences." Under his orders, all of the shops were closed. This situation lasted until his death (around 1920).

Clearly, the attitudes of the Na rulers toward other ethnic groups and their respective cultures depended, above all, on their own political interests. They protected themselves against anything that was likely to harm their power.

PART TWO

Kinship and the

Modality of Sexual Life

Until now, it has been claimed that through marriage all societies are based on the family. The Na, however, seem to have followed another way of life. In the description that follows, I present first the symbolic thinking that relates to their kinship and their basic social unit and then their modalities of sexual life.

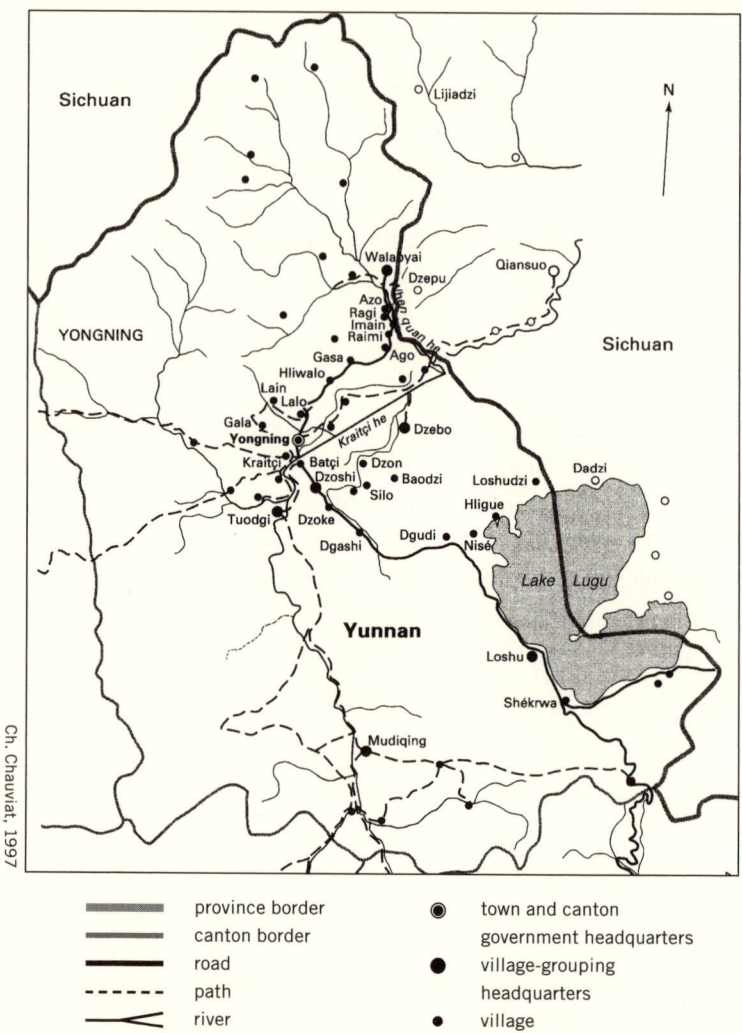

Map 3. The distribution of Na villages in the canton of Yongning.

Source: Map of the autonomous district of the Yi of Ninglang, in *Ninglang Yizu zi-zhixian* (The report of the autonomous district of the Yi of Ninglang) (Kunming: People of Yunnan Press, 1993).

CHAPTER SEVEN

The Foundation of the Na

Kinship System

Genealogical Survey

My field of investigation consists of the following five villages, or *wa*: Ago, Raimi, Imin, Ragi, and Azo. They are in the northern part of the Yongning basin and under the administrative grouping of the Wenquan villages. According to a November 1989 census, Ago had nineteen households and a population of 147; Raimi had four households and a population of 43; Imin had twenty households and a population of 114; Ragi had seven households and a population of 64; and Azo had fifteen households and a population of 106. Therefore, the total population was sixty-five households and 474 people.[1]

I conducted my genealogical survey in public and in the presence of members from each household, and often of other villagers, who were attracted by the spectacle of the discussions. I began by questioning old people (women, for the most part), but not necessarily the oldest, who were not always so clearheaded; their opinions were useful only in confirming the answers of others.

From a given genealogical position, I traced matrilineal relations back as far as the oldest known female ancestor and then followed the reverse process and descended down to the youngest existing generation. In this way, I obtained the entire genealogy of each *matrilignée*. Once the genealogy of a *lignée* was recorded, I repeated the same operation with any other lineages that claimed to have the same female ancestor as my original *lignée*. This process allowed me to uncover the entire range of consanguineally related *lignées*, in other words, the ensemble of this *lignée*'s consanguineal relatives in spite of any eventual splits. This process sometimes made it possible for me to gather other information and thereby confirm the data of one genealogy by comparing it with that of another. Finally, I verified the genealogies obtained in this manner with some of the older people who had known the village's past generations well. They helped me to correct certain errors and to fill in the blanks.

Through this process, I collected the elements that made it possible to retrace the consanguineal *lignées* of all the individuals, whether or not they lived within the geographical confines of my parameters of research, and I was therefore able to determine, without omitting anyone, which *matrilignées* were consanguineally related.

Collecting the chronological data, at least that on past generations, was the most difficult part. In fact, it was almost impossible to find anyone able to recall the names and the consanguineal relatives of his ascendants further back than two generations before his oldest living relative.

The Concept of Procreation

The villagers told me about procreation through several legends:

1. "In olden days, Abaodgu (a good spirit) decided that man would carry the child in his calf. But when the man went to fetch wood in the mountains, the weight was too heavy for him. So Abaodgu decided that the child should be carried by the woman in her belly."

2. "Abaodgu puts the fetus in the bellies of women five months after they are born and nourishes the fetus during pregnancy."[2]

3. "A long, long time ago, to become pregnant, a woman simply had to position herself on a mountain pass and open her vagina so that the wind could enter."

Some sources claimed that a woman could become pregnant without intercourse, but if she did so, she would give birth to snakes, toads, or farts, because she would have met up with evil spirits. The Na understand, of course, that mating between a man and a woman is necessary for procreation.

What then is the role of the man in procreation? After asking about human secretions — tears, sweat, saliva, milk, blood, urine, and sperm (*dZi kra*, or penis water, is also the term used to designate urine; they know, of course, the difference between the two substances because of their appearances) — I did not get an answer. I did, however, get a response when I asked about metaphors, sayings, and popular songs. In fact, one of their metaphorical expressions is "mu o hi mao gi, di go zï mao Zi" (if the rain does not fall from the sky, the grass will not grow on the ground). And frequently they add: "No matter how strong a woman may be, if she is not bedded by a man, she cannot make a baby." The identification of the offspring with grass is revealing, for it implies the initial presence of a seed in the earth (the belly of the woman) whose development is set in motion by a contribution from outside: the rain (sperm). Therefore, to a certain degree, the man is merely a waterer. This corresponds to Abaodgu's decision and is reinforced by the saying "dZiobu dZia i sï," which literally means "having a good time [making love] is a charity to the woman's household." They explained that "in mating, the aim of the woman is to have children, and the aim of the man is to have a good time and to do an act of charity."

My informants added: "If a woman does not get pregnant, it is her problem alone. It has nothing to do with the man because, like other women, she has relations with different men, and other women are pregnant while she isn't. It must be that her sexual parts are blocked." Several sources told me about a famous case of a woman who was considered a beauty and who had had more than a hundred partners without ever becoming pregnant. One of my best sources, a sixty-one-year-old man, remarked, "Some of the men must, probably, have a problem, too. Take me, for example. I went to women's homes all over the place and not one of them had a child with me."

The concept that the fetus comes only from the mother is supported by two other metaphors: "bo mi nu pu, bo zo nu pu" (if the sow has a turned-up mouth, the piglets will have turned-up mouths, too) and "bo mi do ga pu, bo zo do ga pu" (if the sow has a colored head, the piglets will have colored heads), which means "Like mother, like child."

I found no information about the relationships between one human secretion and another. Each time I asked about this, my sources were perplexed.

Consanguinity

For the Na, *ong* (bone) is traditionally considered the carrier of hereditary and racial characteristics. It comes from the mother and is an immutable principle. When I asked "Where does flesh come from?" they were baffled and frequently responded with the phrase: "hing ong hing na dhe da emi gi zé dge" (a person's flesh and bones both come from the mother). They also frequently added: "hing ong hing na dhe giai dZio" (flesh and bones go together), "ong mao dZio, na ti mao di" (without bones, the flesh would not grow).[3] A shaman told me that "bone comes from ChaihondZidZimé." ChaihondZidZimé, according to their myth of genesis, is a goddess who descended from heaven after a flood to cohabit with the only surviving human. However, this was the only shaman I met who linked bones to the legend in this manner.

The Matrilignée

At birth, a child is automatically a part of his or her mother's group. Traditionally, those who have the same true female ancestor living under the same roof are considered *ong hing* in relation to one another. The word *ong* means bone, and *hing* means people (literally, bone people). Anyone who originated in the same woman is designated in this manner, independent of his place of residence.

In this study, I use the word *blood* for *ong* and *consanguineal relatives* for *ong hing*.

In each generation, the brothers and sisters work, eat, and raise the children born to the sisters together. They live together for their entire lives. Normally, this kind of household can stay together for several generations, sometimes more than ten, without separating. The Na residential kinship group is therefore made up of consanguineal relatives and is exclusively matrilineal. This is particularly astonishing since George Peter Murdock, after having treated the problem of relatives grouped by blood and relatives grouped by residence, concluded, "The residential type is always characterized by common residence; the consanguineal type never."[4]

The Na call this group of blood relatives *lhe* and explained it as follows: "dhe lhe dhe ong nié" (every *lhe* comes from the same bone). This term is used only to designate, for example, my *lhe*, your *lhe*, or a specific *lhe*, in which case *lhe* would be followed by a proper noun. It cannot be followed by a number; for example, you cannot say "twenty *lhe*." Another word, *Zï,* is used when referring to the number of households. In their study of the Na,

Chinese ethnologists believed that the Na word *Zidu* designated this group of blood relatives. However, *Zidu* refers to all of the members living under the same roof, without distinguishing blood relationships, and to all of the belongings of this household: the house, land, livestock, clothing, money, and so on, in short, all of their property. In other words, *Zidu* = household + matriamony.[5] The Na use the word *Zidu* to talk about the success and prosperity of a household on both an economic and a human level.

The *lhe* is the fundamental kinship unit of blood relatives as well as the basic economic unit. Within a *lhe,* all property is passed down collectively from one generation to the next.

Using the village of Ragi as an example, Figure 7.1 illustrates the standard structure of a household. I translate *lhe* as *matrilignée*. In the five villages in my parameters of research, there are, in all, thirty-six *matrilignées* of this kind in sixty-three households.

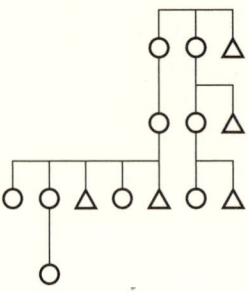

Figure 7.1 The standard structure of a household.

The Matrilignée Chiefs

Within each *matrilignée*, there are generally two *dabu* (chiefs), a man and a woman.[6] According to a Na expression: "The male chief takes care of exterior affairs, and the female chief takes care of interior affairs."

In each household, one of the chiefs plays a greater role in decision making, thanks to his or her qualities and experience. As a result, the female chief dominates in some *lignées*, while in others, the male chief does. Within the parameters of my research, among the sixty-three households, there were fifty-eight female chiefs and forty-seven male chiefs (five households had no female chiefs, and sixteen had no male chiefs, due to a shortage in the *matrilignée* of adults of that sex).

In principle, the female chief takes care of affairs inside the household: the annual distribution of clothing, the management of savings and expenses, the organization of work in the home and in the fields, the daily service of offerings to the ancestors, and the daily preparation and serving of meals. When guests come for celebrations and rituals, it is her responsibility to prepare the feast, gifts, and donations. Prior to 1956, the female chief went on behalf of the *matrilignée* to offer gifts to the *zhifu* on New Year's Day.

The male chief is mainly in charge of dealing with the outside world: the land, the livestock, and helping other villagers on a temporary or annual basis when they are in need. As representative of the *lignée*, he presides over feasts when his *lignée* receives guests and accepts invitations to the homes of others.

The Na have a custom of conducting a service of offerings to the ancestors each time they have something to eat or drink, even a cup of tea. At every meal, the female chief (or the oldest girl, if she is big enough) serves the food. Before eating, she puts a small amount of each dish on the *gwa lu*, a stone tablet directly behind the cooking area. When a member of the *lignée* eats before the others do, because, for example, he is on his way out of the house, he conducts this same ritual. After the harvest of each grain crop, such as wheat, corn, Dekkan wheat, and rice, and in October, when the pigs are slaughtered, each *lignée* prepares a dinner and conducts a more elaborate and solemn service of offerings to the ancestors, inviting them to come back and taste the fresh grain or pork. In most *lignées*, these rituals are conducted by the male chief, who recites as many ancestors' names as he can. He can often recall names as far back as several generations. In the majority of cases, the male chief rules within the *lignée*.

Usually, the oldest daughter and the oldest son learn from the chiefs of the older generation and gradually take over their positions. This is done without an enthronement ritual: the oldest daughter succeeds her mother, while the oldest nephew succeeds his uncle. To be chief, two conditions must be met: competence and impartiality. If the eldest son or daughter is incapable (or refuses the role), another member is chosen. Under these circumstances, authority stems from personal merit. The successor, who does not necessarily have to be from the next generation (for example, he or she could be the chief's younger brother or sister), takes over when the chiefs are too old to do their jobs. Some chiefs, of course, hold their positions until they die.

Chiefs of both sexes do not always belong to the same generation. In households where there are only female members (or only male members; for example, if the mother dies and leaves behind only sons), it is customary to have only one chief. This situation is also found when one of the two sexes does not have an adult representative.

Within the household, the chiefs have no special privileges, and if anything, they work harder than the others. Each member of the *matrilignée* has the duty to work as well as the right to enjoy the fruits of his or her labor. When it comes to important matters (what and how much to grow, the purchase or sale of land and livestock, the pawning and renting of land, the construction of a house, sending a member to do service at the *zhifu*'s residence [before 1956], selecting the son who will become a Lamaist monk, adopting a new member, and making preparations for funerals), a decision can only be reached when all of the members of the *lignée* have discussed it.

As a general rule, the female chief's role within the *lignée* is mainly that of manager. She brought the annual gift to the *zhifu*, for tradition has it that it that a female must bring gifts, not just to the *zhifu* but to anyone. The male chief's role is essentially social: primarily through him, social ties with other *matrilignées* are formed and maintained.

Authority in the Na *lignée* is shared by the two sexes. Given that no individual can survive alone, a *lignée*'s cohesion is crucial, and the chief must use his strengths to keep it together. When a chief finds himself unable to fulfill his duties, custom permits a younger member to replace him. In this way, an inherited authority can become a merited authority, a setup that guarantees the *lignée*'s cohesion.

I should emphasize here that, under the same roof and at the same time, a female chief can have the status of daughter as well as that of sister and mother; while the male chief can have the status of son as well as that of nephew, brother, and maternal uncle.

The Incest Prohibition and the Ban on Sexual Evocation

As is true everywhere, in Na society it is forbidden for consanguineal relatives to mate. The Na say: "dhe krwa dhe raiba Zi mao hin" (those who eat from the same bowl and the same plate must not mate). People who come from the same female ancestor always remain in a consanguineal relationship to each other. No matter where they end up living, sexuality is forbidden between them.

From their ascendants of the same sex, children learn at an early age (somewhere around seven years old) that they must not talk about emotional issues with their ascendants of the opposite sex, nor can they be discussed between brothers and sisters, and that it is a taboo to use coarse, and especially obscene, language. They also learn these kinds of taboos from the villagers in their small talk about sex.

Bu sï nin and the exchanging of gifts on New Year's Day are ways for the younger generation to meet and to remember the *lignée* or *lignées* to which their own is consanguineally related.[7]

When incest does occur, the villagers say: "dgilo mao sï" (they do not know the rules) and "kru Zi ho, zi gi zo ho" (they want to grow horns on their heads and eat grass). In short, they reproach them for turning into *do du* (animals). The term *incest* does not exist in Na vocabulary. The Na consider children born from incestuous relations to be abnormal. They say that they will not grow up and will die very young. The farm animals that belong to a *lignée* with incestuous members can also die as a result. Moreover, the Na believe that the children issued from incest will not have any "bones."

As punishment for those who transgress the ban on incest, there are three known sanctions. The first consists in giving the incestuous couple a rope and a basket filled with grass, which they must eat. They are then ordered to hang themselves with the rope. The second sanction is to dig a grave for the guilty parties, who are tied together with a cowhide cord; after being placed in the grave with the woman underneath and the man on top, they are burned with wood that has been brought from each household, one basketful per home. The third sanction consists of enclosing the incestuous individuals in a cave and leaving them there to die. Many of the older villagers insisted that they had heard about these methods of punishment, but none of them had ever participated in one. The first sanction is, in fact, a Han method, the second is Tibetan, and only the third is Na.

One extraordinary aspect of this incest taboo is what I call the ban on sexual evocation. It is completely taboo to speak of sexual, emotional, or sentimental relationships in the presence of consanguineal relatives of the opposite sex and to make any allusions to sex.

Because of these taboos, consanguineal relatives of the opposite sex are forbidden to take baths at the same time in the nearby hot spring; they must take turns. Before 1974, the spring formed a pond where everyone, men and women, young and old, bathed together. Consanguineal relatives of opposite sexes are not allowed to dance side by side. When a song is over, the participants of both sexes, still being at this moment playfully affectionate, attempt to avoid each other as they return to their different groups.

It is strictly forbidden to use coarse and obscene language. On the rare occasions that someone accidentally does so at home, the others pretend not to have heard, while the one at fault feels so ashamed that he immediately runs off and for several days stays at a friend's house, not daring to return home. Finally, a household member of the same sex has to fetch him. In fact, obscene words have sexual connotations. If consanguineal relatives of the opposite sex happen to see a couple from another ethnic group in the village having a fight, they must distance themselves from the scene right away, because one of them might, at any moment, use coarse language. Even when villagers of the same sex argue, they are careful not to use obscene words. If someone does use coarse language, he risks being spit on by the villagers. This is also why the Na exclude certain ethnic groups — those who habitually use obscene expressions — from their sexual relations.

Consanguineal relatives of opposite sexes cannot accompany each other at night. For example, when going to the movies, my friend (a male) could not give his sister a ride on his bicycle, so she would sometimes ask me to do so. Nor can they sit next to each other, or even in the same row, at the movies. This is for two reasons: young people have a tendency to be physically affectionate during a movie, and at any moment a romantic scene might appear on the screen. During my last stay with the Na, television sets, though still quite rare, were beginning to appear in a few households. A remarkable thing occurred: only members of one sex would sit in front of the television at a given moment. When members of the opposite sex wanted to watch it, they would approach the room with the television and say in a voice that could be overheard that they were going to sit down in front of it. On hearing this, those who were watching would automatically get up, without any discussion, and leave the room. All of this took place as though there was one showing for the women and another one for the men.

When a maternal uncle has something to say to his niece, if it is about something emotional, his only option is to tell it to an outsider who then passes it on to her. On the other hand, if a mother has something to say to her son, she can speak to him directly, but only if she does so discreetly. For example, in the village of Ago, when twenty-two-year-old Luzo from the Jiaa *lignée* began having an *açia*, his mother wanted to give him some advice. However, each time she tried to broach the subject, he fled in shame. He thought that this kind of conversation had to be avoided, even between a mother and son. Because he ran away, his mother had to ask an outsider to give him her advice and also to tell him that in this instance it was not necessary to run away.

This ban is so strictly observed that my questions were repeatedly interrupted each time a consanguineal relative of the opposite sex entered the room where I was conducting my interviews. One day, while I was questioning an eighty-year-old man, his granddaughter suddenly entered the house. The immediate transformation of his calm features into a frozen smile plainly indicated his embarrassment.

The Residence

The dwellings in a village are not uniform. They are connected to the road that passes through the village by paths that lead up to the front door of each home. Traditionally, the houses are built of wood: the walls are made from tree trunks, which fit together perpendicularly through notches at each end. The roof has two gentle slopes so that it can be used to dry grain, such as corn and soybeans. The roof shingles are held down by stones.

The residence is usually surrounded by a garden, which is itself surrounded by a clay wall approximately 1.2 meters high. There are altogether four buildings, which surround a clay courtyard that one enters through the *kré* (the front door). Each building has a name and function (which I will examine later), though not a specific location in relation to the others: *Zimi* (the single story main dwelling); *gahla Zi* (the house of Buddha); *ni dga Zi* (a two-story structure), and *bugwe* (the cowshed), which is where the *kré* is usually found (the *kré* is sometimes located between two buildings);[8] these last three structures usually have two stories. Today, the majority of *matrilignées* live in this kind of dwelling, as opposed to only a third in 1963, but poorer *matrilignées* sometimes have only one or two buildings.

If we enter through the *kré*, we find ourselves in the *bugwe*, where the ceiling height is less than 2 meters. On both sides of the corridor, there are pigs and buffalo. This corridor is at an angle and runs along the wall until it reaches a stairway, which leads up. This stairway opens onto a veranda, about 1.5 meters wide, that is sheltered by the roof and has benches along the railings. The veranda provides access to the three rooms on the second floor: a bedroom; a hayloft, which has no exterior walls; and a room for storing grain.

If we leave the courtyard to go to the other three buildings, we can begin — arbitrarily, since their locations can vary from household to household — by visiting the *ni dga Zi*. The ground floor usually has no walls and serves as both the woodshed and the stable. The second story is similar to that of the *bugwe*, except that its three or four rooms, depending on the size of the building, are usually all bedrooms. However, once in a while, one of them will be used to store grain.

The three exterior walls of the *gahla Zi* are clay. The ground floor is also without walls and serves as both a toolshed and a woodshed. The upper floor follows the model of the two preceding structures, but there are only two rooms: one large and one small. The bigger room is used for Lamaist worship: an altar, holding statuettes and photographs of the Dalai Lama and the Panchen Lama, is against the wall that faces the door, and religious paintings hang on the walls. The Lamaist monk in the *lignée* spends day after day in this room, bent over the sacred books. He sleeps in the other room. It is strictly forbidden for women to spend the night here.

After seeing these three buildings of relatively simple design, we will end with a visit to the *Zimi*, the main dwelling space that every household possesses, even the most impoverished. In this building, day-to-day life unfolds, and the Na receive their guests. A single-story building, the *Zimi* is 10 to 16 meters long and 8 to 10 meters wide. It is divided into five sections: *dzu kru lu* (the corridor), *Zi mi gnao* (the main room), *Zi rai dzo* (the upper room), *Zi cha dzo* (the lower room) and *da kré kru* (the back corridor) or *du pai dzo* (the back room).[9]

On average, the bedrooms are 8 square meters. The bed is quite basic: two trestles support several boards, a straw mattress (the mattress ticking is made of linen), and one or two blankets made from yak or sheep felt. A wooden or a woven bamboo trunk is placed next to it. There is also a fire pit and a small trivet, used for warming oneself or preparing a cup of tea.

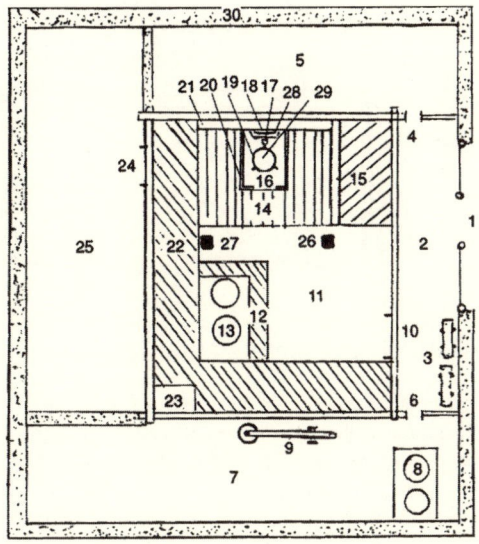

Figure 7.2. The layout of the house's interior.

1. *dzu kru lu kré* (entryway door), this never has a shutter; 2. *dzu kru lu* (the corridor); 3. *dZi gu* (water supply: a container placed on a wooden frame of either wood — a hollowed-out tree trunk — or stone); 4. *Zi rai kré* (door to the upper room); 5. *Zi rai dzo* (the upper room); 6. *Zi cha kré* (door to the lower room); 7. *Zi cha dzo* (the lower room); 8. *dzo gwa* (lower-room hearth); 9. *mu du* (mortar and pestle); 10. *Zimi kré* (door to the main room); 11. *hli du min* or *dha gwa min* (clay lower level); 12. *hwa li bu* (literally, the table of the cat, kitchen table); 13. *ge gwa* (upper hearth); 14. *goli* (platform); 15. *dZio bo* and *Zio* (chest and bed — before 1960, the mortar and pestle were placed here); 16. *mu gwa* (lower hearth); 17. *gwa lu* (stone tablet); 18. *dza ba la* (drawing of a flame with six treasures); 19. *she ké* (iron trivet); 20. *gwa gwe* (stone border of the lower hearth); 21. *shwa gu* (cupboard); 22. *gwa* (bench); 23. *sĭ tu* (altar); 24. *da kré* (hidden door); 25. *da kré kru* (back room or corridor); 26. and 27. *do mi* (central pillars); 28. *gwa ga la* (hearth bodhisattva); 29. *u* (cooking pot); 30. *de bo* (clay wall)

131

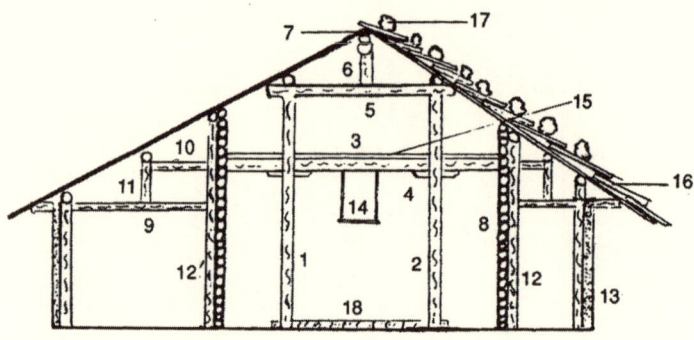

Figure 7.3. The house's support structure and exterior elements.

1. and 2. *do mi* (central pillars); 3. *do dZi* (flat beam); 4. *do mi hlibin* (central pillar hook); 5. *do mi o gra* (top of the central pillars); 6. *gu win* (small roof pillar); 7. *gu sïpi* (top roof beam, top of the roof); 8. *gi do* (pile of logs); 9. *liin mi* (large beam); 10. *win gru* (small beam); 11. *win zo* (small pillar); 12. *odo lhe Rin* (front pillar); 13. *oto lhe Rin* (back pillar); 14. *shwa gu* (suspended frame); 15. *go bu* (second story); 16. *gu prin* (shingle, measuring approximately 1.3 meters long by 0.25 meters wide); 17. *gu lu* (stone roof); 18. *goli* (platform)

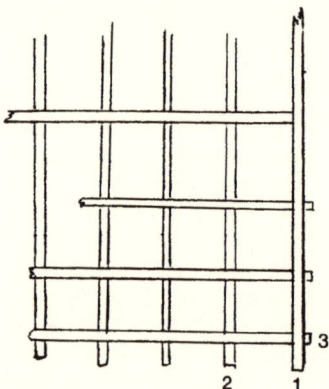

Figure 7.4. Beam construction.

1. *hin ke bo mi* (mother sow beam); 2. *hin ke* (beam); 3. *ru* (beam)

Once we cross the threshold, we enter a corridor and are able to notice a variety of things, which differ from household to household. Hanging above the door, there might be a painting of *pinba* (the guard) or of a tiger, a bear, an eagle, or a weapon (a bow and arrow, an ax or a saber, for example), or there might be a beehive, some eggshells from a chicken, a bear claw, or two goat horns. All of these things are used to ward off evil spirits and to bring good fortune to the household.

The building's walls are made of clay and the main room is surrounded by another wall made of wood. These building materials, which are used to conserve heat in a very cold region, make the room incredibly dark, so much so that when I first entered, it took several minutes for my eyes to adjust before I was able to see anything. Once I was seated on the platform, the light given off by the flames when my host stirred the fire in the lower hearth allowed me to make out the arrangement of the room. It was divided into two sections: one with a clay floor and the other with a platform, about 20 centimeters thick, attached to the ground.

In the middle of this platform, toward the wall, a fire pit had been dug into the ground. An iron trivet (which in the past consisted of three stones) had been placed in this pit and supported a cooking pot. Directly behind it was a square stone tablet, and during every meal and each time tea is served, before any member gets his share, the female chief places a little piece of food on this tablet as an offering, while she says a prayer. Behind this was the altar, which had three steps. On the first, there was another hearth that is used for celebrations and is considered the place where the divinity of the hearth lives. This divinity is a bodhisattva, and there is a statuette of him on the altar. On the higher steps are usually Lamaist statuettes, incense, utensils for serving tea and wine, sifted flour, and various gifts brought back by members of the *lignée* or friends who went away on trips. Finally, leaning against the wall was a bas-relief made of clay, paper, or wood that depicts the *dza ba la*, a fire with six flames which are treasures, shooting out of a lotus, above which is a sun and a moon and beneath it a cat and a seashell.

Seated around the fire pit, members of the *matrilignée* eat their meals and discuss matters on this platform. Each member has an assigned place. If your back is to the wall, the seating arrangement is as follows: children face the *dza ba la*, women are to the right, and men are to the left, seated along the fire pit according to their age, the eldest closest to the wall and the youngest near the edge of the platform. If there are two members from the older generation, and they are the same sex, they sit on either side of the fireplace against the wall. When there are guests, these elders sit on the left according to their age, but without distinction made to their sex, and the same holds true for the members of the *lignée*, but on the right. This arrangement is mandatory: you can usually tell someone's identity and the respect he or she commands from his or her seat placement.

When I began to feel uncomfortable in the darkness and bothered, if not completely suffocated, by the smoke, my hosts explained that the hole through which a ray of daylight enters is covered by a shingle when it rains, and at night they burn pine logs, which are full of resin. Since there is no chimney and the fire is kept going almost all of the time, the interior of the house is blackened, which is thought to be a good thing, since the soot protects the wood from worms, and a house protected in this way can last for more than a hundred years.

In the middle of the room, in front of the platform, are two pillars, each of which sits on top of a stone. The one to the right is ancestral and female; the one to the left is descendant and male. (This is a key point in Na symbolism and kinship, and I will return to it later.) A beam, the "lid" (or top), connects the two. These three pieces should in principle come from the same tree; the lower section provides the right pillar, the middle section, the left pillar, and the top section constitutes the lid. Moreover, the pillars must follow the tree's orientation: before it is felled, its positions are engraved into the bark. If it is impossible to find a big enough tree, one can use two trees, as long as they meet the following criterion: they must have grown together in the same spot, one against the other. Obeying these restrictions guarantees the solidarity of the *lignée*, whereas ignoring them brings about discord.

Two boards are placed about 60 centimeters from the floor on two walls, the one facing the front door and the one facing the platform. The first is used as a bench or a bed, depending on the hour of the day. One-half of the second board, the one closest to the door, serves as a cupboard, while the other half is also used as a bed. In the corner where the boards meet, against the wall in situ, is a wooden altar on which a vase of flowers and several statuettes are usually found. This is considered the heart of the main room. During celebrations, candles, offerings, and butter are also placed on this altar. When a household has no *gahla Zi* (the house of Buddha), the Lamaist monk conducts his rituals in front of this altar. Next to it, along the bench and toward the platform, is a three-part unit on a wooden frame about 1 meter from the floor: the first part is a fire pit used to provide more heat when there are many people in the house; the second part is a hearth (or an upper hearth) that is only used for births and funerals, and in those households that do not have a hearth in the lower room, it is also used for cooking the pig feed; the third part is a kitchen table positioned between the fireplace and the front door. Above this table a round iron plate is hung on which pine resin is burned for light.

Above this room is a loft that is used for drying grain (oats and buckwheat), straw, and fodder. One can reach it by climbing the left pillar — a series of notches makes this possible.

Another door called the *da kré*, which means the door through which one sees nothing, is found in the wall facing the door of the main room, next to the platform. This door must not be positioned directly in front of the door to the main room, or a death may occur, since death can only march straight ahead. This door leads to the back room, which is usually used to store various objects and large vessels of salted vegetables. In the past, this was also the room in which babies were born. Today, women give birth in their bedrooms. When someone dies, the body must be kept in a hole dug in this back room, until the second day of the funeral ceremonies. There is a large chest in front of the *da kré* in which cooked food and meats are stored, safe from the rats. This chest also serves as a bed. Behind the door, bladders are hung from the wall, which the Na believe will protect them from fires.

Since we have now gone through the main room, we will visit the upper room. The room behind the *dza ba la* is called the upper room. It is often used as the bedroom of an old great-uncle or an old woman, or sometimes the bedroom of a young woman. It all depends on how many members the *matrilignée* has. On the other side of the main house is the lower room, in which there is a fireplace for preparing pig feed, a still for making wine and alcohol, a mill, and a mortar and pestle for grinding grain.

On the subject of the structure of this main building and the uses of its various parts, my Na friends emphasized that the roof beam deserves special attention: it is located at the summit of the roof's frame and in Na is referred to as *gu sïpi* (top roof beam). It not only dominates the entire structure of the house but also watches over the behavior of the members of the household, making sure that their actions do not break the moral code. Mothers and uncles frequently advise children not to get into trouble, even when there are no adults around, because the *gu sïpi* is always watching. Another architectural part that merits attention is the *hin ke bo mi* (the mother sow beam) (see figure 7.4). Its function is to link all of the horizontal beams together. Installed on the roof of the house is a wooden trident and a bottle filled with water, providing constant protection from evil spirits and fire.

While we were talking, the female chief of the *lignée* was busy preparing food in the fire pit, that is, the lower hearth. What Westerners would call setting the table is for them placing chopsticks and bowls directly on the platform around the lower hearth. The platform therefore serves as a table. The Na are a very warm and hospitable people; once you are in their home, they will not let you leave without serving you something to eat.

The meal is served by the female chief. Each member of the *lignée* receives an equal-sized portion of meat and vegetables. Because meat is scarce, if a member of the household is not home, his portion is saved for him, so that he can enjoy it on his return. An elder member may give a portion of his share to a younger member if he is unable to finish it. Adults can take more corn, potatoes, wheat, and rice if they like, as long as there is more. Before the 1980s, there was not enough grain. Even today, there are two or three households in each village that run out of grain as early as April. Poor management by the *lignée* chief is often to blame for such a shortage.

When the meal is finished, a daughter cleans the dishes (a man never does), and another daughter sweeps the platform with a broom. At night, this multipurpose platform serves as a bed for the older women and the children. They sleep on roughly woven wool mats and on one or two animal skins or on straw cushions. If they stay close to the fire pit, they keep warm.

A new house is built only if there is a split in a *lignée*, which rarely occurs. During my stay in the field, I had the opportunity to witness one separation. Before taking on the construction of a new home, the household will invite both a *daba* and a Lamaist monk to choose the plot of land, as well as the date for chopping down the trees. To determine the most auspicious day, the *daba* follows the rules of the twelve signs of the zodiac, while the Lamaist monk makes a decision according to the twenty-eight stars. If there is not a *daba*, a Lamaist monk can select the day on his own.

Custom forbids cutting down trees from April 1 until August 15 of every year. During this period, the village households take turns conducting the ritual service of offerings to the mountain spirit. This ritual, in which they burn pine needles, buckwheat, corn, and alcohol, takes place in the morning on a hill behind the village.

Because their buildings are made entirely of wood, a single structure requires as many as 6 hundred to 7 hundred trees (with 10-centimeter radii). Once the trees are felled, they are left to dry on the mountain for one year. They are then transported to the village during the rainy season, by being floated down the river when the water is high. Before cutting down the tree that will be used to make the central pillars, a white chicken must be killed as an offering to the mountain spirit.

Under the supervision of a carpenter, a hole approximately 20 centimeters deep is dug, and a foundation is built out of stones. At the same time, four men cut notches into logs that have been placed on level ground, so that they will fit together well. Once the frame of the four walls is completed, it is dismantled, and then put back together, only this time the frame is placed on the prepared stone foundation. Now the pillars and the beams can be erected. However, before the central pillars are installed, the carpenter must conduct another ritual. He begins by filling a wooden chest or a bamboo basket with grain and by placing a jug of alcohol next to the central pillars. He then takes a chicken and walks it around them. When he has gone around three times, he pierces the thicken's comb and mixes the drops of blood with the grain and alcohol. He then lets the chicken go. If the bird runs to the east, it is a sign of good luck; if it runs in a different direction, it is a sign of bad luck.

After having erected the frame for the four walls, the pillars, and the beams, the walls are made of clay, and boards are installed on the roof. Inside the main room, a shallow pit, approximately 1 square meter, is dug, and its edges lined with stone slabs. A vase filled with metal and grain is buried at the bottom of this hole. This is how they construct the fire pit. This vase is considered the heart of the pit, which is considered the center of the house.

On the day chosen by the *daba*, a ritual of lighting the new fireplace is conducted at dawn. One woman and one man (consanguineal relatives or not) are chosen by the *lignée* of the new home. They must both be monkeys according to Chinese astrology, and the woman must be very fertile, having already given birth to children of both sexes. Carrying a pail of water, the woman enters the main room through the front door; the man, carrying a torch, enters through a hidden door. While the woman pours the water into the cooking pot, the man lights the fire. Then the *daba* comes and removes two pieces of burning wood and passes them around the room. Once this is done, he throws water from a bowl into every corner of the main room. The Na believe that this purification ritual chases away bad spirits and anything else that might bring bad luck. When this is done, the inhabitants of the new residence will be healthy and safe. The *daba* then says prayers to invite the spirit of the mountain and the spirit of the hearth to come forward. He recites an excerpt from the story of genesis: "All of the grains, wheat, buckwheat, oats, and all of the farm animals were brought from the sky by Chai-hondZidZimé, daughter of the celestial gods. Ever since, humans have cultivated crops." He continues by reciting prayers: "The lower hearth is the heart of the house. From this day forward, the fire will never go out but remain lit for three hundred and sixty days a year (the lunar calendar), and the water will never run dry.... To construct the main building, two central pillars, five hundred beams, and seven hundred boards are needed.... Behind the door there is a treasure chest, to the left of it there is a yak and to the right, a tiger. Above the door there is a peacock, and at the foot of the door there is a lion. A golden frog sits in the water jug, and in the low room there is a silver mill.... The right pillar is female, and the left pillar is male," and so on. Having said these prayers, the *daba* pours alcohol on the *gwa lu* (the stone tablet, or the hearth stones) in an offering to the ancestors.

After the *daba* is finished, a Lamaist monk reads several passages from his book. Then the members of the *lignée* invite their consanguineal relatives, friends, and villagers to participate in a feast. The guests bring gifts to their hosts and wish them good luck in their new home. That night, the *lignée* organizes a dancing party outdoors in the village, and the entire village comes.

Finally, in the official residence of the *zhifu*, a *Zi mi* was installed, which was normally used by the servants. However, on New Year's Eve, the *zhifu* and his entire family came to this spot to conduct a service of offerings to the ancestors and to eat dinner.

The Nomenclature of Kinship

Na kinship terminology for the *matrilignée* is strictly classificatory. The entire nomenclature includes only fifteen terms, as can be seen in figures 7.5 and 7.6.

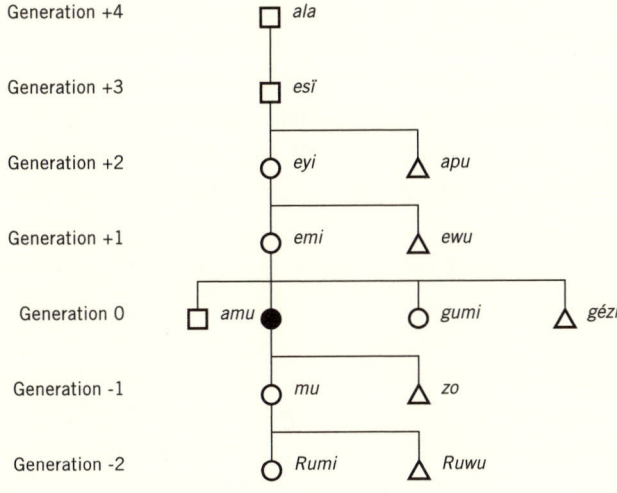

Figure 7.5. Kinship terms for generations +4 through −2.

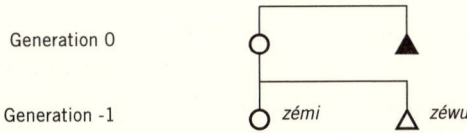

Figure 7.6. Kinship terms for generation −1.

According to this kinship terminology, beginning with female Ego, a member of the +4 generation is called *ala*, no matter what his or her sex.[10] A member of the +3 generation is called *esï*, no matter what his or her sex or age. If there are several members in this generation, this term is followed by the individual's first name.

In the +2 generation, a woman, regardless of her age, is called *eyi*, and a man is called *apu*. If there are two *eyi*, the term is followed by *dgi* for the elder one and by *dZi* for the younger one. The same holds true if there are two *apu*. If there are more than two *eyi* (or more than two *apu*), the term is followed by the individual's first name if he or she is not the oldest or the youngest.

In the +1 generation, the woman, whether she is the Ego mother or not, is called *emi*, while the man is called *ewu*. If there are several members in this generation, the rules for naming are the same as those for the +2 generation.

In the 0 generation, no matter who their mother is and no matter what their sex, all of the elders are called *amu*, while all of the younger females are called *gumi* and the younger males *gézi*.

On the –1 level, all of the female members are called *mu*, and all of the male members are called *zo*, no matter what their age and no matter who their mother is. On the –2 level, all of the girls are *Rumi,* and all of the boys are *Ruwu*, again without any age distinction. Outside of these names, there are no other terms.

When Ego is male, he calls the daughters of his sisters *zémi* and the sons of these same sisters *zéwu*. For all of the other members, whether they are his ascendants or descendants, the nomenclature is the same as that used by female Ego.

In practice, Ego (female or male) calls all of the members of the younger generation by their first name; therefore, the names used to address someone are their individual first names. When addressing someone from an older generation, however, the kinship terms are used.

This terminology was taken from the villages surrounding Kaitçi; in other villages, the terms may be slightly different. For example, *emi* is *ami*, *ewu* is *awu*, *eyi* is *ayi,* and *esï* is *asï*. Both *e* and *a* are prefixes that connote respect. Beginning with *amu*, the elder, this prefix appears in all of the terms. This prefix can also be used to address nonrelated people, to express respect and feelings of closeness. In this case, the Na leave off the first syllable of the person's first name or title and add this prefix. For example, Tsidi is the first name of a sixty-one-year-old man in Ago. The young villagers would call him *adi*. The title of the *zhifu* in Na was *sïpi*, and he was therefore addressed as *api*.

The first distinctive feature of this terminology appears in the prefix with which Ego expresses respect toward his ascendants. The second feature, *mi*, which indicates that a person is female, is present in the terms *emi, gumi, Rumi,* and *zémi*. The other part of each of these terms denotes which generation the person belongs to. The same holds true for the terms *ewu, Ruwu,* and *zéwu*. On the other hand, beginning with the +2 generation, the second syllable of each term designates both the generation and the sex of the named individual.

In his analysis of kinship, George Peter Murdock states, "Within the nuclear family are found eight characteristic relationships.... Despite cultural differences, each of the eight primary relationships reveals a markedly similar fundamental character in all societies, in consequence of the universality of the family's basic functions."[11] As basic units of kinship, both the Na *matrilignée* and the nuclear family in other societies belong to the same place within social organization. However, because of the differences that are immediately apparent between the Na *matrilignée* and the nuclear family, a careful and detailed comparison of the two is necessary. To facilitate this comparison, I will cite Murdock at length:

> These relationships, with their most typical features, are as follows: *Husband and wife*: economic specialization and cooperation; sexual cohabitation; joint responsibility for support, care, and upbringing of children; well defined reciprocal rights with respect to property, divorce, spheres of authority, etc.

Father and son: economic cooperation in masculine activities under leadership of the father; obligation of material support, vested in father during childhood of son, in son during old age of father; responsibility of father for instruction and discipline of son; duty of obedience and respect on part of son, tempered by some measure of comradeship.

Mother and daughter: relationship parallel to that between father and son, but with more emphasis on child care and economic cooperation and less on authority and material support.

Mother and son: dependence of son during infancy; imposition of early disciplines by the mother; moderate economic cooperation during childhood of son; early development of a lifeling incest taboo; material support by son during old age of mother.

Father and daughter: responsibility of father for protection and material support prior to marriage of daughter; economic cooperation, instruction, and discipline appreciably less prominent than in father-son relationship; playfulness common in infancy of daughter, but normally yields to a measure of reserve with the development of a strong incest taboo.

Elder and younger brother: relationship of playmates, developing into that of comrades; economic cooperation under leadership of elder; moderate responsibility of elder for instruction and discipline of younger.

Elder and younger sister: relationship parallel to that between elder and younger brother but with more emphasis upon physical care of the younger sister.

Brother and sister: early relationship of playmates, varying with relative age; gradual development of an incest taboo, commonly coupled with some measure of reserve; moderate economic cooperation; partial assumption of parental role, especially by the elder.[12]

I will now compare the eight relationships within the family, which is held to be the basic unit of society, with the relationships in the Na *matrilignée*, also the basic unit of society. One brief look reveals that three relationships are completely absent for the Na: husband-wife, father-son, and father-daughter. The reason is quite simply the absence of husbands and, consequently, that of fathers.

I begin my analysis of this set of relationships with that between sister and brother, one that exists universally. When comparing the Na with other societies, we find that the husband-wife relationship is replaced to a great extent by the brother-sister relationship. Because of this, the brother-sister relationship has two aspects: one is between the brother and the sister; the other is between the sister and brother and the sister's children. The brother-sister relationship is a more or less intimate friendship during childhood that normally evolves, according to their respective ages and the progressive development of the incest taboo, into a somewhat reserved relationship with economic specialization. The oldest sibling assumes, in part, the role of *lignée* chief from childhood. When the brother and sister reach adulthood, they jointly provide for the sister's children, both materially and emotionally, and educate them, and they cooperate in the economy of the household and respect each other's equal rights to property and each other's sphere of authority.

One characteristic of this relationship deserves particular attention: the residence. Because their sexual lives revolve around the institution of the visit, neither sibling, in most cases, brings an outsider of the opposite sex into the household as a permanent member. Instead, brother and sister live together under the same roof for their entire lives, in spite of the incest taboo. This characteristic reveals a direct contrast between the relationship of brother and sister and that of husband and wife. As participants in the institution of marriage, husband and wife have sexual relations, and they can end their relationship through divorce and thereby separate. Between Na brothers and sisters, despite sharing the same residence, sexual relations do not exist, and they are inseparable, companions for life.

In principle, a separation between brother and sister is not conceivable because of the need to maintain equilibrium within the *matrilignée* to meet the necessities of material life. Moreover, the bond between brothers and sisters, created by their mother and their shared consanguineal identity, is immutable, whereas the matrimonial bond is mutable, as the possibility of divorce shows. As with marriage, the ties forged by an adoption are not unbreakable: while keeping his or her own consanguineal identity, an adoptee, in most other societies, takes on a new consanguineal identity. But this new bond is mutable, since an adoption can be annulled.

For the Na, the connection between sister and brother is not loose but very strong and, in principle, eternal, since this relationship guarantees the economic success of the *matrilignée*.

In the place of the father-son and father-daughter relationships in other societies, we find those of maternal uncle and nephew and maternal uncle and niece in Na society. The uncle is not, of course, the genitor of the nieces and nephews, because of the incest taboo. However, in every other respect, he plays the role taken by the father in many other societies.

When it comes to authority and material support, the mother-daughter relationship is no different from the uncle-niece relationship. Mothers and sons, given the rule of residence, are interdependent in every aspect of life for life. These fundamental constraints are handed down by the mother's mother, since most of the time she is the one who cares for the children. Because the basic Na unit (the *matrilignée*) incorporates several generations, certain jobs done by the mother or the mother's husband in other societies are done here by the mother's mother or the mother's uncle. In Na society, for example, the mother's mother and her uncle mostly tend to the children.

The Na *matrilignée* is generally made up of three generations. Most of the work involved in raising the children and the running the *matrilignée* is shared by the +1 and +2 generations. This work involves: socializing the children (through education and discipline) and providing their material support; handling emotional issues and reciprocal rights between the three generations; teaching the children to be obedient and respectful; insisting on respect for authority and on economic cooperation; introducing the incest taboo; the mother's and the uncle's protection of the children; regulating the closeness between members of the *lignée* during certain periods of their lives; ensuring the companionship and camaraderie of the members; managing productive activities; overseeing the management of one generation by another and of one individual by another.

In other societies, kinship bonds tend to loosen according to how distant relatives become through marriage. With the Na, because they only have consanguineal relatives to consider in the incest taboo, no matter how far apart they are, they maintain the memory of consanguineal ties for life. This constitutes an essential characteristic of Na kinship.

In the nomenclature of Na kinship, there are only elementary terms and derivative terms, for example, *little mother* and *grandmother*, but no descriptive terms, whereas in other societies, there are always descriptive terms. Na kinship terminology therefore corresponds perfectly to their behaviors and attitudes.

In his book *Social Structure*, Murdock, elaborating on the work of A.L. Kroeber and R.H. Lowie, presents nine major criteria of terminological differentiation, which are useful for an analysis of Na nomenclature for kinship.[13]

First, the criterion of generation: above Ego, Na terminology goes as far back as the fourth generation; beneath Ego, it goes down only to the second generation.

Second, the criterion of sex is applied equally in this nomenclature of kinship. But the terms for members of the third and fourth generation above Ego are not differentiated by gender, apparently because it is extremely rare that relatives of both sexes are alive in these two generations, due to poor living conditions.

Third, there is the criterion of a relative's age. The Na make a terminological distinction between older members and younger ones. In addition to *grandmother* and *little mother*, *great-uncle* and *little uncle*, the terminological distinctions made in Ego's generation deserve attention. We have already seen that the oldest brother and the oldest sister are both called *amu* by the younger members and that the younger sister is called *gumi* and the younger brother is called *gézi*. When introducing someone or speaking to others about one's sisters and brothers, a person says that they are his or her *mo mu ni mi* instead of *amu gézi* and *amu gumi*, for *amu gézi* only means brothers and *amu gumi* only means sisters.

Fourth, there is the criterion of gender as it applies to Ego. Murdock describes the criterion of gender terminology as follows: "Kinship systems which recognize this criterion will have two terms for the same relative, one used by a male speaker and the other by a female."[14] This criterion seems to apply in Na terminology as well. When it comes to individuals who belong to the –1 level, female Ego and male Ego refer to the children of female Ego in different ways. But since the rest of the terminology is the same for female Ego and male Ego, male Ego is, to a certain degree, "reduced" to female Ego. There is a certain "identity of opposite sex siblings."

This leads me to think that, for terminological distinction, it is not so much Ego's gender that matters as the incest prohibition, for through the application of this rule, men never have children directly issued from themselves within a *lignée*. In this way, the terminological distinction tallies perfectly with the incest prohibition, an extremely powerful imperative in this society.

What we have here is a strictly consanguineal and matrilineal nomenclature. It has assimilated the collateral line and the direct line. The central Ego is female. The criteria used to classify relatives in this terminology are, therefore, generation, age of individuals in the same generation, gender of the relatives that one designates, and the incest prohibition, as well as polarity. No term exists in this terminology for relatives by marriage (husband, father, brother-in-law, sister-in-law, father-in-law, mother-in-law, collateral relatives, and so on).

Four of the nine criteria listed by Kroeber and Lowie, and taken up by Murdock, are marriage, collaterality, bifurcation, and death. With the exception of the criterion of marriage, which is connected to permanent social features, these criteria, according to Murdock, are based on biological data. We know that the existence of these other three criteria depends completely on that of marriage. Without marriage, none of these criteria would exist. Consequently, in my opinion, they are based on social features as well. Unlike terminologies of kinship in which marriage exercises an influence, the Na nomenclature for kinship constitutes an ordered set.

Unlike the status of a woman in the nuclear family of other societies, a Na woman can be, within her *matrilignée*, a daughter, a sister, a niece, and a mother at the same time; and a man can be a son, a brother, a maternal uncle, and a nephew at the same time.

As the societal unit the Na *matrilignée,* for both men and women, orients them toward the rest of society and is the focus of their procreation activities, if we understand procreation to mean the perpetuation of the line. Because of the incest prohibition, they go elsewhere for their sex life, but this does not mean that the Na understand the *lignée* as regulating their mode of reproduction.

If we take the usual definition of the term *collaterality*, we notice that this concept does not exist in the Na kinship terminology nor in the set of relationships. If we take the ensemble of *matrilignées*, they can be divided into two categories only: those who are consanguineal relatives and those who are not. Their kinship group includes consanguineal relatives only, no outsider is ever considered a relative. We can see here a fundamental correspondence between their kinship terms and their cultural models of behaviors and attitudes.

That their kinship group includes consanguineal relatives only implies that, for the Na, there are only relatives of the first order. The Na kinship bond is eternal. This feature puts their kinship system into direct opposition to the marriage relationship in other societies: marriage, as a rule, while uniting outsiders and making them relatives, occasions a split between blood relatives in every generation. With the Na, consanguineal relatives stay together forever, which explains why solidarity for them rests on the relationship between brother and sister, not on that between brothers.

With no terms for affinal relatives, this kinship terminology obviously differs from the six types of kinship terminology proposed by Murdock. It seems legitimate to consider it a new type.

Adoption

In Na, *shu bo tçi* means adoption or to adopt. As with many Na expressions, it is at once a noun and a verb. The term *hing ke dhu* means adoptee (*hing* means human being; *ke* means thread literally and founder figuratively; and *dhu* means to succeed; literally: a human succeeds from the founder). The Na adopt for two reasons: the first, called *hwa nin* (*hwa* means house, *nin* means to occupy and to take care of), has as a goal to maintain the house. For this, the adoptee must be a consanguineal relative of the adopting *lignée*. The second reason is to augment the workforce. An adoption confers the same rights on the adopted member as the other members have, as well as the same duties. An adopted member can also become a *dabu*, the *lignée* chief.

If there is only one son or there are only boys or if all of the women are sterile in a generation, adoption is the first solution that the Na consider to the problem of creating descendants. A *lignée* can adopt one or two girls or even an entire branch from another *lignée*. When adopting, a *lignée* always prefers a child from a consanguineal *lignée*, but this preference must be subordinated to the number of children in the donor *lignée* being approached: this number must be high enough; there must be at least three girls.

The adopting *matrilignée* first goes to *lignées* that have the same "bone" as they have, for, as a proverb says, "ho zo çi dZio in mao dzai" (a wild chicken cannot become a domestic chicken). Most adoptions fall into this category. If this is not possible, the *matrilignée* will approach *lignées* to which it is not related, but only as a last resort. Another proverb echoes this order of preference: "kra dzé gutu la bi du gu" (kernels of corn are different from oats). This metaphor means that blood relatives are different from non-consanguineal individuals. The donor *lignée* has the same attitude: unless it is having economic difficulties (most commonly, not being able to feed all of the children), it is very reluctant to give a daughter to strangers.

When an adoption occurs between two consanguineal *lignées*, the chief of the adoptive *lignée* goes to the other's home, bringing gifts: 2 or 3 liters of alcohol, a basketful of rice cakes (approximately 3 kilos), and 10 *yuan*.[15] After they have reached an agreement, they ask a *daba* or a Lamaist monk to choose an auspicious day for the ritual. On that day, two or three members of the adoptive *lignée*, bringing the same gifts as before, go to the donor *lignée*'s home. A service of offerings to the ancestors is then conducted to let them know that a member of their *lignée* is being given to another. Traditionally, a *daba* is invited, and, before all of the members present, he recites the following prayer: "May the adopted girl give nine daughters and nine sons to *lignée* X, and may their descendants from generation to generation be numerous." Currently, because of the scarcity of *daba*, the day is frequently chosen by a Lamaist monk, and this prayer is said by the female chief. Once the ritual is completed, the adopted girl is brought to her adoptive home and from that point on takes the name of her new *lignée*.

When an adoption takes place between two non-consanguineal *lignées* and a girl is being adopted (or two girls, or an entire branch) to ensure descendants, the adopting *lignée* invites a village woman who has had several children to accompany its representative (who can be male or female) to negotiate with the donor *lignée*'s chief, most often the female chief. If adopting a boy, the adoptive *lignée* asks an older man from the village, one who knows the customs well, to accompany its representative and to help with the negotiations, which, in this case, are more likely to take place with the male chief. The process of adoption here is no different from that between two consanguineal *lignées*, except that after taking the adopted person home, the adoptive *lignée* conducts a service of offerings to the ancestors to let them know about the arrival of one or more new members. It gives its name to the adopted person, who, from that moment on, becomes a member of the household.

Adopted members who are non-consanguineal take the name of their adoptive *lignée*, but always maintain their original consanguineal identity. Sexual relations between the adopted members, on the one hand, and the consanguineal members of the adoptive *lignée* on the other, are still allowed but on the following condition: if an adopted child is raised under the same roof from infancy with a child of the opposite sex, it is forbidden for them to mate when they become adults. Yet once they have been separated in two houses, the ban is lifted. On the other hand, relations between the adopted child and consanguineal relatives in his or her original *lignée* will always be prohibited.

I will now look at two examples of adoption among consanguineal relatives:

1. Ninety-eight years ago, there was only one man left in the Shale *lignée* in Ago, and he adopted a girl from the Tsikru *lignée* in Imin. At the end of two generations, the original Tsikru household had died out, and Tsikru went back to Imin to inherit the belongings. Now the Tsikru *lignée* lacked descendants, so it adopted a five-year-old girl from the Shale *lignée*. Then, ten years after this adoption, because it lacked workers, it adopted another child from this *lignée*, a fifteen-year-old boy. Here is a case of reciprocal adoptions between *lignées* that are consanguineal relatives. First *lignée* A adopted a girl from *lignée* B, and two generations later, *lignée* B adopted a girl and a boy from *lignée* A.

2. In the Badzi *lignée* in Raimi, Judzu's oldest sister proved sterile. Although she had had a child, it died shortly after birth. When she was thirty-nine years old, she adopted a one-year-old girl, the granddaughter of her grandmother's sister. Ten years later, she adopted another girl, the second-oldest sister of the first adopted girl.

In the following example, non-consanguineal children are adopted once the attempt to adopt a consanguineal relative has failed:

The biological mother of Dindgu (a sixty-one-year-old man) had six children, four boys and two girls who had died when they were nineteen and eight years old, respectively. Before she died, Dindgu's mother presided over the adoption of two sisters, Echedgima and Nadgodgima, whose *lignée* came from the same "bone" as she did. In fact, in the Ibu *gnao lignée*, one of Dindgu's grandmothers had been adopted by a Pumi family from Totçi (3 kilometers from Imin). This woman had several girls, and one of them was adopted by a Na *lignée* from Lakrwa (about 2 kilometers away). This girl also had several girls, including Echedgima and Nadgodgima. Several years after the death of their adoptive mother, when they were grown, they no longer got along with Dindgu and his youngest brother. After a quarrel, they returned to their original *lignée*. With the help of the villagers, Dindgu's *lignée* received a sum of money from the *lignée* of these two girls, in compensation for the money it had spent feeding and clothing them.

Following this separation, Dindgu and his brother decided to adopt two sisters, daughters of Tselidgima, who also had had three boys. Tselidgima's sister had three daughters, and when, at thirty-eight years old, Tselidgima died, the following generation was too numerous to feed. The *lignée* therefore gave its consent to Dindgu to adopt Tselidgima's two girls. One of them, Nadzidgima, was thought to be the offspring of Dindgu: he had had an *açia* relationship with Tselidgima, and Nadzidgima looked like him.

During my interview with Dindgu, I asked him: "Why did you adopt these two girls from another 'bone' than your own, when you know that after you, your *lhe* will disappear, and all your worldly goods will be dispersed?" He answered: "You are right. I did so because I was not successful in adopting *ong hing*. Adopting strangers was the only solution. For us, not having descendants [*min dZi; min* literally means tail and figuratively means continuity, and *dZi* means to break, therefore, the tail (the *lignée*) is broken] is the worst thing possible, and we try to avoid it in every way we can. We must, above all else, guarantee the perpetuation of the name of the *matrilignée*."[16]

Over the course of my interviews, I came to understand the source of this terror of rupturing one's *lignée*: without descendants, no one will take care of the service of offerings to the ancestors; therefore, those without descendants would have nothing to eat in the afterlife.

Here is another example:

In the Baomo *apo* I *lignée* in Ago, Dgubi's mother died when he was one year old. Only he and his great-uncle remained, so his great-uncle adopted seven people from three generations of a neighboring non-consanguineal *lignée*. The great-uncle died in 1959, and Dgubi joined a new household in 1964. His old residence still bears the name Baomo, but its inhabitants are all outsiders. Currently, the female chief comes from a *lignée* of yet another consanguinity. When the male chief dies, this residence, still under the name of Baomo, will be represented for the second time by a group of a different consanguinity.

The following case provides another interesting example:

In the *raimi*'s village, the *raimi*'s *lignée* once (the members of this *lignée* do not remember exactly when) gave a girl to the Abo *apo* *lignée* in Azo. Most of its members, including its son, had died of a contagious disease, and Gézodgima's adoptive mother remained alone with two girls (the daughters of her sister). Since she lacked laborers, she first adopted Kruzotsie, a non-consanguineal boy, and then Gézodgima, a consanguineal girl from the Abo *apo* *lignée*. Because these two adoptees were not consanguineal relatives, they had children together.

The interest in this last example lies in the fact that Kruzotsie and Gézodgima were both adopted. Their situation amounts to the same thing as cohabitation.[17] According to the kinship terminology, they call each other brother and sister, but this does not prevent them from having children together. This, of course, is an extreme case, but it is useful in illustrating that for the Na, in every instance, even in adoption, the consanguineal identity of an individual, acquired at birth, will never change.

The decision to adopt is not always easy. The adoption made by the Miindge *lignée* presents a very interesting example:

If we begin with the youngest generation of the Miindge *apo lignée* in Raimi alive today, a woman in the sixth generation had three children, one girl, named Dgimabuche, and two boys. Since Dgimabuche, when the time came, had only two boys, this *lignée*, as a precaution, adopted Echedgima, an unrelated girl. After this adoption, Dgimabuche had two more children, and one of them was, finally, a girl. After Dgimabuche's mother died, relations between the two lines of different consanguinities became acrimonious. In 1964, these two lines split apart. Nadgotsie, Dgimabuche's daughter, had only one child, a son, and once again the *lignée* faced the problem of providing descendants. Due to their lack of means, they built a wall separating the two houses through the courtyard. The Miindge *apo lignée* had to wait until 1980 before it was able to build a new house and move out. This famous wall, standing between two houses, two groups, and above all between two consanguinities, symbolizes, once more, the power of the concept of Na matrilineal consanguinity.

When there is a shortage of manpower, a *lignée* can bring boys into the household for a certain amount of time without adopting them. Here are two examples:

1. In the Raimi village *matrilignée*, in Sigemi's generation, there were no young boys to do the odd jobs. Sigemi brought in

guarantee descendants. Another astonishing characteristic of Na adoption is the immutability of the adopted member's consanguinity. In most societies, precisely the opposite is true: once adopted, an individual is considered a consanguineal relative of the adoptive parents, and sexual relations are forbidden not only between the adoptee and his or her consanguineal relatives from the original family, but also between the adoptee and the consanguineal relatives of the adoptive family. This change in consanguineal identity represents the most crucial point in the rules of adoption.

There are several consequences to this immutability of consanguinity of the adopted member in Na society. First, an adopted individual who is non-consanguineal becomes a member of the adoptive household but not a member of the adoptive *lignée*. Second, these kinds of adoptees, while assuming the same rights and economic responsibilities as the other members of the adoptive *lignée*, are not subject to the ban on sexual relations between consanguineal members in this *lignée*. Adoption can even bring the possibility of sexual relations between members of the same household. This phenomenon does not occur in households where there is no shortage of fertile women in every generation. Third, when a non-consanguineal female, whether through adoption or through some other form, is brought into a household where there is only a male, her descendants are referred to as sisters and brothers by the children of the men's consanguineal relatives, for example, the offspring of that man's mother's sister who live under another roof. The descendants of the two households could have sexual relations, which means that there can be sexual relations between the children of the woman and the children of her brother — in other words, between crossed collaterals or, according to their kinship terminology, sisters and brothers, not crossed cousins (the concept of crossed or parallel cousins does not exist for the Na). Finally, through the adoption of a non-consanguineal person, some households change their own consanguineal identity, and the consanguineal relatives of the *lignée* end up being dispersed, little by little, in other villages. As we have seen, giving birth to only boys and female sterility play enormously important roles in the structure of Na society. Later, we will examine other factors that influence the structure of the Na lineage.

The Na pay close attention to the continuation of their consanguineal identity. Both oral accounts and statistics on the adoption of consanguineal relatives (nineteen out of twenty-eight cases, or 68 percent) provide concrete evidence for this. The adoption of consanguineal relatives perpetuates the identity of the adoptive *lignée*, and also the *lignée* itself. On the other hand, the adoption of a non-consanguineal individual is a solution to which some *lignées* are forced to resort because there are no consanguineal relatives available. Without this option, the members of these *lignées* would have nothing to subsist on during their old age or after their death. Consequently, in these kinds of cases, only the name of the adoptive *lignée* is perpetuated, not its consanguineal identity or the *lignée* itself, because in their service of offerings to the ancestors, the Na usually recite the names of their ancestors from the past three generations only.

The Breakup of a Lignée

The Na attach great importance to the solidarity of members within the same *matrilignée*. According to Na tradition, all *lignée* members must be treated fairly, and everything in the household must be shared. "The fewer the members in a *lignée*, the more difficult life will be." The Na frequently make fun of the Han living in the Yongning basin in this manner. Because the Han family (based on the nuclear family) is always limited, the Na joke that the couple is left to take care of everything and that their house is always a mess.

Related to the importance of the number of *lignée* members is the issue of separations within a household. These splits bring about a segmentation of the *matrilignée*: the data that I gathered indicated that, since 1956, the number of *lignées* in the five villages within my field of investigation had doubled.

There are two types of separations: *baolu* and *Zidu bubu*. *Baolu* occurs when there is dissension between one woman and the rest of her *matrilignée*, and so she leaves her original household to live elsewhere, usually in the same village.

The following circumstances can lead to this kind of separation:

1. Tension between sisters who have no ascendants and are fighting for authority within a household. The sister who has children remains in the house.

2. Tension created by a woman's strong-willed personality.

3. A man's bringing his partner, with whom his sisters cannot get along, into the house.

4. Tension between a daughter and one of her "mothers" (the sister of her actual mother), who, having other children, does not treat her as well as the others.

Usually, in these kinds of separations, the woman receives nothing but a small plot of land on which to build a cottage, a few kitchen utensils, a sow, a small quantity of grain, and some basic farming tools, such as a hoe. She has no rights to a share of the land, the livestock, or the houses. She is therefore not required to pay taxes, nor in the past would she have been under obligation to do her service for the *zhifu*. To earn a living, she makes an arrangement with a household that owns a great deal of property, and in exchange for working the land, she is allowed to keep the grain harvested from a small plot designated in advance.

The word for this kind of separation, *baolu*, means the construction of a little house. Once a woman has separated from her *matrilignée* in this way, she no longer has the resources to build a proper house. Her new home is usually very small (about 7 square meters) and has such a low ceiling that one must bend over to enter it.

There have never been any male *baolu*. When a young man does not get along with the members of his *matrilignée* (which is extremely rare), he goes to work with craftsmen in the town of Batsïgu, he goes to work in the caravan trade, or he simply goes off, far away to other regions. The Na believe that it would be too difficult for a young man to take care of himself alone.

According to statistics from 1963, among the 157 homes in the nine villages of Yongning, there were thirty-two cases of separation over three generations, out of which twelve, or 37.5 percent, were *baolu*. In the villages within my field of investigation, the old villagers could recall four *baolu* in 1988.

After one or two years (sometimes more), relations between the *baolu* woman and her original *matrilignée* might improve. This usually means that if the *baolu* woman runs into difficulties, her *matrilignée* comes to her aid, and sometimes this results in the reintegration of the dissident into the *matrilignée*.

The other type of separation, *Zidu bubu*, means to divide the household and share the matriamony (*Zidu* refers to the household and the matriamony, and *bubu* means to share).

In general, this second type of split takes place under the following circumstances:

1. In a single generation, there is a surplus of girls, and each of them has children. In this situation, the Na find it difficult to follow the rules of fairness. To protect themselves from eventual discord, the *lignée* members build a new house together, often right next door to the old one, so that one branch of the *lignée* can move in there. During the separation, one of the mothers leaves

her birth house with her descendants (sometimes as many as three generations). As the Na proverb says: "bo mi zo go he, bo zo zo go biai" (the piglets go where the sow goes).

2. When there is discord between brothers and sisters who are the offspring of different mothers who are all deceased and no one is able to maintain cohesion, the members split into groups according to their direct descent; in other words, those who have the same mother stay together. Their belongings are divided equally among them. Sometimes they do not have time to build a new house, so they temporarily stay together, each group with its own autonomy.

3. Two sisters who have no other consanguineal relatives and are living together under the same roof are on bad terms. During the separation, they share the land, house, and livestock, in short, all of the household belongings. This type of segmentation is not considered a *baolu*.

4. A female partner (or a male partner, though this is extremely rare) is introduced into the household and destroys — almost inevitably — the solidarity of the *lignée*, leading some of the members to leave. The intrusion of an outsider into the household is considered a kind of crime, for it transgresses the moral standards. Intrusions of this kind are condemned by the Na.

Below are two examples of *Zidu bubu*:

1. In 1927, in Gesha, a woman, Bima, had three children, two girls and a boy, and left with them. During the separation, the members of her maternal household told her that, as a woman, she had no rights to the land. However, Bima and the other *matrilignées* in the same line unanimously said that she was entitled to her son's share.[18] Since the members of her *matrilignée* were firm in their position, Bima and her children, supported by their neighbors, brought the matter to trial before the *zhifu*. The *zhifu* decided that

since Bima had a son the maternal household was required to give her a piece of property, as well as other belongings, and he ruled that she should receive one-third of the land.

2. Relations between Tsie and her siblings (two sisters and one brother) had soured, and Tsie left the maternal household. Her older sister did not want to give her anything, not even a plot of land to build her cottage on. Tsie would not accept this refusal and filed a complaint with the *zhifu*, who ruled that Tsie, who had no sons, was not entitled to a thing. However, because receiving nothing from her older sister did not conform to custom, the *zhifu* reconsidered and judged that the *lignée* had to provide her with a plot of land for her house, one sow, a big and a small cooking pot, and several articles of clothing, as well as the jewelry bequeathed to her by her mother.

When the group leaving the original household includes a Lamaist monk, this group is entitled to receive a house but not any land or farm animals because a Lamaist monk must not work the land and therefore is not obligated to pay taxes or do service. If a Lamaist monk leaves his *lignée* by himself, he can only acquire one house: his temple.

During a separation, the existence of at least one male member on each side is an indispensable condition for the sharing of goods from the original household. In principle, the share of goods allotted to the original household is always larger than that allotted to the new one. These shares are not made according to the number of individuals on each side. The Na believe that this custom will discourage *lignées* from separating. This desire for solidarity reveals, on a moral level, the power of the concept of consanguinity.

The branch of the *lignée* that stays in the original house is called *ong mi* (*ong* means bone; *mi* is a broad term that signifies maternal, feminine, principal, big, and so on). This expression can be translated literally as maternal bone, or figuratively as founding *lignée*. Another term in current use is *gnao*. It also designates the founding *lignée* or the remaining household (and means at home), as opposed to, in the case of a separation, *apo*, the branch *lignée* or the migrating household.

In fact, separations are rare for two reasons. The first is moral: breaking up a *lignée* is shameful, indeed criminal. The second reason is physiological: the Na population is stagnating due to the sterility of a large number of the women. Therefore, there are *matrilignées*, mostly in the commoner stratum, that have not had a separation for several generations. The Na have two explanations for the high rate of sterility in the women: on the one hand, they believe that when young girls who have not yet reached puberty have sexual relations they become sterile; on the other hand, they think that women who are visited by too many men simultaneously lose their capacity to become pregnant. One reason the villagers did not mention is that several kinds of sexually transmitted diseases are widespread in their community.

No matter what kind of separation occurs, *baolu* or *Zidu bubu*, the two groups maintain their communal consanguineal identity. After the separation, the two *lignées* are considered *krwadhe* to each other. This term refers to a relationship between two or more consanguineal *lignées* that are economically independent. On New Year's Day, no matter what the distance between them, consanguineal *lignées* exchange gifts: a ring of boned pork, several liters of alcohol, cakes, tea, and such. Following the first day of the New Year, one can see women carrying baskets of gifts on the paths in the Yongning basin.

After a separation, maternal uncles and mothers no longer have any rights or responsibilities concerning the nephews and nieces (or sons and daughters) who no longer live under the same roof as they do.

Finally, although children refer to their mother's sisters as mother, they acquire their unique identity through their relationship to their true mother, which enables the distinguishing of the self from others. The bond between a mother and her own children and the bond between true brothers and sisters are considered to be a natural substance and therefore inalienable. For humanity, only the natural bond is unbreakable.

Larger Social Groupings

The Lineage

The social unit higher than the *lignée* is *sïzï*. *Sï* is another word for bone, and *zï* means man (or people) and also true. This expression designates people from the same bone. The Na explain *sïzï* with the expression "dhe sïzï dhe ong nié" (a *sïzï* is from the same bone) and "dhe sïzï dhe krwa dhe raiba go dzi" (a *sïzï* eats from the same bowl and the same plate). A bowl and a plate symbolize a *sïzï*. Today, the only occasion on which one can observe this symbolism is a funeral. Once each *lignée* of the *sïzï* has brought in a platterful of rice and a fried egg, the person who is officiating stands in front of the coffin holding a bowl and a plate in his raised left hand and recites words of consolation about the deceased, while a group of women weep, each of them representing one of the *lignées*.

A village can be made up of one *sïzï* or several. Within my field of research, Ago had three *sïzï*: Sadabu (eight *lignées*), Ago (five *lignées*), and Hababu (nine *lignées*, of which four were located in Raimi). Imin had one *sïzï*: Ibu-Imin (fifteen *lignées* out of twenty). The village of Ragi also had one *sïzï*: Ragi (seven *lignées*), as did the village of Azo: Azo (sixteen *lignées*).

Sometimes there are *lignées* in a village that do not belong to any *sïzï* in that village. For example, in Imin, there are twenty *lignées*: two Ibu, three Imin, three Batsimi, five Adgi, one Dgimat-sie, one Sigebuchi, one Tsikru, two Daba, and two Lama. Among these *lignées*, the first fifteen constitute a single *sïzï*, named Ibu-Imin. The other five belong to *sïzï* in the villages of Ago and Ragi, for the Tsikru *lignée* and the Daba founding *lignée* immigrated here many years ago, and the Lama founding *lignée* immigrated here less than one hundred years ago. About twenty years ago, both the Daba *lignée* and the Lama *lignée* underwent separations, each of them into two parts.

The name of a *sïzï* is usually taken from the first name of a female ancestor, such as Sadabu, Hababu, Ago, and Ibu-Imin. Some of the names, however, come from a male ancestor or from the name of his job. For example, *Ragi* means the one who washes the horse of the dead. Chaman, a male ancestor in the Ragi *sïzï*, had this job, done especially for funerals in the *zhifu*'s family. This is where the *sïzï* got the name Ragi.

A *sïzï* generally includes about ten *lignées*. All of the *lignées* in a *sïzï* claim a common maternal line. The members are not able to reconstruct the relations that tie them to this ancestor and some-times not even those that tie them to each other. But they always know categorically within a *sïzï* who their consanguineal relatives are.

The villagers told me: "dhe krwa dhe raiba i mao hing" (a bowl and a plate must not mate). Now, within every *sïzï*, there is always one or more *lignées* of different consanguineal identity, because of the adoption of a non-consanguineal girl, or a cohabitation or a marriage with an outsider. Therefore, while a *sïzï* always consti-tutes a purely matrilineal group, its *lignées* can fall into two, or even more, groups that are not consanguineal to each other. And between members of the same *sïzï* who are not consanguineal rel-atives, sexual commerce is not, of course, forbidden.

We can take the Ibu-Imin *sïzï* as an example:

166

In this *sïzï* about eighty years ago, the Imin founding *lignée* (after splitting apart into two *lignées*) had no descendants and therefore adopted a Tibetan girl.

About seventy years ago, the Imin *lignée* branch had two daughters and one son. The *lignée* decided to have Dudgi, a man from Walabié, cohabit with their eldest daughter so that their son could become a Lamaist monk. At that time, Dudgi had one brother, two sisters, and two nieces living in his household. After his brothers and sisters died, his two nieces, both minors, became orphans. At Dudgi's request, the Imin *lignée*, which was well-off, agreed to take them in. Ten years or so later, Dudgi died. Conflict between the members of the Imin *lignée* and these two women and their children escalated. Finally, the *lignée* turned them out of the house. Today, these two women and their descendants each make up a *lignée*. The oldest daughter is called Dgimatsie, and her *lignée* bears her first name. Likewise, the *lignée* of the younger daughter, Sigebuchi, bears her first name.

The son of the Adgi founding *lignée* (before the separation) was an only child. About one hundred years ago, he brought a woman from the village of Ago to cohabit with him. In the next generation, the *lignée*, once again, had only one son, and to resolve the problem of descendants, it adopted two girls from one of his *açia*. As a result, these eight *lignées* no longer share the same consanguineal identity as the seven other *lignées*. In fact, the fifteen *lignées* that make up this *sïzï* are from four different consanguinities.

Within a *sïzï*, all *lignées* are equal and have certain mutual rights and responsibilities. Prior to 1956, if a person hurt or killed someone in a fight, the victim's *lignée* would institute proceedings before the *zhifu*. The trial would be undertaken in the name of the two *sïzï* involved in the incident, which would send their elders and/or those who were particularly skilled at presenting arguments. If the losing party's *lignée* was unable to pay the fine, each *lignée* of his *sïzï* was required to help, according to its means. With the exception of the amount that went directly to the *zhifu*, the fine was paid to the winning *lignée*. The other *lignées* in its *sïzï* received nothing. Until 1958, in October according to the lunar calendar, each *lignée* would choose a day to slaughter one or more of its pigs. On that day, all of the *lignées* in the same *sïzï* (some *lignées* only got together with consanguineal *lignées* that lived in the same village) gathered together and invited a *daba* to conduct a service of offerings to their ancestors. If the *daba* did not know the names of the ancestors, he would be told. In 1985, during the era of the People's Commune, a canteen was installed by the local government to replace the individual kitchens of each household. All of the land and grain was gathered for the commune exclusively. Consequently, this ritual disappeared in most of the Na villages.

There are, however, customs that have not changed and continue today. For example, on the second day of a funeral, following the example of the deceased's *lignée*, the other *lignées* in the same *sïzï* must prepare and offer a feast for all of the guests who have come from other villages. On a hill bordering the village, each *sïzï* has a piece of land on which all of its *lignées*, taking turns, come in the morning to burn pine needles and wheat flour as offerings to the mountain god. When a *lignée* depletes its grain reserve, other *lignées* from the same *sïzï* sometimes provide for it. The villagers told me they had never heard of a separation in a *sïzï*.

These examples demonstrate that today's *sïzï* makes up a localized group of matrilineal descent, but one with multiple consanguineal identities that allow for the possibility of sexual relations within it. A *sïzï*'s *lignées* helping each other out during funerals by receiving guests and sharing the responsibility of the service of offerings to the mountain god function to reinforce the *sïzï*'s cohesion.

One *sïzï* undertakes responsibilities vis-à-vis other *sïzï*, and conducts the service of offerings to the ancestors.

I translate *sïzï* as matrilineage. Since the lineage no longer includes exclusively consanguineal *lignées*, I designate the ensemble of consanguineal *lignées* as a consanguineal group.

Today, the *sïzï*, as a social structure, is very flexible. It has no chief, no authority, no common matriamony. The matrilineage no longer goes by the name *sïzï*. Practically no one under the age of thirty has ever heard the word *sïzï*, and those who have heard it are unable to say what it means.

The Legendary Lhe

Beyond the *lignée* and the *sïzï*, there is yet another sort of grouping, the *lhe,* whose number varies from three to six, depending on which shaman one is speaking to. About these *lhe* some of the old people and shamans told the following legend:

> In the olden days, the Na emigrated from Sibuanawa, their original village, to the south. In the LidZiadzï basin, they came across a stag that had just been killed by a wolf. Before sharing this stag among them, each *lhe* made a distinctive sign to mark the path from whence they came:

> Çi lhe zi odu [Çi *lhe* tied grass together];
> Gwe lhe sï pintçio [Gwe *lhe* carved a tree];
> Chu lhe chu odzi [Chu *lhe* stuck the antler of a stag in the ground];
> Hon lhe lu na dzi [Hon *lhe* stood a black stone on end].

> Angry because they only got the intestines as their share, the members of the Hon *lhe* burned all of the marks made by the other

lhe. Therefore, the other *lhe* got lost and ended up taking detours to reach Yongning.

Each *sïzï* belongs to a *lhe*. For example, among the six *sïzï* within the parameters of my investigation, Sadabu is part of the Hon *lhe*, and the others are in the Gwe *lhe*. Each *lhe* has its own itinerary on the route that ends in Yongning. Even today, when someone dies, a shaman must come to the funeral to recite each step of the itinerary of the *lhe* in question, so that the deceased will know which path to follow to be reunited with his ancestors. If this is not done, the soul of the deceased will be lost forever. For all of these *lhe*, the final destination is always Sibuanawa, the original village of the Na. No one, however, was able to identify its precise location. They only knew that this place was somewhere in the north.

Although the shamans did not agree on how many *lhe* of this kind there were, they unanimously claimed that these *lhe* were all *Zi*. *Zi* corresponds to the word *foyer* in French which doesn't have a corresponding term in English. Originally, when the Na began their immigration toward Yongning, they belonged to several *Zi*. Their names were Hon, Gwe, Chu, Çi, Ia, and Bu. No one today knows the meanings of these names. When they arrived in Yongning, there were only the four *Zi* mentioned in the legend. The term *lhe* designates, in a broad sense, a group of consanguineal relatives; it can indicate both *sïzï* (lineage) and *lignée*. On the other hand, the term *sïzï* cannot replace *lhe* to designate the original *Zi*. Because of this, I call this sort of *lhe* the legendary *lignée*.

Beyond their use in returning the souls of the dead, these legendary *lignées* no longer play a role. As is true within a *sïzï*, sex is permitted between those from the same legendary *lignée* who are not from the same group of consanguineal relatives. These original *lignées* do not have a common ancestor, their lineages are not located together, nor do they constitute a political unit. They do not play a religious role. They do not provide a heading for the *sïzï*, nor do the *sïzï* that claim the same legendary *lignée* have a consanguineal bond.

Today, most of the villagers, even some of the old ones, do not know to which legendary *lignée* their *lignée* belongs. There does not seem to be any role for this kind of *lhe* in the social structure; therefore, I believe that the four legendary *lhe* are merely mythical founding *lignées*.

Reciprocity

The term *idi* means cooperative use of buffalo (*i* means "buffalo," *di* means "cooperative use"). Each year, for the sowing of grain (wheat, Dekkan wheat, corn, and, recently, rice) and after the corn is picked, two or three, and very rarely four, households join forces to plow the fields, an arduous task.

As a general rule, before 1959, the year the People's Commune introduced collective arrangements, the households that joined forces were on good terms with each other. Most of the time, they came from the same village, which guaranteed efficient cooperation. However, two households from neighboring villages could, when their property was next to each other, cooperate. The oral agreement to cooperate annually was traditionally negotiated during the New Year's Day feasts. These negotiations were usually initiated by a household that had no buffalo. Since payment in cash was not an issue, the discussion, led by the household chiefs, centered on their respective participation in the farmwork and continued until they reached an agreement satisfying and fair to both parties. The terms of this mutual aid were very flexible, but there was one rule that applied to absolutely every cooperation: during the entire period of the work, the participants would be fed by the *matrilignée* on whose land they were working. For example, if the participants were working on A's land one day, they would eat at A's house; if the next day they were working on B's land, they would eat at B's house.

Another custom was left to the judgment of the parties involved. If household A owned more land than its partner B and an approximately equal number of buffalo and laborers, or if it had a particularly good harvest, A compensated the extra work required by its larger agricultural surface by offering B a gift of salt, tea, grain, or even clothing. Any cooperation, no matter what the circumstances, was always negotiated annually and never resulted in a contract for longer than one year. Because of this, if one of the parties did not behave fairly, the other had the option of not renewing the cooperation. An unfair cooperation was, however, unusual.

Here is an example of a situation that was perceived as unfair: the Tsona *lignée* was made up of three individuals, had 5 *dZia* of land and no buffalo, and harvested 6 *dan* of grain. Its neighbor, the Lafu *lignée*, with two individuals, owned 10 *dZia* of land and two buffalo and harvested 12 *dan* of grain. The Lafu *lignée* gave one or two pairs of pants and 2 *dou* of Dekkan wheat to the Tsona *lignée*. The Tsona felt that they had been wronged but were resigned to this state of affairs for four years, because there was no other household available to cooperate with them.

Cooperation usually lasts for one or two years. But sometimes an *idi* relationship can go on for ten or even twenty years. This phenomenon is most often found when the cooperating parties remain on good terms and have an equal amount of property, owning an almost identical amount of land, buffalo, and laborers. For example: The Dashi *lignée* and the Adzé *lignée* were neighbors. The Dashi had eight members, owned 13 *dZia* of land and one buffalo, and harvested approximately 15 *dan* of grain each year. The Adzé *lignée* had six members, owned 10 *dZia* of land and one buffalo, and harvested 13 *dan* of grain annually. Because the Na traditionally use a two-buffalo plow, these two *lignées* needed to cooperate. They did not give each other anything in the Fall, except when one of them had a bad harvest, because of a natural disaster or some other reason. In this case, one *lignée* gave the other some grain to help out. Their *idi* relationship continued in this manner for ten years.

Take the following situation: households A and B have an equal workforce but great disparities nonetheless. A owns a large piece of land and several buffalo, while B owns nothing. B can therefore harvest 1 or 2 *dZia* of land belonging to A. Between two consanguineal *lignées*, this type of cooperation sometimes continues for several generations. Moreover, in this combination, the two households form an alliance for practically every farming activity. This system continues today.

The only option for households with a workforce but only a small piece of land and no buffalo is to trade their workforce for the loan of buffalo.

Relationships between cooperative households can be broken down into two categories: neighbors and consanguineal relatives. The partners in an *idi* relationship change for a variety of reasons, including that of not getting along. Because of this it is possible for a household, given a long enough time span (as long as several decades), to cooperate with several different *matrilignées*. According to Na custom, when the economic situation of a household improves to the point where it can be autonomous, it is allowed to leave a cooperative.

In 1989, the existing and former *idi* in the village of Ago were as follows:

• Ago, a branch *lignée*, cooperated with Shadga (non-consanguineal but part of the same lineage, and neighbors);

- Baomo, branch I *lignée*, cooperated with AZi (consanguineal relatives but not from the same lineage);
- Zigrai cooperated with BadZi (consanguineal relatives but not from the same lineage);
- Gocho, branch I *lignée*, cooperated with Gocho, branch II *lignée* (consanguineal relatives from the same lineage);
- Baomo, founding *lignée*, cooperated with the Xu (a Han household from the same village), three years earlier, for one year;
- DZiaa cooperated with Miindge, founding *lignée* (neighbors from the same lineage, three years earlier, for one year);
- Abié cooperated with Ago, branch *lignée* (neighbors), six years earlier, for one year.

From 1959 to 1979, the era of the People's Commune, this custom was interrupted, and each Na village farmed the land collectively. In 1982, however, the custom reappeared with the agrarian reforms in which the government redistributed land to each household. This time, the land was distributed according to a head count: 3 to 6 *mu* per person, depending on the village.[19] Since then, the amount of land that each *lignée* owns has stayed the same; the government does not take anything back when someone dies or add anything when there is a birth. The average Na household owns more buffalo now than it did before the People's Commune, and therefore the *idi* relationship has been facilitated.

As mentioned earlier, this cooperative relationship is characterized by its temporary nature: it must be reestablished every year, and, consequently, it can vary from one year to the next. Because of this, if we follow a single household for several decades, we can reconstitute the network of its relationships with other households, and all of these networks intersect. Again, the requirements for a cooperation include: a shortage of manpower or buffalo, availability of resources, and good relations between the two households. This last factor takes precedence over the others. Consanguineal ties also play a significant role. If it is necessary to form a cooperative alliance, households that are consanguineal relatives, and therefore naturally supportive of each other, will join together: they choose each other first, and their *idi* relationship generally lasts.

Birth

To ensure a successful birth and a healthy life for the baby, a ritual must be conducted by a *daba*. First of all, a brother or sister of the pregnant woman must pick a branch from a healthy fruit tree in the mountains. The *daba* then makes a circle from a stalk of flax in the courtyard, and plants this branch in the center of it, reciting: "This tree is strong and very fertile. Snow cannot make it bow, storms cannot beat it. May it now be the guardian of the child, so that he lives a long life after his birth." Once this prayer is said, a sister or a brother of the pregnant woman hangs the circle in a tree near the house.

The birth generally takes place in the back room, the storehouse. If this room is not in good condition, the child is born in the room to the right. The mother of the woman giving birth usually functions as the midwife. No man can be present. Even today, the Na do not give birth in a hospital, unless there are difficulties.

The Naming of the Child

Before the 1960s, a *daba* was invited to the house on the day of the birth, or the following day, to name the baby. The naming ritual began with a service of offerings to the ancestors: a chicken killed by a male member of the *matrilignée*, several slices of boned and salted pork, and a bowl of rice. Using the head of the chicken, the *daba* foretold the future, predicting the fate of the child. While seated in the most important place in the house, to the right of the central hearth, the *daba* held two shells in his hand in front of a wooden tray. He then tossed the shells on the tray and came up with a name for the child according to where they landed, the hour of the child's birth, his or her astrological sign, and the position the baby was in when entering the world.

The Na have adopted the Han astrological system, but they have no recollection of when they did so. The twelve astrological signs are *hro* (rat), *i* (ox), *la* (tiger), *toli* (rabbit), *mugu* (dragon), *buRu* (snake), *Ra* (horse), *iu* (goat), *zi* (monkey), *in* (chicken), *kru* (dog), and *bo* (pig). The aspects of these signs fall into two categories: large and small. The large ones are the east, represented by the tiger and the rabbit, the west, represented by the monkey and the chicken, the south, represented by the snake and the horse, and the north, represented by the pig and the rat. The small ones are the southeast, symbolized by the dragon, the southwest, symbolized by the goat, the northeast, symbolized by the ox, and the northwest, symbolized by the dog. The aspect attributed to the child at birth depends on that of the main house. During my research, I was unable to get a *daba* to tell me the various combinations he used in naming a child.

Once the first name was chosen, the *daba* would say it aloud three times in a row, and the mother responded three times for the baby. Following this, he prayed for a long life for the baby and put a small dab of butter on the baby's forehead, a symbol of happiness. The *lignée* members and several attending villagers then gave presents to the mother and the newborn. The female chief of the *lignée* presented several plates of food to the birth mother and offered her, as well as the other participants, a drink of alcohol. Everyone expressed their best wishes in celebration of the growth of the *lignée*.

One month after the birth, at sunrise, the mother or her sister would place a piece of burning pine, full of turpentine, in the courtyard. Then the birth mother, or her mother, took the baby in her left arm and a sickle, a dried stalk of flax (symbolizing a spear), and a page from the sacred Lamaist texts in her right hand and entered the courtyard. The moment she crossed the threshold, she placed the baby in the sun, praying to the sun to protect him. *Nimi* (the sun) is thought to be a woman (the same is true for *hlemi*, the moon) and supreme in the sky. The fate of every living being depends on her. In order to grow, the newborn must come to the sun. The sickle and the stalk of flax are the weapons with which, with the help of Buddha, the child will vanquish all harm.

On that day, the *lignée* would prepare drinks of alcohol and meat and other things to eat for the old women of the village who came to visit. After having seen the sun, the birth mother left the back room for the main room and got into a bed to the right of the central hearth. From this moment on, she and the baby could have contact with others.

For one month after the birth of a child, representatives from each village household, usually women, brought eggs and rice alcohol to the house with the new baby. During that month, the *lignée* invited the elder villagers for a drink to express its gratitude.

Today, since *daba* have become rare, the naming process has changed greatly. At birth, a child receives a pet name from one of the three people authorized to give it to him: his *eyi* (grandmother), his *apu* (great-uncle), or the first person who visits him, whether it is a consanguineal relative or not, for the Na believe that this person transmits his character to the baby.

When the child is three or four years old, during the New Year celebrations, the mother brings him to a living Buddha, who formally gives him a Tibetan name, taking care not to give him a name already held by a member of his *lignée*. The number of first names is very limited. Therefore, in a village, members of the same sex frequently have the same first name. To distinguish one from the other, the villagers will add the name of the *lignée* before the first name when they are speaking about someone or calling out to someone.

The naming ritual is completed with the living Buddha's caressing the head of the child. From that moment on, the *lignée* members and the villagers call the child by this formal name. Only rarely do the *lignée* members continue to call the child by a pet name.

The Name of the Lignée

In principle, a *lignée* takes its name from one of its members. This member, male or female, is always a chief and recognized by the villagers as the *lignée*'s representative. This person may have been dead for generations, with no one knowing anything more about him or her than the name that was transmitted hereditarily (because of this, I collected a list of very old names that seem Na, not Tibetan), or may still be alive and recently moved out of his or her birth home (in the case of a separation, for example).

When a *lignée* splits up, each part keeps the same name, after which is added the term *apo* (external, or branch) for the *lignée* that moves to another house and *gnao* (internal, or founding) for the original *lignée*. If there is a second separation, the name of the *lignée* chief is used to distinguish between different *lignées* that have the same original name. *Apo*, an adjective, can also become the name of the *lignée;* therefore, following a separation, the following names can result: Apo Gnao and Apo Apo.

A *lignée* is sometimes identified by a nickname given it by the villagers, which, through use, becomes its usual designation. The *lignée* nonetheless keeps the name of its representative, even though it is never used in practice. The most frequent nicknames within the parameters of my research were the following:
- names chosen according to a place, whether it be that of the residence (*gelu:* lakeshore) or the place of origin (Tçime: a

Sichuan village; Logu: Ninglang, the city where the district government's seat is located), or according to the original ethnic group (Han *Rumi:* Han granddaughter; Pumi, Li-su)
- a nickname given because of a physical or moral characteristic of the representative (*iumi:* goat nose; *lamu:* female tiger)
- the position the person holds in the *zhifu*'s administration (*raimi*; *toba:* tax collector)
- a term of kinship (*eyi:* grandmother; *emi:* mother)
- an animal or a plant (*imin:* buffalo tail; *sha:* flax)

Some *lignée* names remain inexplicable. In the five villages in my field of investigation, the name of the *sizï* and of the village was the same, and this was also the name of a *lignée*.

The names of Na *lignées* differ from family names found in many other societies. For the Na, separations result in the new *lignées'* taking new names, whereas in other societies, new families usually keep the same name.

Puberty

The age of thirteen marks the threshold between childhood and puberty. Traditionally, before the age of thirteen, all children wear a simple linen dress, regardless of their sex. The girls wear their hair in a short braid, slantwise across their foreheads. The boys have their heads almost completely shaved, except for a handful of hair on the top or the back of their heads. Han clothing, which was introduced in the 1970s, has progressively replaced this type of dress. The hairstyles of Na children today also resemble those of Han children.

The following legend explains the significance of the age of thirteen:

Once upon a time, humans and animals lived together. They were immortal. The spirit Abaodgu decided to assign a life span to each kind of living being. He warned the humans about it and told them to pay attention to a call he would send out in the night, for the first species to respond would be granted great longevity. After midnight, the spirit began to announce life spans. First, Abaodgu cried out, "A thousand years," but all of the living things continued to sleep, except for a sentry of wild geese. They responded first, so the wild geese could live for a thousand years. Then Abaodgu called out, "A hundred years," which was heard by the ducks. After this, the age of sixty was granted to the dog. It was only when Abaodgu called out thirteen years that man awoke, received the message, and felt that his life span was too short. With Abaodgu's consent, he traded his life span with the dog, on the condition that humans give dogs three meals a day and never beat them. The puberty ritual commemorates the life span originally assigned to humans.

The Na call the ceremony accompanying the puberty ritual *chai dZié* for girls, which means putting on a skirt, and *hli dZié* for boys, which means putting on pants. It is the object of much attention. Celebrated during the festivities that surround the New Year (the first day of the first month of the lunar calendar), it constitutes the main event in a Na's life, anticipated by all involved long before the actual date.

On the eve of the event, while the other villagers prepare the gifts to be exchanged between consanguineal *matrilignées*, all of the children who turned thirteen during the year get together in a separate spot, girls on one side, boys on the other, and express their joy. In the early morning of New Year's Day, with gifts, butter and brown sugar presented to the divinity of the hearth, and an abundance of wood thrown onto the fire, creating flames that light up the otherwise dark main room, the ritual takes place the moment the sun rises above the summit of the mountain.

This moment must be strictly respected, for it is decisive in determining the future of the individual. When it is a girl, the mother presides. The girl stands upright, next to the right pillar, which symbolizes the feminine, with one foot on a salted and boned pig and the other on a sackful of grain. The mother or the grandmother begins by tying a large braid made from the hair of a yak tail to the girl. A bundle of silk threads is then tied to the end of the braid. This long braid, trimmed with little yellow and red beads, is coiled around her head. The mother then helps her daughter out of her old dress and into her new skirt, jacket, and belt embroidered with geometric shapes. Before being put on, the new clothes are hung from the door, and the girl's mother takes them and bangs them against the door to chase away anything harmful that they might contain. After the changing of clothes, the daughter holds several jewels in her right hand and a thread and a piece of linen in her left hand. Now the *daba* addresses a prayer to the ancestors and the divinity of the hearth. He places a woolen cord around the girl's neck, which is a symbol of luck. He takes it off at the end of the ritual and attaches it to a stick that has been stuck into the wall. This cord will keep the girl alive and assure a long life. The girl then prostrates herself before *gwa gahla* (the stone tablet symbolizing the ancestors). She does the same before the divinity of the hearth and before her adult consanguineal relatives, from the eldest to the youngest, as well as before the outside participants, even before me, the researcher. After the prayer, the grandmother usually offers her a gift of jewelry; the other participants, including the outside guests, give her money. Everyone wishes the girl great prosperity, the talent to weave beautiful fabric, and the capacity to have many children: nine boys and nine girls. Finally, the girl calls the dog into the main room and thanks him for trading his life span with humans.

After the guests leave, all of the members of the *lignée* gather near the lower hearth and eat breakfast. The male *lignée* chief conducts a service of offerings to the ancestors and tells them the *lignée* has just added a full-fledged member.

From this moment on, the girl lets her hair grow. As she gets older, the color of her skirt changes. During her youth, she wears a white or a light-blue skirt, during middle age, a dark-blue skirt, and in her old age, she wears black.[20]

The ritual for the boy, who stands next to the left pillar, which symbolizes the masculine, is presided over by his maternal uncle or his maternal great-uncle. The uncle dresses the adolescent in a hat, a pair of pants, a jacket, a belt, and a pair of boots.[21] During the ritual, he holds silver coins and a dagger, symbols of prosperity and bravery. The *daba* then recites a prayer for the boy: "The bud becomes a tree, the child becomes an adult. Today is auspicious, for today X wears pants. May he be as vigorous as a wild duck in the sky and live for a hundred years! May he live a thousand years like the wild goose! May he be a hard worker and a good hunter and vanquish his enemies on the battlefield. May all his battles be victorious! Today, you have pork and grain beneath your feet; in the future, may you have piles of grain and an endless supply of meat. The dagger is your companion and can help you to hunt down beasts and demons. Good health and good luck!"

Long ago, the uncle, before the ceremony, would make a wooden spear about 2 meters long on which he would hang a pennon and a saber from one end and a leather strap from the other. During the ritual, the boy would walk on the roof of the house with this spear in his hand.

After the puberty ritual, the boy braids the handful of hair left on his head into a single plait about 20 centimeters long that hangs down in back or is kept under his hat for the rest of his life. This is thought to promote longevity. The rest of the ritual proceeds in the same manner as the one for the girl.

If there is not a mother or a maternal uncle, the *daba* chooses someone through divination who has the same series of astrological signs. The twelve signs are divided into four sequences: ox, snake, and chicken; tiger, horse, and dog; monkey, dragon, and rat; pig, goat, and rabbit. Those who belong to the same series and are of the same sex as the child can be chosen to carry out the putting on of the skirt or the pants.

This ceremony is all the more anxiously anticipated because it marks the moment when the adolescent becomes a full member of society and has the right to participate in social and amorous activities.

CHAPTER EIGHT

The Furtive Visit

If an essential characteristic of this society is that brothers and sisters from every generation live together for life under the same roof, and if the incest prohibition is not ignored, how do these people have a sex life?

In Na society, four modalities of sexual practices exist: *nana sésé* (the furtive visit), *gepié sésé* (the conspicuous visit), *ti dzï jï mao the* (cohabitation of a couple without a ritual banquet), and *jï the ti dzi* (cohabitation after a feast). In this chapter, I discuss the most common practice, the *nana sésé;* in subsequent chapters, I will discuss the other modes.

Definition

The traditional mode of sexual life practiced by the Na is called *nana sésé. Nana* means furtively, and *sésé* literally means to walk and figuratively means to visit. This expression indicates a secret romantic encounter or a furtive visit that occurs without any consanguineal relatives knowing about it, especially the male adults. I translate the expression *nana sésé* as furtive visit because in this case it means to visit furtively.

Society calls a man and a woman who set up this kind of sexual relationship *nana sésé hing*, which means people in a relationship of furtive meetings; the man and the woman discreetly call each other *açia*. The term *açia* is made up of the diminutive prefix *a* and the root *çia*. The Na add *a* to names and proper nouns to indicate intimacy, affection, friendship, and respect; *çia*, when used as a noun, means lover. The same word is used for both sexes, and as a verb it means literally to lie down and figuratively to mate, to sleep and to tempt. *Açia* means lover.

A Na saying depicts those who are *açia* very well:

açia biai zo çia mao i,
the ge di do çia la nié
[It is not enough to say that we are *çia* for it to be so,
sleeping together once makes (us) *çia*.]

I call this kind of sexuality an *açia* relationship. Such a relationship between two partners can last one night or several nights, weeks, months, or even years. But a furtive encounter between two individuals does not unfold systematically.

Forming the Relationship

Usually, the romantic rendezvous is carried out with the man visiting the bedroom of the woman around midnight (the time varies according to the season: in the summer, it is a little later, in the winter, a little earlier). He comes and goes in such a way that the female members of his *lignée*, and the male members of the woman's *lignée* perceive nothing. He leaves the woman's house at the first crow of the rooster and returns home.

Traditionally, men and women enjoy complete equality. In daily contact, in town, in the workplace, and elsewhere, a woman or a man can make the first advance, expressing interest in, or feelings about, another person. Words or gestures are used to make one's desires known. For example, a girl might say to a boy,

"Tsi hwa nia gi dzi io bié" (Come stay at my house tonight). The boy might then respond, "No emi çi to ié" (Your mother is not easygoing. Literally: your mother knows how to shout abuse). And then the girl might say, "Çi to mao ié; hwa kru nana io" (She won't scold you. Come secretly in the middle of the night). If the boy accepts, he says, "Dze yé" (Okay). If the boy refuses, he says, "Nia no gi yo bié ni mao go; ti i bié ni mao gu" (I don't want to come. I'm not going to come over to sleep). In this case, no matter what the girl says, nothing will change his mind.

When the man takes the initiative for the encounter, he often uses the expression "Tsi hwa nia no gi io bié, dze yé?" (I'll come to your house tonight, okay?), to which the woman responds with a smile or by saying, "Dze ié" (okay). Some come straight out and ask "Açia i a bié?" (Do you want to be my *açia*?). If a woman refuses a man's proposition, she can use a ready-made formula: "Dze mao ié, nia tsi hwa dhe wu dZio" (No, it is not possible. I already have one for tonight). In that case, the man will not insist.

One makes one's desire known through a gesture by taking advantage of a moment in which the chosen person is not paying attention and abruptly snatching away an object he or she is carrying. A woman's smile in reaction to such a gesture signifies tacit agreement. The man can then visit her that very night or the next night, bringing back the object he has taken. On the other hand, firmly demanding the return of the taken object signifies a refusal. When a man is the focus of a woman's lust, he will go to her house if she pleases him. If she does not please him, he will recover his object sooner or later. Male or female, everyone has the right to accept or to refuse. Here is an illustration of this custom:

Jishï (twenty-seven years old), a young man from Kaitçi, began his *açia* life at the age of eighteen. His first *açia* was Tsïe, who was seven years older than he. One day during a conversation, he offered her a cigarette, and she snatched the entire pack. Knowing that Tsïe was taking the initiative to express her desires, Jishï let her do it. Two days later, he saw her again. They exchanged belts and began to meet secretly. In less than a month, Tsïe, who had begun to see another *açia*, abandoned Jishï. He then found a second *açia*. One day, while working in the fields, an old man was chatting with him: "NadZi is beautiful. Go and ask her to be *açia* with you." He thought that NadZi was not only pretty but also very good at her job. Jishï approached her and took the scarf from her head. She did not react at all, neither asking him to give it back nor trying to get it back by force. That night, he began to visit her secretly.

A date can come about after some reflection or spontaneously, but it must take place privately, without any of the consanguineal relatives of the opposite sex of either party present. Usually, be- tween people from the same village or from neighboring villages, the rendezvous is set up at a convenient moment during the day when the concerned parties run into each other. At night, the men gather at the side of the path that passes alongside the vil- lage; after some time spent talking, they leave to find the women.

Before the 1980s, young people would leave the house im- mediately after dinner to gather in the homes of *baolu* women, usually those in their village. These women lived by themselves, without any relatives. Conversations could therefore be uninhib- ited. Any subject might be brought up, in particular those about emotions and love, without having to worry about the taboo on sexual evocation. Around midnight, the young men and women who were getting along would leave together, and the boys who had not found anyone would head out to look for other girls. Of course, because of the incest taboo, relatives of the opposite sex were never simultaneously present in this setting.

Today, to meet in this way, the villagers go to the movies.

Many of them go every day, especially those who are younger than forty; therefore, the movie theater, as the place where one goes to find a date, deserves to be examined more thoroughly.

When I first arrived in Yongning, I went to the movies in a neighboring village, about 3 kilometers away. Once a day, a film was projected outdoors, in a field surrounded by a fence. After dinner, people arrived from the surrounding villages. Seated on the ground, the majority of the viewers were younger than thirty-five. During the film, the young men flirted with the young women. They took them in their arms, caressing them and whispering to them. There was a youth sitting next to me who was behaving in this manner with a young woman, and, after about twenty minutes, got up and left. She was then immediately joined by another young man, and the whole process began anew. Women considered pretty received this kind of treatment and seemed to consent to it. I could not believe my eyes.

I continued to return for several days. The same scenes repeated themselves. I began to understand but was still confused and tried to find an explanation.

It was winter; the weather was dry and cold. The wind was blowing hard, stirring up dust and sand. I was very uncomfortable, but they seemed not in the least bit bothered. After the movie, I went to a hut, where several young men were gathered. A conversation started. My culture shock was such that, risking the embarrassment my lack of discretion might provoke, I decided to question them:

"Why do the young women accept this kind of behavior? Why do they let you do it?"

"If you don't fondle them, they won't be comfortable," answered one of young men.

The projectionist added: "That's exactly what they come here for.

They pretend to be watching the movie, but in fact they don't even understand very much [because they don't speak Chinese very well]."

I, too, pretended to watch the movie, but, in truth, I was not following the story, either. As an ethnologist, I was a spectator of the spectators. My "movie" was the Na. I finally understood that what I had first considered coarse behavior on the part of the young men was in reality an attentiveness that the women were used to.

When the movie was over, everyone would disappear into the darkness of the night. Those who lived in the village returned on foot, while those who came from nearby villages rode home on bicycles (in every village, about half of the young men have bicycles). Those couples who had made a tacit agreement left together.

Today, there are eight movie theaters of this kind in the basin, as well as a real theater with rows of numbered seats in Batsïgu, the government headquarters in the canton. A film is shown in Batsïgu every night. The behavior of the young people is more discreet there than in the open-air theaters. The young men and women purchase tickets and wait in front of the theater, getting to know each other. The men take the initiative more often than the women. They approach the women they are interested in and offer them tickets. One man can offer several women a ticket, just as one woman can offer a ticket to more than one man. Once a ticket is handed over, the man and woman move away from each other and only get back together inside the theater. During the film, the viewers talk loudly, often drowning out the sound from the speakers. If they have had a good time during the movie and reached an agreement, they leave discreetly to spend an amorous night together. This night might be spent in a field or in the woman's bedroom. If they go to the woman's house, custom has it that the man returns home the next morning before dawn. Meetings of this kind usually occur only once; the couple rarely gets together again.

Most of the time, a date is made when the two concerned parties agree to get together. But there is also a collective way in which to express one's desire, for example, when a small group of young men comes across a group of young women. From a distance, they yell, with their right hands held up to their right cheeks: "A hé hé! dzo dzo a grai?" (Hey, hey, do you want to trade something?). If the women are interested, they respond: "A hé hé!" One young man, representing the group, steps up to make the exchange. The object exchanged is usually a belt. The women who are reluctant can always refuse. Armed with his object, the man can visit its owner later.

The Process of the Visit
With first-time visits, the time and place for the secret meeting are usually set in advance. The place can be either outside the house, in a field, in the woods, or in a shed, or in the woman's bedroom. If it is to take place in the woman's bedroom, the man and woman agree on a signal that the visitor will give: he will knock on the front door a specified number of times, or throw pebbles on the roof, or climb the wall and crouch in front of her bedroom window to announce his arrival. There is a popular song that all of the *açia* use: The man sings: "Open the door, the mosquitoes are biting me." "Don't be in such a hurry. Mama has not gone to bed yet," answers the woman. "Open the door. It's windy and cold," insists the man. "Be patient a little while longer. The flames in the hearth are still burning," responds the woman.

Many furtive visits between old *açia* and even some amorous encounters between new partners are not planned in advance. The visitor crawls over the fence, climbs up the wall of the house until he reaches the woman's bedroom, and tries to get her to open the door by whispering sweet words. Since every house has a "she-dog," it is helpful to come equipped with a pork bone or a pinecone full of rice to toss to the dog at the right moment so that it will allow the visitor to enter the woman's bedroom in peace.[1]

In these kinds of visits, the visitors usually know the women they are attempting to see. However, the women do not know who is coming that night. Once a woman finds out who her visitor is, she need only welcome him if she is willing. If the visit is unwanted, the woman always has the recourse of sleeping in her mother's room in the main house, which is an elegant way of turning someone down. Less frequently, she can wake up the rest of the household by screaming "Thief!" Such instances are, however, very unusual.

A subtle consensus within a household allows a man making a spontaneous visit to knock on the front door, without any specific signal having been arranged: in a household where there are women of the age to receive visitors, every evening after nightfall, the men of the house will not open the front door, unless the person knocking calls out the name of a household member.

Usually, when someone knocks, the woman who is waiting for a visit will open the door. In *matrilignées* where two or more women are expecting visitors, for example, the mother(s) and the daughter(s), one of the daughters will usually open the door. If the women waiting are sisters, it does not matter which one of them goes to the door. It sometimes happens that the woman who opens the door is not the desired one, but this causes no embarrassment, since the visitor can go directly to the bedroom of the chosen woman or, if he does not know where it is, ask for directions. However, this would only happen if the man came from a faraway village, because, in general, all of the men know where the bedroom is of every woman in their village and even in the villages nearby. Moreover, the spontaneous visit occurs more frequently with older visitors, who have fewer and more stable *açia* and are less shy than the younger ones.

During an amorous encounter, it is forbidden for the two *açia* to speak loudly. They have to whisper so that nothing will reach the ears of the woman's relatives, above all the men (especially uncles and great-uncles). During the day, amorous meetings are forbidden in the house.

Another way for a young man to visit without a prearranged date is to sneak into the woman's bedroom while she is asleep. The visitor who does this is usually sure that he will be well received. The young men who practice this kind of visit are often quite roguish. They know how to use all of their persuasive talents to get what they want. A young man who has met with a refusal to his request for a date can in this way try his luck. Once the visitor has successfully reached the side of the bed, the young woman can not call out for help from her household because of the taboo on sexual evocation. But no matter what method is used, the success of the furtive visitor who comes without a rendezvous depends on the desire of the woman. No one can force anyone.

If, after having expressed her wishes, a woman is refused by the man she desires, she has no choice but to accept the rejection, since custom does not allow women to visit men. About this rule, there is a legend:

When humanity originated, no one knew how to regulate visits. Abaodgu, the god in charge of setting all the rules, proposed the following test: he ordered that a man be shut up in a house and that a woman be sent to join him. To reach the man, the woman had to pass through nine doors. At dawn, she had reached the seventh door. Then Abaodgu tested the man, who succeeded in passing through only three doors in one night. Because of this Abaodgu, believing that women were too passionate, felt that they must not do the visiting. All of a sudden, his decision was made: the men were to visit the women.

Another type of encounter can take place under the following circumstances. While traveling to or from the town of Batsïgu or some other faraway place, a woman may stop in a village on the route to visit a household of friends or consanguineal relatives and to spend the night. A man in this village can then secretly enter her bedroom, even if the woman does not know, or barely knows, him. Generally speaking, he is welcome.

Here is an example. One evening, on his way back from the movies, one of my friends who was giving an unknown young woman a ride on his bicycle, said to me: "Let's go home!" Then he sped ahead of me and disappeared into the night. The next day, quite proud of himself, he told me about his adventure:

You saw the woman I was giving a ride to on my bike last night? She's a friend of Seno [a woman from the village and a lover of the protagonist in this adventure]. I talked for a while to both of them during the movie. When I brought her back to the village, I found out that she was staying at Seno's house. I parked my bicycle, and after midnight, I climbed over the wall to her house and secretly made my way to the door of Seno's bedroom. She let me in. I told her that it was not possible for all three of us to spend the night together in her bedroom and asked her to sleep in the main room with her mother. When she had gone, her friend wanted to go with her. So I grabbed her by the waist and put her on the bed. She began to complain about Seno, telling me: "She's mean. She asked me to spend the night at her house, but then she has someone come over, and she has abandoned me." I interrupted her by protesting: "Don't say that! Seno is nice. If she stays with you one day, would you be as nice and generous as she has been and invite a young man for her, just as she has done for you?"

At these words, she became quiet. I was then able to take her blouse off, but she held on to her pants and wouldn't let me take them off. She told me that she hadn't done it yet and that she was scared of getting pregnant. I tried to reassure her: "Don't be scared. If you get pregnant, I'm here."[2] She did not seem convinced. I then told her that if she didn't want to, I'd leave. But I stayed put. And since she didn't take her hands off of me and didn't protest, I kept going...."

Before 1964, if a man spent the night at a friend's house, the women of the household would customarily arrange for him to sleep with a woman in the household or with a woman from another *lignée*. These two kinds of situations fall under the category of sexual hospitality.

While the incest prohibition, which is strongly felt, severely restricts the behavior of consanguineal relatives among themselves, sexual freedom is absolute between non-consanguineal relatives — so much so that it makes for bold behavior. The following example appears accurately to illustrate the connection between sexual relations and morality:

One night, a young man secretly crept into the bedroom of a young woman while she was sleeping. The man felt that he was welcome. Initially, the woman was confused, emotional, and modest. She said, "My mother is not easygoing. I'm ashamed."

Her attitude was ambiguous: her expression seemed welcoming, but her words were rejecting. "Ashamed!" the young man responded. "Between our two *lignées*, there is no such thing as shame. We can do anything together!"

Selecting an *açia* is a personal matter. When I broached the subject during interviews, my sources, who were always very proud, claimed that they were quite liberal, unlike the Han, whose older generations were always trying to arrange, and even impose, partners on the younger generations — and this in spite of the principle of freedom in love matters that the government had been propagating for a long time. All of my sources confirmed: "na bu dgï lo thï mao dZio, dhe wu gne dhe wu gai o mao i. dhe wu gne dhe bai zé. nia gne ni fu ni gi bié. no gne nia gwai wo mao i" (The Na do not have that custom; that is, we do not arrange or propose sexual partners for a person. No one can force anyone to do something against his wishes. To each his own. I go with the one I love. No one can stop me).

While rare, there are cases in which a mother, having taken a liking to a young man, offers him sexual hospitality. For example, if a young man has helped her with something, a woman might give him food or a drink. Then at nightfall, taking advantage of his having had too much to drink, she brings him to her daughter's bedroom and locks him in. If the young man pleases the daughter, the partners can become *açia*; if not, after that first night, he will be rejected. In any case, the elders cannot impose *açia* on members of the younger generation.

The Selection Criteria

The criteria that women use when selecting a man are, first and foremost, physical beauty, then a sense of humor, vivacity, roguishness, courage, and work capability, and, last of all, kindness and generosity. The more of these qualities a man possesses, the more likely he is to succeed with women.

In one of the five villages within my frame of reference, there lived a twenty-five-year-old man who was considered very handsome. He had so much success each time he went to Batsïgu that the other men whispered with envy: "Look at him, he's back again to pick up girls." He told me himself, and not without pride, that even if that was not what had brought him to town, that was what people always thought.

For men, the essential criteria in selecting a woman are beauty and charm (physical charm, allure, a gift for conversation, good manners, and kindness to others). The more beautiful a woman is, the more suitors she will have. For example:

1. Adga was a beautiful and hospitable twenty-three-year-old woman. According to the villagers, she had already had 102 *açia*, only one of which had lasted for more than a year. Her twenty-four-year-old sister, who was articulate and very pretty but had a limp, had had fifty *açia*, forty-nine of which were short-lived.

2. Chema, a beautiful and exceptionally gracious woman, had been in *açia* relationships with more than eighty men. When she was about twenty-five years old, several young men from the village could be found in front of her house as soon as the sun went down, waiting for an opportunity to get in.

The young men always claim that "the ideal *açia* is a beautiful woman. We visit women according to how beautiful they are. If we go to an ugly woman's house, it is only to satisfy a fleeting desire." It is not uncommon for several young men to desire the same woman at the same time.

As long as a woman remains young and pretty, men will visit her. However, some women, once they reach the age of thirty, lose their charms and have almost no chance of being visited. Women who are ugly or handicapped also have almost no chance of being visited. There are even some who have never had a sexual relationship.

The following is an anecdote about an unintelligent and ungracious woman who received few visits during her lifetime:

Long ago, among the aristocrats, there was a poet in charge of singing stories, anecdotes, and funny tales. One day, he sang a song for A Shaofu, the *zhifu*'s brother and the chief of the Lamaist religion, about a woman in Imin who refused all visitors, even one who had offered her 80 *bankai* [the silver currency in use during the period]. After hearing this song, A Shaofu thought that if, in spite of the 80 *bankai*, she still refused the visit, she must be very beautiful. He sent an attendant to fetch her. When she was presented to A Shaofu, who was on the second floor at the time, he did not even let her come up the stairs. He ordered that she be given 1 *bankai* and sent back to her home.

This woman was so unintelligent that most of the time she would not even open the door when a man visited her. The boys from the village would therefore sometimes try to trick her, and one of them pretended to offer her 80 *bankai*. This is how this popular anecdote originated.

When a young woman begins to receive men, she usually does not speak about it to her mother or her mothers. If the mothers and grandmothers know about the furtive visits, they do not interfere. Secret encounters are completely natural. The following example provides a good illustration of this custom. A young man secretly gets together with a young woman in the storehouse at night. All of a sudden, the woman's mother comes out of the main house carrying a torch. The man tries to hide in the storehouse, but since the floor, made of loose boards, has holes in it, he stumbles and falls into the stable, creating panic among the animals. Believing that a wolf has entered, the mother approaches. As soon as she identifies the true cause of the turmoil, she exclaims: "Daughter, if you want to receive an *adhu* (friend), you must welcome him properly. Why have you seated him with the cows?"

It is so natural for a young man to visit young women at night in their houses that if a young man who has come to rob a house is surprised by a household member, he can easily get out of this predicament by saying he has come for a furtive visit.

After some time, if the same visitor comes back regularly, the woman can talk about him with her mother. If the mother does not like the man, she will make her feelings known to him one way or another. However, this is rare and only happens under two kinds of circumstances: the mother suspects that objects missing from the household have been stolen by the visitor, or the mother was an *açia* of this visitor in the past. If the daughter respects her mother's opinion, she ends the relationship with the man to maintain the solidarity of the household. However, if the daughter is stubborn, her mother will pretend to scold the animals in the courtyard to chase the visitor away when she knows that he is in her daughter's bedroom at night. But if the daughter wants to continue this liaison, the mother must resign herself to it. For example:

> Thirty years ago when he was young, Ondi from Imin, who is now forty-nine, was an *açia* of Dashidgima, who is now fifty-seven. For the past five years, Ondi has been an *açia* of Tsiedgïma (thirty-six years old), Dashidgima's eldest daughter. Dashidgima was annoyed when she found out that Ondi was visiting her daughter, but since Tsiedgïma wanted to keep the liaison going, there was nothing her mother could do.

Conflict also arises when a daughter does not give in to the wishes of her mother(s). Sometimes, if they are on bad terms with each other, the daughter moves out and lives somewhere else. This is the case for some *baolu*. However, intervention by a mother into the *açia* relationships of her daughter is very rare.

The mother or mothers of a young man must not know anything about his *açia* relationships, except for what they pick up from the neighbors' small talk and gossip. This can be explained, first and foremost, by the taboo on the subject and by the fact that a man's *açia* relationships always take place outside of his house. In any case, whether his ascendants know or not, they do not intervene.

While a mother can encourage or discourage a particular *açia* relationship — something she can do only with a daughter, not a son — she cannot intervene in the way that outsiders, namely society, can, nor can she impose her point of view or hinder her daughter's *açia* relationship.

The Exchange of Gifts

In general, a liaison between *açia* is a purely emotional and sexual affair. However, some visitors, although not many, give a small amount of money or a small gift to their lover of the evening, especially if it is the first visit or one of the first visits or if they are anxious to come back soon, but this gesture is usually not repeated. The amount in question is small, often 1 or 2 *yuan* or, before the 1970s, several *mao* (10 *mao* equal 1 *yuan*), for most young men have limited resources. Likewise, sometimes a woman offers a small gift to a lover with whom she has had many visits over a prolonged period. Here are two examples of this practice:

1. Gezo was a serf from a poor *lignée*. He had had six *açia*. The first was for only one night, and did not include a gift. The second lasted about a year. All in all, he gave this *açia* 3 *bankai*, and the girl gave him a pair of linen pants. He spent three nights with his third *açia*, and no gifts were exchanged. The same was true for his fourth *açia* relationship, which lasted six months. He gave 2 *bankai* to his fifth *açia*, and this relationship also lasted about six months. To his last *açia*, whom he saw for one month, he gave thirty nails for her shoes.

2. Tsidi was from a relatively well-off *lignée*, and he gave gifts to almost all of his *açia*. To his first, whom he visited three nights in a row, he gave nothing. To the second one, whom he saw for about a month, he gave a scarf. He gave an embroidered scarf to the third woman, whom he saw for eight nights, and he received a pair of linen pants in return. He gave a jacket, a pair of shoes, and a pair of ribbons for lacing her legs to his fourth *açia*, whom he saw for one week. In return, she made him a pair of linen pants. To his fifth *açia*, whom he visited for about a month, he gave a pair of shoes, and she gave him a pair of linen pants. To the sixth one, whom he saw for one and a half months, he gave 5 pounds of butter and 7 *bankai*, and in return, he received a belt. To the seventh one, whom he saw for one month, he gave a pair of shoes. To the eighth one, whom he also saw for one month, he gave a jacket and a scarf, and she gave him a pair of linen pants.

The gifts offered are usually articles of clothing, for even today, the region is very poor.[3] The exchange of gifts between *açia* is only practiced by a small number of people. It all depends on their generosity and their economic means. These gifts are not given to every *açia*.

It is true that if a man has money, he will succeed in conquering a woman, no matter who she is. About this there is a saying: "no çia nia çia bié mao zo, yatçia ni dZio ni çia nié" (Don't say your *çia*, my *çia*: *çia* belongs to whoever has money). Those who are rich leave a little something for their *açia* after each visit, which helps to prolong the relationship. My sources told me many times that before 1956, the richer the man, the more furtive visits he had.

Not all women will accept the money or gifts offered to them by a visitor. Some tell their generous lovers: "Let's have a good time if we want to. But don't bother bringing me gifts or money."

Moreover, gifts and money do not play a decisive role in an

açia relationship. Either partner can break off the relationship at any time if he or she wishes to do so. Their custom states: "You are not mine, and I don't belong to you. After you leave me, I will find another." The exchange of little gifts between *açia* is an expression of their feelings. If some men give money to women, it is to make them happy, not to pay them. Only those women who earn a living from selling sex are considered prostitutes.

The Multiplicity of Partners and the Discontinuity of Relationships

The examples above demonstrate that over the course of a lifetime an individual can have a variable number of *açia*. Not only do men and women have the freedom to foster as many *açia* relationships as they want and to end them as they please, but each person can have simultaneous relationships with several *açia*, whether it be during one night or over a longer period. In fact, a woman may receive two or three visitors a night, and a man may visit two or three women in one night.

These relationships are also marked by discontinuity. For example, a woman can establish an *açia* relationship with man A one night, with B the next, with C the night after that, and so on. If A comes back after C, this woman and A do not consider themselves to have been *açia* during the interval between their first and second meeting. In other words, each visitor's departure from the woman's home is taken to be the end of their *açia* relationship. Even if A comes to this woman's house every night but then stops doing so, the last morning he is there marks the end of their *açia* relationship. The same holds true from the man's point of view. If he visits woman A one night, B the next, C the following night, and so on, he is in an *açia* relationship only with the woman he is visiting on a given night, not with the others.

In this context, is important to remember that the word *çia* means to sleep when used as a verb and lover when used as a noun. So when two people are not actually sleeping together, the term no longer applies. They are no longer *çia* for each other. A popular song illustrates this point well:

açia bié la a mao çia,
so kru lai çia çia ing nié,
so hwa lo biai biai ing nyé,
açia bié zo a mao çia,
the ga dhe do çia la nié
[Claiming to be *açia* doesn't make you *açia*,
Sleeping together for three years, then you were *açia*.
But with less than three days absence,
Even if you claim that you are *açia*, you are not,
But sleep together again, and *açia* you will be].

The *açia* relationship does not exist in the absence of the sexual act or in the past evocation of this connection. There is no concept of *açia* that applies to the future. The *açia* relationship is not conceptualized as a static and continuous state in time. It only exists instantaneously and retrospectively.

The following account by Lima (a thirty-three-year-old man) from Zhongshi is a good example of these customs:

I began my first *açia* relationship when I was fifteen. At that time, I was a serf in the *zhifu*'s residence on the island in Lake Lugu. Among the serfs, there were four women. Because I was very young, they often teased me. One day, Tsizo [one of the female serfs] said to me: "Lima, would you like to have an *açia* to have a good time? Dgjaa thinks about you a lot!" I answered: "She is more than ten years older than I am. Besides, I don't know what to do to be her *açia*." Tsizo told me: "All you have to do is join her at night."

In this way, I rashly became her *açia* for a little more than a year. Then she left me, because I was very poor and couldn't bring her any presents. A little while later, I secretly joined up with Tsïe, another female serf. She was intelligent and pretty. Her house was on the lakeshore, facing the island. We often met each other at her house. After noticing our relationship, her mother was very nice to me and proposed that I move in with them. I thought it would make it easier to see her, since her house was so close to the *zhifu*'s residence, and besides, each time I went, I got something to eat, so I agreed. Our relationship lasted for about six years.

During that period, I frequently went back and forth between Loshu and Zhongshi. Each time I passed through a village, if the opportunity arose, I had a good time with other women. For this kind of encounter, I was not picky, I was only looking for someone to satisfy my desire of the moment: one month with Tsïe in Little Loshu; three months with Eche in Dashi; one night with Gezo, Eche's sister in Zhongke; and one night with Dgima in Yumi. I left Tsïe from Loshu when I returned to Zhongshi.

After 1956, I worked in the cooperative with Sola. She is eight years younger than I am. She enjoyed having a good time with me and wanted to be my *açia*. But I didn't like her very much because she was not pretty. But since she was young, I accepted for the fun of it. Now, after the liberation [1956, the year of the Na region's succession to communism], as a cadre, I can no longer see a large number of *açia* at the same time, and I live from day to day with her. Our feelings about each other are lukewarm.

Most of the Na begin their love life with a rapid accumulation of *açia*, especially those between the ages of fifteen and thirty. As we have seen, it is as easy to end an *açia* relationship as to enter one.

When a woman no longer wants to receive a visitor, she can

either tell him not to come back or stop opening her door for him. To avoid a visitor who is in the habit of sneaking into her bedroom, she can sleep with her mother in the main room. In any case, the relationship is over when the woman wants it to be. If a man no longer wants to be with one of his *açia*, he simply stops going to see her; there is no need for explanations. Breaking off an *açia* relationship is a matter of personal freedom; a person wishing to do so has no need to explain why.

Arguments between two *açia* usually do not get very far, since they only discuss their sex life. When together, they never bicker over the worries of day-to-day life. A trifle is therefore all it takes to end the relationship. Even if an *açia* relationship has ended because of a fight, the man and woman can renew their relationship if they so desire. The Na describe such a renewal as: "lai shï lai sï" (to be reborn after death).

Therefore, making or breaking an *açia* relationship follows a particularly rapid rhythm from the start. After people reach the age of thirty, the visits tend to be less frequent. The duration of a relationship and the frequency of visits are measures of the intimacy of two *açia*. The younger the *açia* are, the less they see of each other; the older they are, the more they see of each other. For a tiny segment of the population, the situation is the reverse. Until the age of thirty or thereabouts, they have *açia* relationships that last a long time (several years), and afterward, they have short-term relationships (very brief ones, or one to two years maximum).

Some marginal situations should also be mentioned. A person may have only short-term relationships for his entire life (in general, less than one year). Handicapped and ugly people have almost no sexual experience at all. Finally, there are no cases of an *açia* relationship lasting for an individual's entire sexual life.

When all is said and done, there is no rule for duration: the existence of the relationship depends on the feelings, the temperament, the energy, and the desire of each person involved. An *açia* relationship always progresses by fits and starts. Being involved in an *açia* relationship, and believing oneself to be the *açia* of another, does not exclude relationships with other people. This is clearly expressed in the following saying: "no çia dZio nia çia nié" (Your *çia* is also my *çia*).

Case Studies

I conducted a study of the sexual partners of each villager in my field of investigation, and established a list for each person who had been sexually active, including the deceased, inasmuch as my sources could remember them. Naturally, my sources were, on the whole, more precise in naming partners in their own age-group.[4] On the partners of people in a different generation, the villagers could offer little or no information.

I first attempted to put together individual records, mapped out by cross-checking the testimony from various sources (the concerned parties themselves, their friends, and other villagers) at different times and places. An interesting phenomenon emerged: the responses from different sources about a specific person varied very little on the whole. They all provided more or less the same list, as though the names were classified and clear in their minds. On the other hand, they were unable to reconstitute the chronological order of that person's partners and the duration of his or her relationships.

At one point, I asked an eighty-one-year-old woman to help me with my records. As soon as she understood what I was trying to do, she burst out laughing, saying: "If you want to record everyone, even the ones with whom a person has spent only one night, your piece of paper is too small. You need to get a bigger one. Even a few sheets of big paper would not be enough for that." Then she continued: "These notes require too many sheets of paper. For those who have been furtive *açia* for several nights, I don't know, you have to ask them. Everyone only knows their own. But one thing is certain: you will never manage to record them all." This reminded me that while conducting a study in 1963, my colleagues were told by a Na villager that they would need an abacus to count all of the partners someone had been with, whether for one night or for several nights.

The partners that I was able to enumerate were those with whom an individual had had a relatively long relationship (at least two years) and those with whom he or she had had one or more children. Fleeting relationships were either forgotten or ignored. My experience in the field confirmed this. For example, when I asked about men younger than thirty, people gave me the names of some of their partners, ones that the concerned parties themselves acknowledged without any trouble. However, later, when I became friends with these young men, they opened up and told me all of their romantic stories and adventures. In this way, the number of lovers I had originally tabulated frequently doubled, tripled, or even quadrupled. Some of these young men had had secret relationships with all of the women in their age-group not only in their own village but also in nearby villages. This phenomenon can be found in all of the villages.

Recording every individual's partners therefore became an almost impossible undertaking. Not only was it impossible for me to become friendly with the majority of the villagers, but also the people, especially the oldest ones, could no longer remember all of their lovers, even when they were willing to talk about them.

During my interviews about these lovers, my sources' attitudes were interesting: all of the young people, after telling me their secrets, asked me to be discreet about these revelations concerning themselves and others. Some even refused to speak to me about the subject. On the other hand, the older sources, those around sixty, had a completely different attitude. One day, I was questioning Dindgu (a sixty-one-year-old man), whom the other villagers considered the expert on customs. While we were discussing a woman, he suddenly stopped talking after having given me her visitors' names. Believing he had exhausted the list of her partners, I turned the page in preparation for my next interview, while asking him, "Is that all?" "Wait!" he replied, all of a sudden. "Why?" I asked. "There is still someone else, me, I spent several nights with her, too."

Another time, after having dictated a long list of one woman's partners, an old man hesitated and stopped. Armed with my previous experience, I guessed: "You visited her also?" He answered me with a nostalgic smile and some embarrassment: "Yes. You cannot imagine how beautiful she was! The men who went to her house are too many to count. Me, too, I spent several nights with her."

I can cite several examples here:

1. Dhashi (forty-three years old) was known in all of the surrounding villages for her great beauty. If I include only those whom her neighbors were able to recall, the number of her lovers was close to a hundred and included the *zhifu*, the *mkan po*, rich aristocrats, minor chiefs, peasants, serfs, Han and Tibetan merchants, and Bai.

2. Gezo (thirty-eight years old) was considered a perfect beauty, from head to toe. The villagers believed that she had had more than 150 partners and claimed that when Gezo was at home, visitors never stopped showing up. Besides the Na villagers, she had even been with some Yi slave masters and peasants. The members of the Yi ethnic group who live in the region are usually rejected by Na women because of their reputation for coarseness.

3. Known for their passionate natures, Dgama, a thirty-nine-year-old woman, and Tsïe, her thirty-seven-year-old sister, each had had 150 *açia* from all of the social strata and even other ethnic

groups. The general administrator and the *mkan po*, through their valets, had often called on these sisters.

4. Ondi, a forty-nine-year-old man from Imin who made a good living in the caravan trade and had the reputation of being generous, had had thirty-nine lovers. He described each of them to me, one by one.

5. Gelo had had forty-four partners. The villagers explained that this was because of his good looks and his job as a carpenter, which brought in a good deal of money and grain.

6. Gelo, a serf who was seventy-three years old in 1973, had been a Lamaist monk in his youth but had not been trained in the Tibetan temples. He was very talented and became a carpenter and a tailor without any training. He became sexually active at the age of fifteen. His first *açia* was Hlamu, who lived in his village. She was his age, and she was pretty. During their one-year relationship, Gelo gave her many gifts: a jacket, a scarf, a pair of shoes, and several dozen ancient *yuan* (1 *yuan* equals 2 *bankai*). Hlamu had other Na and Tibetan *açia*; and Gelo, during this same period, saw Buchi, another young woman from the village. Buchi also had several *açia,* and Gelo would only visit her once in a while, when he felt like it. Their relationship lasted about three years and ended when Buchi went insane. During this same three-year period, Gelo was an *açia* of Tsïe, Buchi's sister, who was already the open partner of someone else (that is, she was receiving conspicuous visits; see chapter 9); therefore, Gelo would only visit her when her *dhu zï* was not coming.[5]

His relationship with Tsïe continued sporadically until 1956. After Buchi, he was attracted to Hlatso, a beautiful young woman from the same village. He paid her two visits and gave her two jackets. He also spent two nights with Hlatso's sister and gave her two ancient *yuan*. He then had an *açia* relationship with Nadgo, also from the same village, for about a year. Each time Gelo left to build a house, Nadgo gave him a sack of roasted-wheat flour. Nadgo died during a year of famine. Gelo then became an *aҫia* of her sister, Dashi. Several men were already visiting Dashi, and one of them was her *dhu zï* who only visited her a few times.

Then Gelo had a relationship that lasted for about one year with Iazon, one that lasted for several days with Wagwan Dema, one for one year with Chema, one for two days with her sister Dema, and one for two days with Poshi Dema. All of these women lived in his village. While working as a guardian in the Lamaist temple in Zébo, he had *aҫia* relationships that lasted anywhere from several days to a year. During this period, he was about thirty years old. He then established an open relationship with Dindgu, whose Tibetan partner had gone back to Tibet. This relationship, which produced two of Dindgu's sons, lasted until her death. During their relationship, he would form new *aҫia* anytime he had the chance: he spent two nights with Tsïe from Kaitçi, at whose house he was working as a carpenter; he spent a week and a half with Dgema, who took the initiative while he was repairing the Lamaist room of Sonami. For more than a year, he was the *aҫia* of a serf owned by the aristocrat Chen *bashi*, whom he met while plowing the fields of her master. There were also two other serf women who took the initiative to be *aҫia* with him, one for several days and the other for just one night. Judgu, a girl from the same village, was his *aҫia* intermittently for about one year; and while he was working in the cornfields, he spent two nights with Duzhi from Zhebo.

One spring, while supervising the irrigation of his *lignée*'s fields, he spent a night with Gaozo. Tsiedgïma, a woman from the Bukaeche *lignée*, came to his house to see relatives (through an adoption), and he spent four nights with her. He spent two nights with Nadgo, an aristocrat from Baozi, and he had an open relationship with Achen that lasted for approximately seven years (during that period, he also had liaisons with two open *dhu mi*), from which one daughter resulted.

In addition to these *açia*, he had other spontaneous ones here and there.

7. Sola (male) was from the Hoerguan *lignée* in Baozi. Attached to his *lignée* for generation after generation, the title *hoerguan* became the name of his *lignée*. He was therefore rich and enjoyed a very high status. Because of his position, he got to pass through all of the homes, one by one. He claimed to have had more than 2 hundred *açia* in all of the villages of Yongning.

Idiocy, physical defects, and ugliness can be fatal to a sex life. For example:

1. Nadgo, a seventy-two-year-old woman from Zhongshi, was not good at anything and in her whole life had never had an *açia*.

2. Ayi, a woman born in 1909, was sold during childhood to Poso. No one was interested in her because she was a mute. One night, when she was out fetching water, she met a Naxi, whom she would never see again and with whom she had a child.

3. Sona, a thirty-nine-year-old man in the *lignée* with which I was staying, was kind and handsome. He often worked for other households to help them out. As a child, he had had a serious and prolonged ear infection that left him a deaf-mute. He had never had a sexual experience.

Plurality and diversity characterize an individual's *açia* relationships. A person can be proud of having had a great number of *açia*, and although he might be envied, he is not exalted, while those who have had only a few partners are not, however, belittled. On the other hand, a person who has only one *açia* relationship for a long time, without having any others, will be subjected to mockery by the villagers, who use the following proverb in such a case: "kru da krai bu rai" (a lazy dog will only go looking for food in human excrement). If a handsome and/or rich man has only had a few *açia*, he risks being considered incapable and clumsy. And the few individuals who earn a living from being paid by visitors are not trusted.

Finally, the farther away a visitor lives, the prouder a woman is, because his journey proves the strong attraction of her beauty. The same holds true for a man: the more success he has in far-off villages, the prouder he is, because being welcomed far away from home is a testimony to his desirability.

Jealousy and Fidelity

For a long time, I wondered whether this multiplicity of lovers and the short duration of most *açia* relationships created jealousy in the Na. To find out, I talked to villagers of all different ages. I asked one source:

> "When you arrive at a woman's house and she is already taken, how do you feel?"
>
> "That kind of thing has happened to me many times. When it does, I go looking for someone else."
>
> "Are you jealous?"[6]
>
> "No, not jealous. These are our customs. Even if you are jealous, it's of no use. There is no shortage of women. There is always one next door. It's enough to walk a few steps farther. Besides, a woman doesn't owe you anything. There is no reason to be jealous."

He told me about one of his experiences:

> One night, with one of my wilder friends, I went to Batsïgu, a town of shoemakers. After dinner, we headed in the direction of Walabiéi. At the first house, the sister of the woman I had chosen answered the door and nicely warned me: "There is already some-

one here, come back tomorrow night or the day after tomorrow." I went to see another woman, and there, too, I was too late. The same thing happened to my friend. We left that village, since, in each village, there were only one or two women that we liked. Then we went to another village, and then to a third and a fourth, and continued like this until we reached Walabiéi. That night, we were really unlucky. Having gone through ten or so villages, we got the same response everywhere. Disappointed, tired, and frustrated, we threw some pebbles onto the roofs of several houses while we were leaving the last village. It was almost morning, and we went to the hot springs to take a bath. Then we headed home and went to sleep.

One night after a movie, my young friend Luzo (a nineteen-year-old boy) and one of his male friends came to see me. The discussion turned to the topic of the visit. His friend told me:

"You know, Luzo has not had a lot of *açia*, but he has made many visits. This is because he only goes to the homes of beauties. In particular, he goes to visit Seno, a pretty girl in our village. Do you want to go '*nana sésé*' at her house?" he asked me.

"No! If I go there, Luzo will be jealous," I answered.

"How could I be jealous!" he responded. "You can ask whomever you want. You will see that in this kind of situation, we don't know how to be jealous."

"He's right!" his friend interjected. And to explain himself he added: "Girls belong to everyone. Whoever wants to can visit them. There is nothing to be jealous about."

Another example: Sola has had an *açia* relationship for three years with Dema, a woman from the village of Batçi. One day, Dashi, another boy, spoke to Sola in a joking manner: "Your *açia* Dema, she's pretty cute. How about letting me have a good time with her!"

"Go ahead, if you want to. In any case, she doesn't belong to my *Zidu*." A short while later, Dashi spent two nights with Dema, and Sola knew about it but was indifferent.

About this, the saying, already quoted above, accurately reflects reality: "no çia dZio nia çia nié. nia çia dZio no çia nié" (Your *çia* is also my *çia*, and my *çia* is also your *çia*). In fact, I went many times to see just how a young man would speak to a young woman so that she would let him in. Often, while two or more men are arguing with a woman, trying to convince her to open the door, other men will arrive on the scene, with the same goal in mind. In the end, the one who succeeds in persuading the woman is let in. This activity is a passionate one for the suitors but a tiring one for the observer, because it always takes place late at night.

Within the parameters of my investigation, and in all of the generations that I examined, I encountered one single case in which the two partners loved each other so much that they made a solemn vow of eternal fidelity. After exchanging a lock of hair, they swore: "If you go looking for someone else, I will tell you to die, and you will go to your death." Because of their vows, the other villagers, while plowing the fields or bringing the livestock out to pasture, would make fun of them: "The one who made the pussy vow had better keep away from us. He better not come near us." The women would talk about the man in this way, and the men about the woman. Before their vows, these two partners had had several *açia*, and, of course, their promise to be faithful was not kept. This man is even worthy of being called a champion of the *nana sésé* among his contemporaries.

According to the Na, a vow of fidelity is shameful because it is considered a negotiation, an exchange, which goes against their customs. We can find in this attitude a key concept: no sexual relationship can lead the lovers to promise each other a monopoly on their sexuality nor bring them to give, trade, or sell themselves. Sexuality is not a piece of merchandise but a purely sentimental and amorous matter that implies no mutual constraints.

From a different perspective, this attitude demonstrates that fidelity, as a personal wish and at a given moment, is something that can be promised. But in Na society, this kind of promise is marginal, whereas in other societies, the lack of a vow of eternal fidelity is a transgression of the norm. For a long time, divorce was thought of in other societies as a kind of disaster. As a result, those who did not keep their promise to be faithful risked being scorned and distrusted. With the Na, an *açia* relationship that is sealed by an oath is neither protected nor enforced by society when one of the two partners no longer wants to keep it. It is a purely personal bond. On the other hand, in other societies, the sexual privilege, if not the sexual monopoly, between a husband and a wife is protected and even, if necessary, enforced.

The song quoted above perfectly reflects reality. In the villages, everyone knows about the activities of everyone else. The moment an *açia* stops visiting her or goes away, woman will be visited by other men. In any case, she can easily see different visitors if she pleases. The same is true for a man: once his *açia* is not available or simply when he feels like it, he can see other women. How can one conceive of fidelity when even an *açia* relationship that two partners keep going night after night over a long period does not create an attachment between them? For two former *açia* to become *açia* again, all they have to do is sleep together.

Intra- and Inter-Village Relations

I have already mentioned that the Yongning villages are spread out on the foot of the mountains and that they are connected to each other by a path. The distance between two neighboring villages is 1 kilometer more or less, sometimes only several hundred meters and rarely more than 2 kilometers. It takes only about fifteen minutes on foot to go from one village to the next, a half hour at the most. A man will usually do his visiting in his own village or in the villages next to his. Generally, the farther away the village, the fewer *açia* the men have there. This relatively restricted range for *açia* relationships is quite naturally explained by the fact that the visits take place at night and the men must return home the next morning for work. In other words, not only do they need to have a satisfying sex life, but also they need to be productive to earn a living. Take the following example:

Dashi (a man who was fifty in 1963) from Gala was in charge of business affairs for his *lignée*, which before 1956 owned 10 *dZia* of land. The household was relatively well-off. He began his *açia* life when he was sixteen. His first *açia* was Shada from Gasa. They met each other when she stayed in his village for a few days. Their relationship lasted about one year. Eventually, he found that Shada's village was too faraway for him to continue seeing her.

Since Shada loved him very much, she returned to ask him to continue their relationship after he stopped visiting her, and expressed her desire to cohabit with him. Dashi, however, felt that his *lignée* did not need another member, and because he had sisters, bringing a woman into the household would create discord and only cause problems for him. He therefore refused to see her again and had *açia* relationships with all sorts of women here and there. According to him, in addition to all of the women in his village and in the neighboring villages who were about his age, he also had *açia* living in villages farther away: Lower Kaitçi, Upper Kaitçi, Naha, and so on. When he was twenty-three, he set up an open relationship with a Pumi woman who lived in his village and continued to see other women as usual when the opportunity arose. According to the villagers, he had had twelve *açia*. In 1961, he became *açia* with Nadgo, a woman who had the same genitor as he did.

To give a better account of the distribution of villagers' *açia,* I will examine the grouping of consanguineal *lignées* from the lineage of Ibu-Imin in Imin as an example. This village is made up of twenty households, fifteen which belong to the Ibu-Imin lineage, and five of which immigrated fourteen generations ago, according to the village elders.[7] The consanguineal grouping of Ibu-Imin is made up of the following *lignées:* two Imin, two Ibu, and four Batsimi. The eight other *lignées* in this same lineage no longer have the same consanguineal identity.

I will look first at the number of potential partners per individual in the village. Because the age range from which one can choose a lover is quite large in comparison with that of other societies, I have classified individuals into groups of fifty-year-olds, forty-year-olds, thirty-year-olds, and twenty-years-olds. I then took a given individual and came up with a list of all of the non-consanguineal villagers that ranged in age from ten years older to ten years younger than he or she. The statistics obtained for the grouping of Ibu-Imin consanguineal *lignées* are as follows:

For the women:
- for a fifty-year-old, there are seven potential *açia;*
- for a forty-year-old, there are six potential *açia;*
- for a thirty-year-old, there are ten potential *açia;*
- for a twenty-year-old, there are twelve potential *açia* (this includes males who range in age from seventeen to thirty).

For the men:
- for a fifty-year-old, there are five potential *açia;*
- for a forty-year-old, there are nine potential *açia;*
- for a thirty-year-old, there are twelve potential *açia;*
- for a twenty-year-old, there are ten potential *açia* (this includes females that range in age from fifteen to thirty).

A young woman more readily accepts relations with an older man than a young man accepts relations with an older woman. The method I adopted is not perfectly precise. If other factors that influence the choice of *açia* are taken into account, the number of potential *açia* would be even smaller. I cite the statistics above to give a scale of values close to reality. Contrary to what one might expect, the choice of possible partners is limited within a village because of the large number of consanguineal *lignées*. Therefore, one consanguineal group's network of *açia* depends on two factors: the number of non-consanguineal villagers in its village and the distance between its village and other villages.

The Behavior of the Different Age-Groups

I will now examine where the *açia* of this grouping are located. I took a sampling of villagers who had been or were sexually active and who ranged in age from seventy (including the deceased) to the youngest ones. I arrived at the following figures:

- for the thirteen women from this grouping of consanguineal *lignées,* twenty-five (or 37.87 percent) of their *açia* lived in their village, thirty-one (or 46.96 percent) and came from nearby villages, and ten (or 15.15 percent) came from far-off villages.
- for the twelve men, the figures of their *açia* were nineteen (24.35 percent), thirty-five (44.87 percent), and twenty-four (30.76 percent), respectively.

There are approximately five *açia* per woman and six and a half per man.

It is not unusual in a village, or in a village and its neighboring villages, for a man to have had *açia* relationships with all of the women in his age-group. For the bolder ones, the range of acceptable ages is between ten years younger and five or so years older.

As a general rule, boys begin their *açia* life at about seventeen, and girls at about fifteen. In spite of the puberty ritual at the age of thirteen, I did not find one case of a boy who became an *açia* when he was only thirteen, and girls rarely become sexually active immediately after undergoing the ritual. In fact, a mother will try to prevent a girl as young as thirteen from becoming an *açia*. For example, for several nights in a row, some boys take turns and secretly go to the house of a very young girl. Having spied these furtive visitors in the dark courtyard, the mother speaks to the boys: "Come back later. She is still too young. She is only thirteen years old." "That's okay! By fooling around with us now, she'll grow even faster and better!" respond the boys.

With the Na, sexual activity is accepted between thirteen and fifty years old for a woman and between thirteen and sixty-one years old for a man. To continue one's sex life after these age limitations is frowned on but not forbidden. For example, one day, a dozen villagers came to the house where I was staying to help transport some large sacks of Chinese medicine. Among them was a man, older than sixty-one, who was a former *açia* of the chief of the household. He wanted to take advantage of the occasion to spend an amorous night with her. After dinner, the conversation went on and on. Realizing the old man's intentions, the woman's eldest son began to shout insults at the domestic animals: "Shame on you! A corpse wants to stand up again!" Seeing how opposed to the idea her son was, the disappointed old man was obliged to go back to his own house. The most striking thing about this story is that the old man was the genitor of this boy, and was not ignorant of the fact.

Between individuals of different age-groups, there is some difference in behavior when it comes to the *açia* relationship. At about the age of forty, the villagers usually enter a relatively more stable phase of their sex lives, a change characterized by the following facts: the liaison with each *açia* lasts longer, on average more than a year, and the number of *açia* maintained at the same time diminishes and settles to about three until the sex life is over.[8] The visits themselves become less complicated: the men no longer have to go through the trouble of climbing over walls to get to the women. Most of the time, a simple knock on the door gets one into the home of an *açia*. They also arrive earlier in the evening, at about ten o'clock, and leave a little later the following morning, at about seven. The area in which their *açia* live becomes smaller, usually limited to their own village and to those right next to it. The women, in particular those who are *lignée* chiefs, receive their lovers without embarrassment, all the while avoiding, of course, the males in their *lignées*. While the visits become less secret for middle-aged people, they nonetheless remain subjected to the prescribed standards.

When a woman no longer needs sexual activity, she simply turns away all visitors. For example:

> Getso, a sixty-three-year-old woman from the Ishi *lignée* in Ago, was the *açia* of Dashi of the Imin *gnao lignée*. Their relationship lasted about thirty years. When she reached the age of forty-six, she ended the relationship. Five years later, Dashi died. Getso was informed of his death and of the date of his funeral, however, neither she nor her son Haleba attended. When she was asked, "During your old age, with no contact, don't you sometimes think about him?" She responded, "No, I don't think about him, and he doesn't think about me, either. The Na are not like you. We don't need an old companion."

When older men no longer feel the need to see their *açia*, they stop visiting them. Their sex lives end in a natural way.

From society's point of view, when it comes to sexuality, the tradition is to "let it be," and from the individual's point of view, the *açia* relationship can only occur when the two interested parties are in agreement. An age difference is not a factor in an *açia* relationship. There are cases of a young man seeing an older woman. For example, Gezo's fourth *açia* was twenty years older than he, while his tenth was eighteen years younger. Here is another interesting example:

> Dgama had had seven *açia* in her life. When she formed an *açia* relationship with Tsïe, she was only seventeen years old, while he was fifty. Tsïe's *lignée* was relatively well-off, and he was very energetic. He often gave her grain, money, and other gifts. One day she said to him: "You are very nice to me; almost all of my food and clothing come from you. From now on, I will not receive other men." The year Tsïe turned sixty-one, Dgama was twenty-eight and gave birth for the first time. Not without irony, the villagers nicknamed her son Sixty-one.

Two individuals from different generations and different social strata can have an *açia* relationship. Several examples that I have already mentioned illustrate this.

We have seen that moral standards do not allow women to visit men. In spite of this taboo, there are several exceptions. For example, Sona, a woman from Zhoke, took the initiative to go to Tsïe's house in Baodzi, the neighboring village. Likewise, Chema, another woman from Zhoke, visited Dindgu from Tozhi. She offered him gifts and from time to time would invite him to feasts at her house. These two women were, of course, disparaged by the villagers.

Another example deserves mention:

> In Ago, a seventeen-year-old girl wanted a boy who lived in her village. Because she was not yet sexually active, she was afraid that the members of her *lignée* would discover her. During a secret meeting

outside the village, the boy, who was sixteen, talked her into coming to his house. The next morning, she did not even have the patience to wait for the rooster's crow before going home. After this experience, she was filled with regret. When the boy asked her to do the same thing again, he received a firm refusal. After telling me this secret, the boy asked me several times not to repeat this story to anyone. In fact, he was trying to keep the girl's reputation intact: a woman who takes the initiative to go to an *açia*'s home is considered a "sow in heat charging through the fog."

Disputes between Villages

In certain villages, through insults and violence, young men chase off a visitor who has come from far away and whose only tie to the village is the woman he wants. This phenomenon occurred with some frequency before 1960, mostly in DZyabu, Ga-sa, Hliwalo, Lalo, Aimilo, and Gala.

However, if the visitor made a friendly gesture in advance, a sign of respect to the men who lived in the woman's village, he would be spared any trouble during his visit. After an argument or a fight, inviting the men for a drink was taken as a gesture of apology and a sign of respect and could reconcile everyone involved. The visitor could then recover his clothing, which would have been taken by force during the fight, and come back the next time without incident. The following examples illustrate this kind of situation:

1. Dashi and Ishi were two young men, one from Jabu, the other from Ga-sa. One day, they went to Ragi to see the women. That night, seven boys from Ragi spotted them and began to chase them. Dashi, who was young, succeeded in escaping, but Ishi was caught and severely beaten. After this beating, Ishi filed a formal complaint with the chief of the village grouping (under the *zhifu*'s regime). The chief punished the boys from Ragi by

making them pay for Ishi's medical expenses and fining them 6 *bankai*.

2. Getu and his uncle, both from Ragi, went to Gasa with the intention of visiting some women. A short while later, they were chased away by a group of local young men. After that, the uncle never returned, but Getu, because he invited the young men for a drink, was able to continue visiting his *açia*.

3. An unannounced visit by Gelo to Dzjatso in Dashi provoked the anger of the village's young men. One night, when Gelo was chatting with Dzjatso, ten men entered without knocking and chased him away, warning: "Next time, if you come back, we won't be so nice!"

4. Guma, a young man from the *sïpi* stratum, went to see a woman in Zhoshi without any advance warning to the men of the village. The men surrounded the house in the middle of the night while Guma was with the woman. They tied the feet of one of them to the head of the other and beat them. Guma realized that he had neglected the necessary protocol as far as the local men were concerned. The next day he brought 15 *yuan* and invited them for a drink. After this reconciliation, Guma was free to come and go as he pleased.

Interethnic Relations

Conflict can also arise between individuals of different ethnic groups. Before the 1960s, Tibetan merchants would pass through Yongning with their caravans. Taking advantage of Na customs, they arranged for Na women from various villages to be brought to Batsïgu to sleep with them. This irritated the Na, who, on many occasions, would attack small groups of Tibetan merchants. Following these events, the merchants moderated their behavior. Using money, they bribed the Na chiefs and the men from Batsïgu and bought their cooperation. My sources claimed that as a result of these dealings prostitution developed in their community.

Because the Na are the majority in the Yongning region, their customs have exercised and continue to exercise a strong influence on the other ethnic groups there. The most typical example of this can be found among the Pumi. The village of Loshu, on the hillside that borders Lake Lugu, is cut in half by a path, with one part of the village below it and one above. The lower part of the village is inhabited by the Na, and the upper part is inhabited by the Pumi, with a few Han households as well. The Pumi in this village have adopted the mode of the visit (no one knows when this began) and have abandoned their matrimonial tradition. They still speak their own language, but they also speak Na, just like the Na. With the exception of several notable differences in the way they dress, they have been deeply "Na-ified." Outsiders can barely tell them apart.

Sometimes, Han men from the upper village visit Na women, but Na men never visit Han women. One twenty-six-year-old Han man, with much experience in Na visiting, told me: "I have already decided that I will not get married." "Why?" I asked. "Because if I got married, I would have to take care of everything: plowing the fields, gathering firewood, the children, and so on. And most of all," he emphasized, "after marriage, you are no longer free. Whether you love your wife or not, you have to stay with her. You can no longer see other women, even if you really want to."

In the Yongning basin, Na women will not accept men from other ethnic groups, with the exception of the Pumi, the Han and the Tibetans. The Na told me that the Yi living in the region are especially avoided because they have the habit of using obscene expressions, and the obscene words they use are almost always sexual in nature. This, of course, directly goes against their taboo on sexual evocation, something that has to be watched at every moment. It is therefore difficult for the Na to come into contact with these people.

The Question of Prostitution

Does prostitution exist in Na society?

During the 1930s and 1940s, especially during the war against Japan, many caravans, Tibetan and others, passed through Yongning. Some women who in times of peace received Na *açia* in their homes went to Batsïgu to meet up with the traveling merchants and offer themselves in exchange for money or gifts. I questioned an eighty-one-year-old woman about this who had been an intermediary, arranging contacts of this nature, and had participated in the activity herself. Well aware of Chinese moral standards, she knew this was considered prostitution. During our interview, she appeared to be embarrassed. On the other hand, a fifty-six-year-old woman who also participated in these practices told me, "Each time the Tibetan merchants came back to Yongning, we were happy, and we would meet them with chickens and with hay for their horses. They also brought food. They gave us clothing and shoes. When they left, they gave us some money." "Why were you happy?" I asked. "They were nice to us, and we liked them," she responded. This woman's description of the situation reveals that what we call prostitution she identified as an *açia* relationship.

Before 1956, in the Yongning region, there were several women who earned all of their income by receiving visitors: merchants passing through, as well as local Na men. This practice was clearly understood to be prostitution (in Na *dobu tçi*: to sell your ass) and was disparaged by society.

One final note about interethnic relations: women from other ethnic groups almost never accept visits from Na men. The following anecdote illustrates this contrast. One day while I was talking with Gezo, a twenty-six-year-old man from Imin, the conversation turned to the topic of Han women from Yongshen, a neighboring district, who had dealings with the Na as seamstresses and clothing vendors. Gezo told me, "The girls from Yongshen are charming and nice, but they won't let themselves be hugged." "How do you know?" I asked. He explained: "One day I went to the movies in Batsïgu. I was sitting next to some girls from Yongshen, and we were chatting nicely. But when I wanted to take one of them in my arms, she pushed me away hard and wouldn't let me do it. What's more, she screamed and insulted me. It was embarrassing and strange. With a Na girl, if she agrees to talk to you, you can take her in your arms."

On the same subject, and under the same circumstances, I had been shocked by his culture. Now it was his turn to be shocked by mine. A true clashing of different moral standards.

Men as Genitors and Children as "Bastards"

We have seen that in an *açia* relationship, no one belongs to anyone. Fidelity as a social restriction does not exist, and virginity has no importance. From our perspective, almost all of the mothers are teenage mothers, but for them, this is completely normal.

When their sex lives begin, young women are just trying to enjoy themselves. Only later, after a few years, do they begin to feel the desire to have a baby — if they have not already gotten pregnant, that is. Men are also trying to have a good time; however, they believe that their personal pleasure with their *açia* is at the same time an act of charity to their partner's household. They have an expression — "dZiobu dZia i" — which literally means having a good time is also an act of charity. To explain themselves, they add: "a woman, no matter how strong she is, would never be able to have a baby without knowing a man." This is a very important idea. I have already quoted the Na proverb "If the rain does not fall from the sky, the grass will not grow on the ground." In this proverb, it seems that men are collectively symbolized by the sky, and they all rain the same water. For the Na, the fetus already exists in the woman's womb. To make a baby, it is enough that a woman be watered, and it makes no difference who does the watering. The entire kinship system, even its terminology, leaves no role for a genitor, and men are not interested in having children. What counts for them is that their sister have children.

In keeping with the plurality of *açia* and the intermittence of such relationships, we can observe the following: the Na might guess who has inseminated the mother if the child bears a physical resemblance to one of her *açia*. If the child has no physical trait in common with any of his mother's *açia*, it is impossible to say who the genitor (*ada* in Na) is. They consider the genitor the one who was seeing the mother at the time she became pregnant, if, during that period, she had only one visitor. However, no one is concerned about this. It is not in the least important to know who is the genitor of whom. In fact, there are children for whom the genitor is unknown. During my interviews, when I was recording the individual lists of *açia*, all of my sources confirmed that they did not know who the genitors of certain people were. For others, each source named a different genitor. When this happened, I would finally realize that I was dealing with a case in which the child's genitor was not identifiable.

One day, while I was discussing this subject with several men, they began to make fun of me when I asked if they knew who their genitor's genitor was:

"Are you crazy or what?! Do you know?"
"Yes, of course I know."
"You must be kidding!"
"No, it's true. I do know."

They were puzzled by my response. After a moment, a young man who had been to high school abruptly said: "Oh yes! It's true, for the Han, they do know."

About this subject, a sixty-seven-year-old woman told me that sometimes an older person might know who the genitor was of the genitor of a child in the village. But no one knew who the genitor of their own genitor was. She told me: "No one asks that kind of question. If you hadn't mentioned it, no one would ever have even thought about it."

Usually, a woman does not tell her children who their genitor is, and a man does not tell a child that he is his or her genitor. A child never says who his or her genitor is, even if he or she knows. All of this is because of the taboo on sexual evocation. In general, when people (men and women, or women alone) under thirty find themselves together, they do not bring up this subject. But when there are only men or only older people (men and women) present, they can discuss it, for under these conditions, they find the topic less embarrassing.

At the beginning of my stay with the Na, I asked if there was a word for "bastard," given that the women had more than one *açia*. I asked two men, both over forty, this question. One of them responded: "cha mu cha zo." "Is this word used to insult people?" I asked. "For everyone, it's the same. How could that be an insult?!" he replied. This seemed to me a contradiction: how could the concept of bastard exist in a society in which there were nothing but bastards? Because this conversation was conducted in Chinese, and its logic was more in keeping with my culture than with theirs, I was unable at the time to figure out the true meaning of this expression. Finally, a shaman explained it to me: only those children whose genitor is completely unknown are called *cha mu cha zo*. The word *cha* means an invisible and harmful breath of air; *mu* means daughter; and *zo* means son. But in spite of the existence of this term, children whose genitor is generally recognized are not glorified, and those whose genitor is unknown are not covered in shame. Whether or not the genitor is known has no effect on the kinship system or on a child's status. They are all treated the same within their *lignée* as well as within society.

According to the genealogies and the lists of *açia* I collected, over a period of five generations 206 women had given birth to 612 children. The genitors of eighty-six, or 14.05 percent, of these children were unknown. Among these eighty-six people, twenty-eight were firstborns.

The multiplication of *açia* has another consequence: the possibility for children of the same mother to have different genitors. For example, a mother in the Daba *lignée* from Imin had the reputation of being a well-behaved woman. One source elaborated by telling me that this was because no matter who the furtive visitor was, she always accepted him. She had had four children with four of her *açia*, three of whom lived in her village, and one of whom lived in Ago, right next to Imin. One day, during an interview with the person in charge of women's affairs in the local government, I mentioned this phenomenon, and she told me: "That's not surprising. There are even cases in which ten children of the same mother are from ten different genitors." This phenomenon can be found in all of the villages. What is interesting about the Daba *lignée* woman's story is that the features of her furtive visitors had been so perfectly reproduced in her offspring that each child was the spitting image of his genitor. When I first arrived in the village, one source told me: "If you want to know who the genitor is, in some cases, you don't even need to ask. When you become familiar with the whole village, you will automatically know."

The situation of the above-mentioned *lignée* also shows the absence of rights and responsibilities between *açia*. In this *lignée*, the mother was forty-eight in 1989 (the year of my third stay in the field), and the four children, all boys, were twenty-eight, twenty-one, thirteen, and nine. They were poor and did not manage their lives very well. Every year when March approached, they ran out of food. During the winter, several village households constructed new buildings, including this one. As usual, all of the village households helped one another to erect the buildings' frames and the walls of hard-packed mud. Until this stage of construction, there was no need to pay for anything, since the wood was felled by each *lignée*.

Now, with the wood rationing stipulated by the local government, they did not have enough to finish the roof. Moreover, for the last few years the Na had been covering their roofs with tarps. As a result, it was necessary to spend approximately 1,500 *yuan*. The average annual income per person in the canton was 234 *yuan* in 1989, and the income of this particular household was even less. Therefore, it did not have enough money for the roof. Among the four genitors, two were from relatively well-off *lignées*. Like the other villagers, they criticized the bad management of this household, especially since the rainy season was approaching. However, not one *lignée* wanted to lend it money, because they were all sure that the household would be unable to pay them back. In June, its building was soaked with water, to the general indifference of everyone.

The *açia*, the genitors, and the children often live in the same village or in villages right next to each other. They are on a first-name basis and treat each other like any other villager. In short, they behave like non-relatives toward each other. Everyone thinks only of his or her own *matrilignée*. Between *açia*, attachment is unknown, and between a genitor and his child, there is no special contact, no bond. Sexual ties create no rights and no responsibilities between *açia* nor between the child and the genitor.

It is insignificant that a mother's children are not the offspring of a single genitor. They are always treated equally by the *lignée* and by society. On the other hand, while the children of different mothers are treated equally as long as they live under the same roof, they are differentiated once a separation in a *lignée* occurs. Under these circumstances, the children of the woman who is moving out follow their mother. The direct bond between a mother and her children does play a role.

We can therefore see that in this society "normal" children correspond to those who would be considered illegitimate in other societies. In order to determine illegitimacy, we need to go a degree further. Instead of designating anyone who does not have a social father, the term *illegitimate children* refers to those for whom the genitor is completely unknown. This said, we must not forget that all children enjoy the same status and suffer no discrimination.

The Norms that Regulate the Açia Relationship

From the description above, we can conclude that the Na must observe the following norms in *açia* relationships:

1. Every person has complete freedom to choose his or her partner.

2. Men and women are equals when it comes to taking the initiative in expressing their desire for someone.

3. The amorous encounter can be arranged in advance or take place spontaneously, on the condition that both parties consent.

4. Every person can carry on *açia* relationships with several partners in a given period.

5. Men and women are independent in their sex lives. The constitution, dissolution, and reestablishment of an *açia* relationship depend solely on an individual's desire.

6. In general, sexual activity takes place through the nocturnal furtive visit of the man to the woman in her bedroom.

7. The visitor and the consanguineal relatives of the female *açia*, especially the men, must not see each other during the visit.

8. It is forbidden for women to visit men in their homes.

9. During their relationship, the two partners call each other *açia*.

10. Two individuals are *açia* only as long as they are seeing each other continuously; they are not *açia* during the interval. After an *açia* relationship ends, the partners can become *açia* again if they so desire.

11. The two *açia* are considered outsiders, that is, not related, to each other.

12. Children under thirteen years of age are not allowed to be sexually active. Women over fifty and men over sixty-one who continue to be sexually active are frowned on.

13. It is forbidden for individuals to argue or fight over wanting to be the *açia* of the same person.

As this summary suggests, the furtive visit, as a modality of sexual life, is basically characterized by the following facts: the free will of each person is both necessary and sufficient to establish and maintain the *açia* relationship; the desire of one partner is enough to end it; a multiplicity of partners; and the discontinuity of the *açia* relationship. It includes four restrictions: a woman must not visit a man; a visitor must avoid the male consanguineal relatives of the woman he is visiting; daytime visits are forbidden; and individuals who want the same person must not argue or fight. As a result, a man's sexual life takes place away from his daily life. *Açia* are lovers who remain strangers to each other. The *açia* relationship is independent of all other social relationships. This leads me to define it as a purely emotional, amorous, and sexual relationship. It is a private matter.

The Sixteen Elementary Combinations of the Açia *Relationship*

According to the list of *açia* that I made, sixteen elementary types of combinations can be defined. This corresponds exactly to the number of elementary logical possibilities. The rest of the combinations found in the practice can be presented by confining some of the sixteen combinations. I will first examine the ten possible combinations between two groups that are not consanguineal relatives (see figures 8.1 through 8.10).

Figure 8.1. One woman and one man.

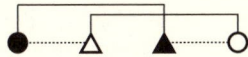

Figure 8.2. One woman and her brother with one man and his sister, respectively.

Figure 8.3. One woman with two brothers.

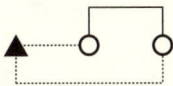

Figure 8.4. One man with two sisters (antisymmetry of figure 8.3).

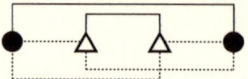

Figure 8.5. Two sisters with two brothers (there are four *açia* relationships in this combination).

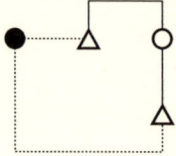

Figure 8.6. One woman with one man and his nephew.

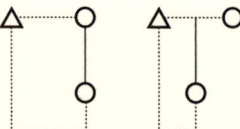

Figure 8.7. One man with one woman and her daughter (this man could be the genitor of the daughter).

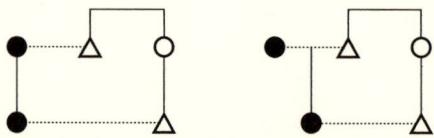

Figure 8.8. One woman and her daughter with one man and his nephew, respectively.

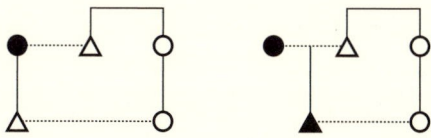

Figure 8.9. One woman and her son with one man and his niece, respectively.

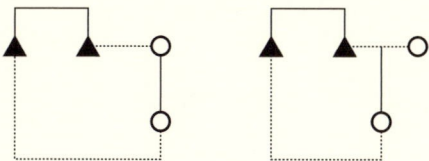

Figure 8.10. Two brothers with one woman and her daughter, respectively.

Now I will look at the five possible combinations formed by three different consanguineal groups (see figures 8.11 through 8.15).

Figure 8.11. One woman with two men.

Figure 8.12. One man with two women (antisymmetry of figure 8.11).

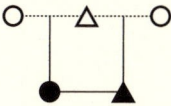

Figure 8.13. One woman and one man with the same genitor are *açia*.

235

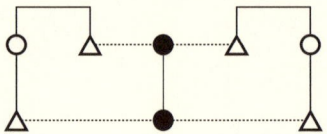

Figure 8.14. One woman with two men from two consanguineal *lignées;* in the next generation, her daughter with the two nephews of these two men.

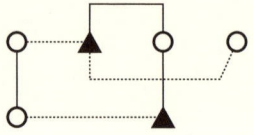

Figure 8.15. The antisymmetry of figure 8.14.

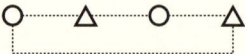

Figure 8.16. Four individuals (two women and two men) from four different consanguineal *lignées*, and each individual has an *açia* relationship with each of the members of the opposite sex.

The combination shown in figure 8.16 is a clear example of a basic characteristic of the *açia* relationship: the multiplicity of partners. I call this multiplicity polyandrogyny. During a given period, the *açia* relationships of each individual constitute a radius that is superimposed on the others. The set of radii makes up a particularly compact network of multi-partners.

CHAPTER NINE

The Conspicuous Visit

Definition

The second traditional modality of sex life, *gepié sésé,* is an institutionalized one: *gepié* literally means to vomit. It signifies getting everything out that is hidden in the stomach (or the heart) or getting everything out in the open. As an adverb, *gepié* figuratively means conspicuously or openly. This expression refers to a visit that a man makes to a woman openly, without having to hide from the members of her *lignée.* I translate *gepié sésé* as conspicuous visit, open visit, or to pay a visit openly.

Forming the Relationship

People who practice the conspicuous visit always begin with the furtive visit. After a certain number of nights spent together secretly, if the partners' feelings for each other have deepened, they exchange belts as a symbol of their desire that their feelings and love for each other will last.

Men and women who practice this sexual modality are called *gepié sésé hing* by society, which means people in a conspicuous-visit relationship. The partners call each other not simply *açia* but *dhu zï dhu mi* (*dhu* means friend or partner, *zï* connotes the masculine and *mi* the feminine). In this study, the expressions *conspicuous relationship* and *open relationship* are used synonymously to express the enactment and the content of the ties that unite *dhu zï dhu mi* together.

As a general rule, once the partners agree to modify their relationship, the woman will talk to her mother to set up a time when the man can be received at home. A man who knows the woman's *lignée* well feels no apprehension and goes to the house alone for this appointment. However, a man who is more timid or from a far-off village, and therefore does not know the members of the woman's *lignée* well, will be accompanied by a *moio* (mediator) so that he will not be too embarrassed during the meeting. About 40 percent of the men in open relationships began in this manner.

The man almost always chooses to be accompanied by a male *moio* who knows the woman's *lignée* well and is therefore capable of carrying on a conversation with them. It is rare that a man will ask a woman to be his *moio*. This only happens when he is unable to find an adequate male mediator. The role can never be filled by a consanguineal relative of the woman's *lignée,* because of the ban on sexual evocation.

The mediator usually belongs to the same age-group as the man, or might be older. The man always chooses his *moio* himself. It would be shameful for a woman to take the initiative here, because if she did so, she would risk being taken for a "sow in heat charging through the fog." After being solicited, the *moio* must talk to the woman's mother to set up a time for the meeting. He is not paid for his services, either in money or in kind, because they are considered a favor.

The Meal Ritual

The meeting traditionally takes place in the main room, around eleven o'clock at night, when the male members of the woman's *lignée* have either left the house or gone to bed. The female chief of the woman's *lignée* always arranges to have all of the consanguineal men out of the way, with the exception of boys younger than thirteen. The other women of the household can be present at the meeting, but they are not required to be. The female chief only needs one helper to prepare and serve the meal.

The man arrives at the house in great secrecy, either alone or with his *moio*. He brings *gwalu pinba* (*gwa-lu* refers to the stone that supports the cooking pot, *pinba* means gifts).[1] These gifts might include tea, raw sugar, and alcohol in variable quantities, depending on the financial situation of the man, but in general he gives several pounds of each. On entering the main room, the man gives the gifts to the *lignée*'s female chief. She then proceeds with the ritual offerings to the ancestors, using the alcohol she has received. When this is finished, she serves a feast to the man (and, if one is present, to his mediator). Chicken is usually served, the only choice dish readily available to the Na. After the meal, if the *moio* lives in the village, he goes back to his house. If not, he will be put up in the woman's house for the night, or he can always, at his leisure, visit one of the women in the household if they have met and taken a liking to each other.

The Exchanging of Gifts

Before the 1960s, the man usually would give the woman, at the very least, a jacket, and she would give him a pair of pants. If the partners were well-off, these gifts might also include a skirt, a pair of shoes, and a scarf for the woman and a jacket, a hat, and a pair of shoes for the man.[2] Usually, the man and woman exchange gifts directly. But sometimes the man will give the female *lignée* chief the jacket he has brought for the woman when he gives her the *gwalu pinba*. In this case, the woman waits and gives him his presents the following morning, or the female chief might give him his gift from the woman after she receives his gifts to the woman.

Sometimes the mediator is in charge of giving the man's gift to the female chief and of receiving the woman's gift for the man.

There are no rigid rules governing this exchange. Sometimes, but not often, if the man does not want a meal ritual, he gives the *gwalu pinba* directly to his partner, who then hands it over to her mother. By not offering his gifts directly to the female chief, he can avoid the dinner.

In the past, the article of clothing given by the woman would have been made of linen. She would have made it, from the growing of the flax to the sewing of the cloth. The jacket that the man gave to her was usually purchased with money he had earned by selling medicinal plants gathered on the mountain.

The Process of the Conspicuous Visit

After this meeting with the female chief, the man tends to come a little earlier and a little less secretly than before for his nighttime visits. From time to time, he will chat with female members of the *lignée* after dinner at around nine o'clock. However, if the male members are present, he will remain silent in a corner for an hour or two, indeed for the entire evening, even if he is normally talkative. Since the main room is very dark, sometimes one can forget he is there. This can be explained by the Na's belief that a man in someone else's home has a very low status, lower even than that of the children. The open visitor does not necessarily come to his partner's house every night. Sometimes he might not feel like it, or he might be busy with something else.

In the morning, he returns home a little later, between seven and eight o'clock. If his village is not nearby, he might be invited to have tea in the morning in the main room or even to have a full breakfast.

The reception for this first meeting or ritual meal always unfolds in the strictest privacy. The other villagers only grasp the conspicuous nature of the relationship by noticing, often not until one or two months later, a greater flexibility in the comings and goings of the man. Sometimes the villagers are unable to determine whether the relationship is open or not. In fact, before the 1960s, very few people practiced the conspicuous visit, and certain furtive visitors, usually the middle-aged ones, would return home at around seven o'clock in the morning, in the manner of open partners. Because of this, my sources were frequently unable to tell whether someone was practicing the conspicuous visit or the furtive visit.

Before the meal ritual, the woman usually manages without any advice from her *lignée*. However, she will sometimes talk to her mother about her love life. The norm is to let each person do as she chooses: no one is allowed to impose anything on anyone else. Usually, the woman's *lignée* accepts the man chosen by her without question, unless he steals things from the household. As far as the man is concerned, as a visiting lover, he is under no obligation to tell the male members of his own *lignée*, and his ascendants often find out about it from the other villagers. In short, when it comes to choosing a partner, individuals enjoy total freedom, just as they do in the furtive relationship.

For her *dhu zï*, it is customary for the woman to make a jacket, a pair of pants, and a belt embroidered with flowers, birds, and fish once a year in the winter. If she has the economic means, she also gives him a pair of shoes, which would be purchased in Batsïgu from a Naxi because Na women do not know how to make shoes. In return, her partner might give her a jacket, a skirt, a scarf, a pair of shoes, some silk thread, a bamboo rain hat, and matches. The gifts exchanged are selected according to the means of the partners. It is rare for a man to be able to give all of the above-mentioned items at once. Older partners often exchange gifts that are not clothing. This annual exchange of gifts is considered an obligation. The person who is unable to give gifts risks being jilted.

Prior to the 1960s, women who received clothing from their open partners would wear it when they went to work in the fields for the fall harvest. Even if they did not actually put them on, they would bring the items to show to other women. The discussion would soon heat up over deciding who had received the prettiest clothes. Indifferent, the men would have nothing to do with these rural fashion shows and debates on style.

In addition to this annual rite of exchanging gifts, the partners sometimes give each other little presents, or one partner might give some tea or salt to the other's mother or uncle. And if needed, they will help each other out in various ways. Although such a phenomenon is extremely rare, if one partner's *lignée* is well-off, it might undertake a small part of the funeral expenses — the candies or rice cakes — when there is a death in the other partner's *lignée*. These sweets will be offered to the participants at the end of the second night of the funeral. But these generous gifts are in no way an obligation. Whether or not they are given depends on the financial situations and the personalities of the concerned parties.

The Sexual Privilege

In an open relationship, the two partners, because of their feelings for each other and by tacit agreement, give each other sexual privilege. This privilege comes close to being a duty, for not only must they respect it but others must also. However, this in no way means that *açia* relationships have to be abandoned. If a woman is engaged with an *açia* when her partner arrives, she tells the *açia* to leave.

Practicing furtive love with a person in an open relationship is called *min kru* in Na. The word *min* means sex, and *kru* means to steal. The expression means to steal sex. While this behavior is traditionally frowned on, it is not forbidden. Each partner in an open relationship can secretly pursue meetings with others when they so desire. Because the *dhu zï* and *dhu mi* do not live under the same roof and do not see each other every day, they have no way of keeping a constant check on each other.

When a man is caught stealing sex by the open partner of the woman he is with, he risks being beaten by him. Nevertheless, everybody knows that each time a man leaves the village for a few days, his partner will receive furtive visitors on the second or third night after his departure. All of my sources confirmed that women in open relationships receive furtive visitors without any hesitation. The villagers told me that "only one out of a thousand women would refuse." And they added: "Everyone knows about this. But you can't stop working because of a woman. When you have to go away, you go!"

When a furtive visitor approaches a woman in an open relationship, he avoids the members of her *lignée* and, above all, her partner. If her partner discovers him, the woman is, in principle, supposed to ask the intruder to leave, unless she wants to use the occasion to end the relationship with her open partner. The same holds true for a man in an open relationship who is visiting other women. It is in his best interest that his partner not find out about it. For example:

> Dgima (female) and Tsidi (male) were *dhu zï* and *dhu mi*. Dgima continued to have *açia* relationships with other men. On three occasions, Tsidi found furtive visitors at her house. When he arrived, they hid or escaped through the back door. Tsidi also visited other women. One time he had secretly gone to see Hlatso in the middle of the night. Suddenly Gedi, Hlatso's partner, knocked on the door. To avoid a confrontation with him, Tsidi hurried out of the bedroom and spent the night in Hlatso's storehouse.

In order to punish a rival, it is absolutely necessary to catch him in the act. A ruse frequently used by men is to pretend to be going away for a long time, and then to come back in secret that very night, or the next night, to catch his partner's furtive suitor in the act.

Jealousy and Tolerance

A *min kru* can provoke conflicts between the *dhu zï dhu mi* as well as between the male partner and his rival. Here are several examples:

1. Dgimatsïe from the Raimi *lignée* in Raimi is a seventy-one-year-old woman who, in her youth, was in an open relationship with Ishï from the Ago *apo lignée* in Ago. He was three years older than she, and died at the age of thirty eight. During their relationship, Dgimatsïe saw *açia*. Once, when she was returning from Zuo-suo in the mountains, Ishï grabbed her and cut her nose with a knife. Dgimatsïe is still alive, and the scar on her nose bears witness to this fit of jealousy.

2. Gemu (female) and Haleba were *dhu zï dhu mi*. Haleba, however, became an *açia* of Dema, who gave him a belt. Gemu found out about this gift. When Haleba came back to her house, she said, trying to hide her anger with sarcasm, "You are very cute in that belt! And now I am going to cut it up." Then and there, she cut the belt into several pieces. And in a sharp tone, she said: "Go to Dema. And never set foot in this house again."

3. Eche (female) and Tsidi (male) were in an open relationship. Eche secretly saw Pitso, one of her *açia*. Tsidi was very unhappy about it, and waited for an opportunity to catch Pitso. When he did, he beat him and chased him away from Eche's house. As a result, Eche would not continue her open relationship with him. A short while later, they separated.

4. Because she was a *dhu mi* of Jïshi, who lived in Ago, Dgama

met Gelo in secret. One day Jïshi came upon Gelo at Dgama's house, but at the time he said nothing. Several days later, when Dgama was passing through Ago, Jïshi began insulting her, and, brandishing a pair of scissors, he cut off her braids and threw them on the path leading to the village. This scene marked the end of their relationship.

5. Lini (female) and Tsïe were in an open relationship. When Lini was told that Tsïe was involved with Gezo (a woman from her village), she and her three sisters undressed Tsïe in public.

Not everyone displays so much character. Sometimes, when a weak man discovers his open partner with one of her *açia*, he simply lets himself be told by her that his place has been taken. Tsïe from the Gocho *lignée*, the secretary of the Communist Party committee of the village grouping, was the lucky witness of just such a situation. He was in the middle of a furtive visit when the open partner of his *açia* walked in. She tried to convince her open partner to be understanding by telling him: "We have our entire lives to spend the night together, but Tsïe is only spending one or two nights here." Rejected, the *dhu zï* returned home without insisting, at least in part because Tsïe had political and economic power and at that time controlled the distribution of the annual grain rations. After telling me this story, my source added: "You might as well say that 'our entire lives' becomes a way to cheat on your partner. Only the heavens know what 'our entire lives' means!"

A pregnant woman continues to receive visitors, whether she practices open or furtive relationships. Two or three months before the birth, she moves into the main room to sleep near her mother and avoid visitors. During these last months of pregnancy, a woman in an open relationship will leave her *dhu zï* alone in her bedroom if he visits her. *Açia* rarely if ever visit pregnant women once the pregnancy is visible. They do not come back for a long time after the birth, because during this period the woman, who is busy with the baby and does not have time to take care of herself, is considered very unkempt.

After a woman in an open relationship gives birth, her open partner's *lignée* brings presents to her *lignée*, whether its members live in the same village or not. If the open relationship between two partners living in the same village has ended before the birth of the child, the *lignée* of her former partner still brings a gift, just like all the other villagers, for this custom expresses the reciprocity between inhabitants of a village.

If the woman who has given birth does not have an open partner, the mother or the sister of one of her *açia* from another village might bring presents; sometimes even the *lignées* of two lovers bring gifts to the house with the new baby. A lover whose mother or sister brings presents hopes to continue his relationship with the woman and eventually establish an open relationship. Whether or not he is the genitor of the baby is of no importance whatsoever.

Before the 1970s, it was rare to see the *lignée* of a furtive visitor from another village bring gifts to an *açia* after she gave birth. Now, because of the influence of Han culture, which is growing stronger and stronger, especially in the generation that is thirty years old, this phenomenon is becoming more frequent. Sometimes it results in an open relationship.

In general, then, the *dhu zï*'s *matrilignée* brings gifts, as long as the relationship between the *dhu zï dhu mi* still exists. Because of the extreme frequency with which they change partners and because they often have several partners at once, the *dhu zï* of the moment is not necessarily the genitor. When I asked how they know who the genitor of the child is, no one ever mentioned the act of bringing gifts as proof.

The Independence of the dhu zï dhu mi

As is the case for *açia*, the *dhu zï dhu mi* can never force themselves on each other. A woman in an open relationship cannot make her partner visit her, and a man cannot oppose the refusal of his partner. A decision made by one of them to end it is enough to break off the relationship. An attempt to monopolize one's partner is always considered shameful and stupid, and the villagers will mock it for a long time.

In this context of freedom and fragility, some *dhu zï dhu mi* show mutual tolerance. Here are several examples:

1. Eji, a woman from Batçi, and Naka, a young man from Zhongke, were in a *dhu zï dhu mi* relationship for six years. While Naka was gone on a caravan trip, Eji saw Natso, a young man from Dapo. When he returned, Naka found out about it. He was also seeing an *açia*, Gonbu. One day, Naka pretended to reproach Eji: "You are seeing other men behind my back."

"Are you saying that I'm seeing others! And what about you? You go to Gonbu's house in secret, and you think I don't know about it?"

"Good! I'm glad that you know. Since you do it, I don't see why I can't."

At the end of this mock argument, Naka concluded: "Let's continue to be *dhu zï dhu mi*. When you feel like seeing Natso, go and see him; and I will see Gonbu when I feel like it!"

This is how they continued their open relationship.

2. Tsïma (female) and Dindgu (male) had been in an open relationship for sixteen years. Each time Dindgu left with the caravans, visitors came to Tsïma's house, including one named Pitso. Now, Pitso was in an open relationship with Çiuba. Ironically, each time Pitso went on a trip, Dindgu took advantage of his absence to see Çiuba. The two women eventually quarreled over this situation. But it did not bother the two men, who believed:

"There is no reason to have a relationship with only one woman. It's enough that my partner be nice to me and not see other men in front of me."

3. Seno (female) and Son-na (male) were in an open relationship. Gezo, who used to be Seno's open partner, went to see her when he returned from a trip, bringing gifts. Seno's youngest mother left them alone so they could talk, and they ended up spending the night together. During the night, Son-na suddenly arrived and knocked on the door. Gezo scrambled to leave, but it was too late. However, seeing that Gezo had sincerely made an effort to give him his place back, Son-na invited him to have a cup of tea in Seno's bedroom and then saw him to the front door. Then Son-na told his partner that if she intended to start seeing Gezo again, he would leave her. Seno explained to him that by inviting Gezo to spend the night she was just being polite, that he had been gone for such a long time, that she had no intention of changing partners, and, finally, that he must not attach too much importance to this incident.

4. Echema (female) and Lima (male) were *açia* and had agreed to see each other outdoors because Echema was Dashï's *dhu mi.* Then while Dashï was away, Lima visited Echema's house. One night, while entering the main room, Lima saw that Dashï was already there. The two men exchanged angry looks. To calm them down, Echema's mother immediately offered Lima a drink and said to him in a kind voice: "Go back to your own house tonight." Crestfallen, he went home.

As a general rule, a person has only one open relationship at a time. I did, however, find cases in which a man simultaneously maintained open relationships with two women from different villages. My sources said that if they had lived in the same village, these women would probably have fought. This kind of situation usually involves men who are rich and generous to their partners. In my research, I came across two such cases, both involving men who were around forty-five years old. It would be almost impossible for a woman to have open relationships with two men simultaneously.

The length of an open relationship depends on the feelings that unite the two partners. It can last for months, years, or even decades. The relationship ends abruptly and without any formalities the instant one partner decides it is over.

In general, men leave their partners more often than women do. The breakup usually occurs when the man finds himself attracted to another woman. When this happens, some women accept the situation without bitterness. Others are unable to accept it. For example, a woman might wait on the road she knows the man usually takes and try to convince him to come back to her; but this is in vain. If the woman in an open relationship becomes enamored of another man, her partner retreats once he knows this and will stop visiting even if the woman wants to keep her relationship with him. According to one Na proverb: "There is always another village on the other side of the mountain, where there are always more women." I observed several brief open relationships, the shortest of which lasted four months. On the other hand, I did not find, nor did I hear about, an open relationship that did not end with a more or less voluntary breakup between the partners. Over the course of a lifetime, an individual will have several open partners one after the other, according to the stage of his or her life.

The continuation of the relationship depends, as I have said, on mutual respect. Because the partners are independent of each other, each living in his or her own home, the slightest incident can provoke a breakup, not to mention bad treatment. For example, during an argument, Ata was on the verge of hitting his partner, Nadgo. Hearing Nadgo's screams, her mothers and sisters came running in and managed to get Ata out of their house. He returned later to apologize, and their relationship was restored.[3]

Some conflicts between the *dhu zï dhu mi* have resulted in serious wounds and even death. In the past, if the partners did not call on the *zhifu*, he generally would not intervene. Here are two instances in which the *zhifu* was involved:

1. Dema (female) was the open partner of Adha (male), who lived in another village. At the same time, she received visits from Tsïe, a young man from her village. Adha was unhappy about this and ended up breaking Tsïe's right arm. Tsïe filed a suit against him. The *zhifu* decided to demote Dema's social status by making her a serf because she had entered into a *dhu zï dhu mi* relationship without respecting its customs. The two men were not sentenced.

2. Luzo (female) and Eche (male) were *dhu zï dhu mi*. Then Sola, a young man from another village, became Luzo's *açia*. When he found out about it, Eche was furious and asked Sïge, a young man from Eche's village, to help him beat Sola. Seriously wounded, Sola filed a complaint against the two. The *zhifu*, who was corrupt, inflicted a light punishment: thirty strokes on the buttocks with a rod for each young man for having attacked Sola, two against one. After this dispute, Luzo left Eche and became *dhu zï dhu mi* with Sola.

In the examples above, we have seen that when a conflict arises, some people are tolerant while others are jealous. At first glance, this phenomenon seems strange, but as we will see when we come back to this later, it is strange in appearance only.

With the exception of the small gifts that the *dhu zï dhu mi* exchange, the partners have no economic ties between them. The children, whether they are born during the relationship or afterward, are always a part of the woman's *lignée*. The Na consider the partners in a *dhu zï dhu mi* relationship *dzé hing* (*dzé* means friendly, and *hing* means people). This expression means friends in the broad sense of the word. The Na include two kinds of relationships in this category. The first is between true friends who keep up close relations. They see each other regularly to talk and eat together, and if they live far apart, they know that if one visits the other, he will always be lodged and fed. The second category of "friends" applies to the *dhu zï dhu mi*. In Yongning, the Na have a saying: "gepié sésé hing krwadhe mao nié. thesïgu dzé hing nié" (people in open relationships are not relatives, they are friends). Of course, when an open relationship ends, this is no longer the case.

My sources confirmed over and over again that before the 1960s only those who were not all that smart practiced the open relationship. Those who were clever preferred furtive visits, because an open relationship was likely to create problems. Within the parameters of my investigations, only two couples were in open relationships before the 1960s.

The Norms Regulating the dhu zï dhu mi *Relationship*

We can deduce from the description above that the following norms apply to the formation and maintenance of an open relationship:

1. Each person is free to choose his or her partner.

2. Men and women are equals when it comes to taking the initiative in expressing their inclination and desire.

3. The meal ritual marks the beginning of an open relationship.

4. The man visits the woman; it is forbidden for the woman to visit the man.

5. The visit must occur at night, but the visitor is not required to avoid the members of the woman's *lignée*.

6. During the relationship, the partners call each other *dhu zï dhu mi*.

7. They exchange annual gifts.

8. The sexual privilege is mutual, as is the respect for this privilege.

9. Transgressing the sexual privilege, by furtive visits, is both reproached and allowed, depending on the circumstances: reproached when it fails and allowed when it succeeds.

10. The *dhu zï dhu mi* remain friends during their relationship and are outsiders to each other and to each other's *lignées*.

11. The partners are independent; each has the freedom to break off the relationship at any time if he or she so desires.

We have seen that an open relationship is always preceded by furtive visits and that an individual's consanguineal relatives do not intervene in the choice of one's partner. Individuals interested in pursuing open relationships are therefore free to express their interest and their desire and mutually to choose each other. The open relationship solely depends on the free will of the concerned parties.

In this context, the meal ritual occupies a special place. With the exception of a few rare cases, it constitutes, for the two partners, a necessary step that marks the transition from the furtive visit to the open relationship for the two partners. It is important to emphasize here that the intervention of a mediator is not obligatory; one is used in about 50 percent of the cases. When someone is asked to be a mediator, he agrees to do so as a favor, and it remains a private matter. Moreover, his role only serves to spare any embarrassment that the man might feel and therefore to help ease the transition. In other words, the mediator does not represent society and does not function, for example, as a witness. His role is therefore not mandatory.

Presided over by the female chief of the woman's *lignée*, the meal ritual requires the presence of three protagonists: the two partners and the female chief. The male adults of the woman's *lignée* are absent because of the ban on sexual evocation. This transition does not even concern the entire *lignée*. I will come back to this when I compare the four modalities of sexual life. Finally, this ritual is conducted in a strictly private manner, with no public announcements. That neighbors and other villagers are not informed about it shows that the establishment of this relationship does not necessitate official intervention.

The meal ritual serves, above all, to make the relationship between the two partners known to the woman's *lignée*. From that point on, the man no longer needs to avoid meeting the household members. This passage from a furtive to an open relationship only needs to be presented to the woman's *lignée*. It does not have to be witnessed or sanctioned by society. The meal ritual is therefore a private matter that concerns only the man and the woman's *lignée*.

Because of the love they feel for each other and the decision they have made to change the modality of their sex lives, the partners give each other the sexual privilege. However, this privilege can only be effective when society recognizes it: others must acknowledge the privileged relationship before they can respect it. The open partners reveal their new privileged status to the public in several ways. The man comes and goes with greater flexibility, and the woman asks a furtive visitor to leave in the middle of the night. Through these changes, the partners assert their sexual privilege. While the assertion of this privilege indicates that it must be respected by others, it is not officially recognized by society. Given that they accord each other this privilege, the partners are held to observe it. It is in principle an obligation. We can therefore claim that the meal ritual also marks the beginning of these rights and these duties: the sexual privilege and the respect of this privilege.

The exchanging of annual gifts is another obligation, one that renews the partners' personal commitment, and the gifts can be taken to be testimonies of the permanence of their mutual love.

Once an open relationship has been formed, the partners continue to work, produce, consume, and live in their own homes with their own consanguineal relatives. They remain members of their respective consanguineal and economic units. It is therefore only natural that there are no economic entitlements or obligations that tie them together. Between the man and the children of the woman, there are no economic or legal rights or responsibilities. Therefore, the man has no obligation to provide for the children, nor does he have a say in matters that concern them. The children are not responsible for taking care of the man in his old age. The open relationship does not strip the partners of their independence in regard to each other. Since the Na have organic ties only to their own *lignées*, it is both natural and legitimate that they consider the *dhu zï dhu mi* friends and not relatives. They are always thought of as outsiders to each other by society. This is a key point in the definition of this modality and differentiates it from marriage. I will go into more depth regarding this comparison later.

The existence of an open relationship only depends on the love that ties the partners together and their free will. According to Na values, sexual freedom is a sacred and intangible principle. If an individual wants to break off a relationship in order to form another one, he or she does so. An open relationship can therefore end naturally, without any formalities or rituals and without any consequences for the respective *lignées* or for society. On the one hand, the meal ritual marking the transition in a relationship in no way makes that relationship official or creates any constraints (when the relationship ends, the partners do not undergo any kind of ritual). On the other hand, because the establishment of this relationship has not been ratified by society, it cannot be reinforced or controlled by it.

As a result of all this, the relationship only depends on the desires of the concerned parties, without any outside coercion. It exists only as as long as there are mutual feelings between the partners. Because of this, I am led to conclude that the *dhu zï dhu mi* relationship is based only on love and sex.

This initial analysis might lead one to believe that, in its ideal state, the open relationship is a form of monoandry or monogyny (not monogamy). However, this is in appearance only. I will now examine another aspect of this modality.

We have seen that, sooner or later, the villagers know about an open relationship. A conflict between an *açia* and an open partner might also bring such a relationship out into the open. The villagers know full well the problems that can arise between the *dhu zï dhu mi* and an *açia*. Everyone knows that open partners also practice furtive visits, and no one finds anything wrong with that. In other words, society tacitly approves of *dhu zï dhu mi* having *açia*. Because custom does not limit their sexual freedom, people in open relationships can continue, each on their own side, to have furtive encounters but will nonetheless try not to be caught in the act by their open partner. The *dhu zï dhu mi* are completely aware of this situation and accept it. As a result, when successful — that is, when one is not caught in the act by one's partner — a furtive encounter during an open relationship is identical to the encounter between *açia*. In such a case, the two partners' sexual privilege and sexual independence harmonize well, for both parties get what they want.

However, when a furtive encounter fails — that is, when one is discovered by one's open partner — the two partners' sexual independence and sexual privilege enter into conflict. Custom gives priority to respecting the sexual privilege. The failed visit is referred to as a *min kru*. That such a concept exists confirms the recognition of the sexual privilege and constitutes a social protection of this privilege, but only in principle. The expression *min kru* is only descriptive, not pejorative. The theft of sex is not in and of itself reproached by Na moral standards, but clumsiness during the theft is, as is, to a certain degree, having the bad luck to be caught! Custom respects the wishes of one of the two partners of the *dhu zï*, or the *dhu mi*, but not those of the intruding *açia*. If the intruder's wishes are denied, why are the wishes of the person who has placed himself or herself in an open relationship and in a furtive visit respected?

The *min kru* introduces an imbalance between the wishes of the two partners that did not exist before. According to the modality of the *dhu zï dhu mi*, each partner enjoys the sexual privilege while reserving the right to see *açia*. But such an injunction and such permissiveness have a hard time coexisting. It is an extremely delicate and difficult combination to put into practice simultaneously. Because the partners' sexual privilege is openly recognized and supported by public opinion, while the furtive visit is only tacitly recognized, as long as two individuals want to maintain their open relationship, the sexual privilege is always judged superior to the right to see *açia* when a conflict arises. Also, when an individual has open and furtive relationships at the same time, his express desire to form an open relationship is respected, while the desire that leads him to the furtive encounter is not. At first glance, then, it seems that the sexual privilege triumphs. However, this is far from the truth. We need to look more closely at the attitudes dopted by the three individuals implicated in this conflict.

We have already seen that the two rivals' attitudes in the conflict vary, depending on the situation. In general, their behavior is dictated by a combination of tolerance and jealousy. Tolerance is by far the most common reaction. Why is this so?

To answer this question, I will first examine the theory underlying the theft. In general for the Na, a successful theft, one in which the perpetrator cannot be identified, does not constitute a punishable offense, as it does elsewhere, whereas a theft that is discovered while taking place does. Of course, both of them are considered amoral. But the metaphorical expression theft of sex does not stem from the same principle. A successful theft of sex has precisely the same result as a furtive visit between *açia*. Not only is it not forbidden, but it is considered completely moral. For an explanation of this particularity, we must turn to the *açia* modality, which, as the usual and preponderant practice, serves as a basis for moral standards in the society.

When a man in an open relationship catches a furtive visitor, there are three possible outcomes, depending on whether he responds with tolerance or jealousy. When the furtive visitor, either willingly or reluctantly, agrees to leave, the open partner can be tolerant and not create a conflict. If this happens, even the neighbors might not find out about it. In the second scenario, the open partner might bully the intruder if he is jealous, but nonetheless, the conflict will not get out of hand. Public opinion in this case will side with the open partner, and there will be no need for societal intervention. A third possibility is that the open partner is so jealous that he becomes furious, attacking and wounding the furtive visitor. In the past when this happened, the injured man could file a complaint with the *zhifu*, who represented society. Then, and only then, would society intervene, not in a civil case, but in a criminal case. When a partner's reaction leads to violent conflict, the woman may end up leaving him, feeling partially responsible for the outcome.

If the man is tolerant, the *dhu zï dhu mi* relationship will continue without any problems. However, if he is jealous, if he harshly reproaches his partner and tries to monopolize her, public opinion will repudiate and ridicule him. In the end, his partner will leave him. By defending one's privileges too zealously, one ends up losing them! This experience teaches that the advantages of tolerance outweigh the benefits one might gain from jealousy. Moreover, if one partner forbids the other from having furtive visits, he is at the same time forbidding himself from the same thing. Therefore, if a person wants to keep his open relationship, it is in his best interest to be tolerant. On the other hand, all of the *dhu zï dhu mi* have experienced the furtive visit, and on this level, the Na mentality, mainly based on the *açia* modality, engenders tolerance.

The society reacts to such conflicts according to their severity. If someone was seriously injured, the *zhifu* usually judged in favor of the sexual privilege of the *dhu zï dhu mi* as opposed to the customs of the *açia*. Under the penal code, society protects itself from violence engendered by a conflict between the *dhu zï dhu mi* and the *açia*. On the other hand, if one open partner tries to monopolize the other, public opinion, by mocking him, swings in the other direction and judges that sexual freedom and *açia* customs are both predominant and legitimate. Mockery works as a social sanction, a moral protection of society against the temptation to possess, which causes conflict. Ridicule kills.

Characterized, on the one hand, by the coexistence of sexual privilege and the freedom to see *açia* and, the other, by society's support of the sexual privilege and its mockery of any attempts to monopolize, the mechanism of this double-sided custom serves as a kind of arbitrator, tempering any jealousy that the coexistence of the conspicuous visit and the furtive visit may incite between open partners. In this manner, it serves as a form of social self-protection.

Therefore, this society protects itself by taking three measures: two private, mutual tolerance and ridicule, and one social, the penal code set up to deal with the dangers that might be incited by the sexual privilege, since it could always threaten the balance of society through the conflicts it engenders.

In these kinds of conflicts, the rivals are not merely two individuals but two modalities: that of the *dhu zï dhu mi* and the *açia*. On the surface, the sexual privilege predominates in the open relationship; but the *açia* modality is always practiced. In reality, the *açia* modality triumphs. In fact, everyone knows an open relationship includes *açia* relationships. Structurally, if the open modality is considered in isolation, it constitutes a form of mono-androgyny. However, if the furtive visit is considered, a true poly-androgyny becomes apparent.

Therefore, the open relationship has two superimposed and interacting layers. On the surface, the *dhu zï dhu mi* behave as though they were exclusive partners in front of each other. If they are never told about or never come across an *açia* of their partner, they act as though they know nothing about the situation. Herein lies the appearance of exclusivity, which I call apparent mono-andry (or monogyny). While it is knowingly constituted, it may nonetheless be a sign of an unconscious desire for exclusive possession. In our society, the sexual privilege exists, but unconsciously there is a desire for multiple partners. In Na society, the reverse is true: sexual freedom and multiplicity exist; therefore, the attraction is toward exclusivity and possession, the very desires forbidden by custom.

On a profound level, the opposite of exclusivity predominates. Everyone knows from the start of an open relationship that the *dhu mi* will receive furtive visitors and that the *dhu zï* will see other women. This is known and accepted as normal. The principle of sexual freedom and the respect for this principle (and for an individual's wishes) constitute the true framework, the basis of this relationship. In fact, we can call the *açia* relationship true polyandrogyny.

The specificity of the open relationship emerges in the interaction between these two modalities: open and *açia*. The distinction between them lies in the existence of the sexual privilege in the open relationship. This privilege, as one person's preference for someone publicly designated, only becomes tangible when it encounters conflict. Therefore, only when the sexual relations between the *dhu zï* and the *dhu mi* and their *açia* are brought out into the open, either through gossip or during a *min kru*, does the sexual privilege exert itself.

The tacit agreement between the parties, existing on both layers, is therefore transgressed. When this happens, the *açia* modality erupts into the open modality. This conflict, this bringing out into the open, necessitates an arbitration to preserve the global balance of society and to maintain the very existence of these two modalities. Each individual reaction, be it jealousy or tolerance, positions him or her in relation to the top or bottom layer. If the *açia* relationship predominates in his or her mind, tolerance will control the response. If the desire for exclusive possession prevails, jealousy will be expressed. Society may then intervene at this point in one of two ways, depending on the reactions of the interested parties: if the apparent exclusivity is claimed as an actual right, and the *dhu zï* or the *dhu mi* reacts with jealousy, public mockery will lead him or her back to the reality of the norm with the reminder that sexual possession, if it is desired, cannot exist in this society. If violence occurs, the penal code will be put into action. On the other hand, a tolerance and a respect for the wishes of the other are the basis of interpersonal relationships.

The sexual privilege is therefore as protected as the *açia* relationship. As a potential source of conflict, through its connection to the desire for possession, it is tempered by the rule of tolerance and society's arbitration in regard to jealousy. The very existence of the conspicuous-visit modality generates imbalance within

society — an imbalance between men, between women, and between the *dhu zï* and the *dhu mi*.

The delicate balance necessary for the *dhu zï dhu mi* modality
to exist makes it understandable that only those who are passion-
ately in love at a given moment would choose to practice it. In
time, they will change. Those who are considered to be unenter-
prising also practice it. After all, this modality can bring stability
to a relationship for a certain period of time.

Finally, there is one more rule of this modality to examine: a
woman is forbidden to visit a man. Logically, the possibility of a
woman in an open relationship walking in on her partner during
a furtive visit with an *açia* should exist. But in practice this is
impossible because women are not allowed to visit men. This rule
also makes it impossible in practice for a woman simultaneously to
carry on two open relationships. Custom demands that the amorous encounter take place in the woman's house. Two men in open
relationships with the same woman therefore could not avoid running into each other. How would they know which of them was
entitled by privilege? If this situation arose, the men would have
no choice but to engage in violent conflict. Therefore, this rule
forbidding a woman to visit a man introduces an asymmetry between men and women in respect to their sexuality and the protection of the sexual privilege.

That the *dhu zï dhu mi* never restrict themselves to a single
conspicuous visit points to another difference between the *dhu zï
dhu mi* and *açia* modalities. An *açia* lives only in the *açia* modality,
while the *dhu zï dhu mi* live in the two. Of course, people in *açia*
relationships also practice the theft of sex, but to them, this behavior is an extension of the furtive visit.

In short, in establishing, continuing, and ending an open relationship, individual desire remains the fundamental, decisive and
imperative factor. Even when the sexual privilege between open

partners threatens the equilibrium of society, in the end, the absolute respect for individual desire prevails. This respect enables the two modalities to coexist and society to maintain itself in a state of equilibrium.

Finally, on a structural level, the small segment of the Na population who practice open relationships do not constitute a network. This is where the fundamental difference between the *açia* and *dhu zï dhu mi* modalities resides. The relationship between the *dhu zï* and the *dhu mi* is purely one of sex and love. In spite of the sexual privilege between the *dhu zï* and the *dhu mi*, its foundation is identical with that of the *açia* relationship.

CHAPTER TEN

Cohabitation

Definition

The third traditional modality of sexual life is the *ti dzï jï mao the*. The term *ti dzï* literally means to sit down and figuratively means to reside or to move in; *jï mao the* literally means not to have drunk alcohol and figuratively means not to have invited guests to a feast. The expression indicates a relationship in which a person has moved into his or her partner's house without going through the formality of inviting guests to a feast. The term *jï mao the* is included in the expression to distinguish this modality from that in which the concerned parties have organized a banquet. When it is clear from the context, the Na simply say "ti dzï." In this work, I translate this expression as cohabitation and the relationship that this expression designates as a relationship of cohabitation.

In this modality, the partners spend not only their nights together but also their days, during which they undertake common activities. They work and produce together, and they share the fruits of their labor. In short, they live together. Those who live together also call each other *dhu zï dhu mi*. However, because of the considerable differences between this modality and the open visit, I call them cohabitants.

Types of Cohabitation

There are three types of cohabitation — uxorilocal, virilocal, and neolocal — which come about for different reasons.

Uxorilocality

Most uxorilocal cases appear in *lignées* in which there is a deficiency in the male workforce. In this case, the goal of cohabitation is to assure the survival of the household. It appears, for example, when a *lignée* has daughters only, or an only child in a younger generation who is a girl, or a single adopted girl. For example:

1. Hlamugézo was an only child. Having had a son with one of her *açia* when she was around thirty years old, she brought Halba, another *açia*, to live with her. They had a son together.

2. In the Ama *lignée*, there were only three daughters, all of them from the same generation. Short on laborers, Dema took in Dedgi, one of her *açia*. During their cohabitation, Dema continued to receive other *açia*, among them Wu, a Zhuang, and Latsa, a Lamaist monk. Dedgi never showed the slightest antipathy toward Dema's visitors. Wu was a carpenter and frequently helped with repairs on the house and made plowing tools for the *lignée*. He was always welcome. Each time Wu arrived, Dedgi left to make room for him without having to be asked. Latsa took advantage of Dedgi's absences to visit Dema. Dema had seven children, some of whom were the offspring of these two visitors. Dedgi, however, raised them with Dema and treated them all equally.

Baolu women also practice uxorilocal cohabitation. Having left her birth home to live by herself, Thema, a woman from Zhongke, initially received furtive visitors. Then she had Jishi, one of her *açia*, move in with her.

Uxorilocal cohabitation may also result when there is a significant age difference between the oldest sisters and the youngest brothers, who are too young to work in the fields or to provide economically for the household. To meet this need for labor, a household brings a man into the home. For example:

> At one time, there were only three people from two generations left in the AZi *lignée* in Ago: NadZi (a woman), Getu (her brother), and Tsiedgema (her daughter). After the death of Getu, who had provided for the household, Tsiedgema brought Lima, one of her *açia*, into the household. Even when NadZi had two more daughters and three sons, the *lignée* kept Lima.

Uxorilocal cohabitation also occurs in households in which two boys from the same generation become Lamaist monks, or only one becomes a Lamaist monk, a merchant, or, in the past, a minor chief of the *zhifu*, or a boy is adopted by another *lignée*. In these cases, one of his sisters has to bring a man into the home. For example:

> In the Gwaidga *lignée* in Ago, there were four generations, one of which included two brothers and a sister. The younger brother went to live with a consanguineal *lignée*. DZiaama, the sister, had Gezodgima, her eldest daughter, with Pitso, one of her *açia*. Then she had a second child with Gigu, a merchant. After two years in an *açia* relationship with Gigu, she had him move in with her. During their cohabitation, she continued to engage in *açia* relationships with other men. Her youngest daughter is the product of one of these relationships. Gigu knew about this but was indifferent and continued to live with her and to raise the three children, treating them all the same. When Gezodgima was about fifteen, Gigu started having a sexual relationship with her, which caused frequent arguments between mother and daughter. After DZiaama died, the *lignée* wanted Gigu to stay on, because otherwise they would be shorthanded. He stayed and cohabited with Gezodgima. They had a son, Dadgu.

Within this *matrilignée*, Gigu was called *ewu* (uncle) by Gezodgima and by Dadgu's brother and sister and *apu* (great uncle) by Dadgu — even though he was his genitor — because of his double status: he was the genitor of two members of the *lignée*, of two generations.

Uxorilocal cohabitation may also arise when a woman, though her *matrilignée* is not short on labor, wishes to cohabit with a man because of his capacity to make money. In this case, the man might respond favorably to the request if he is attracted to the woman's beauty. For example:

> Tsïe was known throughout Yongning for her beauty. With four girls and two boys, her *lignée* did not need another man. However, because Laji, one of Tsïe's *açia*, was a vigorous and talented carpenter, capable of earning large sums of money, she had him move in with her. During their cohabitation, she continued to receive visitors freely. Laji, in turn, continued to visit: each time he left to build a house, he saw other women. Tsïe had four children, three of which were born during her cohabitation with Laji, but he was not the genitor of any of them.

Virilocality

Virilocality is, for the most part, found in *lignées* that have only sons, or an only child who is a boy, or an only adopted son. The goal of cohabitation in this case is to perpetuate the household. Here are some examples:

1. Luzo was an only child from Hliwalo. When he was about forty years old, he brought Nadgo, one of his *açia*, home to live with him. She was thirty-five at the time. Having had several *açia*, she already had a daughter. She and her daughter moved into Luzo's house. During the cohabitation, she continued to have *açia* relationships.

2. Gezo from Tuozhi had one brother but no sisters. He and his brother practiced the *açia* modality. At one point, Gezo asked Dashima, one of his *açia*, to move in with him: "Come and move in with me. You will be household chief right away. You can only win, you have nothing to lose." She went to live in Gezo's house, bringing her two children.

In the past, even when they had sisters, men who had become wealthy through their jobs for the *zhifu* or through the caravans sometimes brought their partners home to live with them. For example, Luzo from Kaitçi was the assistant of a steward. He had had several *açia*, one of whom shared his genitor. Their mothers, of course, were not consanguineal relatives. After five years in an *açia* relationship, he brought Hlatso, a member of the Li-su ethnic group, home with him. During their cohabitation, they had one daughter.

Some aristocrats and people from different ethnic groups cohabit with a partner even when there is not a shortage of female members in the household. Here are two examples:

1. Iudga, an aristocrat, had five brothers and four sisters. He brought Tsidgima home to live with him.

2. Gaodi was the only son in his household. His ascendants were Han. His grandfather had moved to Yongning and married a Naxi woman. His father had lived with a Naxi woman. Completely integrated into Na society, against the wishes of his ascendants, who had counted on his marrying, Gaodi lived an *açia* life. He waited until he was over thirty to give in to his ascendants' insistence that he bring Aji, one of his *açia*, home to cohabit with him. During their cohabitation, he continued to see other women.

Neolocality

In general, the neolocal cases that I came across began as virilocal cases. Men who have made a lot of money from their jobs in the *zhifu*'s administration or through business bring their partner into their birth homes to cohabit with them. This kind of cohabitation inevitably provokes a conflict between the man's mothers and sisters and his partner. In these situations, two solutions exist, depending on the case: either the man's *lignée* is broken up into two or more households, which only happens when the man holds the power in the *lignée*, or the cohabitants are forced to leave and build a new house. For example, Daja had been named chief of a village grouping by the *zhifu*. During his youth, he lived the *açia* life. After forty, he brought Naka, one of his *açia*, into his home. Their cohabitation in his birth house brought about much discord within his *lignée*. After a while, he was forced to build a new house in Tsuiyi, where he resumed his job and cohabited with his companion.

Breakdown of the Cohabitation Types

In the oldest cohabiting couple I found in the genealogies I collected, both members were older than 110. This was a long time ago, around 1880. From that time until 1963, there were only thirteen cases of cohabitation (ten uxorilocal and three virilocal) in my field of investigation.

Among the ten uxorilocal cases, seven of which were motivated by a lack of male laborers, I found:

- two in which the woman was an only child;
- two in which the woman had one brother who had become a Lamaist monk;
- one in which the woman had two brothers, who had both died. Finding herself alone, she was unable to maintain the *lignée*. After she died, her cohabitant cohabited with her daughter (this case still existed in 1963);

- one in which the woman had one sister and two brothers. Her partner was a Han merchant. Their cohabitation lasted for only two years;
- one in which the woman had three sisters and one brother. Because all of the women had children, it was difficult for them to subsist without bringing in another man;
- one in which a Han cohabited with a woman who had four brothers, three of whom had become Lamaist monks. After seven years of cohabitation, he was chased out village by some villagers, among them a young man who was visiting his co-habitant;
- one in which the man had been the full-time farmhand for the *lignée* of his partner, who had one sister and a brother who was a Lamaist monk;
- one in which the man cohabited with his partner without the consent of his own *lignée*. His *du mi* already had two sisters and four brothers.

The three virilocal cases involved the lack of female members to perpetuate a household:

- one in which the *lignée* only had two brothers. The cohabiting woman had been adopted;
- two in the same *lignée*, which had four brothers and no sisters. One brother cohabited with a Na woman and one with a Pumi vagabond (this case still existed in 1963).

Among these thirteen cases of cohabitation, ten, or 76.9 percent, came about due to a lack of members of one sex. By 1963, ten of these thirteen cohabiting couples had died, and of these ten, two had separated before their deaths. Among those still alive was a Na man living in Gala (uxorilocally), outside the parameters of my research. Two couples remained. These four people (including one Pumi) represented 1.2 percent of the 331 villagers who were alive and older than sixteen at the time.

Because there were no aristocrats in within the parameters of my investigation, to give a more thorough account I will examine cohabitations in the nine villages in the village groupings of Zhong-shi and Batsïgu, the center of the Yongning region: Batçi, DZybu, Hliwalo, Yumi, Zhongshi, Zhongke, Kaitçi *gewa*, Kaitçi *muwa*,[1] and Naha. The three social strata live together in this area, as do individuals of other ethnic groups. In 1963, these villages had forty-four cohabitations that included:

- twenty-four uxorilocal cases, five of which had dissolved when the aging male cohabitants were thrown out of the house and four of which had ended because the couples had died; as a result, only fifteen cases remained;
- thirteen virilocal cases;
- seven neolocal cases, of which one couple was deceased; therefore, only six remained.

Among the fifteen uxorilocal cases, there were:

- nine that involved *lignées* with only one child who was a girl or only daughters;
- two (which were already dissolved due to the expulsion of an old cohabitant) in which the woman was an only adopted child and was therefore in the same position as an only daughter;
- three (out of which two were deceased) in which the woman was *baolu*;
- four (out of which one was dissolved because the man had been chased away from the house) in which the woman cohabitant had brothers, but they were too young to work;
- five (of which two were deceased and two were dissolved) in which the mutual attraction was based, for the woman, on the size of her partner's income and, for the man, on the physical beauty of the woman;
- one in which the woman had brothers and sisters and the man was a Zhuang.

Thirteen of the remaining fifteen uxorilocal cohabitations, or 86.66 percent, fall into three categories — an only child who is female (or girls only), a woman with brothers who are too young to work, and *lignées* whose only children are adopted daughters. That is, they are motivated by a shortage of workers. Of the two other cases, one (6.6 percent of the total) came about because of mutual attraction and one because the cohabitant originated in another ethnic group.

When men move in with their partners, several factors come into play: their household might include many members but not own very much land; the man might come from another ethnic group and therefore have the custom of cohabitation; or, if he has been attracted by his partner's beauty, the cohabitation might have been arranged by a master, if the woman is a serf.

The thirteen cases of virilocal cohabitation were distributed as follows:[2]

- eight in which the only child was male or there were only sons;
- one in which the cohabitant was an only child and was adopted;
- two in which there were both brothers and sisters and the cohabitants were wealthy: one of them was a minor chief and the other became rich through the caravan trade;
- two in which the men were aristocrats.

Nine of these thirteen virilocal cases, or 81.8 percent, were the result of a lack of female members, and therefore their goal was to perpetuate the household (the last four do not fall into this category). The women who cohabited in their partners' homes did so because there were too many members in their household and not enough land or they came from another ethnic group.

Finally, the seven cases of neolocal cohabitation were distributed as follows:

- five (out of which one couple was deceased) in which the man had brothers and sisters, originally lived virilocally, and had a job in the *zhifu*'s regime;

- one in which the man had brothers and sisters, became rich through business, and separated from his original *lignée* to cohabit with his partner;
- one in which the partners were both serfs.

The first five neolocal couples began with virilocal residence. Then, due to tension between the male cohabitant's sisters and the female companion he brought into the household, the couple had to move out and build a new house, passing into neolocal cohabitation. It is important to note here that, in the uxorilocal cases, the presence of the woman's companion in a household that includes her mothers and sisters has never caused a *lignée* to separate. But five of the nineteen virilocal cases I observed caused a split in the *lignée*. In uxorilocality, the female cohabitant's brothers will not exclude her companion. But in virilocality, the man's mother and/or sister will rarely accept his companion.

Another phenomenon that should be noted is that among the twenty-four uxorilocal couples, eight men belonged to other ethnic groups, and two men were aristocrats; among the thirteen virilocal cases, four women were from other ethnic groups; and among the seven neolocal cases, two men were from other ethnic groups. Individuals from other ethnic groups accept cohabitation more readily than the Na do for two reasons: first, other ethnic groups have a tradition of marriage and cohabitation and do not remain with their mother, maternal uncles, brothers, and sisters for life; second, members of other ethnic groups frequently arrive alone in Yongning and therefore need to integrate themselves into the society. One of the best ways to do so is to cohabit with a Na. Out of eighty-eight people who had lived or were living in cohabitation, fourteen, or 15.9 percent, were from other ethnic groups (ten men and four women).

Of the thirty four remaining cohabiting couples, twenty-three, or 67.65 percent, were motivated by a shortage of female members or male workers.

In 1963, the nine villages mentioned above had a total of 683 adults of an age to procreate (387 women and 296 men).[3] Out of these 683, 68 people, or 9.95 percent, were living in cohabitation. If I omit the fourteen people from other ethnic groups, this figure drops to 7.9 percent.

In general, in households that have only one girl or one boy, cohabitation for these children begins relatively early, usually when they are between twenty and twenty-five years old. Others begin to cohabit when they are around thirty-five, and sometimes even later, in their forties or even fifties.

Zo min *and* mu min

The Na refer to a man who is cohabiting uxorilocally with a woman from *lignée* X as the *zo min* of *lignée* X. The word *zo* means boy or son; *min* literally means tail and figuratively means perpetuation. This expression designates a man who must see to the needs of the woman's entire household. In this way, he guarantees the continuation of her *lignée* by providing for it. When a woman moves in to her partner's house, she is called its *mu min*. The word *mu* means girl. This expression refers to a woman who lives virilocally to perpetuate a man's household.

In uxorilocal cases, the woman is not considered a *mu min* by her partner's *lignée*. This concept is completely different from that of daughter-in-law, which in other societies is a status a woman acquires once she is married, no matter whether her residence is uxorilocal or virilocal. Similarly, in virilocal cases, the man is not considered a *zo min* by his partner's *lignée*. This concept has nothing to do with that of son-in-law, which in other societies is the status a married man acquires in relation to his spouse's family, no matter where his residence may be. In neolocal cases, the terms *mu min* and *zo min* have no reason to exist.

In general, for a person to live with his or her partner, there is one absolute condition that must be met: the household he or she is leaving must be large enough that the departure will not bring about a shortage of male or female members. If such a shortage would result, a cohabitation cannot even be considered. For example:

> In the Batsimi *lignée* (*apo* III) in Imin, there are currently only three brothers. Tsïedudgi, the middle brother, has been in an open relationship for six years with Nadgodgima, the Badzi *lignée*'s eldest daughter. She has had three children with him. In her household, she has only one sister. Moreover, she and her sister were adopted from another *lignée* twenty years earlier by the Badzi *lignée*. Due to a lack of female members in his household, Tsïedudgi has been asking Nadgodgima to cohabit with him, while Nadgodgima, because of a shortage of male workers in her household, has been asking Tsïedudgi the same thing; but their situation is blocked on both sides. Their relationship continues, but each lives in his or her own household.

Cohabitation is preceded, without exception, by a furtive and/or open relationship. When the partners agree to cohabit, the one who is moving out discusses this with his *lignée*: the man with the male chief in uxorilocal cases and the woman with the female chief in virilocal cases. As a general rule, if the *lignée* has enough members, it must accept the plan to cohabit as an individual choice and respect it. Those who are given the desired consent leave by themselves. They take along their clothing and personal effects, for example, a felt rug or an animal pelt for bedding, if they have them. The members of their *lignée* never accompany them, because bringing along a member does not conform to the notion of solidarity within a *lignée*. The receiving *lignée* sends nothing in return for the departure of the *mu min* or the *zo min*. I call the *lignée* that agrees to let a member leave to cohabit elsewhere the providing *lignée* or the supplier *lignée*. This expression implies not that the *lignée* in question takes the initiative but that it gives its consent to this departure.

In my description of the *matrilignée*, I explained how the seats to the right of the hearth in the main room are assigned to the female members and those to the left to the male members. When there are guests, the household members sit together on the right, and the guests sit on the left. In uxorilocality, the male cohabitant also sits on the left. In virilocality, the male cohabitant sits on the right, and his companion sits on the left, since she is considered an outsider (not a consanguineal relative). This seating arrangement will never change until the cohabitant dies. The cohabitant occupies the place furthest to the left and the *lignée* members fill the rest of the space.

Members who leave their household to cohabit are called *wu dzé* by their original *lignée*, which literally means birds. This expression means that they fly away like birds to other people's houses. When people move in with their partners, they retain the name of their original *lignée*, and will always maintain their consanguineal identity in relation to their original *lignée*. Society considers the cohabitants *dzé hing* (intimate friends) and not related to each other. The Na call them *ti dzï ji mao the hing*, which means people in a relationship of cohabitation without drinking alcohol, and they say, "ti dzï ji mao the hing dzé hing nié, krwadhe mao nié," which means people in a situation of cohabitation are friends, not relatives. They explain that the *mu min* and *zo min* are not relatives because they are not actually given to the receiving *lignée*.

This friendship between the cohabitants and a receiving *lignée* ceases after the death of a *zo min* in uxorilocal cases. However, it continues after the death of a *mu min* in virilocal cases and changes into a relationship of *krwadhe*, because the descent of the cohabitants' offspring is always matrilineal. As for the incest prohibition, the children produced by a virilocal cohabitation can have sexual relations with the members of other *lignées* that are consanguineal relatives of the receiving *lignée*, but not with members of their mother's original *lignée*, nor with members of other *lignées* that are consanguineally related to their mother. In uxorilocal cases, the same logic is followed.

As long as the cohabitation has not ended and their mother's cohabitant is still alive, children who have lived with their mother in a receiving household will bear the receiving *lignée*'s name, even after their mother's death, and are considered *krwadhe* of the receiving *lignée* but not of its other consanguineal *lignées*.

In neolocal cohabitation, the children bear the name of the new household, which can be that of the man, the woman, a place, job, animal, or plant (as we saw in chapter 7 in the section "The Name of the *Lignée*").

Cohabitants acquire different positions within their receiving *lignées*, depending on whether they are male or female. A Na proverb provides a good illustration of this distinction: "A woman who moves in with others will be handed the job of household chief; a man who moves in with others will be treated like a serf." As household chief, the female cohabitant represents a new leader, and she acquires a certain degree of authority, such as planning the daily meals, presiding over the service of offerings to the ancestors before each meal, and keeping the keys to the storage rooms, even if her partner's mother is still alive. This is why some men, to persuade their partner to live with them, say: "As soon as you are in my house, you will be *dabu* (household chief). Now tell me, what's wrong with that?" However, while the female cohabitant does exercise some authority, she does not have the right to preside over rituals and invitations, and she is not entitled to sign contracts for purchases and sales, even if her advice is weighed heavily when making decisions about outside affairs.

On the other hand, a *zo min* who is in his partner's household for essentially economic reasons will work more than he did when he lived at home and will be considered a servant by the members of his receiving household. In a *lignée* with no male members, he might also take on some of the responsibilities of the male household chief, such as the practical organization of daily life, but he will never be household chief and will never represent the receiving *lignée* in rituals or outside affairs. Here are three examples:

1. In the Imin *apo lignée*, Tsïepitso was a cohabitant from the Gocho *lignée* in Ago. He had once been the secretary of the Communist Party Committee for the village grouping. Though retired, he continued to enjoy a certain amount of prestige in Imin. However, during rituals, whenever his receiving household invited representatives of each *lignée* from Imin, it asked an uncle from the founding *lignée* to preside over the ceremonies.

2. In the grandmother's generation of the founding *lignée* of Imin, there were two sisters, Dgima and Guma, and one brother, Luzo (a Lamaist monk). They were financially comfortable and employed a full-time valet, Dudgitsie. After some time, Dgima, the eldest sister, began to cohabit with Dudgitsie, and they had three children. Because he was very capable, the *lignée* became even more prosperous. In 1944, when another *lignée* pawned a piece of land to them, Dudgitsie saw to all of the arrangements. However, Dgima signed the contract, because Dudgitsie did not have the right to do so.

3. When I went to Azo to record genealogies, I first met with a thirty-six-year-old man. He was the only one home, so I spoke with him. Since he was the only male adult in the household, I

asked if he was the *dabu*, even though I knew he was the companion of a woman in the *lignée*. He answered: "No! I am not. How could an outsider become chief of the household?"

The status of cohabitants in a receiving household is determined by these same values today.

Sometimes men move in with their partners without asking for advice from members of their *lignée* first, simply because they do not get along with them. Usually, the members of the receiving *lignée* will treat a man in such a situation as well as they do his partner. But to stay with them permanently, he must work very hard. According to the Na, he occupies the same position in the receiving household as the children do. Public opinion holds him in very low esteem.

A woman never takes the initiative to move into her partner's home. She must always be asked by his *lignée* or risk being taken for a sow in heat. If there is a conflict in her household, there is only one way out for a woman: *baolu*.

Within the household, the female cohabitant's children, regardless of whether or not her companion is their genitor, are always treated fairly, in uxorilocality as well as virilocality. In virilocality, it is to the woman's advantage already to have had children because this shows that she is not sterile and therefore will be able to perpetuate the household. If cohabitation has not occurred by the time the partners reach middle age (after thirty), the question of fertility is one of the main reasons.

As a general rule, not only does the male cohabitant treat his companion's children well, but he does not dare be strict with them and is always indulgent. Therefore, children whose mother is cohabiting and who do not have an uncle or a great-uncle living under the same roof are often quite spoiled. This is even more true in uxorilocal cohabitations.

After children move in with their mother's companion, the members of their original *lignée* no longer have the duty, in principle, to take care of them. During their old age, the members of the original *lignée* do not have the right to ask these children to provide for them. In uxorilocal cases, this problem is not an issue. The situations are not symmetrical.

In uxorilocal residences, the children call their mother's companion *ewu* (maternal uncle). In virilocal cases, the children refer to everyone in the receiving *lignée* as though they were in a purely matrilineal *lignée*. A man always refers to his partner's children as his nieces and nephews, no matter what the residence. The *mu min* and *zo min* refer to their partner's ascendants as though they were their own. In short, the kinship terminology is exactly the same as it is in a purely consanguineal *matrilignée*. The mother's companion and her brothers are all referred to as the mother's brothers. They are all considered *ewu* of the children. The sisters of the mother's partner are called mother, as are the mother's sisters. They are all considered *emi* of the children.

When there are no other adults in the household, the two cohabitants take the platform for their bed. When there are other adults, or if their children are about seven years old, the two cohabitants have separate bedrooms in the house. They behave as though they were consanguineal relatives, so much so that their sex life takes place in secrecy, in the same way as that of the other household members who are practicing the modality of the furtive visit. Conforming to the ban on sexual evocation, it is taboo for the two cohabitants to talk about emotional or sexual topics or to make any allusions to them in the presence of consanguineal household members of the opposite sex. This taboo is so strict that it sometimes results in terminological confusion. For example, during my genealogical research, in some *matrilignées*, there was from time to time a "false *ewu*" among the *ewu* of past generations. Only when I sought verification of these genealogies from the eldest members of the same village was their real status of cohabitant revealed. Members of this *lignée* alive today are too young to know that this *ewu* was in fact a cohabitant of one of their ascendants.

As with the other modalities examined so far, sexual freedom exists in the cohabitation relationship. If the male cohabitant goes away for a more or less prolonged period, men can visit the woman. Similarly, the male cohabitant can visit women while he is away. In fact, when partners live under the same roof on a daily basis, it is more difficult for a *min kru* (theft of sex) to take place. When a cohabitant walks in on a *min kru*, his reactions may range from tolerance to jealousy, just as in the open relationship. Here are several examples of furtive visits during cohabitation:

1. In Tozhi, Gezo, from the Ama *lignée*, had no sisters and therefore brought Dashima into his house. Each time Gezo went away, she received furtive visitors without hiding them from Gezo's mother, who found this completely normal. When Gezo discovered what was going on, he reproached his mother for allowing others into the house. He also criticized Dashima. In spite of all this, they continued their cohabitation.

2. At the age of thirty, Gaozo from Zhongke brought Halba into her house. Before their cohabitation, she had already had two children whose genitors were unknown. During their cohabitation, she had two children with Halba, and she continued to receive furtive visitors.

3. Before her cohabitation with Ana, Pitso, who had three sisters, had had three *açia* and had had one child with Ana, who had been one of her *açia*. When she was eighteen years old, she brought Ana into her household. But at the same time, she was seeing Gezo. Caught in the act, Gezo was beaten by Ana.

4. Abu, a man from Zhongshi, became rich through the caravan trade, and since he was on bad terms with his mother, he left

his original residence. He built a new house and cohabited there with Gezo, one of his *açia*. At the time, Gezo was thirty-one years old. Having already had several *açia*, she had four children (three boys and a girl). The three boys were the offspring of two genitors, neither of them was Abu, and the girl's genitor was unknown. Gezo brought her eldest son and her young daughter to cohabit with Abu, leaving her two other boys with her original household. During her life with Abu, Gezo had eight more children. Busy with her successive pregnancies and with taking care of the children, she did not have *açia*. Abu, on the other hand, continued to pursue his *açia* life and saw ten or more other women.

Sometimes a man cohabits with two sisters at the same time or with one after the other. For example:

1. Tsïe was the only son in the Shale *lignée* from Ago. He was the *açia* of Krumu from the Tsikru *lignée* in Imin. Their union produced two children. Tsïe brought her into his house to live with him. At the same time, he was the *açia* of Diatsi, Krumu's younger sister. Shortly after Krumu moved in with him, Diatsi also came to cohabit in his house.

2. Hlatso from Upper Kaitçi had five sisters and one brother. Ana, one of her older sisters, had cohabited with Lanbuta, a rich merchant from the Labo canton. After Ana's death, Lanbuta cohabited with Hlatso for twenty-odd years. In 1948, he died, and Hlatso began an open relationship with one of her *açia*.

A man may also cohabit with a woman and then with her daughter, as mentioned above.

Cohabitation can last for months, years, or a lifetime. It solely depends on the partners' feelings and the receiving household's needs.

A cohabitation can dissolve for the following reasons:

1. The couple can no longer get along with each other, or, following an argument, one of them leaves.

2. The woman's uncle orders the man to leave because he is no longer rich.

3. The man, having grown old, is no longer considered worth keeping in the eyes of the receiving *lignée*. His companion's children (including those he produced) do not get along with him and, after repeated quarrels, chase him away from the house. He therefore has no alternative but to return to his original household or to live alone in extreme poverty.

4. Having grown old, the partners no longer have a sex life, and the receiving *lignée* no longer needs workers because the children are grown up. Because of his attachment to his original *lignée*, the man voluntarily returns to it. Cohabitants claim that they feel closer to their sisters' children than to their companions' children. This kind of case is only seen when the original *lignée* is in a financial position to take the former cohabitant.

Of the twenty-four uxorilocal cases from the villages of Zhongshi and Batsïgu mentioned above, five couples dissolved their cohabitation. The women's situations before cohabitation were the following: in two cases, the woman was an only child and had been adopted (the equivalent to being an only daughter); in two cases, the woman had one brother only; and in one case, the woman had one brother and one sister.

Here are several examples:

1. Jishi from the Chongla *lignée* earned his living working on the caravans for a wealthy *lignée*. After a period of being in an *açia* relationship, he began to cohabit with Tsïe from his village. After 1956, there was no more work on the caravans for Jishi, and therefore he had no more resources. Moreover, he was getting old.

Tsïe's *lignée*, including Tsïe herself, no longer wanted him. He was forced to leave this *lignée* and, to survive, took a job putting the yaks out to pasture.

2. Dgima had had a great number of *açia* during her youth. When she was thirty-three, she brought Eche into her home to live with her. Each time he went away, she would receive visitors. Thirteen years after the cohabitation began, Eche got into a violent argument with one of Dgima's sons, the offspring of a Tibetan man. Eche returned to his original home.

3. Xu Jiewu, a rich Han merchant, was the *açia* of Nadgo, an only child whose mother and uncle were still living. Xu Jiewu went to cohabit with Nadgo and brought three mules with him. Xu Jiewu and Nadgo were very much in love and had five children together. In the meantime, the three mules were sold. After twenty years had passed, Nadgo's uncle abruptly said to Xu Jiewu one day: "Your three mules have been eaten up, now it's time for you to go!" Feeling that she must respect the wishes of her uncle, Nadgo sent her partner away. Having no means of support, Xu Jiewu returned to his birth home without complaining.

When serious problems arise between cohabitants, the villagers do not intervene as intermediaries or arbitrators.

In virilocal cases, when a couple breaks up, the *mu min* has the right to bring all of her children back home with her if the cohabitation has been short lived, but she has no rights to any of the material possessions. When the woman does not get along with her companion's mother or brother(s) and when the cohabitation has gone on for many years, the receiving *lignée* might insist on keeping one or two of her children, in which case she must leave the child, or children, behind. But she has the right to choose which children she will bring back with her and to demand certain material possessions. However, even when a mother leaves one or more children behind, the others always expect that they will end up joining their mother. The Na express this inevitability with the saying: "bo mi zogo he, bozo zogo bié" (the piglets go where the sow goes).

My sources knew of only one separation of this type and insisted that it was quite rare: In the Bima *lignée* in Emi (outside the parameters of my research), a couple separated after ten years of cohabitation because the woman no longer got along with her partner. She took her youngest daughter with her and left two boys behind with her partner.

The position of a *zo min* is much more precarious than that of a *mu min*. When problems and arguments arise, no matter what the reasons are, the man's only option is to leave, and he has no rights to the children or to the property, no matter how long the cohabitation has lasted. There are even cases in which the man was turned out of the house by the children he had produced. What is more, it is not at all certain that he will be accepted back into his birth *lignée*, especially if he is old, and especially if he initially left without asking for their consent. The members of his original *lignée* might very well say to him: "When you were young and full of energy, you worked for others. Now that you are no longer good for anything, you come back to us. Out of the question." Here are two examples:

1. Dashitsïe, who was cohabiting with Dgimatsïe in Imin, was, during my stay, in the process of being forced out of the house by the children he had produced. His original *lignée* (Baomo) lived in Ago, right next to Imin, and did not want to take him back because he was already seventy-six years old. When I left, in spite of interventions by the leaders of the village grouping, a solution had still not been found.

2. Dudgi, from the Ragi *lignée*, had cohabited twice: once with a woman from the Adgi *lignée* in Imin and once with a

woman from Gala. Turned away by his original *lignée*, he built a minuscule house in Ragi. At first glance, it was hard to believe that the tiny structure could be a home. He was the poorest person I encountered during my stays in the field.

When a *mu min* dies, the receiving household pays for her funeral expenses, and the cremation takes place there. The ashes, however, must be scattered on a mountain slope behind her original village, if she is not from the same village as her receiving *lignée*.[4] For a *zo min*, the same is true, except that today his ashes can be scattered on the mountainside behind his receiving village as well as behind his original village. If a *mu min* has broken up with her partner after a brief cohabitation, her former receiving *lignée* has no responsibility for her funeral; if the relationship falls apart after a long cohabitation, the receiving household is responsible for a part of the funeral expenses.

In the case of an older former *zo min* who has voluntarily returned to his birth *lignée*, his former *lignée* will cover the main expenses of his funeral. The cremation takes place on a spot near his home village. If, because of discord, an aging *zo min* returns to his own *lignée*, his former receiving *lignée* contributes nothing at all, or only a small amount, to the expenses of his funeral. If a breakup takes place shortly after a cohabitation begins, the former receiving *lignée* pays none of the funeral expenses.

Following the death of a *mu min* or *zo min*, during *bu sï nin,* the annual ritual of offerings to the ancestors, the receiving *lignée* does not recite her or his name. It is up to the original *lignée* to include the name in their lists of ancestors.

Cohabitation is an extremely fragile modality that comes about when a *lignée* needs a woman or a man, but its existence is neither reinforced nor protected by society. It is enough that one partner wants to separate for the cohabitation to end, without

any formalities or rituals. To maintain this delicate tie, the cohabitants usually try to respect each other. They are equals within the
household in respect to choice.

The Prerequisite Condition for Cohabitation

The Na place great importance on the cohesion of the *matrilignée*.
In general, a *lignée* does not allow people who are not consanguineal relatives to move in, unless there is a shortage of male or
female members. Take, for example, the following conversation:

> One day I went to meet Alu, one of my sources. He was in the
> process of helping DZiatsi, a fellow villager, to build his stable. After
> introducing me to DZiatsi, Alu and his friend stopped working, and
> we went into the main room. It was their lunchtime.
>
> During the meal, fearful that I would break the ban on sexual evo-
> cation, I discreetly found out from Alu the status of the woman in
> the house. Alu understood my concern and introduced me to all of
> the household members.
>
> Without any embarrassment, he said to me:
>
> "The woman is DZiatsi's companion. We can discuss this freely
> here, you don't have to worry about the sexual taboo." And then he
> abruptly added, looking directly at DZiatsi: "The way you did it
> [bringing his partner into the household] was degrading."
>
> "There were only the two of us, me and my brother," DZiatsi re-
> sponded. "Without a woman, we could not live properly. When we
> came home from work, there would be no one here to serve us tea.
> During the Cultural Revolution, the political situation forced people
> to cohabit [he was referring to the matrimonial reforms of that peri-
> od]. As for us, if we live together, it is the situation of my *lignée* that
> forces us to do so. Without a woman, there would be no one to take
> care of raising the pigs and the chickens, and no one to prepare the
> food. You know very well that men are incapable of that kind of

work. And moreover, when we go away, there would be no one at home to look after the house. The household would no longer be a household."

At that, Alu seemed to remember the tradition and said, "Oh yes! You are right! It is not degrading. Your *lignée*, having only men, brought in a woman. It has always been that way, since ancient times."

DZiatsi, agreeing with him, added, "Of course what we have done is not degrading. But in a *lignée* in which there are brothers and sisters, then it is taboo to bring in a woman! It is even criminal, because it breaks the *lignée* apart. Once a woman arrives in the house, the *lignée* always falls apart."

"Is your cohabitation registered?" I asked him.

"No," he responded, somewhat embarrassed. "They [the civil servants who are in charge of marriage registrations] "came and asked me to register. But I did not want to. What good would that do, registering [for marriage]? If we want to cohabit, we do it. It's all the same, with or without that piece of paper. If we decide that we don't want to live together, even if we had the piece of paper, what would it change? It's a good thing that we didn't register. We didn't waste any paper, and we didn't waste a civil servant's time."

"So, then, does your brother practice the visit?"

"Yes. My brother is still young, he is twenty-five years old. We feel that it is not worth the trouble to bring in yet another woman! To do so would split up the household. It would not be in his best interest, and it would weaken our home. He has no need to bring in a woman. Actually, the visit is our tradition."

Here is an example of an unnecessary cohabitation breaking up a *lignée*:

Didzi was one of the *zhifu*'s stewards. He brought Buchi, his companion, into his house. By doing so, he created discord within his *lignée.* The household was divided into three parts: he stayed in the main room, his older sister stayed in the upper room, and his younger sister stayed in the lower room.

Prior to 1956, under the *zhifu*'s regime, if an individual left to cohabit with someone, and by doing so went against the judgment of his *lignée*, the *lignée* could start proceedings against him before the *zhifu*, who had the power to demote him to a serf. This dissuasion forced descendants to obey their ascendants. Here are two examples of members running away:

1. Dashidgima from the Ragi *lignée* in Ragi is seventy-one years old. When she was seventeen, she had a strong character. She was in love with Tsïe from the Naka *lignée* in Winda, and they decided that she would cohabit with him. Because her *lignée* was shorthanded, Gélo, her uncle, did not consent to her leaving. But, gripped by passion, she and her lover insisted that they live together, even though her uncle had threatened Tsïe with a rifle. Since he could not control his niece, Gélo brought her to the *zhifu*, who put her in prison for several months and demoted her to the rank of serf. When the *zhifu* had her gather grass for the pigs, she escaped with her lover, and the two fled to Wujué, a village in the Muli District. They did not return to Yongning until the 1950s.

2. Gebu had two brothers and one sister. During his youth, he worked on the caravans and therefore frequently traveled in Han country. He and Adga were initially *açia*. They then decided to cohabit at Gebu's house. Fearing that she would be reduced to the status of a serf because her *lignée* did not approve of her decision, Adga took refuge with Gebu in Baiqi, 90 kilometers from Yongning. They worked together there as assistants in a workshop. Several years later, they returned to Yongning and cohabited in Gebu's house. Adga's not getting along with Gebu's mother and sister broke up the household. Gebu's sister was finally forced to leave.

If a *lignée* has practiced cohabitation in one generation and it therefore includes members of both sexes, cohabitation will not be practiced in the next generation. With the exception of some aristocratic *lignées*, I did not find any in which cohabitation occurred in successive generations.

The Norms Regulating Cohabitation

From this description of cohabitation, we can extrapolate the following norms:

1. If a member of a *lignée* intends to bring someone into a household for cohabitation, that household must lack either female members to perpetuate the household, or male members to work and provide for it.

2. An individual is free to choose his or her partner.

3. It is up to the individual whose *lignée* is lacking a member to ask a partner to cohabit.

4. A person who intends to cohabit with a partner must first ask for the consent of his or her *lignée*.

5. The cohabitants call each other *dhu zï dhu mi* ; the individual who has come to cohabit with a partner is called a *mu min* or a *zo min*.

6. The *mu min* and *zo min* keep the name of their original *lignées* and maintain their consanguineal identity forever.

7. The *mu min* and *zo min* are seated in the place of a guest in their receiving *lignée*. The partners are considered friends and not related to each other.

8. In uxorilocal cases, the children keep the name of their original *lignée*; in virilocal cases, the children who live with their mother in the receiving household take its name for as long as the cohabitation lasts, but their descent remains matrilineal.

9. In kinship terminology, a *mu min* is assimilated to her partner's sister and a *zo min* to his partner's brother in the receiving

household. All members of a mixed household (one in which there are individuals of different consanguinity) must be called and behave as though they were all consanguineal relatives.

10. There are mutual sexual privileges of and a respect for these privileges between the cohabitants.

11. The transgression of sexual privileges is reproached when it fails, permitted when it succeeds.

12. The cohabitants have reciprocal rights to the fruits of their labor, as do the cohabitant and the other household members.

13. Whether or not they are the offspring of the male cohabitant, children living under the same roof are treated equally by all of the adults in the household, no matter what their mode of residence; they have the right to inherit the household property.

14. During the cohabitants' old age, the children have the duty to take care of their mother as well as her partner, if he has lived with them for a long time and if they are on good terms with him.

15. The cohabitation's existence is based on the mutual feelings of the cohabitants and the needs of the receiving *lignée*; the cohabitants are free to break off the relationship whenever they wish to do so, and its dissolution occurs without any formalities or rituals.

16. When a virilocal cohabitation ends after only a short time, the woman has the right to take all of her children with her, but she is not entitled to any possessions. If the cohabitation has lasted a long time, the receiving *lignée* is entitled to keep the children, and the woman is entitled to some small possessions. In uxorilocal cases, no matter how long the cohabitation has lasted, the man has no rights to the children or property.

17. Which *lignée* is responsible for the funeral expenses of a cohabitant depends on the duration of the relationship and the reasons for the breakup.

We have seen that the norms of this modality, as distinguished from those of the furtive visit and the conspicuous visit, concern the period before, during, and after the cohabitation.

I will now examine the connections between these norms.

A lack of members of one sex in a generation within a *lignée* is a necessary condition for cohabitation and is therefore the first norm of this modality. It is the main reason for cohabitation and is present in the majority of cases (67.65 percent). This norm is confirmed not only by the motivations for most cases of cohabitation, but also by the consequences of bringing a *mu min* into a *lignée* that already has enough members of both sexes: a separation in the *lignée* often occurs, a split that goes against the moral standards of this society.

In this regard, the most telling examples are those of couples who run off together. Whereas the first examples demonstrate that unnecessary cohabitation is disapproved of, the runaways' stories reveal that a *lignée*'s authority can go so far as to forbid unnecessary cohabitation by appealing to official authority. For official authority to intervene, of course, the decision made by the *lignée*'s representatives is crucial. The older generation will always frown on unnecessary cohabitation, at least until it no longer holds authority. This fact helps to explain why unnecessary cohabitations most often occur between partners over thirty whose *lignées* no longer have any living members from the ascendant generation.

These opposing views of cohabitation — one that is approved of and the other that is disapproved of by society — confirm the definitive importance of this first norm.

Although virilocal and uxorilocal cohabitations follow the same norm, one results from a shortage of girls and the other from a shortage of boys. If a *lignée* without female members behaved as though it were a normal *lignée* — that is, if it continued to live with only consanguineal members who practiced the visit — it would not be able to reproduce. In this instance, the reason for cohabitation is biological: a lack of human support. In the opposite case, a *lignée* without male members is able to reproduce through practicing the visit modalities, but it can only provide for its needs with difficulty. The shortage of males amounts to a lack of human support in this case, too, but here the cohabitation occurs for reasons other than reproduction: the survival of the *lignée*. At bottom, it is a question of material needs, and the reason for the cohabitation is economic.

Therefore, two causes come from the same problem: a lack of human support. These two kinds of cohabitation do not have the same function. Uxorilocality serves to perpetuate the consanguineal identity and the name of the receiving *lignée*, while virilocality serves to ensure that the female cohabitant and, above all, her children, will take care of the male cohabitant during his old age and perform the service of offerings to the receiving *lignée*'s ancestors for two or three generations after the male cohabitant's death. In the end, when everything is taken into account, virilocality only serves to perpetuate the receiving *lignée*'s name.

In households that include members of both sexes in a single generation, if a cohabitation comes about, the powerful Na concept of matriliny, and the exclusivity of matriliny, favors uxorilocality. Neolocality comes about only after virilocality because this mode of residence is the result of a double mishap. The first is a transgression of the necessary condition for cohabitation, and the second is the tendency for conflicts to arise, from one generation to the next, between two groups that are not consanguineal, because the woman who has come to cohabit with her companion gives birth to outsiders. That the majority of neolocal cases originate virilocally constitutes a new asymmetry. This proves, yet once again, the power of the concept of pure matriliny.

Neolocality is therefore merely a derivative form of virilocality. The two fundamental types of cohabitation are uxorilocal and virilocal.

I will now look at the norms observed by the cohabitants from the beginning of their cohabitation until the end. As in *açia* and open relationships, individuals have complete freedom in choosing a partner; moreover, their relationship always begins with one of these two modalities. It is true, however, that the *mu min* and *zo min* are obliged to ask for the consent of their original *lignées*. But the implications of this act are limited to the partner and his or her *lignée*, and do not involve any direct contact between the two *lignées* nor any societal intervention. In this way, the request for consent is a private act.

On a conceptual level, the *mu min* and *zo min* are considered helpers in the household of their partner, from the point of view of both the providing *lignée* and the receiving *lignée*. The meaning of *mu min* and *zo min* corresponds not only to the goal of cohabitation, *min* meaning perpetuity, but also to the cohabitants' status as friends. This is further reinforced by the Na's classifying them as *dzé hing* and by the meaning of *dhu zï dhu mi*, the name used by the cohabitants between themselves. Because the cohabitant of a *mu min* is not considered a *zo min* by her original *lignée*, and vice versa, their *lignées* are never considered more than friends.

What a cohabitant enjoys inside his or her partner's home in terms of status and behavior corresponds to this outsider identity as well: her or she bears the name of his or her own *lignée*, is seated around the hearth in the place reserved for outsiders, does not have the right to represent the receiving *lignée* in accepting invitations or officiating at rituals, and cannot sign land contracts. In short, the cohabitant's role is strictly limited to that of a helper who only works, eats, and lives with his or her partner.

If a *lignée* allows a member to leave, it is because it has many, or even too many, members in relation to the amount of land it owns. It therefore has no need to bring in an outsider itself. When a cohabitation takes place, the receiving *lignée* is never at the same time a provider, since it has no member it could give to someone else. For its part, there is no countermovement, either material or symbolic, to displace the arrival of a *mu min* or a *zo min*. Therefore, this action does not involve an exchange between the two *lignées*.

The bonds brought about by cohabitation include the sexual privilege between the cohabitants. The phenomena associated with this privilege — *min kru*, jealousy, and tolerance and their attendant mechanisms — are the same as those in an open relationship. The only difference lies in the quasi-constant presence of the cohabitants, which makes it more difficult to have a successful *min kru*, except in those cases where the partners no longer pay any attention to each other.

On an economic level, between the cohabitant and his or her receiving *lignée*, there are mutual rights and responsibilities concerning the fruits of their labor. Cohabitants are also responsible for raising the children during their time together. The two cohabitants do not usually have independent resources.

No matter what their mode of residence, the attitudes between the partners are regulated by a respect for the appearance of being consanguineal relatives. The application of a purely matrilineal kinship terminology to the entire household and the installation of separate beds for the cohabitants so that their sexuality is hidden make the cohabitants behave in front of the rest of the household as though they were sister and brother. We also noticed that the public behavior of the cohabitants is identical with that of members in a purely matrilineal *lignée*. Because of this, they can be designated as pseudo-brother and pseudo-sister.

I will now look at the children's status within a receiving household. In virilocal cases, like their mother, they remain outsiders in relation to the receiving *lignée* and keep the consanguineal identity of their original *lignée*. They must therefore always observe the incest prohibition that applies to their mother's group.

The children, from the beginning of their mother's cohabitation or from the moment of their birth within the receiving household, take the name of the receiving *lignée*. Consequently, if they were born before the cohabitation, no matter who their genitor is, the name of their *lignée* will be changed. However, taking the name of the receiving *lignée* is merely a formality, because they are treated as friends, not relatives, by this *lignée*. According to the kinship terminology, they call their mother's partner *ewu*, even though he is not their uncle. They take the name of the receiving *lignée* because they are raised in and live in its house, thanks to the fruits of their mother's and her companion's labor. It is also their duty to look after their mother's partner in his old age. Therefore, with or without their mother, if all of the members of the receiving *lignée* were to die, these children would become its only representatives and would inherit all of its property. In this respect, their relationship to the household follows the same logic as that of an adopted non-consanguineal woman. They become part of the household but not of the *lignée*.

In uxorilocal cases, the children do not change their name because they remain in their birth home. This represents yet another asymmetry between these two modes of cohabitation.

That the male cohabitant treats all of his partner's children in the residence equally, regardless of whether or not he is their genitor, deserves further attention. This phenomenon can be explained in the following way: if he were to favor the children he had produced, he would draw attention to the sexual relations between him and his partner. Such a revelation goes against the taboo on sexual evocation. Moreover, he has no reason to favor a child that he has produced, since, after all, he is nothing but the waterer. On the other hand, an unfair attitude would undoubtedly create discord within the household and might even bring about a separation in the *lignée*, which goes against the very reason for the cohabitation. Another factor that the man must not overlook is that as he grows older, he risks being expelled from the household (in uxorilocal cases only), and it is therefore in his best interest to be appreciated by his partner's descendants and to be on good terms with them.

The male cohabitant's attitude toward the children confirms the representation of the male's role in procreation. In a purely consanguineal *lignée*, my sources repeatedly assured me, the Na man places no value on producing children. It is both essential and vital, however, that his sister have children, and the identity of these children's genitors is never important. A cohabitant's attitude corresponds perfectly to this, to the point that he does not dare be strict with them. I therefore call him a pseudo-uncle.

Conversely, the children's attitude toward their mother's partner is extremely variable. In a virilocal residence, influenced by property, needs, and the importance of getting along, they are predisposed to treat the cohabitant well. Since the household property belongs to the man, the children cannot turn him away. Whether or not he is their genitor exercises no influence. In uxorilocal cases, the children's attitude is different. Again, whether or not the cohabitant is their genitor gives him no special status, but the children know that he is a pseudo-uncle, an outsider. Once the goal of the cohabitation has been reached and the children have grown up, or the cohabitant is no longer productive, they do not need him. If they do not get along with him, they will chase him away with no notion of duty or gratitude toward him, no matter how they felt about him in the past.

In direct opposition to the male cohabitant's situation, an aging *mu min* cannot be expelled from the household, which can be explained by the concepts of procreation and pure matriliny. The children belong to her, and it is unthinkable that they would ever chase her away. If, forced out by her companion, the woman leaves, the children will follow her, and the end result would be contrary to the initial goal of the cohabitation.

Although breaks in this relationship are possible, during the cohabitation, while the receiving *lignée,* on the one hand, and the *mu min* and her children or the *zo min,* on the other, will never be related to each other, they keep up the appearance of being consanguineal relatives and behave as though they were in a pure *matrilignée.*

Throughout this analysis, it has been observed that the ban on sexual evocation, the concept of pure matriliny, and property serve as foundations for moral standards in this society, and constitute the general rules that govern Na behavior in pure *matrilignées,* as well as in households of cohabitants. In other words, with the exception of the sexual relations between cohabitants, and the attitude of the male cohabitant toward his companion's children, the cohabitants' behavior corresponds to that of a sister and brother in a pure *matrilignée.* Cohabitation, as a modality of sexual life, distinguished from that of the furtive and the conspicuous visit, does not have its own code of conduct.

All of the facts concerning cohabitation unanimously confirm that the cohabitants are friends and that, from the point of view of the providing *lignée,* as well as that of the receiving *lignée,* both the *mu min* and the *zo min* are helpers of the receiving *lignée.* Therefore, the relationship between the two *lignées* is also one of friendship.

There are two kinds of relationships in the cohabitation modality between the receiving *lignée* and the providing *lignée,* and their respective consanguineal *lignées.* In fact, the *mu min*'s (and her descendants') and the *zo min*'s relationships of consanguinity to their original *matrilignées* are not altered. However, a bond of friendship is established, on the one hand, between the members of the receiving *lignée* and the providing *lignée* (as well as its consanguineal *lignées*), and, on the other hand, between the *mu min* or the *zo min* and the consanguineal *lignées* of her or his receiving *lignées*. There is, therefore, a double relationship, one that is specific to cohabitation: one of consanguineality and one of friendship.

We have reached the last stage: the rights and responsibilities of cohabitants once the cohabitation ends. The dissolution of a cohabitation depends on the free will of the partners, just as its formation does. The cohabitants do not have the right to impose anything on each other. The three conditions for a successful cohabitation are getting along well, the necessity of a sex life, and the need for a workforce. There are four possible endings to the relationship, two of which are natural, death and the voluntary departure of an aged companion, and two of which are provoked, a change of heart and an aged male cohabitant's being chased away by his partner's children.

In uxorilocal cases, after a *zo min* dies, the friendship between the providing and receiving *lignées* ends. However, in virilocal cases, after the *zo min* dies, not only do all of the receiving *lignée's* possessions go to the *mu min* and/or her descendants, but the relationship between the receiving *lignée* and the *mu min's* original *lignée* becomes purely consanguineal. The friendship between this household and the cohabitant's other consanguineal *lignées* is broken, while the friendship between the *mu min* (as well as her descendants) and her deceased companion and his ancestors continues, for the *mu min* and/or her descendants take care of the daily and annual service of offerings for them. A successful virilocal cohabitation creates a friendship, one that is to a certain degree eternal, between the two *lignées*.

Therefore, in terms of friendship between the two house-holds, the concept of matrilineal consanguinity engenders yet another asymmetry between the two modes of residence (neolo-cality is comparable to virilocality in this matter). The relation-ship in uxorilocal cohabitation is temporary, while that in virilocal cohabitation is continuous. By favoring the female cohabitant in virilocality, this concept brings about another asymmetry: the *mu min* in virilocality is never at risk of being forced out of the house when she grows old. This fact helps to explain why most neolocal cases began as virilocal cases.

Usually, a *mu min* and a *zo min* enter a cohabitation believing that it will be for life. This relationship, based on their mutual feelings and trust, does not imply, at least not initially, mutual rights and responsibilities. However, as long as the relationship lasts, the fruits of the labor done by the *mu min* or the *zo min* increase and accumulate in goods as well as in children, which brings about the growing gratitude of the receiving *lignée*. With this gratitude come certain rights and the implication of the *lignée*'s responsibility toward the cohabitant. Because of this, during a *zo min*'s old age, it is legitimate for the receiving *lignée* to take responsibility for feeding him and, after his death, to pay for the funeral. According to this logic, if the cohabitation breaks up, the receiving *lignée* is indebted and the cohabitant settles its accounts: the longer the cohabitation, the larger the debt.

This same logic applies to the rights of men over the children raised by the couple, to the rights of women over possessions, even if what she is entitled to is minuscule, and to the amount paid for funerals. But when a *zo min* leaves, either because he has a change of heart or because he is chased away in his old age, this logic of accumulation of the fruits of his labor does not entirely apply. Once again, the concept of pure matriliny creates an asymmetry.

This analysis leads me to conclude that the relationship of

cohabitation is one of friendship between the partners and the children produced by the female cohabitant, as well as between their respective *lignées*.

On a structural level, because the two cohabitants usually spend their nights under the same roof, it is less convenient for the woman to receive furtive visitors than it is for a woman in an open relationship. However, the parallel practice of cohabitation and the furtive visit shows that in this modality, monoandry and monogyny are only apparent and that polyandrogyny exists here, too.

From the above, we can extract three characteristics: cohabitation is disapproved of or altogether forbidden when there is not a shortage of female or male members in a generation of a *lignée*; a providing *lignée* is never at the same time a receiving *lignée*; and cohabitation is not practiced by the next generation in the same *lignée*. These characteristics lead me to conclude that the lack of a female or male member, a biological phenomenon that exists everywhere, constitutes the necessary premise for Na cohabitation and that cohabitation is therefore only a temporary measure taken to overcome a crisis.[5] Once the crisis has passed, the household returns to life in the ordinary modality: that of the visit.

The modality of cohabitation is conditioned by the same norm: a lack of one sex in a generation of a *lignée*. But the two types of cohabitation do not stem from the same causes: one is caused by a human shortage and the other by a material shortage. Nor do they fulfill the same functions: one transmits consanguineal identity and the name of the *lignée*, the other transmits only the name.

Finally, as we have seen, adoption for the Na is a preventive measure taken when female or male members are lacking. The function of cohabitation is therefore the same as that of adoption. When adopting, priority is given to children who are consanguineal relatives of the *lignée* in need, whereas in cohabitation, the *lignée* in need can only choose someone who is not a consanguineal relative.

Adoption is the first choice, but it cannot solve every case, because there are not always adoptable children available. That 67.65 percent of the cohabitation cases occurred in situations where there was a lack of male or female members shows that cohabitation offers an alternative to adoption, one that integrates an adult member (and in some cases, the *mu min*'s children) into the *lignée* with the deficit. In this society, cohabitation is a supplementary measure to adoption. This also partially explains why cohabitation usually occurs when the partners are around thirty years old.

CHAPTER ELEVEN

The Marriage of the Only Son

as a Type

Definition

The fourth sexual modality of the Na is the *jï the ti dzï*. The word *jï* means alcohol, *the* means to drink, and *ti dzï* means literally to sit down and figuratively to move in or to reside. In its literal sense, *jï the* simply means to drink alcohol. Figuratively, it means to organize a feast. In fact, this locution is derived from the expression *ban jiu* traditionally used by the Han in the region. The term *ban jiu* is an abbreviation of *ban jiu xi*; *ban* means to organize, and *jiu xi* literally means feast. The feast can be for several occasions. In this case, the expression alludes to a wedding feast. I translate *jï the ti dzï* literally as cohabitation after a feast and figuratively as cohabitation after a wedding feast.

Na vocabulary cannot directly signify the terms: fiancé, engagement, wedding, marriage, to marry, to wed, and to divorce. It is under the heading of giving someone to a *lignée* that the entire procedure of "marrying" a woman (or a man) takes place. This modality is usually associated with virilocality and only rarely with uxorilocality.

The Request to Give a Young Woman

In virilocal cases, the procedure for obtaining a woman usually unfolds in the following manner: After *lignée* A has established a preference for a woman from *lignée* B, A sends its male or female chief to discuss the matter with the male or female chief of *lignée* B. Ordinarily, *lignée* B must have many daughters, otherwise it would never agree. As a general rule, a Na *lignée* does not like to give away daughters to another *lignée* for two reasons: it wants to guarantee its own continuation; and giving a daughter to another *lignée* is considered detrimental to her, because the Na believe that she might be treated badly. When the representative of A returns to household B for a second or even a third time and has received a favorable response from B, A must ask a *moio* (a mediator) formally to express its choice of a girl and to solicit the approval of *lignée* B. The role of the *moio* can be filled by either a man or a woman.

The two *lignées* set a date for the first intervention by the mediator. The mediator introduces himself to the mother or the maternal uncle by reciting the following ritual words, meant to convey his sincerity: "To get to your home, to ask for your daughter, I have worn out nine pairs of straw sandals, and nine walking sticks," and so on. He brings the first of a series of gifts (also called *gwalu pinba*): a piece of linen for a skirt or a jacket, about 100 grams of silver, a jug of alcohol (about a gallon), a box of tea (about one pound), rice cakes, and a ring of boned pork (about 10 pounds), as well as the necessary ingredients for the evening meal.[1] An initial service of offerings to the ancestors is conducted by the female chief or by a *daba* as soon as the mediator arrives, and afterward, the members of B eat the rice cakes and drink the alcohol. When this is completed, B gives its consent. When the evening comes, *matrilignée* B invites one representative from each *matrilignée* in its village to a dinner, which is preceded by a service of offerings to the ancestors; in this instance, a *daba* must preside over the ritual.[2] The ensemble of these activities is called *cho do tçi*.[3] Following this ritual, if the daughter changes her mind and refuses to be given, her ascendants must apologize to *lignée* A and return the gifts they have received.

After this first visit by the *moio*, *lignée* A invites representatives from each branch of its lineage to speak with the future husband, to make him understand that once his future wife arrives, he must never quarrel or fight with her nor separate from her, so that she becomes a member of his household forever. In the meantime, always through the *moio*, negotiations over the price of the daughter take place, a price that varies according to the wealth and social status of the two *lignées* involved as well as according to the beauty of the betrothed.

Once a price has been agreed on, the chief of *lignée* A, accompanied by the mediator, goes to B's home to pay. Prior to 1956, in rich peasants' households, this price was about 30 *bankai*, ten boxes of tea (about 10 pounds), two jugs of alcohol (about 2 gallons), one to three pigs, one to three horses, one to three cows, and, finally, enough linen to make two suits.

Once it has received the payment, *matrilignée* B invites its consanguineal relatives to dinner. The female chief presides over a service of offerings to the ancestors and informs them of the decision to give a member to *matrilignée* A.

Prior to 1956, to accomplish this transfer of a daughter between two *lignées,* the receiving *lignée* was required to inform the chief of the village grouping and the *zhifu*, to whom it had to bring one pig's foot and one ring of boned pork as a tribute. The receiving *lignée* was also required to register with the state at the *zhifu*'s residence, for two reasons: taxes and the judgment on the division of property and children in the event of a separation.

Once a day is chosen on which A will come to get the young

woman, a third meeting is arranged for the night before the ceremony. The mediator brings the third payment to this meeting: a jacket, a skirt, Ace bandages, a belt, jewelry, a shawl, and provisions for the feast on the following day, to which representatives from each *matrilignée* in B's village will be invited.

The Ceremonies

On the day of the ceremony, before sunrise, *matrilignée* A sends a procession to *lignée* B that includes the mediator, a mature woman who has already had many children of both sexes and who has the same astrological sign as the betrothed, two girls, two or three strong and able young men, and a man riding a docile horse.

In the meantime, *matrilignée* B has gathered women from its village, both consanguineal relatives and others, in the main room around the young woman. The three young men and the mediator enter the room, closely watched by the women. After reciting several prayers to the spirit of the lower hearth, one of the young men will suddenly push his way toward the betrothed and whisper in her ear: "Hey, go and have some tea at X's house." Then he runs away with the young women chasing him. If they catch him, they will hit him and poke him with pine needles and tear his clothing. They might also hit the mediator. In response, the mediator and the other young men give silk threads, which have been especially prepared for the occasion, and silver to these women, all the while begging their pardon.

The young woman will then leave for her new home, accompanied by her oldest brother and one or two of her adult sisters, as well as by the procession that has come to fetch her. The young woman's consanguineal relatives and the older women from her village follow her and pretend to prevent her from leaving. While this is going on, the mediator and the young men place a table, taken from the future husband's house, on the road and hand out more silver and thread to the women, who take these tokens back to their village, where they will share them with the other villagers.

Once she arrives in the village of her future husband, the betrothed is also met by a woman who has had many children of both sexes, as well as by the other villagers. This ritual is always the same, even when the two *lignées* are from the same village.

On the day of the ceremony, *matrilignée* A must kill a cow or a pig or, if it is very wealthy, a yak as offerings to its ancestors. During the offerings ritual, an announcement is made to the ancestors, informing them that the household is about to have an additional member.

With the young man and the betrothed united, the *daba* anoints their eyelids and foreheads with butter, a gesture that symbolizes longevity. The betrothed puts her arms around the female pillar in the main room and thereby signifies her incorporation into household A.

The chief of the *lignée* serves food and drink to the young man and the newcomer, who then prays for each ascendant who is present. They, in turn, offer her jewelry and clothing.

For the feast, *lignée* A slaughters goats, cows, and, if possible, yaks and places their skins on the ground in the courtyard. The richer the *lignée* is, the more skins there are. The guests from *matrilignée* B and the representatives of each village household are invited to eat and above all to drink the various white and yellow liquors. Their hosts threaten to poke them with pine needles if they look as though they might not empty their glasses. The idea here is that the more intoxicated the guests become, the more the hosting *matrilignée* will be honored, because their drunkenness demonstrates its ability to provide ample food and drink. In other words, this is a way for them to display their wealth.

During the feast, the young woman's brother and the sister are considered guests of honor. *Matrilignée* A gives the brother 30 grams of silver and enough linen fabric to make a suit, and it gives the sister several coins and some small gifts. The *daba* then recites their story of genesis.

At the end of the meal, *matrilignée* A passes out a piece of beef to everyone. The young woman's brother and sister each receive a part of the cow's thigh and a ring of boned pork. Representatives from A's consanguineal founding *lignée* receive either a rib of the cow or a fleshy part of the spinal column (a symbol of their common stock: "they are issued from the same bone"). Those who are not consanguineal relatives each receive a piece of the beef, a ring of boned pork, and a bowl of rice. A portion is reserved for each *lignée*, and if its representative happens to be absent, its share will be saved. After the meal, all of the villagers go to a field at the edge of the village for dancing. Many others from surrounding villages join the celebration.

Lignée B also organizes a feast on this day, to which it invites representatives of each *lignée* from its village.

The next morning, the people who accompanied the young woman to her new household return home. *Lignée* A sends members to escort them. On the way, the boys from *matrilignée* A will grab the scarves of girls from B's village, who will have to give the boys a few cents if they want to get their things back.

Three days after the ceremony, the young woman returns to her mother's house in the company of several consanguineal female relatives of *lignée* A and remains there for several days in privacy. When the time comes for her to leave once again, her sister and the girls from the village must try, still just symbolically, to prevent her from joining *lignée* A.

In uxorilocal cases, which are extremely rare, when the woman goes to get the man to bring him to her house, the process is pretty much the same as in virilocality: a *moio* is asked to participate, representatives from each *lignée* in *lignée* A's village are

invited to a feast (at least once, the day of the ceremony), a procession is sent to fetch the betrothed man, and then they proceed
to the service of offerings to the ancestors and the various other
stages of the ceremony. A *daba* officiates at the rites of the ceremony, and the newcomer puts his arms around the male pillar
and, like the bride, returns to see his original *lignée* three days
after the ceremony. However, there are usually no, or only very
small, gifts for the man. The ceremonies are also less elaborate. In
short, the entire process is less expensive than it is in virilocal
cases.

Hinshuba *and* Chumi

Through this ceremony, the newcomer becomes part of *lignée* A
and takes its name. The man becomes the *hinshuba* (husband) of
the woman, and the woman becomes the *chumi* (wife) of the man.
The partners and their respective *lignées* have become *krwadhe* in
the figurative sense, but the consanguineal relatives who are not
living under the same roof as the husband's *lignée* are not considered *krwadhe* of the wife and vice versa. In virilocal cases, the
wife is considered a *mu min* to her husband's *lignée*, however, he is
not a *zo min* to his wife's original *lignée*. In uxorilocal cases, the
man is considered a *zo min* to his wife's *lignée*, but she is not a *mu
min* to his.

The Spouses' Rights and Responsibilities

The wife works and produces with the rest of her husband's
lignée. Her rights to the fruits of their common labor are equal to
those of any other household member. She can become chief of
the household if it lacks women or if her husband's mother dies.

The same holds true for uxorilocal marriages. However, in
these cases, the husband is required to do an enormous amount of
work. This is why men do not readily accept this situation, unless

they are from other ethnic groups or extremely poor *lignées*. To explain this discrepancy, the Na say, "A woman who moves in with others will be handed the job of household chief; a man who moves in with others will be treated like a serf."

Given the expense, only rich Na *lignées* can choose marriage.

Min kru: *Jealousy and Tolerance*

In most cases, the marriage is preceded by a furtive and/or an open relationship. The spouses are equals within the household. Their relationship is stable. Usually, they do not give up having furtive relationships, which may be more or less frequent. If a *min kru*, a theft of sex, occurs, their responses are controlled by the same mechanisms as cohabitation.

Sometimes, couples have lovers without bothering to hide the fact. For example:

1. Dazhu (male) from the Shagu *lignée* in Batçi, was married to Sola. During their life together, Sola had more than ten *açia*. She had three children, all of them the offspring of her *açia*. Dazhu never protested his wife's *açia* life. Each time one of Sola's *açia* visited, Dazhu was indifferent. They each had their own bedroom. He would frequently visit one of his *açia*. When he stayed at home, he spent the night in his own bedroom. Nor did Sola pay any attention to her husband's furtive visits to other women.

2. Luzo (male) from the Aijia *lignée* in Lige was married to Dema from Dazhu. Initially, they got along well. Later, both of them saw *açia*. During the day, they worked and ate together, but at night, they each had their *açia*, without any trouble. At one point, Dema's *açia* was Luzo from the Emo *lignée*, and Luzo's *açia* was Bima. They were all from the same village. Sometimes, while going to see Dema, Emo Luzo would come across Aijia Luzo. They would greet each other nicely, with no embarrassment. A short while later, Aijia Luzo became the *açia* of Emo Luzo's niece.

In certain situations, jealousy is not even an issue, as can be seen from the following examples:

The Arranged Marriage

1. Sozha (male) from the Paoso *lignée* in Kaitçi was married to Dema. Their union was arranged by their aristocratic *lignées*. They had no feelings for each other. A short while after the marriage ceremony, Sozha became very cold toward Dema and frequently spent the night with other women. Dema, not content to be left alone, took the household's valet as an *açia*.

2. The marriage of Sade (male) from Loshu was arranged by his *lignée*. Afterward, he continued to visit a Pumi woman in the neighboring village. His wife, in turn, regularly received a Pumi visitor from the same neighboring village.

Polygyny

Gezo (male aristocrat) from Baodzi married a woman, with whom he had a son, Nadgo. Gezo's sister had a daughter with one of her *açia*. While marrying his son to his sister's daughter, Gezo also made arrangements for Nadgo to marry Dema, a girl from the same village. In other words, Nadgo married two women at the same time. Because Nadgo did not like his "sister," he left her to do as she wanted. She received *açia* and had two sons as a result. Dema (the other wife) had a boy. They lived peacefully and raised the three children together.

The Long-Term Illness of a Husband

Sona (female) from Tozhi was married to Tsïe. Because her husband was often sick, she frequently received visitors, and the relationship with one of them lasted intermittently for seven years.

The Sterile Husband
In Tuozhi, Jila (female) was married to Keta. After several years, she was still not pregnant. They agreed to bring Tsïe, one of Jila's *açia*, into the house. All three of them cohabited in harmony, and Jila had four children.

One Woman and Several Brothers
In Tuozhi, there were six brothers in the Buwu *lignée*. Only Tsïe, the youngest, got married. Each time he left the village, his brothers took his wife as an *açia*. His wife gave birth to four children, but not one of them came from him.

One Man and Two Sisters
In the Atsai *lignée* in Tuozhi, there were four daughters and no sons. The uncle brought Pitso, a man from another village, into the household. Before the wedding, the uncle told Pitso that any one of the four sisters could be his wife, leaving the choice up to him. Because the oldest daughter was older than he, and the next oldest one was ugly, Pitso chose one of the younger ones but, in fact, lived publicly with the two youngest.

In some households, especially those with a member in a high level job, the husband will forbid his wife to receive visitors. Some of them say: "Before she comes (as a wife) to my house, she can do whatever she likes. There is no question of telling her not to. But once she has moved in with me, she can no longer do so." The husbands, however, do not stop visiting other women. For example, Dgashi (male) from the DZinbu *lignée* in Batçi had only one brother, who had become a Lamaist monk. His uncle was the chief of the village grouping. He married Tsïe. Afterward, he forbade his wife to receive visitors, but he freely visited other women.

Some husbands are not only jealous but also violent with their wives. This kind of reaction is not common and is disapproved of by society. For example:

1. Gézo had one brother but no sisters. He married Dema, who had known other *açia*. After she moved into her husband's house, she continued to see her *açia*. After relations with a Tibetan, she received a piece of felt as a gift. When he saw it, Gézo beat her. He, however, continued to visit other women.

2. When he found out that his wife, Tsïe, was having *açia* relationships with visitors while he was away, Ishi from the Chen *lignée* (of Han origin and immigrated to Yongning seven generations ago) in Kaitçi hurried home and fired two gunshots in the air in front of his wife to discourage her from doing so again.

A husband is sometimes neither jealous nor tolerant but scandalized by his wife's conduct. For example, Bima, an only daughter, married a Tibetan merchant. Afterward, she had relations with her maternal uncle, which made her husband so ashamed that he hanged himself.

Finally, according to statements I heard, there have been some exceptional couples, who, after marriage, had no other partners.

The Newlyweds' Children in the New Household

Some women move into their husband's house with one or more children whose genitor is not necessarily the husband. For example:

Naka (male) from the Nianxu *lignée* married Nadgo from the Shudu *lignée*. Before they were married, Nadgo had had five children, some of whom were Naka's offspring. It is not easy to tell which child came from which man, and the Na consider trying to do so not worth the trouble. After the wedding, Nadgo brought all of these children to her husband's house. She then had three more. All of the children were treated the same. Only one of these children, a girl, got married (which is extremely rare). The seven others remained at home and followed the *açia* modality.

When the woman already has children, on the day of the wedding, *lignée* A sends clothing for the children to wear. They follow the procession, and if a child is less than a year old, a woman sent by *lignée* A will carry him. While heading toward A's house, the woman accompanying the child must recite the following words: "X, follow your mother! X, follow your mother, who is going to another's home." This is said to ensure the child's soul comes along. If this is not done, the child will lose his soul from fear and will not survive in his mother's husband's house. If the child is older than one year but still very little, the woman who carries him recites nothing, because children who are more than a year old are thought to be capable of bringing their own souls with them.

All of the children live under the same roof as the couple, whether they were born before or after the wedding and whether or not they are the offspring of their mother's husband. They take on the name of the receiving *lignée*, and they are all *krwadhe* of their mother's husband and his *lignée* and are treated fairly.

Children always respect their maternal uncle, as tradition requires. But their mother's husband has authority over them. Their maternal uncle, living in another house, no longer has any rights or responsibilities when it comes to them, which is exactly what happens when a *lignée* separates.

The couple and the rest of the *lignée* raise the children, who, in turn, will take care of the ascendant generation for the rest of their lives. Then they will inherit all of the household's property, the transmission of which is done collectively.

The Kinship Terminology for Married Couples

The terminology used by married people contains two terms in addition to those in pure matriliny presented in chapter 7: *hinshuba* and *chumi*. Only those names that apply to certain people will be presented here.

The children call their mother's husband and any of his brothers living under the same roof *ewu* (maternal uncle). These brothers call the children by their first names and treat them as though they were their *zémi* (nieces) and *zéwu* (nephews.) The husband, however, uses *mu* and *zo* when referring to the daughters and sons of his wife. For example, a married man will say "nia bu zo mu " (my son and my daughter); and his brothers, if living under the same roof, will say, "on zo mu in " (the sons and daughters of our *lignée*). If the brothers live elsewhere, they do not refer to the children in this way, for then the children are not considered their *krwadhe*; they belong exclusively to their mother's husband's *lignée*.

If their mother's husband's sisters live under the same roof, these sisters call the children by their first names and consider them their *zémi* and *zéwu*. In turn, the children call them *emi* (mother). This situation is usually temporary, however, because the marriage of a man who has sisters nearly always results in a breakup of the *lignée*.

The children are still considered *zémi* and *zéwu* to their mother's brothers, and sons and daughters to their mother's sisters, no matter where they reside.

The terms *hinshuba* and *chumi* are not names of reference and can only be used when the children are absent. In daily life, the man calls his wife *Rumi* (granddaughter) or by her first name, and the wife calls her husband by his first name to avoid making any allusion to their sexuality in front of the children.

As for the norms of behavior for the couple, once the wife arrives in her husband's home, the spouses are never side by side in public, including during the wedding ceremony. During the banquet, the couple eat separately, each on his or her own side. After the wedding, they do not have a common sleeping area. The woman sleeps next to the lower hearth, and the husband usually sleeps on the platform against the wall. When they want to be together, the husband must join his wife; she can never join him. When the oldest child reaches the age of seven or eight, the husband must sleep in another room, and the couple's sex life takes place secretly.

Married couples never allow themselves to be photographed together. The same is true for cohabitants and for those in a visiting relationship. This is because of the ban on sexual evocation. When I was in the field, I never saw a photograph of a couple. One day, I asked a man to take me to an island on Lake Lugu. I knew that the woman accompanying us was his partner. On the way, as they were rowing in the stern of the canoe, I wanted, quite innocently, to photograph them. I had only begun to point my camera in their direction when the woman slapped my right elbow with her oar: "You can't just take any old picture!" she scolded. The slap from the oar led me to ask why she had been so mean, and I was informed later about this custom.

In the two modes of residence, since the children are not consanguineal relatives of their mother's husband, sexuality between them and their mother's husband's consanguineal relatives is not forbidden. But sexuality between a daughter and the husband is reproached.

The Dissolution of the Matrimonial Relationship

To express the breakup of a matrimonial relationship, the Na use the term *ti gwai ke*, which means to drop or to abandon. A breakup can come about in two ways: flight without a word or abandonment.

Flight without a word is most commonly resorted to by women who entered into an arranged marriage. After a period of time, which can range from one day to two years after the marriage, some women — because they do not feel comfortable, or because they fight with members of their husband's *lignée*, especially his mother, or with the husband himself, or because they prefer the *açia* life — return to their mother's house. Their husband's *lignée*, in this case, has the right to demand full reimbursement for the price paid for the woman. The Na believe that as long as this debt remains unpaid, the soul of the woman will belong to her husband's *lignée*. Here are some examples:

1. Dema (female) was married to Tsïe from the Asumi *lignée* in Batçi. The day after the wedding ceremony, she ran back to her birth home, refusing the marriage. The gifts that her husband's *lignée* had brought were all returned.

2. In 1950, Gézo (female) from the Jita *lignée* in Hliwalo was married to a Pumi from Bajia. Two weeks after the wedding, she returned to her mother's house and did not want to go back to her husband. Unhappy about losing a wife, this Pumi's *lignée* brought charges against her *lignée* before the *zhifu*, who was in charge of arbitrating such cases. He decided that the woman's *lignée* had to pay back the price of the girl: 15 *bankai*, a piece of cloth, and several pounds of grain.

3. In 1946, Dema (female) from the Maibu *lignée* was married to Chen (a Han) from Batsïgu and gave birth to a child. At the end of one year, she fled with her child to her mother's house. Her husband was reimbursed 100 *bankai*.

The husband's *lignée* does not have to exercise its right to reimbursement. For example, Adgi was married to a *tusi*'s brother from Langqu (a neighboring region that has a patrilineal society). One year after the ceremony, taking advantage of a trip back to her original house to see her consanguineal relatives, she refused to return to her husband's home and began once again to live in the *açia* mode. Her husband did not demand reimbursement.

In uxorilocal cases, the only time a husband returns to his mother's home is when his original *lignée*'s economic situation has clearly improved. In this case, there is never a question of paying back the price if one was paid, because the work he did while living in his wife's house is considered payment enough. In addition, he is entitled to a share of his wife's possessions. However, while my sources claimed that such a situation could arise, not one of them was able to come up with an example.

The husband and wife usually live on an equal footing, especially those who had an *açia* relationship and an open relationship before they were married. If there is ever a fight between the couple, or between the wife and her husband's consanguineal relatives, the wife will run back to her mother's house or to the house of consanguineal relatives. Several days later, when they both have calmed down, she returns. During the conflict, if one of them wants to end the marriage and the other will not accept the separation, representatives from each *lignée* in the village will try their best to reconcile the couple. If the fighting begins again and the couple is unable to continue their relationship, the representatives will intervene to judge how their possessions and children should be shared.

When a wife instigates the end of a marriage after only a few years, and she takes all of the children back with her, her *lignée* reimburses only a part of the price paid for her. For example, Jiatsu (male) from Batçi married Dema from Abu. They were together for approximately six years and had one child. In 1945, Dema took her child and returned home to her mother, not wanting to go back to her husband. She started once again to receive visits. Jiatsu was able to get only some of the gifts back as reimbursement.

If the husband (or his *lignée*) wants to dissolve the marriage (the objective of perpetuating the *lignée* makes it rare that the man's household, especially the older generation, would recommend doing so), he loses the right to a reimbursement of the price paid for his wife, no matter how long the marriage has lasted. However, the husband has the right to claim one or two of the children, depending on how long the marriage has lasted and how many children it produced. In this instance, custom is as follows:

If their marriage has been brief and the woman has not had any children, the wife leaves by herself without any possessions. My sources insisted that there had never been a case of this kind, because it goes against the best interests of the husband's *lignée*.

If there is only one child, the mother takes him with her.

If there are two children, each of them keeps one. If it is a girl and a boy, the girl goes with the mother.

If there are three children, and they are all girls, two go with the mother, and one stays with the father. If there are three boys, one follows the mother, and two stay with the father. When there are two girls and one boy, the two girls leave with their mother, and the boy stays with his father; in the reverse situation, the one girl will go with her mother, and the two boys will stay with their father.

If they have had several children, the wife can only bring them all with her if the husband's *lignée* relinquishes its rights to them.

But the villagers claim that, even if one or more children have been chosen to stay with their mother's ex-husband, such a situation will be short-lived, because "the piglets go where the sow goes."

The children who stay with their mother's ex-husband after the dissolution of the marriage continue to be his *krwadhe*, however, the children that go with their mother do not. If a child who has stayed with his father decides, when he grows up, to join his mother, *lignée* A has the right to demand a reimbursement in goods or in money from *lignée* B.

A woman whose husband has ended the marriage is forbidden to return to her birth home. Her only option is to become a *baolu* with her children, because, during the wedding ceremony, the *daba* told her that she must not return in tears. If she came back crying to her mother and the other members of her *lignée,* it would be considered bad luck for them all.

In uxorilocal cases, if the marriage has lasted for many years and the woman wants to end it, the husband is entitled to some of the possessions (up to half of all the material goods) but not the children.

If the discord between the husband and wife results in violent arguments, the concerned parties will institute proceedings to dissolve the marriage before the *zhifu,* who will make a settlement according to the criteria listed above.

When a wife is sterile, the couple will first try to adopt a girl from one of her sisters. The husband can, however, take the initiative to dissolve the marriage because of the sterility. Once he does so, he forfeits his right to a reimbursement. For example:

1. Echedgima from the Apo *gnao lignée* in Azo, was married to Gilo from the Remi *lignée* in Iiwalo. When she was still not pregnant after one year, she returned to her mother with all of her belongings. Her husband's *lignée* gave her a plot of land and did not ask to be reimbursed.

2. In Yumi, Gaozo and his mother were separated from their original *lignée,* Goge. To perpetuate the household, his mother insisted that he marry, so he married Tema. After eight years of marriage, in 1963, he divorced her because she was sterile. He was not reimbursed. After the divorce, he returned to an *açia* life.

When the woman proposes divorce, the husband retains his right to be reimbursed, but in general, he does not exercise it.

When a spouse dies, whether it is a virilocal or a uxorilocal case, the receiving *lignée* is responsible for the funeral expenses. It will scatter the ashes of the deceased on the mountain slope outside its village, just like it does for its own deceased members, and his or her name will be added to the list of ancestors and be recited during the annual offerings services.

The original *lignée* of a woman who has returned to her mother's house and for whom no reimbursement has been made cannot arrange her funeral, because her soul is thought to be with her husband. In this case, her *lignée* must bring *pinba* to her husband's *lignée* so that it will invite a *daba* to send her soul to join her husband's ancestors.

Since there are very few married couples, divorce is extremely rare, even exceptional. After speaking to all of my sources, spread out over ten villages, I only heard of two cases. The norms concerning divorce are for the most part based on suppositions.

Those who marry people from ethnic groups outside of Yongning are considered to have become members of those ethnic groups. When they die, they join their spouses's ancestors and their names are not included in the list of their original *lignée* that is read during rituals. People who leave the area to work elsewhere are still considered consanguineal relatives by their *lignée*, as long as they do not marry someone from a different ethnic group. When they die, their names are recorded on their *lignée*'s list of ancestors.

Finally, when a man who has sisters and brothers marries, in five out of nine cases, he moves out of his original household and lives elsewhere. The notion of consanguinity in these cases excludes the possibility of another woman in the household.

Why Someone Would Choose Marriage

As with cohabitation, the main reason that commoners and some aristocrats marry is because a given generation of their *lignées* lacks representatives of one of the sexes, for example: when there is an only child, when all of the children are the same sex, or when there is an only adopted child. Other factors also come into play, such as when one of the partners is from another ethnic group that has a matrimonial tradition or when the man is a *huotou* of a village grouping far from Yongning where the inhabitants practice marriage only or he is a merchant who frequents other places and has been exposed to other traditions.

I will cite two examples from my research:

1. In the Ago *gnao lignée* in Ago, in the generation before the oldest generation alive today, there was only one son. Initially, his *lignée* chose a young woman from the AZi *lignée* in Ago. After the first gift, the young man began to visit her openly. With the formal ceremony, they were married. After about a month, following a series of arguments, the woman left and went back to her birth home. Representatives from each *lignée* in the village all judged that she had been wrong to leave in this way. But her *lignée* refused to reimburse the gifts. After this episode, the Ago *gnao lignée* succeeded in adopting a young woman for this son. Unfortunately, in the following generation, once again, there were no girls, only two boys. To rectify this situation, the previous providing *lignée* took the initiative and proposed one of its daughters to the Ago *gnao ignée* as a reimbursement for the first failed marriage. All of the economic requirements were reduced to a minimum: only the receiving *lignée* invited representatives from each *lignée* in the village.

When he was seventy-two, the old man who was married in the above example told me: "Before, practically no one 'prepared the feast.' As for me, my *lignée* did not have the means. Without a sister, we were obliged to bring in a woman. Those who have sisters do not follow this practice. This is the way it has always been and continues to be, even today."

One day, on the side of the road, I was interviewing an eighty-one-year-old woman for my list of the villagers' *açia* from her age-group when the old man mentioned above walked by with a buffalo. The woman said to me in a low voice: "If you want to know someone who has only known one woman in his entire life, he is the only one. After the feast, he never left his house." Before I had time to write this down, she corrected herself: "No, that's not so! Before the feast, he had had several girls, but afterward, only one."

2. In the Dodgo *lignée* in Raimi, there were three generations alive in 1974. Hlamudgima, the oldest daughter in the second generation, did not get along with her mother. Through furtive visits, she had already had two sons. Since she had a sister, she went to cohabit with a Han in 1974, the year of the last matrimonial reform. But the following year, her sister died in childbirth. The newborn was a girl, who died after only six months. The *lignée* tried to adopt a girl but was unable to do so.

When Hlamudgima's mother died, Gézo, her eldest son, was seventeen years old, and he began to make furtive visits. Among his *açia* was the second oldest daughter from the Ago *apo lignée*. Gézo's uncle thought about bringing her to live with them. He expressed this plan to the Ago *lignée*'s great-uncle, who discussed it with his *lignée*'s female chief. Since they had five daughters and two sons, she agreed. After this initial discussion, Gézo began an open relationship with the young woman. About two years later, the wedding took place.

Gézo told me: "If I had sisters, even one sister, we would not have asked Dgima to come. We are counting on having two boys and two girls. It is important to have descendants but also to have a workforce." Gézo's is the only case of spontaneous marriage after 1956.

Within the parameters of my research in 1988 and 1989, there were only five married couples who spanned five generations over more than a century. They were all virilocal, and all came about in response to a lack of female members. As I did in the chapter on cohabitation, to present a more thorough survey, I am going to include statistics for married couples in the nine villages of Batsi, DZybu, Hliwalo, Yumi, Zhongshi, Zhongke, Kaitçi *gewa*, Kaitçi *muwa*, and Naha.

Between 1929 and 1963, there were thirty-five married couples (belonging to all three social strata) in these nine villages, out of which thirty-one were virilocal and four were uxorilocal. Of the thirty-one virilocal couples, twenty-two, or 70.9 percent, resulted from *lignées* that had an only child who was a boy or had only boys. In the remaining nine virilocal couples, there were four cases of men bringing their wives to live with them under the same roof as their brothers and sisters. Among these were one Han commoner, two merchants, and one Na commoner. The other five couples left their original *lignées* and moved into a new house after their marriage; they include one aristocrat, two *huotou*, and two merchants.

Among the uxorilocal cases, three of the four women, or 75 percent, were only children.[4] Three of the four men came from other ethnic groups.

In 1963, these nine villages had 683 adults of an age to procreate (387 women and 296 men). If, from these thirty-five couples, we take away the twelve people (eight men and four women) from other ethnic groups, we are left with fifty-eight married persons in all (thirty-one women and twenty-seven men), or 8.49 percent of the adults of procreating age.

An interesting case deserves mention: one of the marriages cited above took place in a *lignée* that had nine sons. They lived under the same roof, one husband and eight men who practiced the visit. This situation provides a typical example of the function of marriage in most cases: to perpetuate the household.

In the majority of marriages, those of the virilocal type, the reason for marrying is the same as it is for most cohabitations. What is it, then, that would lead someone to choose marriage rather than cohabitation? My sources explained this choice in the following way: "Bringing a woman into your house through the means of *jï the* is a much surer way of keeping her than a simple *ti dzï jï mao the* [cohabitation]." The villagers explained that when a man has sisters and marries, he does so to show off his *lignée*'s wealth, to impress the other villagers, and to earn the respect of society. In fact, many villagers said that the Na pay much attention to wealth. Before 1956, if someone was very rich, he would have a certain superiority over others. People would treat him with respect, even the *zhifu*.

The last important points concerning marriage are as follows: synchronically, within a given generation of a *lignée*, it never happens that all of the brothers or all of the sisters marry nor that all of the brothers and all of the sisters marry; diachronically, a *lignée* that lacks a representative of one of the sexes and therefore has a member marry will generally revert to the custom of the visit in the next generation, once it has children of both sexes or even once it has a girl. Consequently, marriage never occurs successively from one generation to the next within a household.

There is however one exception, and only one: the *zhifu*'s household. I will examine this unique case in the next chapter.

The Norms Regulating Marriage

From this account of marriage, the following norms can be extracted:

1. Spouses must be outsiders, not consanguineal relatives.

2. It is up to the receiving *lignée*'s chief to take the initiative and express its intention to the providing household.

3. Marrying off a member of a household is thought of as giving someone.

4. A formal wedding ceremony and the participation of society are required.

5. The partners become *hinshuba* (husband) and *chumi* (wife); the given person becomes the *mu min* (or the *zo min*) of the receiving *lignée;* the husband and wife and their *lignées* become *krwadhe* to each other, and the husband becomes *krwadhe* to his wife's children, whether he is their genitor or not.

6. After the wedding ceremony, the wife and her children adopt the receiving *lignée*'s name in cases of virilocality; the husband does the same in cases of uxorilocality. When a person who has been given dies, his or her name will be included in the receiving *lignée*'s list of ancestors.

7. In the two modes of residence, the given individual has the right to become chief of the receiving *lignée*.

8. A large gift and a dowry are indispensable especially when the husband's *lignée* is the receiving household.

9. The entire household shares the receiving *lignée*'s possessions and the fruits of their common labor; the household property is passed down collectively from one generation to the next.

10. Husband and wife have the right to end their marriage. Depending on the duration of the marriage, the giving *lignée* must reimburse the gifts, or the couple can share their possessions and their children; the distribution is conducted according to social judgment.

11. Reciprocal sexual privilege and the obligation to respect it exist between husband and wife.

12. Transgressing the sexual privilege is disapproved of when it fails and accepted when it succeeds.

13. Social intervention is necessary to dissolve a marriage.

14. It is taboo for a wife whose husband has ended the marriage to return to her original home.

I will now examine more closely the marriage of the only son as a type.

In the receiving *lignée*, the idea of marrying someone almost always comes from the potential husband's ascendants rather than himself. The *lignée* makes the decision collectively. The chief must express this plan to the chief of the other *lignée*, who will also settle the matter collectively. Because of these practices, marriage appears from the outset to be an affair between groups. Moreover, the intervention of the mediator, the *daba*, and representatives of the *lignées* from both villages, the registration with the *zhifu* (before 1956), and the wedding ceremony itself serve to inform society — including the deceased ancestors — of this union so as to receive its recognition and its protection of the rights and responsibilities of the involved *krwadhe*. What is at stake here is of a social nature.

This kind of marriage includes a series of mechanisms to ensure that the partners will remain together and that their union will be successful: the intervention of representatives from each *lignée* of the future husband's village, who tell him to live peacefully with his future wife forever; the intervention of the mediator, who formalizes the purchase and serves as a witness; the intervention of the *daba*, who transfers not only the body but also the soul of the girl to her husband's home; the return of the wedding gifts if the woman leaves; and the ban on a woman's returning to her original *lignée* if she is repudiated. This modality of sexual life is associated with privileges and duties that implicate all of society, not just the couple and their *lignées*.

In principle, once something has been purchased, it cannot return to its previous owner. A married woman has been sold and should not divorce. We have seen the many measures that are taken when uniting two individuals to avoid a divorce. If the wife does not make enough of an effort for the marriage to succeed, she will be repudiated and fall into the situation of a *baolu*, which is in some ways that of a pariah. The husband must try to behave in such a way that his wife wants to stay and the marriage will succeed. For him, the failure of the marriage would be a catastrophe. The logical result of this matrimonial strategy would be a ban on divorce. But the Na fundamentally value an individual's free will in choosing a way of life. Therefore, with the possibility of divorce, the free will of each individual is respected, but the sanctions are effectively dissuasive.

The rules concerning divorce are interesting. If the union fails shortly after the wedding because the wife is unable to adapt to her new life, her *lignée* is obliged to return the payment so that the receiving *lignée* can form a new union with another *lignée*. When the divorce takes place after many years of marriage, the husband has the right to keep some of the children in exchange for not getting the marriage payment back. The rules are established, in both cases, to ensure the perpetuation of the receiving *lignée*. These rules show that while divorce is permitted, it is conditional and has sanctions. These matrimonial rules are accompanied by coercive measures.

When choosing a wife, a husband places no importance on virginity and does not exclude the children born from her relations with other men before or during the marriage and treats them all fairly. Even husbands who try to monopolize their spouse's sexuality treat the children well because procreation is the goal of the marriage. This characteristic can also be found in cohabitation, as analyzed in chapter 10. But in establishing affectionate ties with one's wife's children so that they will remain in the receiving household forever, what counts more than anything else is that the husband provide for them and take care of them. It makes no difference whether or not he is their genitor. As discussed above, the genitor and the father to the children can be different people. When a married woman's children are the offspring of two kinds of relationships, they belong, without exception, to the husband's household.

We can therefore understand how matrimonial relationships and *açia* can coexist. In response to a *min kru* during a marriage, the couple's attitudes and behaviors are regulated by a mechanism that is practically identical with that of the conspicuous visit. Quite simply, if the husband is always at home, it is not easy for the wife to receive visitors. But when the husband will be away for a few days of work, and presumably visit other women, his foreseen absence constitutes an opportunity for the wife as well. They are on an equal footing in this regard.

In this kind of union, the discourse is explicitly influenced by the ban on sexual evocation. During the wedding, instead of saying to marry someone, they say to give, because matrimonial vocabulary does not exist in Na. What is interesting here is that the Na have not invented words, nor have they borrowed terms from other cultures. In fact, all words concerning marriage refer to emotional life, so they are forbidden under the ban on sexual evocation. Under this taboo, it seems to me, even the idea of inventing a new term cannot enter their minds. Therefore, the procession that fetches the young woman does not bring her to her wedding but invites her for tea. We can see by this that the Na ban on sexual evocation protects their kinship system against the influences of other cultures.

In day-to-day life, the terminology that makes the wife analogous to her partner's granddaughter (or makes the husband analogous to his partner's brother) within the receiving household, the change in her *lignée* name, the secret sexuality of the husband and wife, and the attitudes of the husband and wife, as well as those of the husband toward the children, including the way he addresses them, all point to the fact that everyone in the household behaves as though they were a purely consanguineal *lignée*. Households that include a marriage follow the same code of conduct as pure matrilineal *lignées* do.

In the kinship terminology, the husband is called *ewu* by his wife's children and is therefore another pseudo-*ewu*. In this domain, two new terminological situations arise in relation to normal *lignées*. First, a married man uses the terms sons and daughters to designate his spouse's children. This marks the appearance of paternity. Second, when a married man's sister lives under the same roof as he and his wife, which is rare, she refers to the wife's children as nieces and nephews. Within the kinship terminology, she should call the children of her brother's wife — the pseudo-granddaughter — son and daughter. However, because the children are her brother's, if she referred to them in this manner, it would imply an incestuous relationship. To circumvent this ambiguity, she refers to her brother's children as nephew and niece. The introduction of marriage into a *lignée* that does not lack female members therefore necessitates meticulous adjustments in terminology so that no confusion will arise regarding the incest prohibition.

The symbolic act that the providing *lignée* puts on when it tries to prevent the young woman from leaving as she goes to her future husband's home shows that the household embraces the values of a purely matrilineal *lignée*: it is for solidarity and against separation.

Only in the economic domain does marriage not create great changes. The members of households that include a married couple behave exactly as those that do not. They share the wealth and the fruits of their labor and pass on their property collectively from one generation to the next.

The following rule applies to the distribution of property and children in the case of divorce: the longer the marriage, the more each spouse will receive, and the more children they have had, the more children the husband will get. This division depends on the fruits of their common labor and therefore the duration of the marriage counts for much. The equation they use in this situation is: work = goods + children.

In the majority of cases, the main cause for getting married is a lack of a female representative in a generation.[5] Why is this so? In other words, why is marriage rarely seen in *lignées* with one or more daughters?

For a *lignée* with no female descendants, bringing a woman into the household becomes an absolute necessity. If it is impossible to adopt a consanguineal girl relative, two choices remain: cohabitation and marriage. If the *lignée* is rich, it will lean toward marriage, because of its stability. For *lignées* that lack male descendants, this stability means little, since they can have children through visitors. Cohabitation is sufficient to address the labor-shortage problem. This is why a higher percentage of cohabitations are uxorilocal.

Furthermore, the concept of pure matriliny confers an advantageous and powerful status on the woman in her husband's home, since she can become the household chief. It is therefore in her best interest to remain in a place that enhances her position even more than her original *lignée* did. This, then, encourages virilocal unions. This asymmetry is also due to the Na concept of consanguinity.

In regard to the function of marriage, the most telling fact is

331

that a married man and a married woman are considered the *zo min* and the *mu min* of the receiving *lignée;* that is, they are classified in the same category as a cohabitant would be in such a *lignée*. Since inherent to this terminology is the idea of bringing in someone to perpetuate the household, the essential function of marriage, in the majority cases, is identical with that of cohabitation.

Unlike cohabitants, however, the married *mu min* and *zo min* are no longer friends but *krwadhe* as soon as they move into their partner's home. However, since married individuals will never be consanguineal relatives and the Na have no concept for affinal relatives, *krwadhe* is used figuratively. Moreover, the *krwadhe* relationship between the woman's receiving *lignée* and her original *lignée* is based on her physical presence in the receiving household, not on the union itself.

In this kind of matrimony, a person is passed from one *lignée* to another as a gift. But my sources stated correctly: "We say 'give' when in fact we mean 'sell.'" Actually, this sale is more of an exchange: a woman for material goods. However, because the crisis, as well as its solution are temporary, a receiving *lignée* is never, generally speaking, a giving *lignée* at the same time (with the exception of several dignitaries' households which I will examine later). It follows that this society does not know restricted or generalized exchange. When I refer to marriage as the exchange of a woman for material goods, it is because most receiving *lignées* lack female representatives. In the case of uxorial marriages, the majority of husbands come from other ethnic groups and are living alone in Yongning; therefore, the receiving *lignée* would not even know to whom to allocate the payment.

By uniting a woman with an outside *lignée*, this type of marriage creates a new relationship that, in ethnological terms, can be defined as kinship. This is above all characterized by the ties between husband and wife, as well as by the ties between the husband's *lignée* and that of the wife, without extending to their consanguineal *lignées*. It is also characterized by the ties between the married man and his wife's children.

With the appearance of these ties, the kinship structure of the household changes. Synchronically, when a marriage occurs in a household, ethnologically speaking, kinship = consanguinity + affinity. Diachronically, in the next generation, all household members will follow the custom of the visit exclusively, and the kinship structure will revert to its original composition: kinship = consanguinity. But the household has changed: the consanguineal identity of the providing *lignée* has replaced that of the receiving *lignée*.

If we compare affinity and consanguinity, we see that in this society, affinity is a relationship that people can establish after birth through marriage and that they can dissolve through divorce. In addition, this relationship of affinity will almost certainly disappear after one generation. It is therefore temporary. On the other hand, consanguinity is a relationship that one is born with and that can never be changed or suppressed. It is immutable. In fact, simply because we consider this relationship one of affinity does not mean that the Na consider it so. They have never conceptualized the notion of affinity.

In this kind of marriage, there is a kind of counter-payment to the dowry. This does not, however, constitute an exchange of goods. In the next generation, the receiving *lignée,* once its members die, loses not only its consanguineal identity but all of its material possessions, since the inhabitants of its household are now consanguineal relatives of the providing *lignée*. The end result is exactly the same as that in the adoption of an outsider or in cohabitation. Ensuring the continuation of offerings to the ancestors and the care of the receiving *lignée*'s members during their old age are also motives for marriage. Since the members of the receiving *lignée* know that the extinction of their consanguinity is inevitable, we can see that the perpetuity of the household takes precedence over consanguineal identity for the Na.

Because the marriage modality is not practiced by all of a *lignée*'s generations, nor by all of the *lignée*'s in Na society, it differs from marriage in other societies, where it is practiced by all members all of the time.

The marriage modality appears as a supplementary measure to confront a structural crisis. This crisis most commonly arises for the Na when a *matrilignée* lacks a female descendant. Marriage proves a safer measure than cohabitation because it engenders greater stability. The practice of this modality concerns not only the married couple and their two *lignées*, but the rest of society as well, and it includes coercive measures.

Structurally, in a generation, the practice of this modality transforms a unary kinship (kinship = consanguinity) into a binary kinship (kinship = consanguinity + affinity). In the next generation, the *lignée* changes its consanguineal identity, and the structure of unary kinship is reestablished. The diagram in figure 11.1 illustrates this kinship structure.

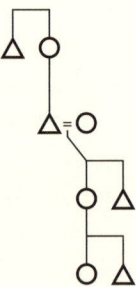

Figure 11.1. Kinship structure in a *lignée* that has a marriage in one generation.

Chapter Twelve

Kinship in the *Zhifu*'s Family

The phenomenon of successive marriages over several generations existed only in the *zhifu*'s family.[1] I will now look closely at
the reasons for these successive marriages.

The Rule for Transmission of Consanguinity and Status

According to the last *zhifu*'s descendants, within their group, consanguinity (*ong*) comes exclusively from the maternal line, as is
true for the other Na.[2] Everyone with the same true female ancestor is consanguineal (*ong hing*). Children are exclusively consanguineal to their mother and are only *krwadhe* to their father.
Between consanguineal relatives, sexuality is forbidden, not to
mention marriage. Sexual relations between father and daughter
are also forbidden.

Children born to the *zhifu*'s official wife (or wives) belonged,
from the moment of birth, to the *zhifu*'s family and enjoyed the
same status (aristocratic) as their father.

Usually, only the eldest son had the right to inherit his father's
position as *zhifu*. But if the *zhifu* died and left no sons, his brother
would inherit his title.[3]

For the eldest son, marriage was an obligation. It was forbidden for him to marry a woman from his mother's consanguineal

group. However, he was allowed to marry a woman from his paternal grandmother's consanguineal group. In practice, the *zhifu*'s wives were all from groups of distinct consanguinity, with the rare exception of a case in which one of the two wives was a daughter adopted from a non-consanguineal *lignée*. They did not therefore share the same "bones." Figure 12.1 shows the possible combinations for the *zhifu*'s family.

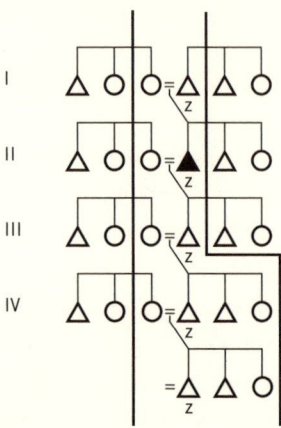

Figure 12.1. The *zhifu*'s family. Z = *zhifu*; the numbers indicate distinct blood groups.

A *zhifu* (consider him Ego, as in figure 12.1) could marry a woman belonging to any social stratum or to another ethnic group. When the *zhifu* married a commoner and she had children, her consanguineal relatives were divided into two strata: commoners and aristocrats. The same held true for the *zhifu*'s family, which contained both aristocrats and commoners (some of the wives).

After marriage, Ego and his wife lived in the *zhifu*'s residence. She was considered to have been given to the *zhifu*'s family (which I will call A). After that, she and her original *lignée* (which I will call B) became *krwadhe* of A.

In the next generation, when Ego's eldest son became the *zhifu* and therefore represented A, B became a consanguineal relative of the representative of A, and of his brothers and sisters, but remained *krwadhe* to the other members of A.

During the transfer of power to the third generation, B became *krwadhe* once again to the representative of A, all the while maintaining a consanguineal relationship to the preceding *zhifu* and to his mother, brothers, and sisters.

Following the death of Ego's eldest son, all relations, consanguineal as well as *krwadhe*, ended between these two households. On the other hand, the consanguineal relationship continued between the consanguineal descendants of Ego's wife and her original *lignée*. In other words, those born of the same true mother remained consanguineal relatives forever. Figure 12.2 illustrates this rule.

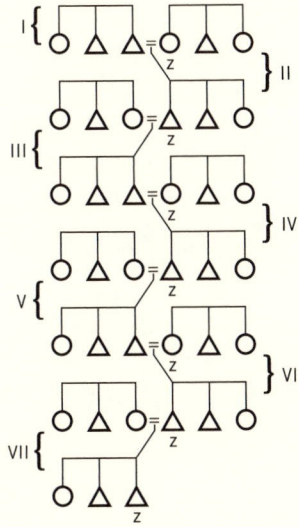

Figure 12.2. The consanguineal relationships in the *zhifu*'s family in successive generations. Z = zhifu; the numbers indicate distinct blood groups.

Branche II

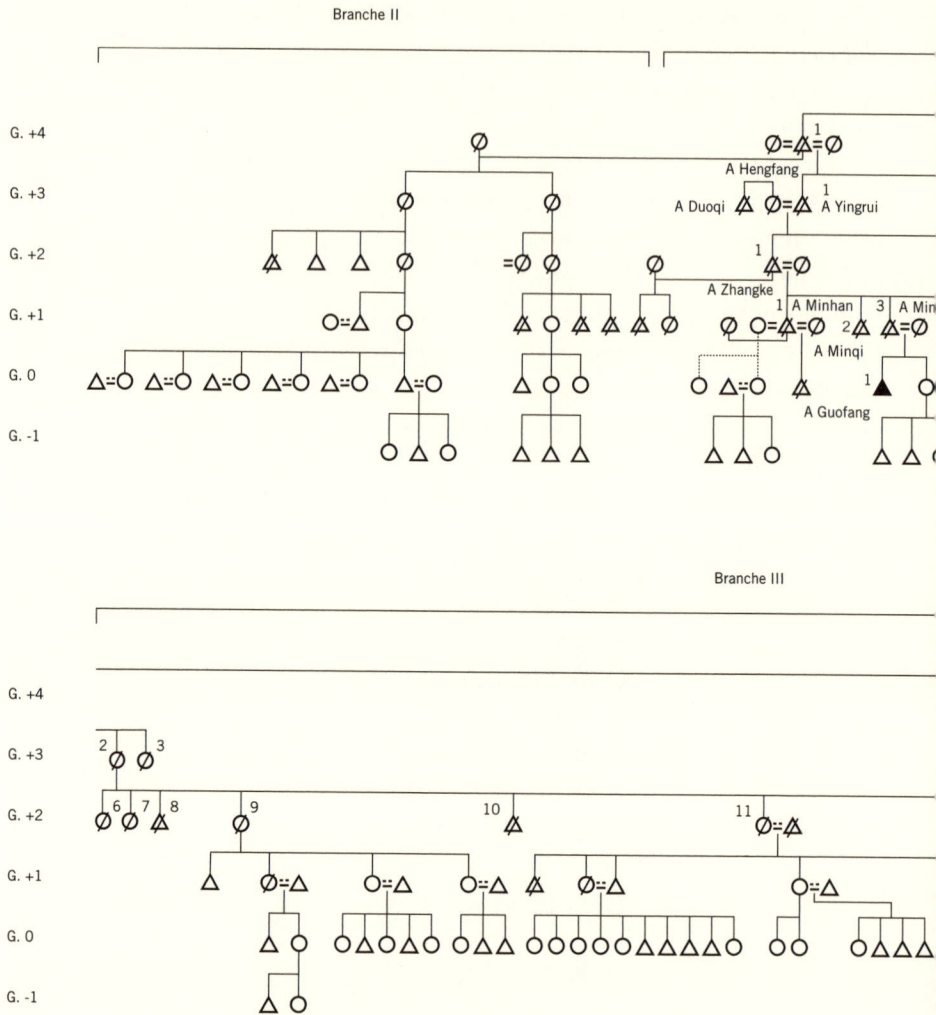

Branche III

Première partie

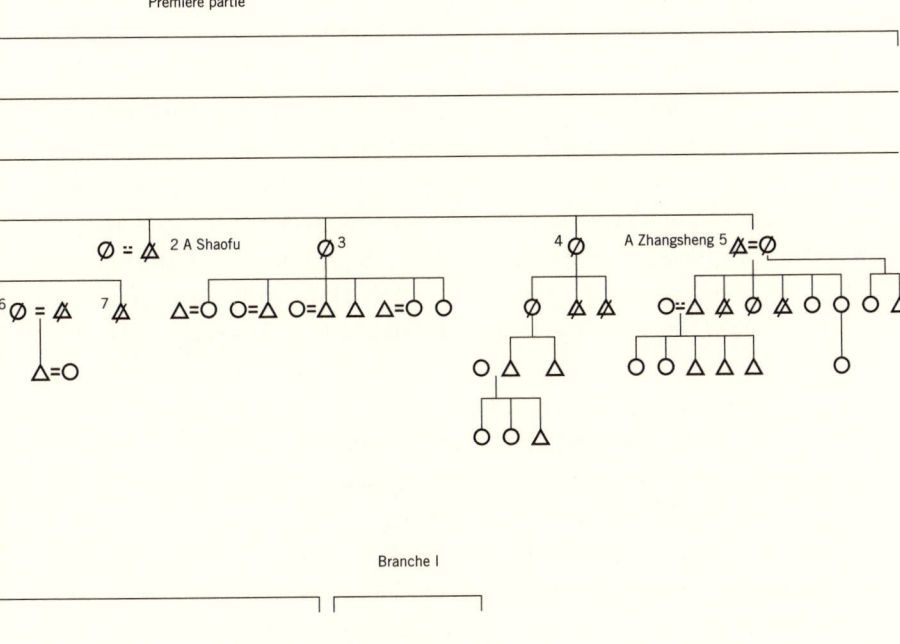

Branche I

Figure 12.3. The genealogy of the *zhifu*'s family.

The Modality of Sexual Life

Since A Hengfang, the oldest person that the descendants of the *zhifu*'s family were able to provide a description of today, all of the *zhifu*'s eldest sons have married. The genealogy that I recorded on the field in 1988–1989 and in 1992 is shown in figure 12.3.

This genealogy includes six generations and twenty-nine households connected to A Hengfang (*zhifu*). I refer to this ensemble of people as the *zhifu*'s group. According to the last *zhifu*'s descendants, it has four parts. I refer to the first part as the trunk, and the three other parts as branches I, II, and III. Gézodondgi (fifty-one years old, generation 0), the last *zhifu*'s eldest son, is considered Ego in this genealogical tree.

I will now examine the modality of sexual life practiced by this group, keeping in mind that, to guarantee the transfer of power, the *zhifu* could resort to polygyny.

A Hengfang (+4.1) had two brothers and no sisters.[4] His first wife was Echedgima from the Chen *bashi lignée*, a Han *lignée* that immigrated to Yongning seven generations ago and is now practically Na. His first two children were girls. As a precaution, A Hengfang married a second wife, a *tusi* daughter from Langqu (the neighboring region), but she was sterile. Fearing he would not have a successor, A Hengfang called in a *daba*, who, through divination, chose a Pumi woman for him from Tuodian (a neighboring region that borders the Jinsha River). This woman, a commoner, already had a son. She married the *zhifu*, and her son, who accompanied her, was adopted by the Busa *lignée* from Kaitçi to perpetuate that household.

This third wife gave birth to A Yingrui (male +3.1), Hlatso (female +3.2), and Naka (female +3.3). A Yingrui succeeded his father. He married Iudgé, the daughter of the general administrator. Since she quickly gave birth to two sons, he did not have to resort to taking more wives. All in all, he had three sons and two daughters. The eldest son, A Zhangke (+2.1), never held the position of *zhifu* because his father outlived him. A Zhangke's first wife was an aristocrat. His first child was a son, and his second a daughter who died eight months after birth. His son had a feeble constitution, so A Zhangke married a second wife as a precaution. It was a good decision: his first son died at fourteen years old, and his second wife gave birth to seven children, four boys and three girls.

The eldest boy, A Minhan (+1.1), replaced his grandfather. A Minhan first married a Tibetan woman, the sister of an influential living Buddha. This marriage, arranged by his father, took place against his will. Several months after the wedding, his wife died. This time, he took extra precautions and married two women, Sonna and Tsïe, at the same time. Sonna belonged to an aristocratic *lignée* connected to the *zhifu*'s family. She was the offspring of an *açia* relationship, and her genitor was A Zhangke, A Minhan's father. She therefore had the same genitor as her husband. Tsïe was from the general administrator's *lignée*. This double marriage was kept a secret; the new brides did not find out about it until their wedding day and were jealous.

Because Sonna was sterile, she was moved out of the *zhifu*'s residence. Tsïe's son died several months after birth. A Minhan died at the age of thirty-eight.

In the absence of a successor, Tsïe, A Minhan's mother, took over and exercised power for two years. Only when she died did A Minzhu (+1.4), her third son, inherit the position. As an adult, A Minzhu had left his father's residence and moved to Batçi, where his ascendants had already prepared a house for him. He then married Dashidgima, a serf with whom he had already had two children while they were in an *açia* relationship.

During the succession in 1949, he returned to his father's residence, where he inherited all of his property, as well as Tsïe, his brother A Minhans's third wife: this is the only known leviratic case. According to A Guofang (Ego in this genealogy), this exception was due to the following circumstances: first, Tsïe was young (thirty-one years old) and in good health, while A Minzhu's wife was in very bad health; and second, being from the powerful family of the general administrator, she held the purse strings of the zhifu's family under A Minhan.

In 1956, the year of the communist succession, A Minzhu was thirty-five years old. He died in prison a few years later. Because of the change in regimes, the family lost its power. A Minzhu had had one son, A Guofang (0.1), and one daughter, Tsïeiuzo (0.2). I refer to the zhifu and all of his descendants since generation +2 as the trunk of this genealogy.

We have seen that a zhifu had recourse to polygyny if his first wife was unable to give him a son and that the function of successive marriages was to ensure that the zhifu had a male descendant to whom he could pass down his power. But was this its only function?

All of the chiefs, the zhifu, the general administrator, and the mkhan-po practiced, without exception, açia and dhu zï dhu mi relationships before marriage. After marriage, they continued to practice furtive visits. Taking advantage of their power and prestige, they openly and easily had their valets bring pretty women into the residence for the night. When they traveled, they were accompanied by charming female companions. All of the chiefs from the different generations had several dozen or even a hundred mistresses and were known for their exploits in this domain. For example, according to my sources, "A Yingrui [a zhifu who married only one woman] and A Duoqi [the general administrator] were very famous throughout all of the villages, far and wide, for the number of lovers they had."

Among the women chosen, most of them accepted willingly, a few reluctantly. They could not refuse. However, even though

342

they visited their *zhifu*, their reputations were not blemished. On the contrary, the women were honored.

These aristocrats could even choose, if they so desired, women in open relationships, which they were then required to end. Moreover, women involved with the chiefs were discouraged from having other visitors at the same time. For example:

1. Dashi (male) risked meeting Nadgo while she was being frequented by the former *mkhan-po*. He was caught and was required to pay a fine of one mule and one rifle to the injured party.

2. Ishi took up with Badgi, a young woman from his village and an *açia* of the general administrator, while the general administrator was away. When the general administrator found out about it, he felt that his honor had been sullied and blamed it on the young lover, who, as a result, lost an ear and was condemned to pay a fine of two mules.

3. A Minzhu had a relationship with Iudgé, the daughter of the *tusi* of Qiansuo. While Ishi was passing through Qiansuo, he formed an *açia* with Iudgé. Sometime later, with the help of Niche (another young man), Iudgé went to Ishi's house. When A Minzhu found out about it, he fined Ishi 15 *liang* of gold (about 1 pound) and Niche 100 *yuan* (*bankai*).

Two chiefs, however, could visit the same woman during the same period as an *açia* or a *dhu mi*. A Minzhu and A Shaoyun, for example, took turns visiting Sigedgima during a certain period.

Many children were born from these visits by the chiefs. But they always belonged to their mother's *lignée* and to her social stratum. They were strangers to the chiefs and had nothing to do with their genitors.

Like her husband, the *zhifu*'s wife had *açia* before she married. However, once she was married, since her official responsibility was to provide sons for the *zhifu* so that he would have a successor, and it was absolutely necessary that there be no question about the identity of the genitor and therefore the legitimacy of his eldest son as the heir apparent, she was required to end her furtive relationships. This constraint was imposed not only by her husband but also by herself, or rather, she voluntarily restrained herself because to have children with her husband, especially sons, had two advantages: first, it reinforced her position within the *zhifu*'s family, and second, bringing an heir into the world, an aristocratic descendant, increased the standing of her consanguineal identity. Once this task was completed, she no longer needed to restrain herself and could take up *açia* relationships once again, especially when her husband, who was often occupied with his mistresses, no longer paid attention to her. But the degree of her freedom was limited in relation to that of her husband. For example:

1. The only wife of A Yingrui (a monogamous *zhifu* with a reputation for having had many lovers) was already seeing Gouni as an *açia*, the *daba* who officiated at rituals for the *zhifu*'s family. Bousa, a frequent guest at the residence, became her new lover. He was very possessive and ended up strangling his rival on the *zhifu*'s property. The *zhifu*, fearing that the affair would damage his reputation, forbade any witnesses of the murder to talk about it. Because of this, Bousa was never condemned.

2. Dgima, the first wife of A Minhan, had had several *açia* before she married. After she was married, she carried on a relationship with A Minqi, A Minhan's second brother. Full of rage, A Minhan, accompanied by two large armies, went after A Minqi and even had him fired at. After this episode, A Minqi broke off his relationship with Dgima.

The wives of other chiefs also pursued furtive relationships after they were married. The degree of their sexual freedom was, however, limited, as the following anecdotes illustrate:

344

1. Before her marriage, Sonna, the first wife of A Shaoyun, was the *açia* of the *mkhan-po* and had a child with him. After she was married, she had furtive relationships with the servants.

2. Ana, the wife of Nazo (A Shaoyun's brother), had several lovers after she married. She had three children, and only the eldest boy was from her husband. She formed *açia* relationships whenever she pleased, so that from time to time she was placed in quarantine in the general administrator's residence. In the meantime, her youngest son was sent off with the valets to look after the trading caravans.

Prestige, however, would also work in a wife's favor. If she was from an influential home, and her husband was not a powerful aristocrat, she could take greater liberties. For example:

1. Sona, A Shaoyun's older sister, was married to an aristocrat from Zébo. Several days after the wedding ceremony, she returned to her birth home and took up once again an *açia* lifestyle, seeing several men and giving birth to two daughters as a result.

2. Adgi, a daughter from the aristocratic Gepai *lignée* in Bodzi, was married to an aristocrat from Langqu, but she found her husband both too tall and too ugly. After a while, she could no longer stand him and returned to her birth home, where she once again took up an *açia* lifestyle.

Unlike their husbands, chiefs' wives did not have the freedom openly to form relationships with their lovers. The chiefs knew very well that their wives received visitors, and as long as these relationships were discreet, they would be tolerant. Therefore, in contrast with their husbands, the women were simultaneously involved in marriage and in furtive visits only. This asymmetry between husband and wife stemmed from political power.

I will now examine the sexual modalities practiced by the

brothers and sisters in each generation and their descendants.

In each generations, the *zhifu*'s sisters (nine in three generations) and brothers (seven in four generations) were required to leave his residence and move elsewhere when they were, at the very latest, twenty-seven or twenty-eight years old. In their situation, marriage or cohabitation necessarily brought about neolocal residence. In general, they were free to choose whatever sexual modality they desired, however, the father sometimes intervened to arrange a strategic marriage.

Custom permitted the youngest sons to marry or cohabit with women belonging to any social stratum. The rule for residence was therefore virilocal. The daughters only enjoyed this freedom of choice among strata when cohabiting. If they married, the preferred choice for a husband was an aristocrat; therefore, the rule for residence was also virilocal.

Six of the sisters practiced the *açia* mode exclusively, and three married aristocrats from Yongning, but one of them ended her marriage and returned to an *açia* life. Of the brothers, four married, and three lived in *açia* relationships.

In the +4 generation, A Hengfang had two brothers. One of them, Echedudgï (+4.2), was adopted by an aristocratic *lignée* from Baodzi that had no descendants. He married and had four children who never married. The eldest, Dgïmahlamu (female +3.4), only had a daughter, Agema. Agema had no children, and therefore adopted Tsïe, a consanguineal relative. Tsïe then cohabited with a woman from Zébo. Bimahlatso (+3.5), Dgïmahlamu's younger sister, had a boy who died when he was young. Finally, A Hengfang's younger brother (+4.3) became a Lamaist monk. He lived in the *zhifu*'s residence his entire life.

I refer to Echedudgï and the group of his descendants as branch I. The last *zhifu*'s descendants do not consider the current descendants of branch I consanguineal relatives or *krwadhe*.

We know that Echedgima, the first wife of A Hengfang (+4.1), gave birth to two girls: Dgima and Sonna, who, with their mother, left their birth home. I refer to these three women and their descendants as branch II. Both Dgima and Sonna had children. At the birth of generation +1, this branch divided into two *lignées*. Until then, Sonnadgima, Sonna's daughter, was the only one in both of these *lignées* to be married, in this case to the second son of the *tusi* of Zuo-suo. (For the descendants of this branch, see figure 12.3.) The members of this branch are not consanguineal relatives of the last *zhifu*'s descendants, but they are *krwadhe*, even today.

Let us now look at Hlatso (+3.2), A Yingrui's sister, and her descendants. When they reached adulthood, A Yingrui's two sisters, Hlatso and Naka (female +3.3), left home. Initially, they moved in together. But after two years, angry with each other, they separated into two households.

Hlatso's father, A Hengfang, wanted her to marry the *tusi* of Langqiu. A Duoqi, the general administrator at the time, was one of her *açia,* and she had had two children by him. He opposed this marriage and proposed that she marry him instead. Hlatso refused and set herself up in a cohabitation with Sige, a serf, braving the disapproval of her father. In the end, it was her younger sister Naka who established a conspicuous relationship with A Duoqi.

Hlatso had nine children from various visitors: four girls and five boys. Her daughter Nadgo (+2.12) refused a marriage proposal from A Zhangshen (+2.5.)[5] She became involved in an incestuous relationship with Sonna (+2.8), her brother. They had four children together. At the time, this scandal was sensational news, known throughout all of the villages. The general administrator wanted to punish them, but the *zhifu* looked the other way. They were never punished, and of their four children, one son is still alive today. The only life that Hlatso's daughter Judgédgima (+2.9) knew was that of an *açia*. She had four children. Her eldest

347

son was the offspring of a Chen *bashi*, her oldest daughter was the offspring of a Tibetan, and her two youngest children were the offspring of a Lamaist monk. Among them, only the youngest daughter married. Her husband was a *huotou* living on the banks of the Jingsha River, where the habitants have a strong tendency toward marriage. Hlatso's daughter Tsïe (+2.11) left her birth house to cohabit with Dudgi in Zhongshi. Hlatso's son Jishi (+2.14) cohabited with a woman named Tsïe.

I will refer to Hlatso and her descendants as branch III. In this branch, there was only one marriage (see figure 12.3). This branch is still considered *krwadhe* by the *zhifu*'s descendants but not consanguineal relatives.

I will now return to the body of this genealogy.

In the +2 generation, A Yingrui's second son, A Shaofu (+2.2), became the *mkhan-po*, chief of the Lamaist religion in the region, and lived in the temple. He had a reputation for having many *açia*. As a Lamaist chief, he was not allowed to marry. When A Shaofu was fifty years old, his nephew, returning from Tibet, took over, and A Shaofu finally brought one of his *açia*, Getu (a serf from Zébo) to cohabit with him, and they lived in a house that was part of the monastery.

Once Dgima (+2.3) left the *zhifu*'s residence, she moved to Tozhi and had *açia* relationships exclusively. She had six children, out of which two girls and two boys got married, and the two others practiced *açia* relationships.

Nadzi (+2.4) moved to Kaitçi and had *açia* relationships for her entire life. The same was true for her children.

A Zhangshen (+2.5), the third son, moved to Tozhi. He married a commoner from the *lignée* of a Chen *bashi*. Before marrying, this woman had already had two children with different *açia*. A Zhangshen did not want his wife to bring them to the house. They therefore stayed in their original household but were nonetheless *ong hing* in relation to the children produced by A Zhang-shen, since they had the same mother. They were therefore considered *krwadhe* to A Guofang. "If these two people were not born of the same mother as the descendants of A Zhangshen," A Guofang told me, "they would not be thought of as *krwadhe*."

A Zhangshen's marriage produced five children, none of whom married. The eldest son completed his studies in Lijiang and taught in an elementary school. He later cohabited with one of his *açia*.

In the generation +1, A Mingqi (+1.2) took over the role of *mkhan-po* from his paternal uncle, once he completed his studies in Tibet. He also practiced the *açia* life.

Nadgo (+1.4), after having had *açia* relationships, married A Shaoyun, the general administrator. Because she did not tolerate her new life very well, she frequently returned to the *zhifu*'s residence to receive furtive visitors. Among her *açia* was a Chen *bashi*, whose genitor was A Zhangke, her own father, yet one more case in which two lovers share the same genitor. She also fell in love with Atçi, a serf, and their relationship lasted for five years. When her husband found out, he ended their marriage and Atçi was fined two rifles and a mule. Afterward, Nadgo returned to the *zhifu*'s residence and stayed until 1956. Without the communist succession, she would have had to move somewhere else.

Iudgé (+1.5), after having had *açia* relationships, including one with a Chen *bashi*, with whom she had had a daughter, married Jishi, a man from the general administrator's family. She brought her daughter with her. Dgima (female +1.6) married an aristocrat from Zébo. Dinba (+1.7) only had *açia* relationships. He is the only one who did not leave the house. My sources said that it was "because he was still young and idle."

Leaving is the rule for all of the *zhifu*'s children. The last *zhifu*'s descendants explained that the aim of this rule was to preserve the peace between brothers and sisters, as well as between their descendants, who, being consanguineally distinct, might fight if they continued to live together.

My sources explained the matrimonial tradition of the *zhifu*'s group in the following manner: "If some of them get married, it is to show off their wealth and their capacity to get even richer. They do not have to get married. The others, they get married because they are lacking a female or a male member in their *lignée*." In the first case, the marriage usually provokes a separation in the *lignée*, since the groom's sisters almost never get along with the bride. Just as cohabitation tends to provoke a breakup of the male cohabitant's *lignée*, so does marriage, and for the same reason: matriliny excludes outsiders.

Finally, all married people, including members of the *zhifu*'s family and their descendants, practiced the visit at the same time.

In the generations +4 to +1 of this genealogy, there were sixty-two people (twenty-seven women and thirty-five men, not including the outside wives and outside female cohabitants) older than seventeen in 1956. In this pool, fourteen, or 22.58 percent, were married (five women and nine men). Eight people (five women and three men), or 12.9 percent, cohabited. Those who practiced the visit exclusively were 64.4 percent of the total.

Most of the members of *lignées* that have separated from the *zhifu*'s family do not practice marriage, for two main reasons: first, the modality of the visit is customary, and second, marriage frequently involves a separation in the *lignée*. and therefore a division of property. Because *lignées* do not generally have increasing land resources, they would become poor after only a few generations at best and risk being demoted to the rank of commoner or, indeed, even that of serf. In this instance, marriage clashes not only with custom but also with their economic and social interests.

For members of aristocratic *lignées* (except for those in which there is a lack of female descendants) who enjoy a strong political position and therefore a strong economic position, marriage serves to display their wealth and to bring them even more social prestige. But for those who have not succeeded in political life, marriage can ruin their *lignées*. Because of this, marriage provokes both positive and negative responses, depending on one's social and economic position.

Besides the households included in the genealogy of the *zhifu*'s group, there were seventeen aristocratic households that claimed to derive from the *zhifu*'s family but were unable to trace the connection. I recorded their genealogies as best as they were able to recall them, and they included, at the very most, five generations. Within these generations, there were 158 people (80 females and 78 males) older than seventeen (including the deceased), out of which 32, or 20.2 percent, were married (15 women and 17 men). Twenty people (16 women and 4 men), or 12.7 percent, cohabited, and 108 people, or 67.1 percent, lived exclusively in the visit modality. These statistics point to two things: the majority of members in the *zhifu*'s group did not marry, and those that did continued to practice the custom of the visit. For them, marriage coexisted with the furtive and/or open visit.

Daily Behavior

I will now look at the daily behavior of aristocrats. In the *zhifu*'s house, the ban on sexual evocation was strictly respected, just as with the rest of the Na. They had to avoid any allusions to their love life. Until A Yingrui, the *zhifu* and his wife still lived in the *Zimi* (the traditional main house), each with his or her own place for sleeping. Changes did not come about until A Zhangke took over and began to imitate the Han lifestyle. At the beginning of the twentieth century, he had a group of houses built, using Han architecture, that served as both a dwelling and an office. He installed a Han bed, the first double bed in Yongning. When A Minhan became *zhifu*, he inherited this bed. At the time, even his brother A Minzhu did not own one like it.

The place to the right of the lower hearth was reserved for the *zhifu*, and the place to the left for his wife, no matter what her original stratum might have been. After the *zhifu*'s death, his successor would take this place or, if there was not a successor, the regent. The same arrangement held true for the other sons in their own households (in cases of marriage or cohabitation). However, after their deaths, their wives would take this place to the right of the fire. This rule applied to the daughters, wives, and female cohabitants of aristocrats. On the other hand, if the sons lived with a commoner, they automatically had the place on the right.

When an aristocratic woman married a nonaristocratic man, she took the place on the right. There is only one example of this, and it was a virilocal residence. This kind of marriage was discouraged, for the descendants would belong to the stratum of the husband, which was considered a decline.

In households where no one married, the oldest brother took the place on the right, and the sister took the place on the left. This is the case with A Guofang today.

This custom of giving the most important place to the *zhifu*, or to the husband or the brother, shows that the principal member of aristocratic households is male.

Inheritance

Within the *zhifu*'s *lignée*, the eldest son inherited his father's title as well as most of his property. The other sons, when they left the residence, would usually be given an administrative position ruling over several villages, as well as money, land, houses, livestock, serfs, and so on. They lived independently. Usually, the younger sons inherited less than the eldest son did. However, there is a counterexample of this that deserves attention. When A Zhangke died, A Minhan, his eldest son, who was twenty-two at the time, became *zhifu*. A Zhangshen, A Zhangke's younger brother and A Minhan's uncle, was only twenty-four years old and had not yet left the *zhifu*'s residence. When he did leave and moved to Tozhi, he took all of the valuable objects and more than half of the material goods from the *zhifu*'s residence. While he was extremely upset, A Minhan could not do anything about it, in spite of his position as *zhifu*, "because A Zhangshen is his *ewu* [paternal uncle]." As my sources explained: "An *ewu* is an *ewu*! For us, there are no exceptions to the principle of respect for one's *ewu*."

In the *zhifu*'s residence, only paternal uncles were present. The children did not have daily contact with their maternal uncles. They knew that these uncles were their father's brothers, but they adopted the same respectful attitude. Therefore, a paternal uncle was not only called by the same kinship term (*ewu*) as a maternal uncle; he was also identified with the maternal uncle. They enjoyed the same status in relation to the descendants of their brothers as they did in regard to their sisters' children. In fact, the nephews' attitudes toward their uncles showed no distinction between maternal and paternal uncles.

When the daughters left the *zhifu*'s residence to live in *açia* relationships or to cohabit, they were also entitled to receive certain material possessions, just as their married or cohabiting brothers were (with the exception of the eldest son), and were sometimes given a position as *huotou*, but this was rare. When a daughter married another aristocrat, she received a large dowry from her parents in the form of money as well as other material goods, but she did not receive land, livestock, or a house.

Kinship Terminology for the Zhifu

Kinship terminology in the *zhifu*'s *lignée* was the same as that for commoners and serfs (the base terminology), except for the addition of four new terms: *hinshuba, chumi, abo,* and *abò.* According to my sources, the word *abo* is borrowed from the Pumi.

Male Ego (for generation 0) called his brother's wife *Rumi* and his sister's husband by his first name.[6] Male Ego called his wife *chumi* and referred to his sisters-in-law and brothers-in-law as though they were his own sisters and brothers: he used *amu* for those older than he, regardless of their gender, *gumi* for females who younger than he, and *gézi* for males younger than he. He used the same terminology for his wife's ascendants as she did, that is, the general terminology. For the +1 generation on his mother's side, male Ego called all females *emi* and all males *ewu,* just as he would have in a pure *matrilignée.*

On the other hand, there were two modes of address for his mother's spouse: *ewu* and *abò.* Therefore, A Minghan called his father (the *zhifu*) *abò,* while A Guofang and his sister called their father, the *zhifu*'s brother, *ewu,* even after he became *zhifu* when his older brother died. I found that the term varied, depending on whether or not the *zhifu* was the eldest brother.

Male Ego called his father's sisters *emi* and his father's younger brothers *ewu* or *abo.* If his father's sisters and brothers married, their husbands were called *ewu,* and their wives were called *emi.*

In the +2 generation, all of the females were called *eyi,* and all of the males were *apu.* Members of the +3 generation were all called *esï,* regardless of their gender. Ego called all of the +4 generation *ala.* Male Ego called any members of the generations beneath generation 0 by their first name.

In the −1 generation, the daughters born directly from the couple were *mu,* and the sons were *zo.* If the daughter was married and lived virilocally, her husband was considered a *mu bu hin-*

shuba (daughter's husband). The son's wife was considered a *zo bu chumi* (son's wife) and called *Rumi*. In the −2 generation, the females were *Rumi,* and the males were *Ruwu*. The words *mu* (daughter), *zo* (son), *Rumi* (granddaughter) and *Ruwu* (grandson) were only terms of reference.

Female Ego called her spouse *hinshuba*. She referred to the others with the same nomenclature used by her husband.

All in all, this nomenclature of kinship included nineteen terms.

This kinship terminology is characterized by the following points: *hinshuba, chumi, abo,* and *abò* correspond to the existence of marriage; *hinshuba* and *chumi* are only terms of reference, because of the rule forbidding sexual evocation; a man has his own sons and daughters, but the term that the children use to designate their father is borrowed, not Na; and the terms of kinship for pure *matrilignées* are the foundation for this terminology. Of course, these kinship terms are used here to designate not only the mother's consanguineal relatives but also, and above all, non-consanguineal individuals.

About the Zhifu's Kinship Group

Until 1956, the *zhifu*'s family and members of branches II and III would gather in each of their homes on a rotating basis during *bu sï nin;* the annual service of offerings to the ancestors. This ritual was carried out just as it was in other Na lineages. However, the *zhifu*'s group did not have a name for its lineage. Branch I never participated in their ritual, for it was no longer part of this group.

During the ritual of offerings to the ancestors in the *zhifu*'s home, taking 1956 as a reference point, to the right of the lower hearth in the main room, a *daba* would recite the names of the twenty-six *zhifu* who had preceded A Mingzhu. After saying each name, he would place a piece of meat and a little grain in a bowl.

Then this bowl and another one full of water were placed on a tray, and the *daba* would pass it to the *zhifu*'s wife, who would bring it out to the courtyard and throw the food and the water onto the roof of the main house for the ancestors.

The other two branches would also have the names of the *zhifu* recited. However, for branch II, before reaching A Heng-fang, the *daba* would begin with the two generations of female ancestors, and a tray containing plates of meat, vegetables, grain, and water would be thrown on the roof of the main house for these ancestors. Then a second tray for A Hengfang and his ascendants would be prepared and thrown on the roof of the building that faced the main house, since these people did not die in this branch's house. Branch III would also begin by reciting the names of female ancestors. The offerings were prepared and given in the same manner as they were for branch II.

Currently, since there is not a *daba*, A Guofang officiates at this annual ritual for his *lignée*. He begins by reciting the three generations on his mother's side, and his sister carries the offerings to them. On his father's side, he does not recite any names further back than his father. As for A Minhan's second wife, Sonna, on her mother's side, she makes offerings to three generations, and on her husband's side, she recites only her husband's name and his father's name. The offerings are thrown onto the two roofs in the same manner as described above. For this ritual, the descendants of branches II and III include only their female ancestors.

For a long time now, the other aristocratic *lignées* have been making offerings to their matrilineal consanguineal ancestors only, and to the wife who used to live in their *lignée*'s house (if marriage has occurred), but not to those who left their birth homes to marry or cohabit.

Today, as a result, there are no *lignées* that make offerings to any *zhifu* before A Yingrui (him included). This phenomenon can be explained in part by the events of 1956, the year the communist authorities banished the *zhifu*'s entire family and occupied his residence. I know of one Na household that only makes offerings to ancestors who died in the house they are now living in.

While aristocratic *lignées* like the *zhifu*'s family do not make up a lineage, they do all belong to the *Gwe lhe*, one of the four legendary *lignées*. To join their ancestors, all of their deceased must follow the itinerary of this legendary *lignée*. That commoner and serf *lignées* also belong to the *Gwe lhe* proves that social stratification occurred quite late.

This description makes it clear that for the *zhifu*'s descendants, the rule of consanguinity remains purely matrilineal. However, for the other elements of kinship, such as rights to the children, the transfer of title and family name, residence and inheritance, and belonging to the legendary *Gwe lhe*, the rules are paternal. Therefore, the children have two opposing identities: one that is consanguineal and counted in the maternal line, and one that is familial and counted in the paternal line. This opposition is essentially one between the rule of matrilineal consanguinity and the rule of hereditary chiefdom in the paternal line. Because of this opposition, throughout the centuries, the *zhifu*'s family had two sides. First of all, a male chief had his own children, and these children took his name and formed a group with him. They lived together under the same roof and were an economic unit. They shared the same resources and material goods. However, they also formed a kinship unit in which a consanguineal relationship existed only between the mother and her children. But in this family, the relationship of consanguinity never continued for more than two generations. Herein lies its distinctive feature.

This distinctiveness brings us to the second side: through this interalliance, *matrilignées* gave a woman, and therefore a son, to the *zhifu*'s family. With the passing centuries, *matrilignée* A gave

357

to a *zhifu* a woman who bore a son, this son then married a woman offered by *matrilignée* B, the son of this wife then married a woman from *matrilignée* C, and so on. As a result, after the first generation, the *zhifu*'s original *lignée* was made up exclusively of these women and their children. They provided the power and the name of the founder of the *zhifu*'s family. Therefore, with each generation, the power changed hands, as though these *matri-lignées* shared the power between them. Each one represented the *zhifu*'s family in a given generation. In other words, since there was not a consanguineal relationship between father and son, power was transmitted from one *krwadhe* to another. We can therefore see that over the course of history, groups of different consanguinity came to share power, as figure 12.2 illustrates.

That each *matrilignée* represented the *zhifu*'s household for a short period of time helps to explain why the *zhifu*'s family placed the *zhifu*'s wife's consanguineal relatives who remained in her original household (where there were four generations at most, beginning with the *zhifu* of the moment) outside the *zhifu*'s kin-ship group and why only those *lignées* that had separated from the *zhifu*'s family two generations earlier were exempt from paying taxes and excused from the duty of working the public land.

When aristocratic *lignées* that originated long ago in the *zhifu*'s family have declined to the rank of commoners, this rule of kin-ship exclusion plays an important role, beyond its political and economic functions. This rule is controlled by the principle of matriliny. In other words, the rule of familial identity that counts in a paternal line is based on matriliny, according to which con-sanguineal relatives will remain kin forever, while the relationship between *krwadhe* is only temporary. Therefore, matriliny takes precedence over paternal rule, and the kinship of the family al-ways functions, in spite of its appearing patrilineal, in conformity to the matrilineal principle.

Because chiefdom in the *zhifu*'s family disappeared while matrilineal consanguinity continues, after several generations, the *zhifu* existed only in the archives, with no living person to serve them something to eat during the service of offerings to the ancestors.

That marriage was not an obligation for all of the *zhifu*'s children, but only for the eldest son, shows that the successive marriages of the eldest son functioned to transfer the *zhifu*'s power from generation to generation within the household. Was this, then, its only function? Before answering this question, I will first examine the conduct of aristocrats outside the *zhifu*'s group.

The General Administrator's Household

According to my sources' recollections, the position of general administrator was appointed to members of the Dashi *lignée* from Dashi and to members of the Rishi *lignée* from Zhongshi. Beginning at the end of the nineteenth century, this position was transferred from one member to another within an aristocratic *lignée* in Dapo. The *zhifu* always assigned this post. In imitation of the governmental system, the position was passed down from father to son. However, the *zhifu* did not copy the court's legislation of the transfer of power exactly. An adopted son could also inherit his father's position.

For example, Luzozonba, the eldest son, replaced his father. He practiced the *açia* modality his entire life. Consequently, he was obliged to find a successor. A Hengfang's second wife was the offspring of a *tusi* from Langqiu. Before her marriage, she had given birth to Judgédgima and A Duoqi, that is, to two "illegitimate children." Since the Nahing in Langqu are a patrilineal society, these two children found themselves in an awkward situation. Since Luzozonba had no descendants and was in need of a successor, he adopted them. A Duoqi, an adopted son, therefore rose to the position of general administrator.

Marriage, then, was not a requirement for the general administrator. Nor was it a requirement for any of the other *lignées* derived from the *zhifu*'s household. Even if the administrator's transfer of power was conducted from father to son in imitation of the mode of transfer used by the *zhifu*, the possibility of adoption allowed for the avoidance of marriage.

The Displacement of Power

In the next generation, Judgédgima (the adopted daughter) married A Yingrui, and A Duoqi married three women, including A Hengfang's daughter Naka, thereby forming a double alliance between the *zhifu*'s family and the general administrator's. A Yingrui and A Duoqi therefore became maternal uncles for the following generation of the *zhifu*'s family. This was a promotion in kinship for A Duoqi, one that was manifested in A Yingrui's eldest grandson A Minghan's becoming *zhifu* and A Duoqi's not dismounting from his horse when he rode past the *zhifu*'s residence and not having to kneel when he went there. He was therefore nicknamed the standing chief. My sources explained this situation in the following way: "The great-uncle was the general administrator, and the great-nephew was the *zhifu*. As far as we are concerned, there is no reason for a maternal great-uncle to be afraid of his great-nephew!" After this period, the *zhifu*'s power was weakened, and the center of gravity of that power gradually shifted to the general administrator.

In the next generation, A Shaoyun, A Duoqi's second son, inherited his father's position because his older brother died at the age of twenty. Before he took over as general administrator, he married his sister, Sonna (whose mother was not a consanguineal relative of A Shaoyun's mother), and moved in with her (uxorilocal residence) in Dapo. When he was chosen to succeed his father, he moved to the general administrator's residence. Sonna died when she was twenty-nine years old, without having had a child. A Shaoyun then married Nadgo, A Zhangke's daughter, and later he married Huang Jizhen (a Naxi) and Bima (a serf). Not one of them had any children.

During this era, the *zhifu*'s power fell definitively into the hands of A Shaoyun, the *zhifu*'s uncle. He even went so far as to take possession of the *zhifu*'s seal and genealogy (in Chinese), a sign of power in the eyes of the central government. In fact, his family had neither an official seal nor a written genealogy.

This displacement of power illustrates that in political life respect for the *zhifu*'s power was, under normal circumstances, a convention for all of the Na, including the aristocrats. However, when this convention conflicted with the Na tradition of absolute respect for the uncle, the matrilineal custom prevailed. Na moral standards determine attitudes.

That A Duoqi and A Shaoyun easily succeeded in using Na customs to manipulate interpersonal relationships and politics leads me to conclude that in their usurping of the *zhifu*'s power, the conception of kinship, in addition to their politically advantageous positions and their personal skill, played an important role.

The Modality of Sexual Life for the Last Zhifu's *Descendants*

In 1956, the year of democratic reform, the *zhifu*'s family lost its power. In 1961, after completing his studies at the school in Lijiang and later working for three years as a bricklayer, A Guofang (Ego, the last *zhifu*'s eldest son), who was at that time twenty-one years old, returned to Yongning. He lived with his sister. The following is a transcript of one of our conversations:

"Will you tell me something about your life ? Who gave you your first name?"

"Our Na first names are given to us by the living Buddha, our Han first names by the Han secretary that my uncle [A Minhan] had brought in from Heqing [a Han region]. Since my father's older brother had no sons and since I was the only boy in my generation, I was the only possible heir. Ever since I was eight years old, my grandmother had me live with her in the *zhifu*'s residence, before my father succeeded his brother. She adored me. After A Minhan died, my grandmother became the regent for two years. During that period, A Shaoyun, the general administrator, wanted A Zhangshen to take over. My second uncle, the *mkhan-po* and the *tusi* of Zuo-suo [also a Na], was against this idea. Therefore, in the end, it was my *ewu* [his father] who became *tusi*.

"I went away to school when I was eight years old and received my diploma when I was fifteen. Between 1958 and 1960, there was a famine. I went to Lijiang to work as a bricklayer. After returning to Yongning, I lived with my sister. I worked to feed my entire *lignée*. My sister was busy taking care of her children, who were still young."

"Does your sister follow the custom of the visit or ... "

"She lives a life of the visit. All of her children are the offspring of the men who visited her."

"And you?"

"I practice the visit, too. Outside, I have had many *açia*, but I only have visiting relations with them, because when you have a sister at home, you cannot bring another woman into the house. That is our Na custom."

"According to tradition, the eldest son of the *zhifu* must marry. Why not you?"

"In some ways, it's because of the circumstances of life, especially because the *tusi* regime is completely over now. I never thought about being a *tusi*. It's true, the *tusi*'s eldest son used to have to get married. But today this rule no longer exists. We only think of survival."

"You see different *açia* simultaneously?"

"Yes, sometimes, during certain periods. But for the most part, I see one after another."

"Do you still have relationships with them?"

"No. For several years now, I have not visited anyone."

"Have you ever thought about getting married?"

"No. Why would I? The mode of the visit is our custom. Ever since my father was put in prison, my sister and I have lived together. My sister has four children. We are bringing them up together. If I were to marry, I would have to separate from my sister, and she would be unable to raise the children all by herself. Therefore, I live with her, and, conforming to our tradition, I visit other women."

"What do you think of marriage today?"

"If I got married, I would have to move in with others. I feel that my sister is closer to me than any other woman I have known. I prefer living with my nieces and nephews and my sister. I'm better off this way."

Today, A Guofang's sister's older son and older daughter are also following the custom of the visit. The younger son and daughter are not yet sexually active.

The communist succession in 1949 gave rise to many changes in China. The new regime put an end to the practice of marriage in the *zhifu*'s family. In fact, A Guofang's sister said: "At the time of the democratic reforms, we no longer resembled human beings. How could we marry? If it weren't for 1956, at least my brother could have married."

This raises a question: for the *zhifu*'s household, did the changes that 1956 brought about remove the possibility, or simply the necessity, of marriage? Two facts help shed some light on this issue:

1. During the 1950s in China, the chiefs of other ethnic groups, both Han and non-Han, underwent the same sort of

political situation as the Na aristocrats did. However, their descendants never stopped marrying.

2. Prior to the 1950s, in the Muli District of Sichuan Province, a grouping of Na villages was under the rule of a Pumi *tusi*. His subjects were required to pay a tax per household, and the household had to be represented by the eldest son whose name, along with his wife's name, was recorded in the *tusi*'s records. This meant that over several generations, the eldest son of each household in these villages got married and that these households were very large, because no one wanted to break them up, for this would mean paying more taxes. Since the communist succession overthrew this *tusi*, not a single eldest son from these villages has married. They all reverted to the custom of the visit.

It seems legitimate to claim that once their power was lost, marriage within the *zhifu*'s family lost its role and therefore became unnecessary for them. Moreover, what A Guofang stated above confirms this: "the *tusi* regime is completely over now"; "today this rule [that the eldest son must marry] no longer exists."

The examples of other ethnic groups show that the possibility of marriage still exists. In fact, for them, the question does not even come up. Even after they lost power, they continued to marry, because that was their way of life. If they chose not to marry, they would not be able to support themselves, for, quite simply, there were no alternatives.

However, for the last Na *zhifu*'s descendants, other ways of life were an option, their own way of life. This is why A Guofang mentioned Na customs before citing the abrogation of the *tusi* regime as the explanation for the end of marriage in his *lignée*: with a sister in the house, he could not bring in another woman. Living with his sister is what his tradition demands. In other words, A Guofang remains unmarried not because there is no possibility for him to do so but because he no longer needs to get married; indeed, he must not get married.

Today, there are eighteen *lignées* in this genealogy. Among them, there were thirty-nine people under the age of seventeen in 1956 and over the age of seventeen in 1989, out of which there were only two married men, or 5.1 percent of the total. One of them was an only child, and the other had two brothers but no sisters. Sixteen people, or 41 percent, practice cohabitation; and nine of these cases came about due to the matrimonial reform of 1974. The other 53.8 percent practiced the custom of the visit.

Governmental Rules Regarding the Transfer of the Zhifu's Power

If successive marriages of the *zhifu*'s eldest sons only served the function of providing a successor, then a question would arise: in this strongly matrilineal society, was the chief's political power ever handed down from maternal uncle to uterine nephew? If the answer is yes, why and when did the chief adopt the mode of transmission from father to son?

In addition to the genealogy presented above, the information available on the genealogy of the *zhifu*'s family comes mainly from two sources: ancient Han texts and oral accounts of the *tusi* successions by a *daba*.[7]

According to *Yuan shi* (History of the Yuan), under Niyuewu, a Na ancestor, the Na expelled the Tibetans from the Loudoudan (Yongning) region to establish themselves there.[8] In 1253, Kublai Khan, heading south to conquer the kingdom of Dali, passed through Yongning. At that time, Hezi, the thirty-first great-great-grandson of Niyuewu, was overthrown by the Mongols. The Han texts have only a few fragments about these two historical characters, so it is impossible to identify them.

In 1381, Budugeji, the Na chief, led his subjects to submit to the Ming dynasty. In several precise details, the Han texts, which are all from the Qing dynasty, provide more information about him and his successors: from 1381 to 1894, there were twenty-four *tusi* successions, out of which seventeen were handed down from father to son, five from older brother to younger brother, one from paternal uncle to nephew, and one from grandfather to grandson (see figure 12.4).[9] The last Han text in question concerns A Minhan's demand of succession. If we include A Minzhu, the last successor who inherited the title in 1938, there were twenty-six *tusi* in all.

In the Han texts, the first four Na chiefs have Na first names only. The fifth and sixth *zhifu* are the first to use a Han last name (阿), but their first name is still Na. From the seventh *zhifu* on, not only are their last names Han but their first names as well.

The chronology in figure 12.4 comes from the oral account of a *daba* who officiated at the *zhifu*'s home and therefore would recite the names of the *zhifu*'s ancestors during various rituals held prior to 1956. The *daba*'s account includes twenty-seven first names (A Zhangke is included only as an ancestor), without specifying the kinship relation between each chief and his predecessor, as the Han texts do. For the first thirteen chiefs, the *daba* lists only a first name. Starting with the fourteenth chief, the name of each chief is followed by the name of his wife or wives.

From the first chief through the fifteenth, as well as for the wives of the fifteenth and sixteenth chiefs, the names are exclusively Na. With the second through the fifth chief, the last syllable (or the last two syllables) of the previous chief's name becomes the first syllable (or first two syllables) of the successor's name. This phenomenon of linking the first name of someone to the first name of his successor by one or two syllables exists in several ethnic groups belonging to the same Yi linguistic family. From the seventh *tusi* on, all of the first names, including the wives', are

List according to the *daba* (The Na Oral Tradition)			List according to the Chinese Texts	
Chronology of Position	Chief's Name	Wife's Name	Chief's Name	Kinship Relation to Predecessor
1	Aachï		Budugeji	
2	Chïyimu		Gejibahe	son
3	Mudgïgo		Busa	son
4	Godgïlulu		Nanba	brother
5	Luluyiyi		A Ju	son
6	DZibulu		A Chao	brother
7	Lubibu		A Gui	son
8	Yansiyan		A Hui	son
9	Yanlumutu		A He	son
10	Mutuditu		A Ying	son
11	BudhukadZi		A Xiong	brother
12	KadZinaba		A Chengzhong	nephew
13	Nabayaya		A Quan	son
14	Yamaa	Yudgumu	A Zhenqi	son
15	Muniachi	Gutuse	A Tingkun	son
16	DZyatsïdgu	Hlamuchï	A Jinhui	son
17	DZigusha	Datçidgima	A Jinxian	brother
18	Dgibutsïe	DZyaadgïma	A Youwei	son
19	Iuchuladi	Pitsodgïma	A Shichang	son
20	Sonaladi	Sonadgïma	A Qichang	brother
21	Dudgïdziatsï	Adhïbuchï	A Liangfu	son
22	Tsowudindgu	Tsïedgïma	A Huiyuan	son
23	Gochodhashï	Echedgïma, Dgïmahlatso, Tsïedgïma	A Hengfang	grandson
24	DudgîdZiatse	Yudgédgïma	A Yingrui	son
25	Nimadhashï	Tsïedgïma, Dgimatsïe	A Zhangke*	son
26	Gezotsïe	Yudgédgïma, Sonnahlamu, Tsïedgïma	A Minhan	son
27	Tsïepitso	Dhashïdgïma	A Minzhu	brother

*A Zhangke was not a *zhifu.*

Figure 12.4. Na chiefs through 1956.

Tibetan. That the chiefs were given Tibetan names is of great importance, for it proves that Lamaism had acquired a dominant status in the Yongning region. This information therefore provides concrete evidence about when Lamaism spread throughout Yongning.

While both sources provide the same number of *tusi,* there is a striking difference in the information they include that raises a question. The father-son relationship between some successive chiefs that the Han texts cite seems to imply that these chiefs were married. But the *daba*'s account only confirms the existence of wives for the last thirteen chiefs. Since the *daba*'s vocation for each generation was to recite the chief's ascendants at least five times a year during services of offerings to the ancestors, memorizing the names of the twenty-six chiefs and of their spouses must not have been a difficult task. It therefore seems legitimate to deduce that if the first thirteen chiefs were married, their wives' names would have been recited. Were these first thirteen chiefs married?

On further analysis, I noticed that these two documents reveal not only a difference but also a point in common: beginning with the fourteenth *tusi,* all of the chiefs are married.

The fourteenth chief is named Yamaa in the oral account, and A Zhenqi in the Han texts. He is a crucial figure in several respects. First, beginning with him, the wives' names appear. Second, all of the genealogical versions, whether in the annals, the accounts of Yunnan Province, the district records, or the genealogy of the *zhifu*'s household, unanimously confirm that he was the one who led his subjects to submit to the Qing army in 1659, which in turn accorded him a formal mandate and named him *zhifu.* Moreover, there is only one legend concerning the foundation of the chiefdom, and it is about this fourteenth chief. According to the legend: "Yamaa is the thirteenth successor of Aachï, the first chief of Yongning. It was he who bowed down before the invading Naxi troops led by Mu, the *tusi* of Lijiang. On his way to the capital to claim his rights before the emperor, he met Yudgumu, a Na woman. She fell in love with Yamaa and gave him her jewelry so that he would be able to complete his voyage. Once in Peking, Yamaa won his case, and the emperor named him the legitimate *zhifu* of Yongning and at the same time assured the hereditary possession of this position within his household.

"Once he returned to his land, Yamaa took measures to consolidate the power he held and strengthen his people: each household had the right to cultivate a certain area of land for its own use but remained liable for duty to work the *zhifu*'s land. Those who did not want to cultivate the fields became permanently attached to the *zhifu*'s estate. This is the origin of the three Na social strata. Yamaa also decided to find Yudgumu, a task that he conferred on two Han merchants. They carried out their mission and brought her back to Yongning. A wedding ceremony was conducted with great pomp, and for the occasion each Na village brought a gift for the *zhifu*. Yamaa asked his seconds in command to record each present from the villages and decided to make this gesture a permanent one. From that time on, the villages were required to send a tribute to the *zhifu* each year in the form of a gift. The two merchants were given the hereditary position of assistant stewards as thanks."

This oral tradition retraces the appearance of three fundamental social elements for the Na: the *zhifu*'s marriage, the annual tribute to the chief of Yongning, and the division of society into three social strata. It marks the historical passage of an egalitarian society to a stratified society. Symbolically yet explicitly, the idea of a discontinuity between the traditions is expressed. As it turns out, the role played by the two merchants is all the more important since they became assistant stewards in charge of written correspondence to the government. Another interesting element here is that a woman brought wealth to Yamaa, thereby allowing him to acquire power from the central government, and that is why he married her. Even if this story is pure myth, its structure is particularly eloquent.

Oral tradition, the Han texts, and this legend all seem unanimously to confirm that beginning with Yamaa all *zhifu* were married.

We have seen that the succession of a new *zhifu* had to be ratified by the central government and that if this was not done, it would not be valid. I will now examine the central government's policies on ethnic minorities during the Qing dynasty.

From the beginning of this dynasty in 1644, the emperor promulgated a series of rules: once an ethnic minority had been subjected, its chief was required to hand over to the court the formal mandate and seal given to him by the preceding dynasty. This gesture granted him permission by the court to keep the same title and guaranteed that his position would remain hereditary. If an indigenous chief had inherited his position, he was required to go in person to Peking to receive his title. This rule was overturned in 1673. No document in the Han texts attests to the existence, during this period, of any conflicts between the Na and the Naxi in Lijiang. On the other hand, Yamaa's voyage to Peking seems to confirm this last rule, since he was the first Na chief under the Qing dynasty and was subjected in 1656, in the middle of the period covered by this last regulation.

According to decrees from the Qing dynasty, the rules on the transfer of power were as follows: when an aging *tusi* becomes ill, and if he asks to be replaced, "his position may be inherited by a son produced by his first official wife or his grandson born of the first wife of his son; if they do not exist, his position will be handed down to the son born of his second wife or to his grandson born of the second wife of his son; without these sons or grandsons, the position will be inherited by his brother or by a member of his lineage (patrilineal, for example, a cousin); among his wives and offspring, if there is someone whom the natives obey, he will be allowed to hand the position down to one of them."[10] "The succession of the *tusi* must conform to the usual rules, and it must follow this order: from older son to younger son, from son of the first wife to son of the second wife, and it is forbidden to select one's favorite son or an adopted son to be the successor."[11] "The court will accord an official mandate to anyone who assumes a hereditary position. His achievements, his heritage, and his position must be recorded on this mandate. Each time that a descendant requests succession, the general secretary of the government of the province [*Zhangyin dusi*] or the bureau of the provincial governor [*Buzhen si*] verifies the old mandate and draws up a report that is sent, together with the old mandate, to the minister [of the army], who, once he has verified it and confirmed it, gives his approval for the succession. He notes the date of the succession and the ascendants of the successor on a new mandate and gives it to him to replace the old one."[12] "The government also gives a seal to the chiefs of the *fu, zhou,* and *xian*."[13]

To avoid fraudulent successions, there was a rule specifying "that the request by the heir apparent must be accompanied by written testimonies from the indigenous chiefs of the neighboring regions." "If the one who obtains power does not have a clear heritage, or if he is trying to pass himself off as the heir apparent and has lied about his genealogy, or if he has usurped the power of the heir apparent, once he is revealed, he will be deposed. Those who have provided him with false written testimony will be punished according to custom."[14]

Successions among ethnic minorities created many problems. In 1659, the provincial governor of Guizhou (in charge of military and judicial affairs) presented a report to the emperor. In it, he stated: "The descendants of the indigenous chiefs succeed as it pleases them and with complicity among them. Disputes arise because of the confusion between *lignées*, which results in conflict." He advised: "Beginning today, at the end of each year, every indigenous chief must present the provincial government with his civil status, which must state whether or not he has had a child that year. Every three years, he must go to Peking and prostrate himself before the emperor, as a precaution, he must also present his civil status at the ministry at the same time. When a request for succession occurs, if more than one person claims the right to inherit the position and a conflict ensues, the government will immediately resolve the issue by referring to the registry. Once the measures are set and clear, the source of conflict will be eliminated."[15] Once the emperor approved this measure, it was added to the rules. When a child was born, the indigenous chief was thereafter required to report the birth to the local government, which would then transmit it to the court.

Furthermore, the court stipulated: "For the son of an indigenous chief to obtain approval to assume power, he must be fifteen years old." "If the indigenous chief has a son, but he is too young, and another member of his lineage or his mother has the capacity to control the regency until he is of age, the provincial government can choose, among them, someone to serve as regent until the son is fifteen." All of the responses to the court's demands can be found in A Hengfang's request for accession to power.[16]

The rigidity of these rules is shocking. They are also accompanied by a series of preventive measures.

Among the possible candidates enumerated in the regulations, a brother of the Na chief could be presented as a successor. But it would be inadmissible, from the court's point of view, for a Na chief to present his brother as a successor from the start, for the rule states that the eldest son of the first wife is first in line in the list of candidates and that all of the regions' indigenous chiefs must absolutely respect this order. As a result of such legislation, a Na chief had to marry in order to hand down his power. Without marriage, a man would never have a son who would be recognized by the court. Therefore, the Na chiefs were under an obligation to marry, at least during the Qing dynasty, if they wanted to keep power within their household. We can deduce from this why the Na chiefs could not hand down power to a uterine nephew. A last question remains, however: can we find a precise origin for their marriages?

Recall that in the *daba*'s account, wives' names only begin to appear with Yamaa. The first thirteen chiefs undoubtedly must have been from the preceding dynasty, the Ming. If these chiefs were not married, power must have passed mainly from maternal uncle to uterine nephew or, occasionally, from older brother to younger brother, or perhaps in other combinations, but not from father to son. To shed more light on this situation, I will once again turn to the Han texts.

Emperor Zhu Yuanzhang, the founder of the Ming dynasty, decided to confer on his newly subjected chiefs the same positions that they had held under the previous dynasty. In 1368, the first year of his dynasty, he stipulated that "the heirs must appear in Peking, following the chief's death, even if they lived more than 10,000 *li* away."[17] After fourteen years, in 1382, he replaced this rule with one that named the indigenous chiefs on the spot and gave them their mandate and their official costume (which varied according to the rank of the mandarin).[18] On the subject of heirs, the court stipulated: "Whether the heir is his son, his brother, a member of his lineage, his wife, his daughter, or *his son-in-law or his uterine nephew, no matter who the heir is, it is agreed that they do as their custom requires*" (emphasis added).[19]

This rule is astonishing. Under the Ming dynasty, the central

Chinese government established a new column in the official annals of the court wherein it compiled the names of all the *tusi*. Hundreds of them exist. To my knowledge, only the Mo-so required such a rule. The emperor, wise, broad-minded, and knowing, comes to resemble a sociologist here.

This document explicitly states that the transfer of power from maternal uncle to uterine nephew was allowed. Therefore, the three types of sources that I have just presented lead me to conclude that the chiefs who came before Yamaa did not marry, that their power was mainly handed down from maternal uncle to nephew, and that marriage of a Na chief first appeared with the Qing dynasty. The practice of marriage came about in response to the rigorous demands of the central government's legislation. In light of the historical context, we can understand it as natural and legitimate that, once the power of his household was confiscated, the last *zhifu*'s son would no longer consider marriage necessary.

To gather more information about the relationship between the chief of Yongning and the central government in previous eras, I propose quickly to finish this course through history. Under the Qing and Ming dynasties, the Na chiefs always received an official mandate from the court; but under the Mongolian dynasty, according to the Chinese historical texts, while the Na chief was entitled to continue his rule in Yongning, he did not receive an official mandate from the court. Beyond the Song dynasty, the texts provide no further specifications about this.

Before concluding this section on the transfer of power, I will attempt to explain the existence of sons among the first thirteen chiefs in the genealogies in various Chinese texts, including that of the *zhifu*'s family.

First, these texts all date from the Qing dynasty. If we compare the genealogy of the *zhifu* of Yongning with that of the Naxi chiefs from Lijiang (which have been profoundly sinicized since the

Mongolian dynasty, if not before), we can see the difference right away: in the genealogy of the Lijiang chiefs, the text clearly states each chief's wife's name, the name of her original family, and the number of children she had. This is not the case in the genealogy of the Yongning chiefs, which simply states that it is the son, brother, or nephew who inherited power, without mentioning anything else. It is easy to claim that someone is a son without it being true but a little more difficult to invent a wife and even more difficult to invent a birthplace, *lignée*, and number of children for her. In fact, we know that the social usefulness of a written genealogy lies in that it can be modified to the advantage of its holder. From this perspective, this aspect of the Yongning chiefs' genealogy no longer seems reliable.

I should point out that since 1956, at the same time that the aristocratic descendants were giving up marriage, those who were employed as cadres by the authorities were required, without exception, to marry. And this is true even though the current constitution and the autonomous regulations for the Ninglang District officially authorize and protect the traditions of ethnic minorities. The power of the Na communist cadres is, of course, no longer hereditary, but if a cadre starts to practice the visit, he will be immediately expelled from the party and will therefore lose his job in the party and/or the government. Between 1956 and 1980, there was no shortage of cadres who made this kind of "mistake." I will return to this later. Now it is no longer heredity that plays a role, but Han moral standards and the evolutionist theory that advocates the superiority of monogamy over other lifestyles and judges Na moral standards to be "depraved customs." Despite the general avoidance of marriage by the *zhifu*'s descendants after 1956, spontaneous marriage continued to appear, just as it did before, in certain *lignées* that lacked female descendants. Marriage, then, continued to play a role. In my research, one out of five marriages took place during this period.

The historical account above suggests that the successive marriages of *zhifu* resulted from administrative policies of the central Chinese government and therefore of the diffusion of Manchurian culture. Na society, while integrating the structures imposed on it externally, succeeded in fundamentally maintaining its own kinship customs.

The introduction of marriage into Na society provided a more reliable way than cohabitation for wealthy commoners and serfs who lacked female descendants to keep an outside woman. For aristocrats, it was yet another way, besides cohabitation, to face a crisis caused by discord between members of a *lignée*, and for them to display their wealth and acquire greater social prestige.

Throughout Chinese history, from the Qing dynasty until the era of the republic, no matter what its method of transferring power, the central government always advocated the right of inheritance of political power for ethnic minorities. But only the Ming and the Qing set up strict rules specifying the successor in the indigenous chief's family.[20]

The Ming law harmonized with Na custom, since it accepted that a uterine nephew could be the heir. In 1644, the Ming dynasty was replaced by that of the Qing. In the hope of diminishing, indeed of obliterating, any conflicts and destabilizing tensions created by wars of succession, the dynasty established new legislation on the transfer of power that conflicted with Na customs. Moreover, this legislation was accompanied by a series of strict measures to guarantee the authenticity of the eldest son as heir.

This regulation falls under the heading of legal and political orders. Because marriage, in the eyes of the court, was natural and therefore universal, the court did not take the kinship systems of ethnic groups into consideration when it established this new legislation. Consequently, it demanded authentic kinship relationships between each chief and his successor. These relationships were strictly watched under the strong administrative structure. But the court imposed no specific kinship system. Its government confirmed the request for succession once the heir presented was authenticated as the *tusi*'s eldest son. For their part, the Na chiefs paid no attention to the court's kinship system. Their only adaptation to it was to produce the required son as an heir. The understanding on both sides states that the father-son relationship was necessary and sufficient to preserve the *zhifu*'s family's power and political autonomy. This gave the Na chief freedom to apply the law however he saw fit.

Now, the father-son relationship immediately presupposes marriage. This legislation therefore implied the practice of marriage among the Na chiefs without explicitly imposing it on them. As a result, the right to inherent political power necessitated successive marriages from one generation to the next among the Na *tusi*, and indirectly bound the Na chiefs to this practice. This combination of freedom and obligation gave birth to changes in the kinship rules for the Na chief's *lignée*, which from that point on were made up of a mixture of concepts.

On the one hand, the concept of consanguinity was exclusively matrilineal, which meant that the incest prohibition determined those women one could not marry and that the children of a chief's wife were only his *krwadhe*. Their *krwadhe* relationship was established through the woman, the wife-mother. On the other hand, the right to inherit political power only existed in the paternal *lignée*, which engendered the concept of paternity and the necessity of the name father for the chief. In terms of the mode of residence, Yamaa was the first to live virilocally; with his successors, patrilocality started. Moreover, the children's membership in the group, as well as the transmission of names, status, and property, was passed down from the paternal *lignée*.

Therefore, with the exception of the family name and belonging to a particular social stratum, both of which came about through contact with the central government, the elements traditionally associated with purely matrilineal descent were detached from the mother-children bond. The connection between mothers and children was consanguineal, while that between fathers and children was *krwadhe*.

As a result of this combination of pure matriliny, the rule prohibiting incest, and the demand for successive marriage, two unprecedented things occurred: first, the *zhifu*'s consanguineal identity changed with each generation; and second, each time a *zhifu* died, all of his consanguineal relatives, those from his mother's original *lignée* as well as those from his sisters and brothers, were no longer *krwadhe* of the *zhifu*'s family and were therefore no longer a part of it. The consanguineal relatives living in the mother's birth house were, on the one hand, excluded on the principle of matriliny and by the rule of paternal *lignée* because they no longer had any consanguineal relatives in the *zhifu*'s family, and, on the other hand, not *krwadhe* to the new *zhifu*. The sisters and brothers of the recently deceased *zhifu* were only excluded by the matrilineal principle. According to this logic, the dead *zhifu* and his wives were not *krwadhe* to the family of the living *zhifu*, in spite of appearances: they were recorded in the genealogy of the *zhifu*'s family. They were then pseudo-*krwadhe*. Their names were registered in the genealogy only to testify to the legitimacy of their successor's power.

This legislation created new behaviors and attitudes in the members of the *zhifu*'s family in relation to the other Na. The chiefs excluded children born out of wedlock but not women who were not virgins. Here too, they only partially conformed to the court's mandates, which stated that a woman who lost her virginity could not be married. The Na chiefs practiced monogamy as well as polygyny, depending on the fertility of their first wife. The chiefs' wives reverted to the furtive visit only after they had succeeded in producing a son. In contrast to Na moral standards that advocate solidarity of the *lignée*, separation was mandatory in the *zhifu*'s family and occurred in every generation. The purpose of all this was to guarantee the authenticity and status of the eldest son as the heir apparent, thereby avoiding any conflicts between the eldest son and his brothers, as well as between the others.

On the other hand, while the chiefs adopted the modality of marriage, they continued to practice the visit, since it in no way interfered with the production of a male heir. However, by taking advantage of their power, they were able to transgress the main rules of the conspicuous visit: the sexual privilege of the open relationship and the taboo forbidding women to visit men. Many of their visits were no longer conspicuous in the correct sense of the term, but deformed by their prestige, and would more properly be called forced visits.

The practice of marriage gave rise to the concept of paternity in the *zhifu*'s family and was marked by the appellation *abò*. The term *abò* was used by the *zhifu*'s children, while the children of the *zhifu*'s brothers, who would not, a priori, be heirs, continued to use the term *ewu* for their father. This difference leads me to believe that the term *abò* was borrowed for the sole purpose of making the relationship between each chief and his successor an authentic father-son relationship, both in form and in content. Therefore, it was a measure taken to privilege the position of the eldest son when he became a father.

I will now look at the separation of brothers and sisters in each generation. Once they left, the eldest son took on the appearance of being an only child. He sat on the right side of the hearth because he now represented the highest power and was the sole representative of the *zhifu*'s family, just as though he were an only child. The departing brothers and sisters received property in the form of shares; only the eldest son received property in the form of an inheritance.

The marriage of the eldest son appears to have been regulated by the same mechanism that regulated an adoption of a girl from the outside, a cohabitation with an outside woman, and a marriage of an only son. There was, however, one important difference: while the *zhifu* needed a male successor, the *lignées* in these other cases were searching for a female successor.

The mechanisms of this kinship system, in their excluding the brothers and sisters as well as their descendants from the *zhifu*'s family, suggest that Yamaa must have been the only member of his *lignée* living in the *zhifu*'s residence. Once he died, his *matrilignée* must have immediately lost its political power, which is completely contrary to the logic of the rule of political inheritance preordained by the court. After Yamaa's death, his *lignée* held its power in name only, for in reality it was held by another *lignée* of a different consanguinity. Through this process, we can see that the title of *zhifu* was only a label and his residence only a shell. With each generation, once the *zhifu* changed, a new consanguineal group took over. This group not only acquired power but also became the producers of an aristocracy of great consanguineal diversity. Even though power did not remain within the same consanguineal group, it remained within a family that had the same name. This was enough to satisfy the court, even if it was only a formality, for this formality fulfilled the central government's regulatory demands and succeeded in making the transfer of power peaceful.

This analysis shows that social stratification came about because of the marriage indirectly imposed on Yamaa. Without this, the development of a single *lignée* originating in Yamaa never would have transformed into a social stratum, and therefore the two other social strata would not have appeared either. Moreover, this society would not have had the same landownership regime. The consequences of this imposition of marriage were therefore far-reaching. We can now understand, and verify as accurate, the Na claim that the "*we* social stratum did not exist before Yamaa."

In matrimonial affairs, the *zhifu* referred to marrying a woman as giving a woman. Except when referring to his wife or wives and his children, he used almost the exact same terminology to refer to his *krwadhe* as the common Na use to refer to their consanguineal relatives, as though his family were made up of consanguineal relatives only. Until the time of A Zhangke, the *zhifu* never had a double bed, and, like the rest of the Na, could only see his wife in secret; but he could transgress the taboo of the open visit when it no longer concerned his household members. These facts lead me to conclude that the chiefs' behavior also strictly conformed to the ban on sexual evocation.

In the *zhifu*'s family, the father had authority over his children. When the maternal uncles came from a lower social stratum, which was usually the case, they had no rights over their uterine nieces and nephews. On the other hand, a paternal uncle, even if he was not of the same blood as his nieces and nephews, had certain rights to the material possessions of the *zhifu*'s residence if he continued to live there after his elder brother's death, and enjoyed a superiority over his nephew, even if his nephew had already inherited the position of *zhifu*. Once he left his birth home, however, he no longer enjoyed these rights. Therefore, within the *zhifu*'s family, respect for the *ewu* was transferred from the maternal side to the paternal side. This corresponds to a general Na principle: it is necessary to respect one's ascendants, no matter what the position of Ego.

The rule regarding the inheritance of power was a political

one. In the central government's view, marriage, as an administrative measure, was not a matter of kinship — even though I am looking at it from that perspective — but a matter of politics.

In 1956, when the *zhifu* lost power, a successor was not needed; therefore, marriage did not have a role and was no longer practiced by the family. This provides proof of the political nature of marriage in the *zhifu*'s family.

Before 1644, there was no matrimonial system in Na society. After this date, marriage was imposed indirectly on the Na chief by the Qing government. From the *zhifu*'s family's point of view, its only function was to produce a male heir to inherit the position of *zhifu*. In this way, the *zhifu*'s *lignée* was transformed into a family and remained so for almost three centuries (see figure 12.5).

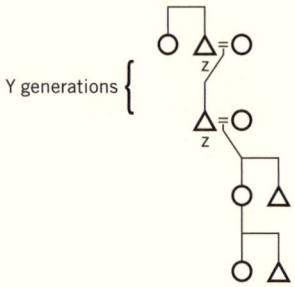

Figure 12.5. Structure of the *zhifu*'s family.

The diagram in figure 12.5 differs from that produced by the marriages of only sons, but the mechanism behind it is the same: first, the transformation of a *lignée* into a family (unary kinship has become binary kinship) and the change of consanguineal identity, and then, after a period of time, once the necessity disappeared, the restoration of the *lignée* (and a return to unary kinship.)

From the discussion above, we can see that the *zhifu* adopted marriage for political reasons; then the rich borrowed the practice. Their wedding ceremony closely resembled that of the Manchurians. The *zhifu*'s *lignée* passively accepted marriage and practiced it over a certain time span, while the others actively adopted it then followed it sporadically, never continuously. In both categories, the practice of marriage was not a constant necessity: there was a lack of universal application. This absence of universality, which was synchronic as well as diachronic, proves that matrimonial customs inside and outside the *zhifu*'s family were the same.

Marriage was practiced only by a small segment of Na society and without continuity, while the institution of marriage in other societies is followed continuously by, at least in principle, every member of every generation of every family. Herein lies a fundamental difference between these two types of marriage.

For more than three hundred years, the Na managed to integrate a social system imposed indirectly by the dominant ethnic group in China. At the same time, they succeeded in ingeniously preserving the essentials of their own kinship system and their own values.

CHAPTER THIRTEEN

The Matrimonial Reforms:

1959–74 and 1980s–90s

In this chapter, I examine the fate of the Na way of life after 1950, as well as the current situation.

Na Moral Standards as Viewed by the Local Government

In 1950, a "democratic government of the multiple united ethnic groups" was established in the Ninglang District. The main leaders were Han. After its first contacts with the Na, this local government judged that the tradition of the visit constituted a "backward and primitive custom." This custom contravened the matrimonial legislation of the People's Republic of China and, according to the government, led to the decline of morals.[1]

The arguments raised were the following: because of their licentious sexuality, more than 50 percent of Na adults in Yongning are afflicted with various sexually transmitted diseases, especially syphilis.[2] A significant percentage of the women are sterile (no statistics are available), and people are deformed. Na women gather in the town of Batsïgu to solicit the Han and Tibetan merchants from the caravans, and the Na chiefs impose sexual relations on the women. What is more, their custom of the visit is counterproductive in two ways: it disrupts their productiveness at work because the men think of nothing but running off to visit

385

someone; and it disrupts their sex lives because during the high season of work in the fields, they come home too late to go visiting. The district government therefore thought it was necessary progressively to reform this "marriage of the visit."

The first measure taken to change the custom dates from 1956, the year of the agrarian reform. To encourage Na men to leave their maternal *lignées* and form nuclear families, the government drafted, in "The Regulation for Peaceful Negotiation and Democratic Reform," the following article: "In the region in which the inhabitants follow the matrilineal system, the distribution of land will occur according to the residences of the men. If a man wants to set up a home by himself, the land will be distributed to him, instead of being distributed to his maternal family."[3] During the agrarian reform, not a single Na male showed the slightest interest in this article. The government could not understand how it was possible that the Na men did not want to have their own land. They did not understand the ineffectiveness of their measure.

The First Reform (1958): The Advocacy of Monogamy

During the Great Leap Forward movement in 1958, the local powers in Yongning developed the first matrimonial reform, which was intended "to propagate matrimonial legislation" for the Na and to promote "the superiority and posteriority of socialist monogamy as compared with the *açia* system in the various stages of the evolution of matrimonial forms."[4] They also arranged discussions with older villagers and tried to persuade those who had been in a "long-lasting *adhu* relationship"[5] to stabilize it. The government hoped, through stabilization, "to make this relationship a de facto monogamous marriage."[6] On the other hand, with the help of a work group sent by the superior authorities, the local authorities began to urge young people to marry each other or cadres from other ethnic groups.[7] Some cadres and "activists" went ahead and registered with the local government and received their marriage licenses. The local government arranged their nuptials in such a way that even if there was no banquet, there was much festivity, so that they would serve as examples for the other villagers.

I can cite as an example the canton of Wenquan (which falls within the parameters of my research). During this reform, seven couples married. They all came from *lignées* that had members of both sexes. The first obstacle the local authorities encountered was that the receiving households considered the person who moved in a stranger. In general, the married couples got along well. However, the wives who moved into their husbands' households were often unable to live peacefully with some members in the receiving *lignée*, in particular, the women. For example:

> Atçidgima (female) from Walabiai had a brother named Pitso. With the government's encouragement, they both married and took up virilocal residence. Since Atçidgima could not get along with her husband's mother, she returned to her birth house. Shortly after she came back home, her brother's wife, a Pumi, could not get along with her. Since the Pumi ethnic group is patrilineal and has the custom of setting up nuclear families, Pitso's wife proposed that he leave his household and move somewhere else, but he would not agree to this. Finally, he sent his wife back to her original family. A little while later, he stopped visiting her and began to see other women in his village. He said: "We are closest to our mothers, our maternal uncles, and our brothers and sisters, and they are the most reliable. A wife is just someone to have fun with when you are young. Will you get along in the future? No one knows. To leave your mother and sisters for a wife, that would be shameful."

Because of conflicts with members of their receiving *lignées*, four wives out of the seven returned home to their maternal *lignées* shortly after their marriages began. The other couples were not far behind in breaking up, one after the other. In this way, the first reform ended in failure.

, According to the conception of the Han who directed the local government, one spouse was a relative of the other, indeed, a close relative. How, then, was it possible that he or she could be considered a stranger? This represented for them then, as it does today, an enigma.

In their investigative reports, two groups of ethnologists in 1960 and 1963 unanimously recommended that this backward matrimonial system be progressively reformed and that, with planning, the Naxi (Na) could be guided toward monogamy. To instigate these reforms, the ethnologists proposed the following strategy to the government: it must lead the Naxi men and women to set up nuclear families, to constitute economic units, and to raise their children together.

The Second and Third Reforms (1966 and 1971): The Imposition of Monogamy

In 1966, at the beginning of the Cultural Revolution, Mao Zedong incited the Chinese people, especially the youth, to "sweep out the *sijiu*" (the four ancients: ancient customs, ancient habits, ancient morality, and ancient culture).[7] With the help of a work team sent by the district government, the leaders of the People's Commune of Yongning launched the second matrimonial reform. Their argument for this reform had three points:

1. It is shameful not to know who one's genitor is.

2. Youth are running off in all directions to go visiting, and this disturbs the means of production.

3. In this custom, some of the old people are abandoned, in spite of their many descendants.[8]

The work team tried to impose marriage on any villager involved in an open relationship. Once it left, however, the majority of couples who had married broke up. For example, in the production brigade of Wenquan (the current administrative grouping of the villages), forty-six out of seventy-three couples dissolved a short while afterward. With the exception of several couples that included cadres, the others did not last much longer. This campaign for matrimonial reform also ended in failure. A third reform, in 1971, was undertaken in the same manner and had the same results.

The Fourth Reform (1974): The Imposition of Monogamy through Administrative Constraints

In 1974, bringing leftism to its height, Mao urged the people to continue the revolution under the dictatorship of the proletariat. He drew attention to the class struggle in the ideological domain. The provincial revolutionary committees reacted according to the local situations. During this era, the Na in Yongning were subjected to the fourth matrimonial reform.

The previous reforms had been enacted rapidly according to the decisions of the Ninglang District committee. Moreover, they had been subsidiary tasks for the local governments, which were preoccupied mainly with political work.

In contrast to the first three attempts, the fourth campaign for matrimonial reform was undertaken by the director of the revolutionary committee of Yunnan province, the provincial governor. In the beginning of 1974, after personally inspecting the area, he noted: "We must resolutely reform the backward matrimonial system of the Naxi in Yongning. The reformation of this ancient matrimonial system comes under the framework of the class struggle in the ideological domain and therefore constitutes a revolution in the domain of the superstructure."[9]

Conforming to his directive, the authorities of the Lijiang prefecture, those of the Ninglang District, and those of the People's Commune of Yongning — in other words, all levels of local authority — became engaged. Considered the most capable of mastering the situation, the committee of the People's Commune of Yongning was put in charge of preparing a report and a plan. As soon as they had done so, they presented them to the district committee, which endorsed the methods proposed to instigate the reform.

The report listed "seven serious crimes of the *adhu* marriage":

1. This custom prevents the realization of the class struggle among the people, which is unfavorable to the dictatorship of the proletariat. For example, some members of the Communist Party and the revolutionary cadres, because of their lapse in revolutionary vigilance or from a lack of experience of class struggle, have fallen into the trap of the enemies of the class. Since 1956, the number of cadres (including a secretary and several members of the Communist Party committee of the canton of Yongning), communists, and members of the League of Communist Youth who have committed the error of extra-conjugal relations with Na women has reached thirty. They were all punished according to the discipline of the Communist Party and the law of the state.

2. This custom affects the means of production, especially for those who travel far to visit. Each time they leave, they are away for several days.

3. This custom is harmful to the solidarity between husband and wife. The fact that married couples are able to form *adhu* relationships with others most certainly creates mutual suspicion and disagreement.

4. This custom is detrimental to the raising and education of children, since the children and their father belong to two different families. They have no reciprocal duties to each other, nor any mutual feelings. Raising and providing for the children falls exclusively on the mother, who must work in the fields and take care of the housework.

5. This custom is harmful to the health of the people and unfavorable to the growth of the population. Many of the people are afflicted with syphilis.

6. Some old people are *wubaohu*, even when they have many children.[10]

7. This custom harms the formation of communist morality and communist quality among the masses. It is unhealthy for the physical and mental growth of the youth.[11]

Given the failures of the previous reforms, the local government concluded: "Education and persuasion alone are not enough to maintain couples; they must be backed up by administrative constraints." The committee of the People's Commune of Yongning therefore stipulated:[12]

1. Everyone under fifty who is in a relationship that has lasted for a long time must register as a couple at the People's Commune headquarters, for the express purpose of getting married.

2. Every woman who has children, even if she is no longer with the man, must state who the genitor of her children is, and then proceed to the registration office to marry him.

3. Those older than fifty and involved in a long-lasting relationship are not required to undergo the formality of marriage, and they are allowed to maintain their present situation: each may stay in his or her separate home. If a man and a woman request of their own free will to undergo the formality of matrimony in order to become formally united as husband and wife,

their wishes must be respected, and the necessary arrangements will be made for them.

4. After marriage, the *Gongfen* [the work unit of the era; the distribution of grain after the harvest depends on its number] and the annual rations of grain for the couple will be counted and distributed by the production brigade on which the couple depends. If a spouse has asked for a divorce and returns to his birth home without the divorce being granted, his annual ration of grain will be suspended and kept in the brigade's storehouse. He will only receive his ration once a reconciliation between the spouses has taken place or once he has completed all of the official steps required for a divorce.

5. Any child born out of wedlock will not receive an annual ration of grain until his mother designates with certitude who his genitor is. His means of survival must be taken care of by this genitor until he is eighteen.[13]

Because the Na in Yunnan and Sichuan were practicing visit relationships, the Ninglang District committee thought it would be more effective to undertake the reform in cooperation with neighboring districts. It contacted the committees from Yanyuan and Muli Districts in Sichuan and proposed proceeding with this reform together. They in turn reported this proposition to their authorities, but they never followed through with it. Therefore, the reform only took place in Yunnan.

The work group distributed its members in all of the brigades and began by holding meetings, night after night, with the goal of propagating its conviction — the superiority of socialist monogamy and the harm of the "marriage of the visit" — and of inculcating matrimonial legislation. They tried to make the villagers understand that anyone who wanted to be united as husband and wife was required to register officially at the Government Service for Civil Affairs, where they would receive a marriage license. Only after this formality was completed would sexual relations be recognized and protected by the law. Visit relationships were illegal.

In the earlier reforms, it was always the older women who openly blocked their descendants' departure; they were therefore considered the most entrenched in tradition and ancient ideas. This time, the work group paid particular attention to them and set about trying to convince them on a one-on-one basis.

The brigade chiefs were required to provide a list of the people involved in open relationships and the number of women who had had children in each village. The work group could then, according to this list, order the villagers to form couples in the following manner:

A woman who had one or more children and was currently receiving an open visitor was required to register her relationship with this visitor and to live with him under the same roof. It did not matter whether or not he was the children's genitor.

The supposed genitor and/or the one designated as such by the brigade chief was obliged to marry a woman who had had one child and was not in an open relationship with anyone.

A woman who had several children, each from a different genitor, and who was not in an open relationship, had to choose one of the genitors and marry him.

If a mother truly did not know who her child's genitor was or if she did not want to reveal his identity, the ration for her child would be suspended; the work group would continue their persuasive tactics.

Those in open relationships without children were required to register and to live together; if one partner did not want to register and preferred to break off the relationship, the other partner had to agree. In any case, it was forbidden to continue the visiting.

Those found practicing the furtive visit had to register and then live together.

"During that period," remembered one of my sources, "the tension was so high that our thoughts never strayed from this subject. No one dared to make a furtive visit. Before, we were like roosters. We took any woman we could catch. We went to a woman's house at least once a night. Sometimes, we would even visit two or three a night. But, with that campaign, we got scared. We did not want to get married and move into someone else's house, and as a result, we no longer dared to visit anyone. Because of this, we took a rest for a few years."

Once all of the brigades had succeeded in uniting a first series of couples, the Ninglang District government sent a Jeep filled with marriage licenses to the People's Commune of Yongning. Ten and twenty at a time, couples were rounded up in the villages under the brigades, and a leader would take their fingerprints on the marriage form and hand them each a marriage license. They would then be given a date for the wedding ceremony. Once the day came, horse-drawn carriages were sent into the villages to provide transportation for the "newlyweds" to the brigade headquarters. The ceremony took place in the following manner: they each received a cup of tea, a cigarette, and several pieces of candy, and then everybody participated in a traditional dance. The government called this "the new way of getting married" as opposed to the old way: "organizing lavish banquets." Because of these regulations, several members within one *lignée*, belonging to two, even three generations, were married at the same time.[14] Following the ceremony, communal residence was required for the two spouses. If they did not come from the same brigade, one of the two had to move in with the other partner and work in that brigade.

Because mothers would not accept their daughters' leaving to live with others, nor would they accept other women in their households, the People's Commune encouraged couples to set up nuclear families. It was therefore necessary to build more houses, but the People's Commune did not have the means to build the number needed by the newlyweds. In the end, the majority of cases were uxorilocal. Sometimes, the couples were rejected by both of their *lignées*. Living like vagabonds, they moved from place to place, borrowing a room from a consanguineal relative or staying with a neighbor, while they waited to build a hut.

This matrimonial reform created social upheaval. No other ethnic group in China underwent as deep a disruption as the Na did during the Cultural Revolution. To understand the trouble this reform caused in Na society, it is enough to imagine a reform in our society, but with the reverse logic.

From January to August 1975, within the parameters of my investigation, the work group succeeded in forming twenty-eight couples.

The Villagers' Reactions

I will now look at how some villagers, during that period and today, criticized the arguments of the work group and that event: "The policy of that reform was to forget about the older ascendants." "It dismembered the *lignée* and destroyed the solidarity of its members." "One wife and one husband [monogamy] is a Han trait. We Na don't live that way. Visiting women without uniting as a couple, that is our trademark. If we all have to practice one wife and one husband we will become Han, and the Na will disappear." "In the one wife and one husband campaign, they [the members of the work group] ravaged by force one healthy *lignée* after another."

The villagers unanimously felt that "the practice of 'wife and husband' provoked discord within the *lignées*." Even those in an open relationship who wanted to continue being so did not want to cohabit. They said: "For the time being, we are together, but it is only for compliance to the government's policy. We hope that we will both be able to return to our birth homes, later on, when the policy lets us do so. Let's hope that the policies will let us live in the mode of the visit."

No matter where the residence, discord immediately arose, either between the receiving *lignée* and the *mu min* or the *zo min* or, in neolocal cases, between the spouses. Chaos reigned in every village.

Several months after the work group left, some marriages dissolved because of conflicts between the wife and the husband's mothers or sisters in virilocal cases or between the husband and the mothers and other members of the wife's *lignée* in uxorilocal cases. For example, Gézo from the Sonnami *lignée* in Kaitçi told me the story of one of his brothers: "My brother was forced to move in with his open partner during the one wife and one husband campaign. He and his girlfriend still had feelings for each other, but this woman did not want to leave her mother. At her house, her mother and her brothers and sisters all despised my brother. There was no room for him. His status there was not even that of a three-year-old child. He was given women's work and was not even considered part of the household. It was very hard for him. His situation there hurt all of us. Once the work team left, I went to get him. We brought him back to our house."

The couples that turned out to be relatively stable were either those who formed a nuclear family or those whose receiving *lignée* had only a few members.

From June 22, 1976, until August 5, 1976, one year after implementation of the reform, four researchers from the Historical Institute of Yunnan went to the field to observe the results. In their report, they stated that they believed the biggest obstacle to the reform was the structure of the traditional family and traditional conceptions of the Na. For the reform to get the better of this backward custom, the following effort needed to be made:

- reinforcing propaganda so that the Na abandon the idea that only members of the same "family" are intimates and therefore stop their tradition of excluding members of other "families."

To strengthen the united couples, the researchers recommended:

- reinforcing the work on women's affairs in order to reconcile wives and husbands who are not getting along;
- continuing to place constraints on the annual rations of grain;
- authorizing couples to cut down trees so that they can build new houses and make additions when they have children;
- providing more medicine and contraceptive devices and reinforcing medical services to guarantee surgical sterilization.

One situation particularly disturbed the research group: "Even after the reform, the young people still do not know how to behave in their love life. Instead of moving ahead one step at a time — meeting someone, getting to know that person, thinking about marriage, and proceeding to the wedding ceremony — they jump right to sexual relations the moment they meet each other. Because of this, they lapse very quickly into the mode of the visit."[15] Consequently, the research group proposed that the local government teach the young people the correct procedure for love.[16]

Another puzzling aspect for the research group also deserves mention. These researchers asked the questions: how was this matrilineal system able to persist through the various stages of the evolution of human society? China today is in the socialist stage; the Na are therefore already several stages behind, that is, several thousand years behind. Why are the *adhu* marriage and the matrilineal family of the Na forever in a state of stagnation?

Within the parameters of my investigation, one year after the work group left in August 1975, more than half of these arranged marriages had failed: sixteen out of twenty-eight couples had broken up.

The Current Situation

In 1976, extremism met its downfall. The regulations that suspended annual rations for a child born out of wedlock were suppressed in 1981; however, having a child out of wedlock is still considered immoral and illicit.

Since 1981, the year the government instigated a family-planning policy, the Ninglang District government has stipulated two new rules:

1. A fine of 30 *yuan* per year per illegitimate child is imposed. The child's mother's *lignée* is not required to pay this fine if a man acknowledges that he is the child's genitor. When a man acknowledges that he is the genitor, he must take responsibility for the cost of raising the child until he or she is eighteen.

2. Each Na woman (as is true for several other ethnic groups that have small populations) has the right to have three children, instead of two, as is the case with Han peasants. But if she has a fourth, her *lignée* will be fined 20 *yuan* a year until the child is eighteen.

The local government's attitude toward enforcing these two rules is currently very ambiguous. First, because the family-planning-service cadres are Na, each time one of them fines a *lignée*, he is alienated from that household, spreads fear among the villagers, and loses popularity. Therefore, the cadres do not strictly enforce the rules when a *lignée* breaks them. Second, since the Na leaders want the Na population to grow, they only look after the work of family planning when the authorities demand statistics. Third, since each *lignée* obtained its own land in 1982, the villagers do not depend on the local government for much (they do, for example, receive a ration of chemical fertilizer). With more freedom, they resist the administrative rules more and more and find ways to avoid paying these two fines. For example, in my research, one villager would claim to be the genitor each time a *lignée* was in danger of being fined, and he had done this for the children of several women in different *lignées*. This is what he told me:

> "When someone is recognized as the genitor of the child, the fine is lifted. These poor women, I always want to lend them a hand."
>
> "You claim to be the genitor of children from various *lignées*, and the cadres find this plausible every time?"
>
> "It's enough that I spend several nights with the woman for them to recognize it. In any case, partners come and go, don't they?!"

These two rules also exist on the Sichuan side. Each fine there, however, is for 1,200 *yuan*, payable in one lump sum. This is not a small amount for the peasants. If a household is unable to pay, the cadres take its buffalo and mules by force, the main sources of labor and transportation for the Na. Two young Na women from the Yunnan side were adopted by a *lignée* in Sichuan, about one kilometer away from their original village. Because they were quite young, they did not understand the serious consequences of these rules. Once in Sichuan, they received furtive visitors as they had before. After the women gave birth, no one wanted to be recognized as the children's genitor. As a result, their *lignée* lost all of its domestic animals.

Clearly, the two provinces do not have the same policy in regard to the Na. The situation in Sichuan can be explained by the fact that this province has felt the strongest pressure from overpopulation in all of China. More than 100 million people live in

Sichuan, in other words, one-tenth of the Chinese population. Consequently, the government, on every level, has proved extremely sensitive to this problem.

Beyond these campaigns for monogamy, other Han cultural factors are exercising a latent influence on the Na way of life. The first has to do with schooling. Before 1950, there was only one elementary school in Yongning which had been established by the Guomindang government, with only some twenty students in all. Now there are about forty elementary schools and one middle school, with approximately six hundred students.

Because the Na have no written language, the instructors sent to Yongning during the 1950s and 1960s, all from other ethnic backgrounds, had great difficulty teaching. They did not speak the Na language, and the students did not speak Chinese. Moreover, all of the textbooks were in Chinese. But little by little, in the last two decades, the government has succeeded in educating the Na, who, with a diploma from high school or elementary school, have gradually replaced the teachers from other ethnic groups. These instructors, extremely sinicized, set to sinicizing Na children in turn and did so much more efficiently than their predecessors had. All of this takes place so subtly that the Na are not even aware of it.

Written in Chinese by the Han, all of the textbooks are impregnated with Han ideas and values. By the end of elementary school, that is, after six years of instruction, Na children are still not all that sinicized, because they have not yet completed their socialization. However, those who go on to middle school, and especially those who finish high school, are deeply sinicized.

I will limit myself to citing three anecdotes. The first: when students graduate from middle school, they must complete a form that includes a column requesting information on their civil status. Unable to fill in the blank asking for the name of their father, they suddenly become aware they do not have a father, while their classmates from other ethnic backgrounds do. Some of the Na students, usually the most brilliant ones, find a quiet spot where they can cry in private. Throughout their education (twelve years), Na students use the primary-school and middle-school textbooks in which children always have a father whenever the subject of kinship and family comes up. No case is made for the maternal uncle. In other words, these textbooks are full of Han ideas of kinship. The more outstanding the student, the more affected he is by these values. The message is clear. For them, unconsciously, there is only one culture that is legitimate, and that is Han culture (that of the majority ethnic group). During a conversation I had with a twenty-year-old high school student, after telling me the above story about the form, she said:

"I do not follow the custom of the visit."

"Why not?"

"We are four brothers and sisters. According to the villagers, we each have a different genitor. It's no good, not having a father!"

She said she wanted to get married later on. However, at school, her teachers never explicitly stated that it would be better to get married. This shows how effectively the school system today spreads Han culture and how far-reaching its influence is.

The second anecdote comes from an interview with a twenty-two-year-old female teacher. She had completed twelve years of study and had had one year of professional experience teaching first-grade students.

"What language do you teach in?"

"Na and Chinese, half-and-half."

"Do the children understand Chinese?"

"A little. The higher up one goes, the less Na we use in the classroom."

"According to your own experience, what kind of Han influence do you feel you underwent after your many years of study?"

"A very great one."

"Is your life more Na or more Han now?"

"At home, I have to behave in a way that conforms to Na customs, but away from home, for example at school, I live like a Han."

"The main lifestyle for the Na is the visit. In the future, what are you thinking of doing?"

"I will get married, for sure."

"Why?"

"Because for those of us who work in the *danwei* [a work department: factories, schools, the government, and so on; any place that is dependent on the state], we must, willingly or not, prepare a banquet. A wedding is indispensable. On the other hand, those of us who stay in the village continue to live the life of the visit, naturally."

The third anecdote came up while discussing the idea of Na procreation with an old man. My young guide put in a word at the end of our conversation: "In fact, it is your interpretation [of procreation] that is correct, ours is wrong. The fetus is formed by an egg and a sperm. Right?"

The students take courses in biology at school. They consider everything they have been taught in class as Han ideas, even if some of these ideas do not belong to the Han at all.

In addition to the influence of the educational system, Communist Party and government disciplines continue to be rigorously applied to matrimonial legislation. This is true for Communist Party members and for cadres, who work in various Communist Party organizations and the government and are therefore paid by the state. They are forbidden to practice the mode of the visit, and anyone who does is immediately dismissed from the Communist Party and loses his or her job. The status of a salaried employee is greatly admired, so such a sanction is a great deterrence. In fact, any Na salaried employee is required to be officially married in order to have a sex life. Moreover, for anyone living in the city of Ninglang, it is difficult, if not impossible, to practice the mode of the visit, because there are not many other Na there from Yongning.

On the other hand, since 1981, the year Na cadres were placed in leadership positions in the Communist Party and in the government of the Yongning canton, some cadres working there have been practicing the open visit, and this is tolerated. But it is out of the question for them to change partners frequently, as the villagers do, or to practice the furtive visit at the same time.

The Na leaders' attitude in the district toward the custom of the visit is very interesting. In regard to the Na in Yongning, they have adopted a laissez-faire policy. To researchers and journalists, they claim that the villagers are in visit relationships and that the couples are stable. They explain that the visit is traditional and that the stability of the couple is, in fact, a marriage. They therefore feel that the current situation of the Na people corresponds to tradition and to matrimonial legislation.

As for the *furtive visit* and the *open visit*, these expressions remain unknown to Chinese ethnologists and to journalists, even today; they do not exist in Chinese. If a journalist asks a question about the current situation of the short-term *açia*, some Na leaders will object: "That does not exist, and it never has. What the researchers from 1963 wrote about in their books concerned only a few exceptions."

In fact, the Na leaders have adopted a double strategy. On the one hand, they have inserted into the "Rule of the Autonomous District of the Yi of Ninglang" the following clause: "The Mo-so have the right to follow their traditions, if they so desire." On the other hand, they do not disclose the villagers' sexual practices to those in charge of reporting facts to the superior authorities. This tactic has had the effect of protecting their society.

What can we say about the situation in 1988, thirty years after the first matrimonial reforms?

Even though the customs remain the same, the behavior of young people has nevertheless changed. A large percentage of those around twenty-five years old are involved in open relationships. The practice of the furtive visit, of course, continues at the same time.

For example, Gézo (twenty-three years old) from the Adgi *lignée* in Imin formed an open relationship with a young woman from Hliwalo. At that time, he was visiting her practically every day. One day, he asked me:

"Are you going to the movies tonight?"

"Yes, I am."

"Tonight, after the movie, I'm going out to climb some walls."

"You're not seeing your girlfriend anymore?"

"No."

"Why not?"

"She is not clean. She hasn't let me do anything since the night before last."

"It's called her period. Once a month, women bleed."

"Oh, so that's it! She told me the same thing last night."

In fact, that night after the film, he went off to see another woman.

Another example: the treasurer of Imin was a young man of twenty-nine. He had completed five years of elementary school. A few days after I arrived in the village, he came to see me. He showed me the book *Yongning Naxi zu de muxi zhi* (The Matrilineal System of the Naxi of Yongning), and said to me: "They have no idea about anything that they are saying in this book. Why bother coming to research us. What good will it do?" His words threw me into a state of total embarrassment.

Ten days later, I went to the movies. Seated on the ground, I watched the film. At one point, I felt someone behind me fidgeting; he seemed uncomfortable and very nervous. All of a sudden, he grabbed the young woman sitting next to me and began fondling her. Later, when I asked him what he had been doing that night, he replied that he had wanted to demonstrate their custom for me. During his open partner's pregnancy and after she gave birth, he frequently saw other women.

These are not unique cases. According to my sources, everyone involved in an open relationship today also pursues furtive visits. No one decides not to: the only difference is in their frequency.

Why are there more people in open relationships today than before? On this subject, a twenty-nine-year-old man gave me his opinion:

> "Today, the policies of Deng Xiaoping are not bad. We can once again have a good time with the women, like we did before. Just for that, we hope that Deng sticks around for as long as possible."
>
> "Do you have an open girlfriend?"
>
> "Yes."
>
> "But if you love having a good time with the young women so much, why are you in an open relationship?"
>
> "Politics can change, you know. If I practice an open visit with a woman, it's because I don't want to wake up one day and have the political situation changed once again and have them force just any old woman on me simply because I slept with her a few times. If they

make me get married, I'd rather do so with a woman I like a little better than the others."

Between two periods of open relationships, a person makes furtive visits. When I came back to the field in the fall of 1992, the treasurer of Imin whom I had met in 1988, having broken off his relationship with his third open girlfriend, only had furtive relations. Nadgodgima, the oldest daughter in branch I of the Imin *lignée*, had a child in 1990 with her former open partner. She was therefore free, for he no longer came to see her and was frequenting other women. There are more and more examples of this kind.

Within the parameters of my research, the statistics on the number of people living according to each modality of sexual life provide a broad picture of the current situation: in 1989, the five villages had 277 sexually active people — the base group of my calculations — out of which there were 158 women and 119 men. There were 158 people, or 57 percent of the whole, who practiced the furtive visit exclusively, out of which 92 were women and 66 were men. In this category, 42 women and 22 men had been, at various times, in an open relationship. There were 79 people, or 28.5 percent of the whole, in open relationships, out of which 44 were women and 35 were men. Among these couples, there were only 23 in which both members were within the parameters of my research. In 33 of the couples, only one of the partners was from one of the five villages, out of which 21 were women and 12 were men.

Only five people, three women and two men, or 1.8 percent of the whole, were voluntarily cohabiting. Among these couples, one of them fell within the parameters of my research and had the consent of both of their *lignées*. In the other two couples, one cohabitant was from Lijadzï, a remote mountain village, far from the Yongning basin, where life is more difficult. The other came from Dgepu. One man moved to Gala without the consent of his original *lignée*.

There are currently seventeen couples, or 10.1 % of the whole, formed by the various reforms. Out of these people only sixteen women and twelve men fall within the parameters of my research. Out of these couples, one was formed in 1958; four were formed in 1966 (one of these had been formed in 1958 but had fallen apart in 1959; since the man was the village chief, he got back together with the same woman in 1966); and twelve were arranged in 1975.

During the last reform, twenty-eight couples were created within the parameters of my research. Sixteen of these fell apart shortly after the campaign, that is, in 1975 and 1976.

I asked the villagers, including some of the couples that were formed during the monogamy campaigns, if they were considered *jï the hing* (those that were organized with a banquet) or *ti dzï jï mao the hing* (cohabitants). They responded: "*ti dzï jï mao the hing*, because they were forced to get together without a banquet." I have therefore classified them as cohabitants.

There were three voluntary marriages, whose members make up 2.16 percent of the whole, within my frame of reference. Two of them took place approximately sixty years ago, and one of them took place in 1983. There was also one marriage between a Na man, who represents 0.4 percent of the whole, and a Li-su woman. The man traveled extensively in his youth and was recruited by the state as a woodcutter. He married this woman from another ethnic group and years later resigned his job and returned to his village. Figure 13.1 shows the breakdown of statistics for sexually active people in 1989.

Among those who had never been sexually active were three Lamaist monks, one deaf-mute, four mentally deficient people (one of whom was a woman), and a person with a clubfoot. The three Lamaist monks were over seventy years old. The ages of the others ranged from thirty to forty-five.

	Furtive Visit	Conspicuous Visit	Cohabitation	Marriage
Female	92	44	19	3
Male	66	35	14	4
Total	158	79	33	7
Percentage	57	28.5	11.9	2.56

Figure 13.1. Number of people who practiced each modality of sexual life in 1989.

The chart in figure 13.2 shows the statistics, recorded in 1963 by Chinese ethnologists, of the nine villages discussed in previous chapters: Batçi, DZybu, Hliwalo, Yumi, Zhongshi, Zhongke, Kaitçi *gewa*, Kaitçi *muwa*, and Naha. There were 683 adults alive in these villages, out of which 387 were women and 296 were men.

	Visit	Cohabitation	Marriage
Female	326	30	31
Male	245	24	27
Total	571	54	58
Percentage	83.5	7.9	8.5

Figure 13.2. Number of people who practiced the three modalities of sexual life recorded by researchers in 1963.

During the reforms, the work groups and the villagers reproached each other for their lifestyles: for "breaking up the 'family'" and for "undoing solidarity." The terms *family* and *solidarity* were used, but they did not designate the same thing and did not cover the same concepts. For the work groups, a family was a husband, a wife, and children. For the Na, it was brothers and sisters and the sisters' children in every generation. Because these two types of families were completely different, the idea of solidarity could not be homogeneous. Therefore, from each side's perspective, the reproach was legitimate. This conceptual opposition seems to be the most profound reason for the failure of the reforms.

We must not forget that the marriages that took place during the reforms were arranged marriages. Ironically, one element of the ancient institution of Chinese marriage that was criticized and forbidden by the matrimonial legislations was the arranged marriage. Of course, by this the authorities meant a marriage arranged by parents and a mediator. It is easy to force people to stay together physically, but mentally, it is difficult.

Whereas forced attempts to reform marriage have failed, the schools have certainly succeeded: by proceeding peacefully and taking their time. Under these conditions, one mentality can be replaced by another. For this reason, the schools, it seems to me, have been more effective than force in changing Na culture.

What is behind this series of matrimonial reforms?

On an ideological level, evolutionism was taken to be a sacred doctrine, and monogamy was seen as the final stage of evolution in human sexual relations. During the years of extreme leftism, two sayings of Marx were often quoted as maxims: "The proletariat will not be completely free until all of humanity has been liberated," and "Before, philosophers only wanted to explain the world. Our duty is not only to explain the world but also to reform the world." Among the extremists, these sayings became an obsession.

On a legal level, matrimonial legislation legitimized monogamy only. It protected the rights of women and children so that they would not be abandoned, and it neither recognized nor protected premarital relations. From this point of view, it is obvious that Na moral standards did not correspond to Chinese matrimonial legislation. With this legislation, matrimonial reform seemed inevitable. But since this legislation was, above all, for a society of marriage, these matrimonial reforms were, at bottom, the manifestation of an intercultural conflict.

Given the pragmatism of Deng Xiaoping, who became the leader of China in 1981, it is now understood that the more the government tries to "liberate" other ethnic groups, the less it will be supported by them. A more moderate policy toward ethnic minorities has been adopted. In Yongning, those who practice the custom of the visit can still be fined, but matrimonial reform is no longer justified. The Na tragedy of 1974 was a product of extreme leftism, while today, intercultural conflict continues but in a more tempered way.

Na customs are tenacious, resistant, and extremely vivacious. This is the only possible conclusion one can come to in the face of these reforms.

In social science, it is difficult, if not impossible, to conduct an experiment. The social test that the extremists dared to carry out demonstrates what a scourge ethnocentrism and evolutionism as world visions can be and how society can react. At the same time, however, these reforms provide an opportunity to observe the mechanisms of this kinship system.

PART THREE

Comparison and

Theoretical Discussion

Throughout this ethnographic description, some of the differences and similarities between Na culture and other cultures have been apparent. In this section, I conduct a comparative study between the four modalities of Na sexual life and marriage in other societies and between the Na *matrilignée* and the family. By doing so, I hope to add to the understanding of the modality of institutionalized sexuality and basic social organization.

The Comparison of the Four Modalities of Sexual Life
The incest prohibition is present in all of the modalities. I therefore posit the observation of this rule as the first characteristic
of each modality. In most societies, there are three categories of
people for Ego: consanguineal relatives (in the sociological sense),
relatives by marriage, and outsiders (including friends, acquaintances, and strangers).

I will begin by examining the furtive visit. The first characteristic of this modality is the observation of the incest prohibition.
The furtive relationship is characterized by equality between the
sexes, in both its formation and termination. A furtive visit occurs
only with the mutual consent of the partners, and the relationship
takes place exclusively in the form of a nocturnal visit from the
man to the woman in her house (a woman visiting a man is forbidden). The second characteristic of this modality lies in its
being a matter between two individuals only, that is, a private
affair. It is completely private because its establishment, existence, and breakup concern no one except the visitor and the visited. Because of the ban on sexual evocation, the visitor must
avoid the woman's male consanguineal relatives during the course
of the visit. The third characteristic of this modality is the multiplicity of partners during a given time span. The fourth characteristic, discontinuity between the partners, stems from the third.

These four basic attributes lead me to classify the *açia* as an
acquaintance (outsider); the *açia* are acquaintances only to each
other. Why not classify them as friends? As is true elsewhere, a
friend for the Na is someone with whom one is familiar, indeed
someone with whom one is intimate, someone who will stop by
to see you and know that he will always be fed and housed if necessary. A visitor, on the other hand, can never eat at his *açia*'s
home because of the furtiveness of the relationship. During my
research in the field, I discovered the word *dzé hing* (friends), a

category that includes both *dhu zï dhu mi* and friends in the more general sense of the term, and I wanted to know if there was a word that identified *açia* as a category in Na conception. When I asked this question, the villagers were perplexed.

I will now examine the conspicuous visit. Observation of the incest prohibition is the first characteristic of this modality. The second characteristic is the meal ritual, which involves the intervention of the visited's *lignée*. This ritual abolishes the need for the visitor and the woman's male consanguineal relatives to avoid each other and therefore permits a new behavior on the part of the visitor, as well as on the part of the woman's male consanguineal relatives. All this constitutes the social aspect of this modality. The concept of social here is used in opposition to that of individual or private. This social aspect is, however, very limited. The meal ritual involves only the womans' *lignée*, while the villagers, including the man's *lignée*, only find out about it later. The decision to form the relationship, however, is made by the partners on their own. The consent of the womans' *lignée* is requested only to facilitate the visit, and the maintenance of the relationship depends on the partners alone. The relationship ends when one partner wants to terminate it. The woman's *lignée* does not intervene, and moreover, it cannot, because of the ban on sexual evocation. Therefore, this kind of relationship depends entirely on the wishes of the partners, and its private aspect takes precedence over its public aspect. Indeed, the supposedly social aspect of this relationship might better be called semi-social. The third basic characteristic consists of having a single partner. The fourth concerns the continuity of the relationship. Based on my observations in the field, four months seems to be the minimum duration for this kind of a relationship. The fifth characteristic is the sexual privilege and its partial protection. The sexual privilege is only partially protected because people in open relationships also

	açia	*dhu zï dhu mi*	*Cohabitants*	*Married Couples*
Essential conditions				
Non-consanguineal individuals	+	+	+	+
A lack of members of one sex in a generation and an unsuccessful adoption attempt			+	+
Ways of forming a relationship				
Equality for both sexes in taking the initiative	+	+		
Mutual consent	+	+		
Consent of the *lignée(s)*		+	+	+
Social consent and recognition				+
The receiving *lignée* making the request, and never at the same time being a donor			+	+
Prestation				+
Maintenance of the relationship				
The mutual feelings of the partners	+	+	+	
Being on good terms with the receiving *lignée* (in uxorilocal cases)		+	+	
Social coercion				+
Conditions for ending a relationship				
The will of one of the partners	+	+	+	
Social intervention				+
Forms of the relationship				
In space				
Nocturnal visits by the man to the woman's house	+	+		
Living together on a permanent basis			+	+
In time				
Discontinuity	+			
Continuity		+	+	+
Taboos				
Women visiting men	+	+		
Meetings between the visitor and the woman's male consanguineal relatives	+			
Fighting between rivals over the same woman (or man)	+			
Returning to one's birth home following a separation				+

	açia	*dhu zï* *dhu mi*	*Cohabitants*	*Married Couples*
Combination of formal partners within a given time span				
Multiplicity of partners	+			
One partner		+	+	+
Rights and responsibilities of the partners to each other and between them and the descendants				
During the relationship				
Sexual privilege and its partial protection		+	+	+
Symbols (annual exchanging of gifts between the partners)		+		
Economic relationship			+	+
Economic rights following a breakup			+	+
Identification of the individuals in the relationship				
A change in the *lignée*'s name for the displaced partner				+
The children taking the name of the receiving *lignée*			+	+
The nature of the relationship				
Private affair	+			
Semi-social in appearance only, private in reality		+	+	
Social				+
Identity				
Outsiders				
Acquaintances	+			
Friends		+		
Mu min zo min			+	+
Hinshuba and *chumi* (can be designated as spouses)				+
The recording of the name after death, on the list of the receiving *lignée*'s ancestors				+

Figure 14.1 The constitutive elements in the four modalities of sexual life.

practice, without exception, furtive relationships. This makes their sex life appear as a diptych: one part takes place as a conspicuous visit, and the other takes place as a furtive visit. They, too, then, have multiple partners. Consequently, if the partners want to keep their open relationship going, they must accept each other's furtive relationships when they are discovered, since the furtive relationship is the primary modality of sexual life and the basis of Na values and moral standards. The contradictory effects of the mechanisms of these two modalities make it inevitable that respect for the sexual privilege is only limited. The sixth basic characteristic is the annual exchanging of gifts between the two partners, a symbol of their attachment to each other.

These six basic attributes lead me to conclude that the relationship between the *dhu zï dhu mi* has two aspects, one private and one semi-social. But its character is, in the end, private. The *dhu zï dhu mi* are friends (outsiders), which is also the meaning of *dhu zï dhu mi*. Moreover, the Na have traditionally identified them as such.

A comparison of the furtive visit and the conspicuous visit reveals the following commonalities: the nocturnal visit, the ban on women visiting men, and the mutual consent of the partners. On the other hand, the following oppositions reveal their differences: the rule mandating that the visitor avoid the visited's consanguineal relatives in her home versus not needing to avoid them; multiple partners versus one partner; discontinuity versus continuity; no sexual privilege versus sexual privilege; no exchange of gifts versus the annual exchange of gifts; and, finally, a private affair versus a semi-social affair. The nature of the relationship between the partners in these two modalities also differs in that an *açia* relationship is between acquaintances, while a *dhu zï dhu mi* relationship is between friends. In terms of kinship, that is, in comparison with the relationship between affinal relatives (for the moment, we will rely on common sense and broach the question of just what the relationship between affinal relatives is later), these two kinds of relationships belong in the category of outsiders. One partner is an outsider in relation to the other.

Now I will examine the modality of cohabitation. Once again, the observation of the incest prohibition constitutes the first characteristic. The second characteristic is that it is a last resort to perpetuate a household, one that comes after all adoption attempts have failed. The third basic attribute is its semi-social aspects given its procedures: the mutual consent of the partners; the intervention of both *lignées*, or of only the receiving *lignée* in some uxorilocal cases; and the desire of only one partner being enough to break off the relationship. The fourth characteristic is that the partners share the same fire and the same pot. The fifth characteristic of cohabitation includes continuity of the relationship, one partner, and the partial protection of the sexual privilege. The sixth trait is that, in virilocal cases, the children take the name of the receiving *lignée*. The seventh is the economic relationship between the cohabitants and between them and the female cohabitant's children, expressed in the communal sharing of the receiving *lignée*'s possessions and the fruits of their labor. Finally, the eighth essential characteristic is that the cohabitants are labeled *zo min* in uxorilocal cases and *mu min* in virilocal cases.

I will compare this modality to the furtive and the conspicuous visit at the same time. First of all, for *lignées* that have members of both sexes (or in some *lignées*, of just the female sex), the furtive and conspicuous visits are the norm and are perfectly adequate for filling the *lignée*'s reproductive needs. The reproduction of the *lignée* is not something a man would be concerned about under normal circumstances. But when a *lignée* lacks a member of one of the sexes, especially a female member, furtive and conspicuous visits cannot meet its reproductive needs. Cohabitation is turned to when the possibilities for adoption have been exhausted. Besides the incest prohibition, there is a second restriction on cohabitation: it is only permitted when there is a lack of one sex in one generation. For this reason, one cannot but observe this modality as conditional. It was created to overcome a crisis provoked by a biological phenomenon.

When compared with the furtive visit, cohabitation shares only one-half of a point: the establishment, maintenance, and dissolution of the relationship are based on the mutual consent and free will of the partners. In all of its other characteristics, this modality differs from the furtive visit: concubinage versus the nocturnal visit; permission for a woman to live with a man when his *lignée* lacks female members versus the ban on women visiting men; continuity versus discontinuity; one partner versus multiple partners; economic ties versus no economic ties; rights and responsibilities regarding the children of one's partner when the relationship ends versus the opposite.

I will now compare cohabitation and the conspicuous visit. Here, there are more points in common: the manner in which the relationship is formed and dissolved; the receiving *lignée*'s intervention in uxorilocal cases (both partners' *lignées* intervene in virilocal cases, but this is a difference, not a similarity); staying on good terms with the members of the receiving *lignée* in order to maintain the relationship; one partner; continuity; and the sexual privilege. The differences between cohabitation and the conspicuous visit are the following: concubinage versus the nocturnal visit; the existence of economic ties versus the absence of economic ties; rights and responsibilities regarding the children when the relationship ends versus the opposite. There is one last difference: the children taking the name of the receiving *lignée* in virilocal cases versus the children keeping the name of their original opposite is also true: the providing *lignée* is never a receiving *lignée* in the same generation. As a rule, marriage is not repeated from one generation to the next, once the receiving *lignée* has a girl and a boy. Therefore, this modality occurs only rarely and not consecutively. Its second characteristic is the at once horizontal and vertical discontinuity of its development. To form a marriage relationship, the following conditions must be met: mutual consent of the partners' *lignées*, agreement to marry by both partners, prestation, intervention by representatives of each *lignée* in the village as witnesses, and, in the past, registration with the *zhifu* — all of which constitutes formal social recognition of this relationship. To maintain the relationship, there is the rule preventing a partner from returning to his or her original household following a separation. Moreover, a separation can only occur after representatives of the village *lignées* have intervened (in the past, when this intervention did not bring about a reconciliation between the spouses, there would be a trial before the *zhifu*). From the beginning to the end, every process concerning this relationship is social (as opposed to private or personal); in other words, it is a relationship between groups. It is a simple and pure social affair, and this is its third basic characteristic. Its fourth basic attribute includes having only one partner, the continuity of the relationship, and the sexual privilege of the partners. Given that the partners share the same pot and the same fire, the fifth essential characteristic is that they form an economic unit. Because the woman and her children take the name of the man's *lignée* and because the woman's name will be recorded on the receiving *lignée*'s list of ancestors, the partners acquire two new social qualities while remaining non-consanguineal: spouse and affinal relative. In addition, on an economic level, the man and his wife's children have mutual rights and responsibilities. From an ethnological point of view, the children, too, have become relatives by marriage of the woman's partner and therefore constitute a new community of kinship. This constitutes the sixth basic characteristic.

I will now compare marriage with the furtive visit. With the exception of the observation of the incest prohibition and the mutual consent of the partners, these two modalities have no points in common. All of their other basic characteristics are not only different but in direct opposition. Here are the opposing pairs:

- specific practice versus general practice;
- permission for a woman to live in her partner's home versus the prohibition against women visiting their partners' homes;
- a social affair versus a private affair (or an affair between groups versus an affair between individuals);
- one partner versus multiple partners;
- continuity versus discontinuity;
- the presence of the sexual privilege versus its absence;
- sharing the same pot and the same fire versus the nocturnal visit;
- new social positions created by the relationship — husband and wife, spouses and relatives by marriage, and a new community of kinship — versus no new social position created by the relationship (each partner continues to belong to his or her own *matrilignée*);
- economic ties between the partners who create a new economic community, versus the absence of economic ties;
- rights and responsibilities between the man and his partner's children versus no such rights or responsibilities;
- the partners' entitlement to claim a share of the property and the children when the relationship ends versus no rights to the property or the children (this is unthinkable) when the relationship ends.

I will now compare marriage with the conspicuous visit. In addition to the observation of the incest prohibition and the mutual consent of the partners, these two modalities share having one partner, continuity, and the sexual privilege. Since the duration of an open relationship varies from several months to ten years, but never a lifetime, and a marriage almost always lasts for life (recall that we came across only one case of divorce in the Na), the difference between these two modalities seems not one of degree but one of nature. As far as their basic attributes are concerned, they differ from and are in direct contrast with each other in the same ways as marriage and the furtive visit. By extension, in comparison with marriage, the two types of visits are of the same nature.

I will now compare of marriage and cohabitation. This comparison is somewhat complicated, because among the Na marriage only occurs virilocally, while cohabitation can occur virilocally or uxorilocally. However, since the relationship is much less stable in uxorilocal cases than in virilocal cases, I will first compare marriage with virilocal cohabitation and will address uxorilocal cases later, in the discussion on the nature of the relationship between cohabitants.

The two modalities have the following points in common: an exceptional practice; the *lignée* lacking in female members being the receiver and never the donor within a single generation and, conversely, the donor *lignée* never at the same time being a receiver; the consent of the partners and their kinship groups; one partner, continuity, and the sexual privilege; the partners sharing the same pot and the same fire, establishing economic ties, and forming a new economic community; each partner being entitled to a share of the property and the children when the relationship ends after a long communal life together; the children taking the name of the receiving *lignée*; and the existence of rights and responsibilities between the male partner and the female partner's children.

The differences between and cohabitation are the following: a social versus a semi-social affair; the partners becoming husband and wife and forming a new community of kinship versus the partners remaining outsiders to each other; the woman taking the name of her partner's *lignée* versus the partners keeping the names of their own *lignées*; and the woman's name being added to the list of her partner's ancestors after her death versus not having one's name added to the receiving *lignée*'s list of ancestors after death.

This initial comparison demonstrates that these two modalities have their own specific features, such that, in order to discern their natures, it is necessary to enlarge our field of comparison. This second stage of comparison will come later.

The comparison above leads to the following conclusions: compared with Na marriage, the furtive visit and conspicuous visit are not of a different nature from each other. They represent only a sexual bond. In the Na way of life, the norms of these two modalities together constitute an institution, one that I call the visit. This institution is essential and basic; it is the preeminent modality of sexual life in this society, and in a sense everyone is forced to follow it, its practice being determined not just by individual will but, because of its preponderance, by a sort of societal coercion. The practice of cohabitation, on the other hand, is much less common and is permitted under only one circumstance: when a generation in a *lignée* lacks a member of one sex. The rigidity of this rule is evident not only in its observation as prerequisite condition for cohabitation and marriage but also in the consequences for breaking it, illustrated most glaringly by the examples I cited of runaways. Finally, it is imperative for an individual to follow the institution of the visit. However, an individual can practice the furtive visit, the conspicuous visit, or the two types of visits at the same time. Under this institution, an individual therefore has a choice, which does not hold true in a marriage society, where there is only one institutional modality for sex. The existence of this choice marks the great particularity of this institution.

Cohabitation is auxiliary and complementary to the institution of the visit. This modality is necessary for Na society in that it allows it to function, no matter what the circumstances. But while this modality is institutionalized, it does not constitute an institution. As is true in certain unilineal societies, the kind of biological phenomenon that necessitates cohabitation — that a couple has only one child, for example — obliges an only child to follow a way of life that goes against the norm of his society. For example, in Han society, which is patrilineal, the receivers only take in girls, as a general rule, and the residence is virilocal. But when a couple has only a daughter, it is obliged to take in a man to marry her, and the residence is therefore uxorilocal. Clearly it is normal for a society, especially a unilineal one, to have an auxiliary modality.

I will now return to the institution of the visit. Its complete opposition to the mode of marriage makes us confront, for the first time ever in the course of human history, a society based on an institution other than marriage. The existence of this institution provides a new type of institutionalized sexual life that makes it possible to consider marriage as only one modality of institutionalized sexual life. We can therefore posit the visit and marriage as different types of institutionalized sexual life and treat them as separate categories.

Until now, every theory of social structure has stated that no society can exist without marriage. However, Na society is based on an alternative institution, the visit. Does this mean that it has completely passed over marriage? What is the essence of the modality of Na cohabitation? Is it identical with or different from that of marriage?

What Is Marriage?

Having considered the particulars of Na cohabitation and marriage, the identification of these two modalities immediately raises the following question: what is marriage? In response to this question, which has obsessed ethnologists and been studied and restudied, many definitions have already been proposed. But none has been recognized as adequate, even by the authors themselves.

I am forced, then, to return to the definition of marriage, and I propose to organize my thoughts on the subject in three steps: (1) an examination of the term *marriage*; (2) an in-depth study of the definitions of marriage proposed by E. R. Leach and in an article by P. G. Rivière on the subject; and (3) an attempt to define marriage and state what the institution of marriage is.

I will begin by examining the semantic fields of the term *marriage* in English and French. The word *marriage* has two meanings in the natural language:

1. The ritual of marriage: for example, when we say "when did your marriage take place?" or "to attend a marriage," we are using the term *marriage* as an action in a specific moment in time. Its synonym in this case is *wedding*.

2. The institution of marriage: for example, when we say "they are united in marriage" and "the legislation of marriage."[1]

Marriage in this second case encompasses the first meaning. In the sense of a wedding, marriage is a ceremony — but defining the ceremony does not get us any further. Since an institution consists of a set of rules, it does not need to be defined. On a linguistic level, then, we are blocked. Moreover, the difficult here is not

427

merely linguistic but also cultural. For in defining *marriage*, we are dealing with a concept whose medium is a particularity of language, in this case in both English and French. Therefore, the block has arisen from Anglo-Saxon or French culture.

Finally, surrounding the terms *marriage* and *to marry* there is an expression that refers to neither an action nor an institution but to a state: "Are you married?" To define this state is the equivalent of listing the rights that are customary or stipulated by the legislation. This does not, however, help us solve our problem. This state supposes the existence of something else: relations, what we call matrimonial relations or matrimonial ties, that are not the same as rights and responsibilities.

At the outset, we were attempting to define *marriage*, but nothing else. The stumbling block arose from the fact that only the word *marriage* was taken into consideration instead of observing the facts. Consequently, if instead of focusing on the word we focus on the object of study itself, we can see that it is precisely these matrimonial ties that must be defined. Moreover, this is the only object that requires a definition and that is definable.

I cite here the definition of marriage put forward by E. R. Leach (I have emphasized certain words that I will discuss further on):

> The institutions commonly classed as *marriage* are concerned with the allocation of a number of distinguishable classes of *rights*. In particular a *marriage* may serve:
>
> A. To establish the legal father of a woman's children.
> B. To establish the legal mother of a man's children.
> C. To give the husband a monopoly in the wife's sexuality.
> D. To give the wife a monopoly in the husband's sexuality.
> E. To give the husband partial or monopolistic rights to the wife's domestic and other labour services.

F. To give the wife partial or monopolistic rights to the husband's labour services.

G. To give the husband partial or total rights over property belonging or potentially accruing to the wife.

H. To give the wife partial or total rights over property belonging or potentially accruing to the husband.

I. To establish a joint fund of property — a partnership — for the benefit of the children of the marriage.

J. To establish a socially significant "relationship of affinity" between the husband and his wife's brothers."[2]

First, the three "marriages" contained in this definition do not seem to designate the same thing. It is clear that the first "marriage" means the institution of marriage, whereas the second and third do not clearly denote the institution, but rather the action, as discussed above. Above all, in this definition, it seems that the second and third "marriages" can only be included if they are considered the ritual of marriage.

Second, it is clear that this definition in no way constitutes a real definition of *marriage*, no matter what the meaning of the term might be. What I mean by this is that first of all the author was trying to define an object but was limited by the common usage of the word *marriage*. Therefore, he could only take, for lack of anything better, marriage as a ceremony or a ritual as a point of departure among the various factors that he drew from social acts. But in defining it, he has only presented a list of the functions of marriage inasmuch as it is a ceremony. Besides, "function creates the organ." The organ decides the function. Leach's approach results in circular reasoning. Finally, as long as one is not rid of the obstacle of his or her own culture — that is, as long as one is trying to define the term *marriage* instead of grasping the reality of the facts first — it will be difficult to avoid this double pitfall: that is, defining marriage as a wedding or as an institution.

Third, Leach has understood the husband and the wife as axiomatic: he has not specified in his definition what kind of man and what kind of woman can become a husband and a wife. This, however, is strictly prescribed in every society that has the institution of marriage. His definition therefore lacks an essential factor: non-consanguinity as the concerned parties' social quality. In addition, this definition contains terms taken by the author to be axiomatic, such as "legal father" and "legal mother" and "relationship of affinity." Who can become a "legal father"? And who can become a "legal mother"? What does "relationship of affinity" mean? All of this still needs to be defined.

Finally, Leach only sees rights in the institution of marriage. Therefore, his approach reveals that the essence of marriage is underlying in other societies, as well as in that of the author. Other existing definitions of marriage contain the same problems and confirm the same findings if we closely analyze them. In spite of all these caveats, among the various definitions of marriage, Leach's has great practical and analytical value.

Before presenting my own definition of marriage and the rules that constitute the institution of marriage, I will quote from an article by P. G. Rivière, "Marriage: A Reassessment," which is especially interesting because it takes into account the various methods with which to approach the question of marriage and because it can serve as an object of analysis for discerning the latent obstacles that anthropologists (Rivière included) bring with them in their approaches to marriage.

First of all, Rivière believes that "all functionalist definitions and explanations of marriage belong to the conscious model, and because of this the functions of and the reasons for marriage become confused";[3] "the marital institution and its function are being used to define each other"; "there is no place for one without other, and the argument is purely circular."[4] Therefore he concludes: "I do not think there is anything wrong with functionalist approaches to marriage other than that they are inadequate."[5]

One question can be raised about this part of Rivière's argument: What definition of *marriage* has actually treated the cause of marriage?

Subsequently, he advises us to take our eyes off "what the institution does in order to look at its composition, its constituent elements, and the relationships between them."[6] This does seem to be a good suggestion. But just what are the constitutive elements? He states: "The constituent units of marriage are men and women, and this seems to be marriage's single, universal feature. Thus the study of marriage must in the first place concentrate on the categories of male and female and the relationship between them."[7]

Rivière does not begin, as Leach does, with the husband and the wife. However, by placing all men in one category and all women in another, without distinction, as Leach does, he has not said anything about the kinds of men and women. Moreover, Rivière is also blocked by his language and his culture. The proof is that he has indicated that "one is trapped in one's own argument and in the terminology employed in it."[8] But two pages later, he suggests that we apply Leach's definition of marriage, under the angle of typology, as the second stage in the study of marriage. It is not enough simply to state that others are prisoners of something to avoid being a prisoner oneself.

His pessimistic conclusion is: "We mislead ourselves by describing with a single term relationships which in different societies have no single feature in common."[9] (The set of facts that come under the term *marriage* remain a labyrinth for the author.) He goes on to say, "if we are to retain marriage as an analytic category we are condemned forever to examining marriage in terms of what it does. This does not mean that I think there is no such thing as marriage (as I have been accused), although I would say that part of our difficulties springs from its too obvious existence."[10] Treating marriage as a category does not condemn us to study it in terms of what it does. On the other hand, the too obvious existence of marriage does pose certain difficulties, and it is precisely for this reason that many factors connected to marriage have been taken to be axiomatic and that we encounter circular reasoning in studies of marriage. However, this does not mean that marriage cannot be regarded as a unitary and coherent object of study, as Rivière concludes: "I would certainly agree with Leach that there is no single definition of marriage";[11] "neither a definition nor explanation of marriage" is possible.[12]

It must be said that that to consider marriage as a category in order to distill its essence constitutes a necessary and even sufficient approach. However, because of the above-mentioned obstacles, this is difficult. It would be easier methodologically if we could pass to a higher level and consider the institution of marriage as a type, instead of a category. If we could then find another type that is also made up of institutionalized rules, we could compare the two. The task of defining human beings is facilitated when we take them to be a type and place them side by side with primates, also considered a type, because we can then pick out the essential characteristics of each and the differences between them and therefore extricate the nature of man. Knowledge of the Na case seems to provide such an opportunity.

Following this lengthy examination, I can now clearly articulate my definition of *marriage*. Contrary to Rivière, I propose to consider marriage from the perspective of ties and to approach what it is and what it implies from this angle.

I propose the following definition of marriage. I give to marriage the same meaning as a double sexual and economic bond between two social, non-consanguineal individuals of the opposite sex, established on the basis of the acceptance of the two parties, and with the consent of their consanguineal groups with prestations. This double bond is recognized and constrained by society. The constitution of this double bond has the following implications:

1. The formation of a sexual and economic community between the partners and thereby their privilege of mutual possessions, which leads society to conceptualize their reciprocal sexual and economic rights and obligations.

2. Conceptualization of two new social qualities for the man and the woman: husband and wife, which leads to the conceptualization of another quality for them: spouse.

3. A common residence for the spouses immediately following, or a specified time after, the wedding.

4. A link of specific interest that is more or less intense depending on the society and that is translated by a particular solidarity between the spouses' membership groups, or between the spouses and each of their membership groups. Society identifies the husband and the wife, as well as the members of their groups, and conceptualizes a new category for them — affines — and labels this bond of particular interest affinity.

5. Conceptualization of a new social quality for the husband, that of father of the children born to the wife, and a new quality for the wife, that of mother of these children, and a new quality for the couple, that of parents vis-à-vis these children. This is because procreation is generally a consequence of marriage. Society names the bond between the father and these children paternity and the one between the mother and these children maternity.

6. The partners' responsibility for the children born of the wife and rights and responsibilities between the parents and the children. The parents raise and provide for the children; the children (or some of them) take care of the parents during their old age.

If we are to accept this definition, let us specify some of the terms used. By *prestation*, I mean a variable quantity of goods (people can be included, but then they must be considered goods) that passes from one group to the other in one direction only or reciprocally or from the two groups to the new couple. No matter what the amount of these goods, which might even be symbolic, they always serve as a sign of mutual recognition of the groups. By *constrained*, I mean that society watches over the concerned parties to make sure that they fulfill the rights and responsibilities that come with the establishment of this double bond and also over the other members of the couple's community so that they in turn respect the rights of this couple.

The symbolic and public act conveyed either in a ritual or in a legal procedure, or in several actions — the engagement and the wedding, for example — is not shared by every society that practices marriage. On the other hand, recognition of this double bond is common ground for all. Therefore, these acts are not necessary conditions for the constitution of the double bond. In any case, as Claude Lévi-Strauss says: "It matters little whether group intervention is explicit or tacit; what matters is that each society has at its command a means of differentiating between de facto unions and legal ones — a means arrived at in several ways."[13]

From this definition of marriage and its implications, it is possible to introduce a set of rules that make up what we call the institution of marriage:

1. Marriage is a double sexual and economic bond established between two individuals of the opposite sex who are non-consanguineal (in the sociological sense).

2. It is forbidden for two consanguineal relatives to form this double bond.

3. Every marriage must be formed with the agreement of the partners and the consent of their membership groups and recog-

nized by the representatives of the community to which they belong or in which they are integrated.

4. The establishment of this double bond must be accompanied by a prestation.

5. After the creation of this double bond, the man becomes the husband of the woman, and the woman becomes the wife of the man, and they are identified as spouses to each other.

6. At some point after the foundation of this double bond, the two spouses must live under the same roof.

7. The two spouses have the sexual privilege in regard to each other, and they must respect this privilege.

8. In relation to each other, they possess partial or exclusive economic rights to their current and future property, as well as to the fruits of their labor.

9. After the constitution of this double bond, the partners become affines, and at the same time, through them, the members (including the spouses) of the spouses' groups become affines to each other.

10. The husband is the father of the children born to his wife, and she is their mother.

11. The parents are responsible for providing food and lodging and bringing up the children, and the children (or some of them) are responsible for taking care of the parents during their old age.

Is this approach to the subject of marriage (as matrimonial bond) adequate? Or, in other words, given that as a social convention, marriage and its implications emerged together, could marriage thus defined and its consequences be understood as resulting in a tautology? It seems not.

The reasons are simple. First, the formation of this double bond between two non-consanguineal individuals can never occur without the agreement of the partners, even in cases of arranged or prescribed marriage. Whether it is voluntary or forced, the partners' consent is an absolute necessity. The absence of consent could provoke the suicide of one or both of the partners. An arranged marriage can only succeed on the condition that it is accepted by the partners; if not, it will fail. There is no shortage of these kinds of situations in societies in which arranged or prescribed marriages exist.

Second, both the sexual bond and the economic bond can be established between two individuals according to their desires and without the consent of their membership groups and even against the wishes of these groups. In this case, the relationship imparts neither the quality of spouse nor that of affine. Situations of this kind can only occur in societies in which the matrimonial convention exists. For the partners to be identified as spouses, this double bond must be formed communally, with not only their consent but the consent of their membership groups as well. In other words, the existence of this double bond is necessary, but not enough in and of itself, for the partners to be considered spouses and relatives by marriage. It is not because the concepts of spouse and affine exist in a culture that the individuals who have formed this double bond can automatically be considered spouses and affines by marriage. This is precisely the case in concubinage (in the traditional sense of the word), which provides a perfect counterexample of marriage. In this case, the legal situation of the partners comes not from a socially known relationship (often a concubinage relationship is notorious because it is considered a scandal in many traditional societies) but from a socially recognized relationship.

As with arranged marriages, there are two solutions for concubinage: either the couple gives in to the pressure from society and separates, or their membership groups give in and the story ends with their social recognition of this bond.

the incest prohibition; the need for the consent of the partners and their membership groups, in both the formation and maintenance of the bonds; the social recognition of these bonds; communal residence; one partner; the mutual sexual privilege; economic ties between the partners; and continuity in the relationship.

The differences between them are as follows. Cohabitation is a conditional modality, while marriage is a general modality. For *lignées* that lack a member of one of the sexes, cohabitation is not an obligation. Adoption is always the first choice, and cohabitation a last resort. Marriage, on the other hand, is the only institutionalized modality available in other societies and therefore constitutes a social constraint. It is almost an obligation. Cohabitation is done without prestation; marriage is accompanied by prestation. In cohabitation, the receiving *lignée* is never a donor in the same generation and vice versa. This is in contrast to other societies, where a family is usually a receiver and a donor at the same time. In cohabitation, unilateral intention is enough to end the relationship. This is in direct contrast to marriage, in which social intervention is required to sever the matrimonial bond. Cohabitation is a semi-social affair, whereas marriage is a social affair. The cohabitants take on the quality of *mu min* and *zo min* and are considered friends, whereas the married couple become wife and husband and are considered to be affines. A cohabitant is never considered a father, whether he is the genitor of his partner's children or not; he is never more than their mother's friend. The bond of friendship between the two *lignées* of different consanguinity necessarily disappears after one generation with the death of the male cohabitant. This is in contrast to the two families of the married couple, who remain relatives by marriage. A *mu min* and her descendants have the responsibility to conduct the service of offerings to the male cohabitant's ancestors for several generations following the *zo min*'s death. In uxorilocal cases, however, the *zo min* never conducts the service of offerings to his receiving *lignée*'s ancestors, and moreover, he might be chased away in old age, especially when the female cohabitant's children are grown.

This comparison demonstrates that in terms of sexual and economic bonds between the partners, Na cohabitation and marriage are exactly the same. Even if cohabitation is conditional, once an individual's situation meets the prerequisite condition, it is socially approved and therefore has become legal. However, when this modality as a whole is placed in its cultural context, a context that I approach from a dynamic and structural point of view, it becomes clear that four of the basic characteristics of cohabitation are in direct contrast to marriage. First, as a general rule, cohabitation is illegal and forbidden, whereas marriage is legal and even, to a certain degree, prescribed for everyone all of the time. Second, cohabitation is semi-social. Society does not intervene when the two partners separate. And while they have economic rights between them, they do not own each other. The bond between non-consanguineal individuals, whether it is sexual or economic, depends exclusively on the free will of the concerned parties. This is the golden rule in Na society. The two partners have economic rights in relation to each other, but these rights do not extend to the *zo min* and his partner's children. This is one reason why the children can chase away their mother's companion when he grows old. Third, as someone who has come to the aid of a *lignée*, the *mu min* or *zo min* becomes a part of the economic unit of the receiving household but not of the kinship unit. Moreover, there is an asymmetry between the aide and the aided, because cohabitation is a unilateral need. A husband and a wife, on the other hand, are completely symmetrical, because marriage is a bilateral necessity. Fourth, in cohabitation, the relationship between the two *lignées* only lasts one generation. Once the male cohabitant dies, the female cohabitant and her descendants no longer have any relationship with his consanguineal *lignées*. Even the service of offerings to the receiving *lignée*'s ancestors conducted in virilocal cases merely constitutes a favor performed by the *mu min* and her descendants for her dead partner. It is still a matter of aid. The bond between two cohabitants is therefore not between groups but between individuals.

As mentioned above, in the semi-social relationship or affair, the private part is far larger than the social part. In the open visit, the social part only entails the *lignée*'s consent with the goal of facilitating the visit. In cohabitation, the social part is constituted only by the choice of the *lignée* that is lacking a representative of one of the sexes. Moreover, as we have seen, cohabitation takes place quite late in life. In virilocal cases, when a choice is made by the ascendants of the man who is going to cohabit, it is the last resort. This, of course, is not the case in marriage societies, where the question is not whether one will marry but whom one will marry, since the modality of taking is already established. In any case, in a marriage society, it is unthinkable that a marriage could be replaced by an adoption. In some uxorilocal cases, a woman decides to cohabit following the deaths of her ascendants, who, in all likelihood, had insisted that, with the children born to her, the difficulty caused by the lack of workers in their household would resolve itself. In this situation, cohabitation becomes a completely private matter.

Assessing these contrasts from a structural anthropology point of view, it seems legitimate to state that as a Na social act cohabitation is fundamentally different from marriage and that cohabitants can be considered friends, exactly as the Na claim, rather than affines. Therefore, in relation to the first two modalities (the furtive visit and the conspicuous visit), cohabitation adds nothing new to Na kinship.

Finally, since the analysis of marriage in chapters 11–13 was quite exhaustive, I will simply recall the distinctive features of Na marriage here. Marriage was initially imposed indirectly by the Qing dynasty, and then later imposed directly by the extremists during the Cultural Revolution. Anything that could be directly imposed was (such as the labels husband and wife), but the concepts of being affines and of a relationship of affinity never successfully penetrated Na thought. On the one hand, for the government leaders, it goes without saying that if two individuals were married, they were automatically endowed with the qualities of being spouses and relatives. The government leaders took these two concepts so much for granted that they never thought to include them in their propaganda. On the other hand, the Na were completely unconscious of and unfamiliar with these concepts. It is not easy for someone who is mute to impose a concept on someone who is deaf. The following anecdote provides a good illustration of this situation. When the work group sent by the provincial government succeeded in uniting several couples, they could not understand why the members of the receiving *lignées* tended strongly to reject the spouse. They wondered how "they were capable of separating from a relative, but not of accepting one." Moreover, the imposition of marriage affected only a small segment of the population, even under the extremists, and was never universalized among the Na, neither horizontally nor vertically, not even within a single *lignée*. All of this leads me to conclude that while the local authorities succeeded in sporadically imposing marriage on Na society, they did not succeed in imposing all of its implications. In other words, they were never able to impose the institution of marriage. The existence of the institution of the visit prevented the imposition of the institution of marriage, because the existence of the second would require the disappearance of the first. It is absolutely impossible for them to representing the body — that is, the roles the society attributes to a man and a woman in reproduction. In societies in which the rule of transmitting consanguinity is patrilineal, cognate (or undifferentiated), or bilineal, the institution of marriage is indispensable. Otherwise, it would be difficult for a man to own the child of whom he is the genitor. When the rule is matrilineal, a society can function without the institution of marriage. Now, in reality, most matrilineal societies have not failed to institute marriage. Therefore, the system of representing the body constitutes a necessary reason for the institution of marriage, but, for the moment, not one that is sufficient to answer our question. Therefore, the explanation must lie elsewhere.

We have already seen that the essential difference between the institution of marriage and the institution of the visit is that in marriage the partners generally belong to each other because of sexual and economic prestations, whereas in the visit they have neither the sexual privilege nor mutual economic rights. In short, in the first institution the partners own each other and, as a general rule, must live under the same roof, whereas in the second one the partners are independent and must live separately.

There is an entire series of basic human desires, among them the desires to possess one's partner and to have multiple partners, that can help to explain these two institutions. By claiming this, I am presupposing that these two desires are factors, among many others, that govern Man's behavior, and this in spite of all the changes that have occurred over the course of history. Therefore, they are two invariants. Since they are closely tied to love between partners of the opposite sex, I will briefly discuss what I mean by this formula.

When certain physical and cultural traits of an individual (his or her personal character) please another individual, they are appreciated by this person. Through spontaneous glances, seduction, and words, this person makes his or her feelings known, all the while watching the other and attempting to discern his or her response. If the two parties find that the character (in the broad sense of the term) of the one corresponds to the taste of the other, they adore each other.

This process has a duration that varies according to the couple and the circumstances and includes a whole series of communications, identifications, and interactions that unfold circuitously. In short, there is an exchange of signals that give the two parties both physical and cultural pleasure. Everything happens with these pleasures in mind. The exchange is presented as a process of expressing one's feelings. It is at once a manifestation, a proposition, a request, an acceptance, a donation, and an affirmation of feelings, that is, an actualizing of feelings. At the same time, this exchange constitutes the confirmation of these feelings and the means for maintaining them. Once the feelings of one partner disappear, this exchange ends. In the opposite case, when their penchant reaches a certain level, it is sublimated into passionate feelings.[15] Therefore, when we say "love," we mean a passionate feeling created by the interaction of two individuals. It is true that passionate feeling can arise in one individual. But if it receives no positive reaction from the other, it usually subsides rapidly and dies, like water without a source or a tree without roots. Love can be actualized only between two people. Reciprocity is the first rule of the game.[16]

I will now return to examining the human desire to possess and to have multiple partners. Under the effect of love, possessiveness pushes the two parties further. Partial possession, that of feelings, is no longer enough for them. They want to control not only each other's feelings but also each other's bodies, so that one belongs only to the other, as well as, through implication, everything that they own and are able to produce. This is the case, par excellence, in many societies when two individuals get married.

For an individual, passionate feelings cannot be aroused by just anyone, nor can they be aroused exclusively by a predetermined single individual. Every human being is capable of being attracted to several personality types. Since each individual is physically determined and, to a certain degree, culturally determined, passionate feelings aroused by an individual can only last for a more or less long period of time. While one can enjoy a partner forever, one cannot, in general, be thrilled by him (or her) forever. Monotony kills. Consequently, natural and cultural diversity and human curiosity place these individuals in an ongoing search for the fulfillment of pleasure and lead them to love successively or simultaneously several different types of personalities. From the desire for diversity is born the desire for multiple partners. Herein lies the logic of love, if there is one, and its fatality.

An individual is capable of loving several people successively or even simultaneously but also desires to possess them. To respond simultaneously to the request for sexual equality and for possessiveness, it would seem that an equal number of women and men would have to possess each other.

There are three known types of matrimonial modalities: monogamy, polygyny, and polyandry. Logically speaking, there is a fourth possibility, the one mentioned above. But it does not exist. Was it beyond the scope of our ancestors' imaginations? It is, however, not a difficult concept to come up with. Then why, according to current anthropological knowledge, was it never institutionalized? The answer is probably quite simple: several individuals simultaneously possessing several other individuals poses a contradiction, for in this situation it is a question no longer of possessing but of sharing. If one respects the equality between the sexes and if one desires several partners, one can no longer possess them. Therefore, to maintain equality between the sexes, we are left with two possibilities: either possession without the pleasure of diversity or the pleasure of diversity without possession. In the first case, the partners lose their freedom, while in the second they maintain it.

Man is always led by his desires for physical pleasure and for cultural pleasure, for possession and for diversity, and from this stems the desire to possess one's partners and to multiply one's partners. The mechanisms of these last two desires often come into conflict.

When a society gives preeminence to the desire of possessing one's partners, it must inhibit the desire for multiple partners. Conversely, if it gives preeminence to the desire for multiple partners, it must repress the desire for possession. Institutionally speaking, society cannot simultaneously satisfy these two desires completely. As a result, from these two desires come two opposing institutions: marriage and the visit.

By legitimizing one of these desires and by advocating one of these forms of behavior, each institution can go as far as repressing or even forbidding the other. Of course, by admitting one of these two desires into its institution, society can never completely eradicate the other, for these desires originate in the most profound needs of human nature. For this reason, in marriage societies, prenuptial and/or extra-nuptial sexual freedom is more or less present, depending on the society. When this sexual freedom does not exist, fornication and adultery will always accompany marriage. Moreover, as economic and technical developments in medicine evolve, marriage societies tend to confer more and more freedom on the desire for multiple partners, without, however, going so far as to give it preeminence. In fact, today, through marriage, divorce and remarriage, individuals are able more or less to satisfy their desire for multiple partners. With the Na, the institution of the visit gives preeminence to the desire for multiple partners, but it also allows an individual to remain with his or her partner for a more or less long period of time, as can be seen in the modality of the open visit. This society could function perfectly well without this last modality. But it is necessary because of human possessiveness and has been instituted in response to this desire. Here, of course, it is a matter of limited possession, because it does not extend to an economic level. As we have seen, in this society, there are instances in which a young couple runs off together, carried away by the burning fire of their love, in order to possess each other completely. In this case, their desire for possession clearly rules their desire for multiple partners.

An interesting phenomenon emerges from this comparison of these two institutions. In both the marriage society and the visit society, the fire of love is not always accommodated. When a society has the custom of arranged marriages, elopements often occur. When a marriage society gives its members the freedom to choose partners, divorce often results. When a society confers preeminence on the desire for multiple partners, this preeminence can also result in the couple running off together. The fire of love can always create problems for a society. As they say, "love is the enemy of society." We can now better grasp the logic of opposition between these two human desires and the mechanisms of love. This also makes it easier to understand why unary kinship and binary kinship are heterogeneous and have completely different and mutually exclusive functions.

This examination leads me to propose the following hypothesis: in the institution of the visit, the effective cause is the desire for multiple partners. In the institution of marriage, the effective cause is the desire to possess one's partner. When society attributes preeminence to the desire for possession, it applies the law of possessiveness, and in the opposite case, it applies the law of multiplicity. These two laws are regulated by a single principle

CHAPTER FIFTEEN

Various Types of Domestic Groups

From the hypothesis proposed at the end of chapter 14, we can deduce that a society without marriage must necessarily be without family, given the absence of a husband and father. Consequently, to compare the various types of Na domestic groups with the family, I will begin by defining *family*.

What Is a Family?

Family, like *marriage*, has suffered from an overabundance of definitions. For example, George Peter Murdock begins his book *Social Structure* with a definition of the family: "The family is a social group characterized by common residence, economic cooperation, and reproduction."[1] In this book, by *family* he means family in a broad sense, one that envelops what he calls the nuclear family, the polygamous family, and the extended family. According to his definition, it is entirely appropriate to point out that the family is a social group. Now, common residence and economic cooperation between spouses are the rules for the institution of marriage but not essential characteristics of the family.

He then specifies that the family "includes adults of both sexes, at least two of whom maintain a socially approved sexual relationship, and one or more children, own or adopted, of the sexually cohabiting adults."[2] First of all, in a family, it is not necessary that all of the children be produced by the couple. Take, for example, the Samo of Burkina Faso or adopted children. In his presentation of the composition of the family, Murdock makes clear that among adults of both sexes, "at least two ... maintain a socially approved sexual relationship." Here, too, we have one of the rules for the institution of marriage. Therefore, we can observe that he has taken the characteristics of marriage to be characteristics of the family. However, Murdock himself warns that we must not confuse marriage and the family: "The family is to be distinguished from marriage."[3]

About the nuclear family, he quite simply states that it "consists typically of a married man and woman with their offspring, although in individual cases one or more additional persons may reside with them."[4] This, however, is not a definition of the nuclear family either.

I will now move on to the definition provided by Kathleen Gough. The family is "a married couple or other group of adult kinfolk who cooperate economically and in the upbringing of children, all or most of whom share a common dwelling."[5] Gough, too, places the crown of marriage (economic cooperation, common residence, and raising children) on the head of the family.

These kinds of definitions of the family abound. But as Françoise Héritier-Augé has noted: "As with marriage, there is no hard and fast definition.... By insisting on the conditions for its emergence — the necessary social recognition of the union of the two sexual partners, the fact that they are procreators and form an economic cooperative with common residence, blood ties, or in time the transmission of blood — we can certainly see a model being sketched out that has a tendency to define what a family, the base cell for all of society, does, but one that does not provide a universally correct definition that is not somewhat tautological:

the family serves to create children in order to reproduce society, while society creates the obligation of exchange and the constitution of the family, which cannot be perpetuated without this obligation."[6]

Why do the existing definitions systematically revert to tautology? Why, when my predecessors approached the institution of the family, did they write so much more about marriage than about the family? In short, why do they always confuse these two objects?

About this, Murdock remarks at the end of his chapter on the nuclear family that "marriage is the regular means of establishing a nuclear family, because the marital relationship forms the very warp of the family fabric," and "the regulation of marriage through sex taboos produces far-reaching effects upon family structure itself."[7]

In fact, marriage and family are closely linked. The definition of marriage and the first four implications presented in chapter 14 are necessary and sufficient for marriage to exist. But the story does not end there. Once formed, marriage gives birth to a new community made up of a man and his wife. And then, as a corollary to marriage, the sexual relationship between husband and wife usually results in procreation. The birth of offspring is not only a necessary consequence of the sexuality between husband and wife but also a vital necessity, for "no one who lacks the cult of self provided by descendants can hope to achieve the rank of ancestor."[8] In addition, in many traditional societies, the husband and wife would not be able to provide for their needs during old age without procreation. This is the main reason that adoption becomes indispensable when a couple is deprived of children, due to sterility or because of an accident.

Therefore, within the framework of the institution of marriage, the last two implications of marriage raised in chapter 14 imply the birth of a group that is structurally complete. As long as we are unable to circumscribe the marriage, we are unable to trace a border between these two objects of study. Their confusion is inevitable. Because existing definitions of marriage consist of circular reasoning, definitions of the family likewise fall into tautology.

Given that we have discerned what marriage is, I propose definitions of three kinds of families. First, the limited family is the basic unit of kinship and economy and is composed of a man, his wife, and a child (or children) born of the wife or adopted by the couple. This kind of family is produced by monogamous marriage. And, as Claude Lévi-Strauss states, in this kind of unit "other relatives can eventually gather" without changing its essence.[9] Second, the polygamous family is a basic unit of kinship and economy made up of either a man, his wives, and the children born to his wives or of a woman, her husbands, and her children. This kind of a family is produced by polygamous marriage. As Lévi-Strauss points out, it can only be widespread in societies in which "either the children of one of the two sexes are destroyed ... or life expectancy differs according to sex."[10] Third, the extended family is a basic unit of kinship and economy made up of two or more men, their wives, and the children of the wives. The relationship between the men can be father-son and/or brother-brother; the relationship between the wives can be mother-daughter and/or sister-sister. It is only possible to speak about the extended family on the condition that after the marriage one segment of its members (children, brothers, or sisters) do not separate economically from the family and from their relatives (in the broad sense of the term).

Since the presence of a man, his wife, and their children constitutes the essential framework for all three types of families, I will take it as a reference point in the following comparison.

A Comparison of Various Na Domestic Groups with the Family

We have observed that in Na society there are five types of domestic groups. The first is the purely consanguineal *matrilignée*. It represents the majority of cases and is therefore the standard form among all types of domestic groups. It is characterized by the presence of two or more generations and by having both sexes in each generation, a communal residence, and a communal economic existence, as well as by the consanguineal relationship of all of the members. Figure 15.1 illustrates this type of domestic group. I define the purely consanguineal Na *lignée* as follows: a basic unit of kinship and economy made up of a sister (or sisters), her brother (or brothers), and the children born to this woman (or these women).

Figure 15.1. The purely consanguineal *matrilignée*.

Like the family, this type of domestic group constitutes the basic unit of kinship and economy for the society. But these two types of domestic groups are completely different structurally. In a family, the members are heterogeneous. At the very least one member is non-consanguineal to the other, in this instance, the husband and the wife, no matter what the rule of descent is. In the Na *lignée*, the members are homogeneous: they are all consanguineal relatives. This fundamental difference leads me to conclude that the standard Na *lignée* cannot be considered a family.

The second type of Na domestic group is the *lignée* that has adopted a non-consanguineal individual (or two or indeed several belonging to two or three generations). Its essential characteristics are the presence of members of both sexes in two (or more) generations, the presence of non-consanguineal individuals, communal residence and economy, and, finally, that it becomes purely consanguineal at the end of a generation. Figure 15.2 illustrates this second type of domestic group.

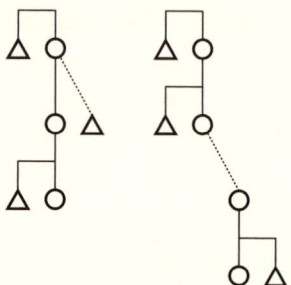

Figure 15.2. A *lignée* that has adopted a non-consanguineal individual.

This type of *lignée* cannot be identified as a family for two reasons. First, the adopted person (or persons) is non-consanguineal in relation to the members of the adoptive *lignée*, but he or she is not in an affinal relationship to them; he or she is only a member of the household. Second, after one or two generations, following the death of the receiving *lignée*'s members, the adopted members become the only members in the household. The identity of the adoptive *lignée* is replaced by that of the adoptee. The household becomes, once again, purely consanguineal. Synchronically, this type of domestic group, a transient model, differs from a purely consanguineal *lignée*, but only from the point of view of the household. Diachronically, this type is identified with the standard *lignée*.

The third type of domestic group is a *lignée* that has a member who is practicing cohabitation. Its essential attributes are identical with those of the second type. Figure 15.3 illustrates this type of domestic group. This type of group cannot be considered a family for the same reasons that the second type cannot.

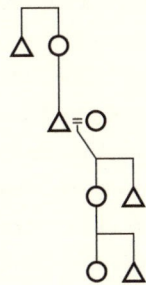

Figure 15.3. A *lignée* with a member practicing cohabitation.

The fourth type of domestic group is a *lignée* in which a member lives according to the modality of marriage. It shares the essential characteristics of the second type with one addition: the man has become a husband to the woman, and she has become a wife to him. Because of these new relationships, from an anthropological point of view, this type of *lignée*, within a given period, is a kind of family. But it manifests a fundamental difference from the family defined above: as the basic social unit, the family is a constant phenomenon in other societies, whereas in Na society, this type of group is singular and only sporadic and temporary. Usually only one generation within a household practices this modality (see figure 11.1). Here it is interesting to note that marriage can create a bond between two individuals only. It can therefore set up a nuclear family. Without the institution of marriage, however, the existence of marriage alone is not enough to create an alliance (in the exact sense of the anthropological theory of alliance).

The fifth type of domestic group is the *lignée* of the *zhifu* (see figures 12.1 and 12.5). In addition to the basic attributes of the fourth type, this one is characterized by the fact that the children use the term *father*. In appearance, this *lignée* presented itself, for almost three hundred years, as an extended family. Now, when compared with the existence of the family in other societies, three hundred years is a short time. Brought about by changes in policy under the Qing dynasty and gone after 1956, as we discussed in detail in chapter 12, this extended family is only a temporary phenomenon. Moreover, this *lignée* had another essential attribute: it was composed of as many kinds of consanguineal relatives as it had generations. So there were usually three consanguinities at the same time: that of the great-grandmother, represented by the grandfather, that of the grandmother, represented by the father, and that of the mother, represented by Ego. This is never the case for the extended family in other societies, whether the rule for descent is unileal or other. Because marriage was only partially imposed in Na society, the family never could fully evolve there. Therefore, in its archetype, Na society was based exclusively on the purely consanguineal *lignée*, and since the Qing dynasty, it has continued to be based, for the most part, on the purely consanguineal *matrilignée*.

From this comparison, it is clear that along with the basic family, the purely consanguineal Na *lignée* constitutes another type of basic unit of kinship and economy.

In fact, the institution of the visit, like that of marriage, rests on the incest prohibition; therefore, it falls under the heading of a social act (here social is the opposite of natural). Nevertheless, the two institutions do not have the same outcomes. The institution of marriage unites two non-consanguineal individuals through sexual prestation (service) and mutual economic rights, making them affinal relatives and giving birth to a new family. With the institution of the visit, the participants remain non-consanguineal individuals, and do not give birth to any new unit of kinship and economy. In Na society, the number of elementary units of kinship and economy only increases when there is a separation within a *lignée*.

The regimentation of sexuality is not a phenomenon exclusive to the family; it also exists within the Na *lignée*. It comes under the heading of institutionalized sexual life. A lack of descendants can create problems for a family in terms of reproduction, just as it can for the purely consanguineal *matrilignée*. This is where adoption enters in. Personal or legal identification is regulated, for the most part, by the rule of descent. As is true for a family, the name of the purely consanguineal *matrilignée*, as a basic unit of kinship and economy, serves as a point of reference, but only secondarily in the *lignée*. Therefore, we can see that in a marriage society there is an institution of marriage but, contrary to preconceived ideas in anthropology, not an institution of the family at all.

CHAPTER SIXTEEN

Conclusion

For the Na, everyone who originated from the same female ancestor has the same *ong* (bone) and the same social quality. Through
this bond, they are considered *ong hing* (people of the same bone,
consanguineal relatives). According to their system for representing the body, the man is the waterer in mating, and an individual
has no bond to his genitor, who is not necessarily known and does
not need to be known. The quality of consanguinity of each individual is therefore determined exclusively by the links to the
mother. An individual is consanguineal to his mother and therefore a consanguineal relative to his mother's other consanguineal
relatives. It is a matter of absolute and pure matriliny.

The concept of pure Na matriliny is completely primordial.
According to the logic of their representation of the body, the
female gender is anterior and the male is posterior, for within the
Na *matrilignée*, people are born of women, never of men. The
arrangement of the two main pillars in the center of their main
room perfectly reflects this logic: on the tree from which these
pillars are made, the section of the trunk closest to the roots provides the female pillar, while the section above is the male pillar.

Governed by the concept of pure matriliny, their rule for the
transmission of consanguinity is exclusively matrilineal. It serves

as the primary parameter in an individual's social identification. The mother alone suffices to legitimize a child.

Those who have the same female ancestor are always consanguineal relatives, no matter how close or far apart their relations. For them, the degree of distance has no effect on the quality of personal consanguinity, neither in direct nor collateral lines. Their quality of personal consanguinity is immutable, and their circle of consanguineal relatives is determined only by the bonds of matrilineal consanguinity. Na consanguinity therefore constitutes a social fact entirely different from biological consanguinity.

Mating is prohibited between consanguineal relatives in this society, as it is everywhere else. Inasmuch as sexual relations are not forbidden (even if they are disapproved of) between a woman and her genitor (whom she does not necessarily know as such), and even between a *zo min* and the daughter of his cohabitant (who is not his offspring), their circle of consanguineal relatives certainly corresponds to the field of application of the incest prohibition. Between consanguinity and the incest prohibition there is, therefore, a perfect correlation.

In this society, the basic organization of kinship is the *matrilignée*. It is made up only of consanguineal relatives. Each *lignée* has a name, which all of its members take. The rule for the transmission of the *lignée*'s name is matrilineal in accordance with the rule of transmission of consanguinity. But when a separation occurs, the branch *lignée* does not necessarily keep the same name as the founding *lignée*. The members of such *lignées* will not have the same *lignée* name, but they are nonetheless identical in regard to their quality of consanguinity. Therefore, the rule of transmission of the *lignée* name serves only as a secondary parameter for personal identification, versus that of consanguinity.

In addition to the bond of consanguinity, there is a second bond between the members of a *lignée*, that of economy. They live in the same residence; they work together and share the same pot and the same fire. Within a *lignée*, property is communal; there are no individual possessions. All members enjoy the same rights and have mutual responsibilities: the older generation raises the following generation, and the latter, in turn, takes care of its ascendants in their old age. In other words, they belong to each other. From one generation to the next, property is handed down naturally without any concern about issues of inheritance to make, as is often the case in other societies. The rule of property transmission is matrilineal; therefore, there is a concordance between the rule of transmission of consanguinity and the rule of transmission of property.

There is a sexual division of labor within the *lignée*. Each *lignée* has two chiefs, one male and one female. The management of the *lignée* is the responsibility of the eldest sons and daughters of each generation. The most prominent division is that between the maternal uncle (the male chief), who takes care of matters outside the household, and the mother (the female chief), who is in charge of matters within the household. The heavy labor is usually done by the male members. The idea of pure matriliny does not, however, imply that authority be allotted mainly to the female chief. That there is no father does not mean that the mother has a monopoly on domestic authority. In this respect, the individual's ability prevails. But, in most *lignées*, the male chief is more influential than the female chief.

The ascendants have the right to supervise the descendants and the duty to pass down to them a moral and technical knowledge (this is done separately for the two sexes). Between the older and younger generations, there is a relationship of subordination and obedience. In this society, male dominance is relative, that of seniority is absolute.

Consanguineal relatives of different generations of a *lignée* live together permanently. Between them there is a third bond, that of emotion. Na society promotes a spirit of solidarity in the matrilineal *lignée* that discourages separations. The members of a *lignée* always tend to maintain this solidarity forever. Normally, separations do not take place unless there is a demographic necessity.

Therefore, from the concept of pure matriliny three matrilineal rules ensue that regulate the bonds of consanguinity, economy, and emotions between the consanguineal relatives. I call this set of rules *the institution of consanguinity*.

An essential characteristic of Na kinship terminology is that it takes into consideration the incest prohibition. Within the *lignée*, the man does not have sons or daughters, and symmetrically, the children do not have a father — neither in their kinship terminology, nor by right or in fact. Because terms for affines are lacking, the women do not have husbands, and the men do not have wives. This kinship terminology corresponds to the experience of the members of the *lignée*. It is clear that this is different from the six types of kinship terminology that George Peter Murdock has defined. It seems legitimate to consider this kinship terminology as a new type. I call it *a terminology of matrilineal consanguinity*.

There are, then, four elements associated with this type of *matrilignée*: (1) the rule of absolute matrilineal descent; (2) the rule of matrilocality; (3) communal property; and (4) a kinship terminology that is purely matrilineal and consanguineal.

For the Na, those who are not descendants of the same female ancestor do not have the same "bone" and therefore do not have the same quality of consanguinity. They are therefore not consanguineal to each other. If we consider consanguineal relatives the same, then non-consanguineal individuals are different. Generally speaking, it is this opposition which is the primary one in the kinship of every society.

The institution of consanguinity is positive. It expresses the sharing of the same quality of consanguinity between, at the very least, the members of the *lignée*, and the belonging of a given individual to a given group, and therefore, their identity. And it calls for cohesion and solidarity to rule over the consanguineal relatives. In opposition to the institution of consanguinity, the incest taboo is a negative rule. It bans mating between consanguineal relatives, and therefore implies that they can only mate with non-consanguineal individuals.

Influenced by the incest prohibition, the Na mode of sexual life is carried out under the institution of the nocturnal visit to the woman by the man. This institution includes a coercion forbidding conflict between two individuals who covet the same partner. This institution implies a second restriction: for it is forbidden for two non-consanguineal individuals to cohabit if they both have brothers and sisters. Finally, two partners' taking an oath of fidelity is considered by Na morality a matter of commerce, and something shameful. Through its rules, notably its negative and coercive rules, the institution of the visit does not result in the exchange of women or men between non-consanguineal groups. However, because of the incest prohibition, there must be a certain degree of reciprocity between non-consanguineal *lignées*.

For a Na man, over the course of his life, the visit is never focused on a single partner since it is spontaneous and the choice of the evening and is conditioned by opportunity and the availability of the woman he has designs on. In short, it is up to chance. Moreover, in his sex life, a man's only goal is sexual gratification. The Na consider mating in and of itself a kindness on the part of men toward women, since "if the rain does not fall from the sky, the grass will not grow on the ground." Mating is necessary for procreation. Therefore, the institution of the visit implies a reciprocity of generalized kindness between non-consanguineal *lignées*. Yet, obviously, this cannot be read in the sense of the principle of exchange as proposed by Lévi-Strauss.

In addition to this abstract reciprocity in sexual matters, other forms of reciprocity appear in other levels and are based on the villagers. During the construction of a house, at the moment of a birth, during funerals, and so on, the villagers bring donations to the household in question. This household keeps track of the amount received so that it can send similar donations when the same events take place in other *lignées*. During the high seasons in the fields, when a *lignée* is unable to finish its work on time, the neighbors help out. When the villagers help a *lignée*, they eat with its members. All of this constitutes various exchanges, and the Na are perfectly conscious of them as such.

The conception of pure matriliny also exercises a dominant influence when there is a lack of one of the sexes within a *lignée*. When in need of a member, a *lignée* will first try to adopt a consanguineal relative. The adoption of a non-consanguineal individual and cohabitation are last resorts. When non-consanguineal individuals are adopted, the conception of pure matriliny protects the adopted woman and disadvantages the adopted man. The same holds true in cases of cohabitation. These kinds of situations can have serious consequences: a change in the consanguineal quality of the receiving *lignée* and the banishment of the grandmother's or the mother's companion in his old age.

I have grouped the furtive visit, the conspicuous visit, and cohabitation together as a modality of sexual life in order to study them. However, the two visit modalities differ from cohabitation on the levels of both cause and effect. The institution of the visit was instigated to direct and regulate the sexual relations of all members of society, whereas the cohabitation modality was set up in response to an exceptional circumstance, a lack of a member of one of the sexes within a *lignée,* and aims to the perpetuate the household. In contrast to the institution of the visit, which is in complete compliance with the institution of consanguinity, the modality of cohabitation goes against consanguinity, in the same way that the adoption of a non-consanguineal individual does. But this is allowed because in such situations the practice of the visit cannot resolve the problem of a lack of descendants. Therefore, the two visit modalities do not share the same character as the cohabitation modality.

Neither the institution of the visit nor the cohabitation modality will make non-consanguineal individuals affines. For the Na, only consanguineal relatives are kin, and non-consanguineal individuals are outsiders from each other forever.

The following characteristics may be observed of Na kinship. Its matriliny is absolute. Its concept of consanguinity is completely social as opposed to biological. Brother and sister never separate. The brother-sister relationship is at the center of consanguinity and therefore at the center of Na kinship. A consanguineal relationship with the mother is all that is required to legitimize the children. The maternal uncle plays a role in relation to the children that is equivalent to that of the father in other societies, without being the genitor. Here, kinship is made up of three genres only: consanguinity, economy, and emotions.

Traditionally speaking, in this society there are three institutionalized modalities of sexual life, whereas in other societies there is, in general, only one, that of marriage. In contrast to other societies, within the Na basic unit of kinship and economy, the members maintain economic relations with each other but no sexual relations. And partners in a sexual relationship have no economic relationship, even if their sexual relationship lasts for a long time, as is the case with open partners.

The cohabitation modality, which in principle is illicit, may become licit on the condition that it is done from a need to perpetuate the household.

This community is therefore characterized by logical mechanisms of behavior and attitudes that differ from those found in all other societies, and it provides new knowledge about the diversity of human behavior.

The sexual relationship is indispensable for this society to perpetuate itself, but it does not create another kinship relationship, that is, it does not create affinity. Descent proceeds without recourse to alliance. Here, there is only one opposition: between consanguineal relatives and non-consanguineal individuals. And this model is completely original. Therefore, in contrast with the kinship of other societies where kinship equates consanguinity plus affinity, Na kinship is only constituted by consanguinity. From the number of components in these two models, I call the first one binary kinship, and the second unary kinship. They are indeed two fundamental structures of kinship.

Therefore, in this society, the institution of consanguinity, the terminology of matrilineal consanguinity, the institution of the visit, the modality of adoption, and the modality of cohabitation are all regulated by the concept of pure matriliny. Being exclusively made up of an institution and a kinship terminology of consanguinity, the Na kinship system is, properly speaking, *a system of consanguinity*. It is a society without marriage.

A comparison of the family with the Na *lignée* reveals two basic differences. The first stems from the condition of their existence and the mechanisms of their construction. As a general rule, a Na *lignée* can subsist without recourse to non-consanguineal individuals. The second difference can be found on the structural level, that is, in the social qualities of their members and the relationships between them. This structural difference can be illustrated by comparing the diagram that Lévi-Strauss proposed for the atom of kinship for the family (see figure 16.1) with the one I propose for the structure of Na kinship (see figure 16.2). Thus it seems logical to say that a society without marriage is also necessarily a society without family.

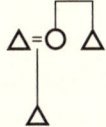

Figure 16.1. Lévi-Strauss's kinship structure.

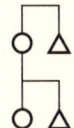

Figure 16.2. The Na kinship structure.

By comparing the two, we can see that among the characteristics attributed to the institution of the family, some of them — a sexual relationship between the spouses, a common residence, and economic cooperation — fall under the order of the matrimonial institution. The regulation of sexuality is not a phenomenon that belongs only to the family; it also exists within the Na *lignée*. It is above all regulated by the incest prohibition. A lack of descendants can create a concern for the reproduction of the family, just as it can in the purely consanguineal *matrilignée*. This is where adoption enters in. Personal identification or legal status is regulated, for the most part, by the rule of descent. The name of the purely consanguineal *matrilignée*, as is true for the name of the family elsewhere, assures personal identification, but only secondarily. Therefore, we must admit that in a marriage society, there is indeed an institution of marriage but no institution of the family at all.

Before the Qing dynasty, Na society had a flexible relationship with the central Chinese government. The government's regulations over ethnic minorities were not actively enforced. The indigenous chief named by the court and the *raimi* were in all likelihood the only political representatives. The only real evidence of Na society's submission to the central government was the annual payment of a symbolic tribute to the court. Because information is lacking, the landownership regime of the Na during this period remains unknown. Under the flexible and inspired rules of the government concerning the transfer of power of the *tusi*, Na kinship remained intact. Until this period, the Na had never known marriage.

To consolidate its power, the Qing dynasty took much more rigorous measures than its predecessors had. Ever since then, as was true for other ethnic minorities in China, the regime of the *tusi* was subjected to new regulations instituted by the central government, which were carried out more strictly in Yongning. The Na were required to pay not only a tribute but also a tax to the central government. These new regulations and their enforcement marked the general and effective influence of the Chinese imperial court over Na society.

However, in politics, the Na maintained, at least partially, their tradition, as can be seen in the ambivalence of the *raimi* and the arbitrating role of the *zhifu* in moments of crisis. However, new legislation concerning the transfer of the *zhifu*'s power brought about the following consequences for their kinship system. To present an heir, the *zhifu* was obliged to adopt the concept of paternity, as well as the modality of marriage. To guarantee the hereditary status of the eldest son, the *zhifu*'s *lignée* was required to separate consecutively, and this created an aristocratic stratum. The servants of the *zhifu*'s family, people who had lost their means of survival, and criminals formed the serf stratum; to manage this group, the *zhifu* created the concepts male-lineal and female-lineal. As a result, Na society became stratified.

While they applied the rules of paternal transmission of name, title, and property, the *zhifu* and the members of certain aristocratic *lignées* did not adopt the rule of paternal transmission of consanguinity. Patriliny remained unthinkable for them. In their sexual life, their behavior strictly conformed to tradition, observing the principle of matriliny, the incest prohibition and the strong ban on sexual evocation. In fact, while living according to the marriage modality, the *zhifu* never stopped practicing the visit modality. He maintained and protected this way of life. The fact that he married never stopped him from demoting to the rank of serf anyone who cohabited, that is, when they had a brother or a sister.

When a *zhifu*'s maternal uncle belonged to an inferior social stratum, he had no authority over his sister's children. Only when he originated in the *lignée* of the general administrator could he lean on tradition and enjoy a certain degree of superiority over his nieces and nephews. In this situation — the relationship between the *zhifu* and the general administrator — a *zhifu*'s weakness in character could have important consequences. On the other hand, the paternal uncle had a certain authority and a certain influence over his nephews and nieces, as long as he lived in the *zhifu*'s residence. But once he left his birth home, he lost this authority.

The marriage modality was borrowed inconsistently by some aristocrats with political connections and by some of the wealthy. For them, the father had authority over the children, and while the maternal uncle was highly respected, as tradition dictated, he had no rights to the children nor any responsibility for them, which is precisely the case when a *lignée* separates.

By adopting the marriage modality the *zhifu*'s *lignée* was transformed from a unary kinship into a binary kinship. In spite of the existence of this structure, which lasted for about three hundred years, unary kinship was restored in 1956. Once the *zhifu* was stripped of political power, the necessity of marriage for his descendants was gone. For other married couples, this cycle of transformation from unary kinship into binary kinship and then the return to unary kinship was usually accomplished in a single generation.

Na society had no marriage prior to the Qing dynasty and has never had the institution of marriage. Even today, it functions, for the most part, according to the institution of the visit. I therefore refer to it as a society of the visit.

Toward the end of the fifteenth century, at the latest, Tibetan Buddhism was universally accepted by the Na. And since the beginning of the twentieth century, if not before, it has been a powerful social organization led by a Na. This was not without political consequences. Given that the legitimacy of political power and religious power emanated from different cultures, they were unable to come together in the hands of one single person, as is the case in Tibet. The holder of political power has therefore always tried to master religious power by placing a member of his family at the head and in this way rule the region effectively. But while the diffusion of Tibetan Buddhism had an impact on the political life of the Na, it did nothing to change their kinship system.

The *gaituguiliu* campaigns did not reach the Yongning region. Until the Guomindang era, the Na *zhifu* still had great authority. But psychologically, this campaign profoundly influenced the Na *zhifu*, so much so that he adopted different attitudes toward the

Han and the Tibetans. He forbade anything that might harm his power: the learning of Chinese by Na commoners (all the while encouraging his sons to learn Chinese in preparation for their accession to power), the cultivation of rice, the immigration of the Han, and even the opening of stores in Yongning. At the same time, he welcomed Tibetan culture with open arms. The attitude of the Na ruler toward these two ethnic groups was based on his political interests.

In 1956, the authorities abolished the *tusi* regime and the system of stratification. Therefore, the tradition represented by the *raimi* in political life also came to an end. Until 1981, the Na were under the rule of non-Na government administrators. Only with the rule of Deng Xiaoping were Na administrators installed in government posts in the Yongning region.

The agrarian policies of the Qing dynasty and the Guomindang effected certain status changes among the Na. For example, most of the serfs lost their land. However, these policies did not affect their kinship system.

Since 1956, as is true for all of the people of China, the Na have been subjected successively to several policies: that of the distribution of land to each household, the cooperative group, the People's Commune, and the system of familial responsibility. Once again, not one of these regimes influenced their kinship system, with the exception of the disappearance of the *bu sï nin*, which came about because, between 1958 and 1960, every harvest was allocated to the People's Commune.

During a period of twenty years (1960–1980), all religious activity was forbidden.

Since 1959, led by ethnocentrism and the doctrine of evolutionism, the local authorities have forbidden the Na cadres to follow the mode of the visit and instigated four matrimonial reforms, the last of which, under the influence of extremists, went as far as to use administrative measures to impose monogamy on the Na. But it was all in vain. In 1981, the means used to enact this last reform were officially recognized as wrong. In 1988, the government of the autonomous district of the Yi of Ninglang stipulated that it would not force ethnic minorities to reform their customs. But as a local government, it is obligated to obey the law. Therefore, in conformity with Chinese matrimonial legislation, it set up a fine for children born out of wedlock.[1] While much more moderate, of course, this measure shared the spirit of the measures taken during the Cultural Revolution.

In addition to their general conversion to Buddhism, from the Qing dynasty until today, the Na have gone from being an egalitarian society to being a socially stratified society, and then returning to being a society without social stratification. They have experienced two different types of political regime — that of the *tusi* and the current one — and several types of landownership regime. In spite of all this, and in spite of the matrimonial reforms instigated by the extremists, only the modality of marriage was successfully introduced, not the institution of marriage. Over the course of this long history, despite the influence of two patrilineal cultures (Han and Tibetan), the Na kinship system has displayed a tenacity and a great compatibility with all kinds of situations.

While coercive measures did not succeed in changing this kinship system, scholarly education and the lifestyle of salaried employees have begun to alter it, because education, especially courses in biology, brings about a change in the system of representing the body. In the upcoming years, it is foreseeable that education and the probable industrialization of the Yongning region will make this kinship system disappear altogether.

Marriage, affinity, alliance of marriage, family — these kinds of concepts, no matter what their definitions may be, are essential to anthropology, but seem absent from this culture. The Na case attests to the fact that marriage and the family (as well as the Oedipus complex) can no longer be considered universal, neither logically nor historically.

Every society, with the exception of the Na, knows marriage and/or the family in one form or another. The two great theories of social structure, of which those of A.R. Radcliffe-Brown and Lévi-Strauss are the most representative, were based precisely on the relationships between family members. Their divergence stems from the fact that they each emphasize one aspect of these relationships: descent or alliance.

Radcliffe-Brown based his thesis on the universality of the model of the basic family. According to him, the "unit of structure from which a kinship system is built up is the group which I call an 'elementary family,' consisting of a man and his wife and their child or children, whether they are living together or not.... The existence of the elementary family creates three special kinds of social relationship, that between parent and child, that between children of the same parents (siblings), and that between husband and wife as parents of the same child or children."[2] For Radcliffe-Brown, "the basic family, founded as it is on natural requirements, forms the hard core around which any social organization re-volves.... The relationship between parent and child occupies the first place... [among the ties created and developed by the family] ... filiation is the fundamental notion. From this point of view, families can be compared to threads which it is the task of nature to warp in order that the social fabric can develop."[3] Since the Na have no family, they completely unground this theory. Moreover, contrary to the views of Radcliffe-Brown, it is, it seems, a matri-monial relationship that creates the family and not the other way around.

Lévi-Strauss's theory takes the institutionalized exchange of women by the alliance of marriage to be the central point of kinship. It sees "the transversal networks of alliances" as "the lines of power that underlie and even engender all social organization."[4] Without marriage, the Na provide, here too, a counterexample. Moreover, the Na case contradicts fundamental arguments of this thesis, given that Lévi-Strauss believes that, because of its universality, the incest prohibition necessitates marriage, that the division of labor according to gender makes marriage indispensable, and that, without marriage, no society could sustain itself, and without the family, no society, or even humanity itself, could exist.[5] The incest prohibition not only exists in Na society but also is particularly prominent, and the same holds true for the division of labor. They were not, however, instigated by marriage.

Obviously, the incest taboo in every society only forbids sexual relations, not marriage. If the division of labor according to gender is also governed by a sexual ban, as Lévi-Strauss has claimed, how can we explain that the cooperation between a brother and a sister must be dissolved in order for each of them to collaborate with someone else who is non-consanguineal? Is it because siblings do not cooperate as well?

If other types of societies that fall outside of these two theories are nonetheless established with the help of marriage and the family, Na society functions without these characteristics. The very existence of this counterexample indicates in a striking manner the limitations of these two dominant theories in the field and makes our current knowledge relative. From now on, marriage can no longer be considered the only possible institutionalized mode of sexual behavior. Without marriage, a society can maintain itself perfectly well and function as well as any other.

Of course, the hypotheses of these two authors were difficult to refute before the study of Na society. It was almost inconceivable that a society could give preeminence to the desire for multiple partners. Especially when we consider, as Lévi-Strauss said, that "nothing permits the assumption that humanity, from the time it emerged from the animal condition, was not endowed with a form of social organization that, in its fundamental structure, scarcely differed from later ones."[6]

Therefore, as far as kinship is concerned, we can conclude that there are only two constancies: social consanguinity and the incest prohibition. The correlation between them constitutes a social constraint on human sexual behavior. We can call this universal constraint the principle of sexual exclusion of consanguineal relatives. Because this principle does not require the institution of the visit alone or of marriage alone and only constitutes a prerequisite condition that they must absolutely obey, something must exist between this principle and these institutions. An examination of the parameters currently available to social anthropology leads me to think that this something is the desire principle. This principle consists of the desire to possess one's partners and of the desire to have multiple partners, two needs rooted in the innermost depths of human nature. When a society wants the desire for possession to prevail over that for multiplication, it implements the institution of marriage. When a society wants the desire for multiplicity to prevail over that for possession, the institution of the visit is put into practice. The institution of marriage necessarily implies, by its very definition, the appearance of the family, whereas that of the visit forces the consanguineal members of a group to stay together and maintain a purely matrilineal and consanguineal group, such as the Na *matrilignée*.

From these two opposing desires two types of opposing institutions were born (that of the visit and that of marriage). From these institutions, two types of basic units of kinship and economy, also opposed to each other, ensued (the purely consanguineal *matrilignée* and the family). And, finally, two structures of kinship were therefore constituted (unary and binary kinship). In the oppositions to each of these three pairs, each pole constitutes the negative form of the other. It is obvious, then, that the incest prohibition is not the negative form of the family.

The desire principle that makes up the basis of these two institutions also represents what these institutions are responding to: it directly creates and regulates them. Once one acknowledges this principle, the marriage/family paradox disappears. In a marriage society, the order of causal succession can only be the desire to possess one's partner, followed by marriage and then family. The opposite no longer seems tenable. Besides, contrary to what was automatically believed until now, the institution of marriage does not have as a goal the guarantee of human reproduction. As long as mating is possible among a segment of the population of a society, reproduction will ensue smoothly.

Social anthropology is faced, for the first time in the history of the knowledge of humankind, with a society that is without fathers and husbands. Born of the confrontation between the institution of the visit and the institution of marriage, between the purely consanguineal *matrilignée* and the family, the relativization of anthropological knowledge acquired until now allows a fuller understanding of the elements of kinship, the relationships between these elements and the structure of the human spirit in this field.

Notes

A Note on the Transcription of Na and Chinese Words

1. He Jiren and Jiang Zhuyi, *Naxi yu jianzhi*. For more on the Naxi, see "Official Identification" in chapter 1 of this book.

2. Pinyin is the official transcription of Chinese.

Introduction

1. The Cuan lived in eastern Yunnan from the third to the sixth centuries and ruled over several ethnic groups. See You Zhong, *Zhongguo xinan de gudai minzu*, pp. 60–61.

2. Xie Zhaozhe, "The Account of the Ethnic Minorities, "in *Dian lue*, vol. 9. Dian, a Chinese character, is an alternative name for Yunnan. The edition of this work that I consulted in the Library of Yunnan Province is a handwritten copy that has neither an exact date nor page numbers. The original is in the Library of Shanghai. Several other works that I refer to later are in a similar state.

3. Yongning is a canton in the autonomous district of the Yi of Ninglang in Yunnan Province. The Na also live in the Yanyuan and Muli Districts in Sichuan Province.

4. I use the French terms *lignée* and *matrilignée* because there are no terms in English that convey the same meaning. See *lignée* and *matrilignée* in the glossary.

5. Fan Ye (398–445), "Xinan yi zhuang," p. 11.

6. Li Jing, *Yunnan zhilue*.

7. *Yanyuan xianzhi* was written during the era of Daoguang (1821–1850) under the Qing dynasty.

8. *Yanyuan gaikuan*, an anonymous account, dates from the era of the Guomindang (1911–1949).

9. Zhou Rucheng, "Yongning jianwen lu," p. 169.

10. Polo, *Devisement du monde*, pp. 296–97. Gaindu is located in the modern city of Xichang. It is a region that neighbors the Yanyuan District.

11. The note on page 300 of *Devisement du monde* is incorrect. *Iaci* is not "the indigenous name of the current city of Kunming, capital of Yunnan." One of the dependent districts under the Han dynasty (206 B.C.–A.D. 220) of the prefecture of *Iaci* was called Dingzuo. Under the Tang dynasty (618–907), the name of this district was changed to Kunming. Today it is Yanyuan.

12. Rock, *The Ancient Na-khi Kingdom*, vol. 2, p. 391.

13. These researchers were all trained as historians.

14. Since 1980, two changes in administrative funding have taken place in China. The People's Commune of Yongning was divided into two cantons. Today, Yongning is the name of only one of these cantons. During this period, the cantons became administrative villages, which I refer to as village groupings.

15. Some of the researchers mentioned above returned to the field. Zhan Chengxu, Li Jinchun, Wang Chengquan, and Liu Longchu, *Yongning Naxi zu de azhu huyin he muxi jiating*; Yan Ruxian and Song Zhaolin, *Yongning Naxi zu de muxi zhi*.

16. Zhan Chengxu, Li Jinchun, Wang Chengquan, and Liu Longchu, *Yongning Naxi zu de Azhu huyin he muxi jiating*, p. 18.

17. Cai Hua, "Discussion du système de parenté mo-so (Naxi) de Yongning (Yunnan)," p. 120; "Une société sans père ni mari," pp. 55–74.

18. The administrative village is at present the basic administrative unit and comprises several villages.

19. Françoise Héritier, "L'enquête généalogique et le traitement des données," in Cresswell and Godelier (eds.), *Outils d'enquête et d'analyse anthropologiques*, pp. 223–65.

CHAPTER ONE: GENERAL PRESENTATION

1. The first appearance of the term *Mo-so,* in Fan Ye's *Houhan shu,* dates from the third century A.D. Different terms can be found later in various Han texts, such as the Chinese annals of the dynasties and the records from Yunnan Province and its districts. Yet, in spite of changes to Chinese characters due to the different transcription style of each era, the pronunciation has stayed the same, that is, *Mo-so.*

Currently, fifty-six ethnic groups are officially recognized by the central government in China. The Han, the majority, are 92 percent of the total population (according to the 1991 census).

2. *Yongning* is a Chinese term that means eternal tranquillity. This place-name first appeared in Chinese texts from the Yuan dynasty (the Mongols). Before then it was called Loudoudan or Dalan. The Na call it Hlidi, which means that place.

3. *Zhao* literally means chief or king; figuratively, it means principality.

4. See *Naxizhu jianshi,* pp. 1–15.

5. To confirm that these are in fact two dialects further study is necessary. The difference between them might not be any bigger than that between one of them and another recognized language from the same linguistic family.

6. Kublai Khan was an emperor of the Yuan dynasty. In 1253, on his way to conquer the kingdom of Dali, west of Yunnan, he stationed his army in Yongning.

Na aristocrats in Yongning also claim to descend from the army of Kublai Khan. Even if it is true that Kublai Khan installed Mongolian chiefs in this region, over the course of history they were integrated among the Na, not the contrary.

7. According to the Chinese constitution, when a group demands official recognition from central and provincial governments, the People's Assembly of the Province only has the right to grant permission for the designation *ren,* which indicates that the group remains to be categorized. For the Na, recognition as Mo-so *ren* means that they are no longer considered part of the Naxi. But only the People's National Assembly has the power to recognize them as a *zu* group.

8. *Manqing* is a plant with an edible root.

479

9. The villagers used their yards as latrines and continue to do so today.

10. The Yi, a neighboring ethnic group living high in the mountains, cultivated opium.

11. Throughout Chinese history, the terminology for territorial and administrative units has undergone many changes. In this work, I generally translate these Chinese names in the following manner: *zhou* as sub-prefecture and *xian* as district; *fu* as prefecture; and *shen* as province.

12. The term *sïpi* means the one that is strongest and dominates others of its kind. For example, the main beam at the top of a roof is called *gu sïpi*. The word *gu* means milieu, the *gu sïpi* dominates and watches over those who live in the house and everything that goes on under its roof, above all the behavior of its inhabitants. In chicken and buffalo fights, the winners are also called *sïpi*.

CHAPTER TWO: SOCIAL STRATIFICATION UNTIL 1956

1. See "The Residence" in chapter 7. The representation of power and status connoted by round central pillars continues even today. During my fourth trip to Yongning, the secretary of the Communist Party committee for the canton of Yongning, who had held this position for three years, was in the process of expanding his house. While reconstructing the main building, he decided to use two round central pillars. His younger brother, the chief of a village grouping, was able to do the same.

2. For the sake of simplicity, I use *sïpi, dzéka,* and *we* as adjectives in certain contexts.

3. The statistics for the three social strata come from data collected by Chinese ethnologists in 1963. See *Yunnan shen Ninglang.*

4. The four modalities of sexual life constitute a main part of this book. See chapters 8, 9, 10, 11, and 12.

5. I deliberately use the term *male* here instead of *paternal* and especially instead of *patrilineal* to avoid the multiple connotations of these concepts of descent.

6. A Chinese unit of weight, 1 *dou* is approximately 6 kilograms; 10 *dou* equals 1 *dan.*

7. The *bankai* was a unit of silver currency in circulation in Yunnan during the first half of the century.

8. Yamaa is a male ancestor of the *zhifu*.

9. A unit of Na land, 1 *dZia* is equivalent to the surface of land that two buffalo can work in a day; 1 *dZia* equals approximately 0.17 *ha*.

10. Statistics for these two types of households are not available. The statistics for the three strata in 1956 come from the investigative reports of Chinese ethnologists (see *Yunnan shen Ninglang*) and do not distinguish between the two types.

CHAPTER THREE: THE POLITICAL REGIME UNTIL 1956

1. Sima Guang, *Zizhi tongjian*, vol. 198, p. 6247.

2. Under the Yuan dynasty, the Han, the ethnic majority of China, became *yi*, that is, they became natives in relation to the Mongols in power.

3. Zhang Tingyu, *Ming shi*, p. 5166.

4. The rule of heredity for the position of *zhifu* will be discussed thoroughly in chapter 12.

5. The following story explains this Han name for the *zhifu*'s family: During the Ming dynasty, between 1403 and 1424, a Na chief went to see the emperor in Peking, who asked his name. The Na chief responded, "A ..." The emperor took this to mean that his name was A and gave him the Han name (阿). Rock claims that in this context the *A* means "I don't understand" in Na. This explanation, however, seems wrong. In Na, "I don't understand" is *nia mao nu*. *A* is either a prefix that expresses respect, as in *Api*, a term that the Na use for the *zhifu* (*pi*, in this case, is an abbreviation of *sipi*), or a prefix that expresses "what" or "how," as in *azi*. Therefore, what the emperor took for a family name must have been the prefix *A* and not the sentence "I don't understand." What does seem true in this anecdote is that the *zhifu*'s receiving a Han name was preceded by a meeting with the emperor.

6. The position of *Zongguan* was filled by individuals from several *lignées* that had separated from the *zhifu*'s family sometime earlier.

7. See chapter 4.

8. The village and the *lignée* in question here are both named Raimi after the title of a member of this *lignée*.

9. The Pumi are another ethnic group living in the Yongning region.

10. The majority of the Pumi are patrilineal.

CHAPTER FOUR: LANDOWNERSHIP

1. The Na use the Han lunar calendar.

2. A *dan* is a Chinese weight measurement: 1 *dan* equals approximately 60 kilos.

3. When the Na asked the *zhifu* for anything, they were required to prostrate themselves in front of him the moment they entered his reception hall.

4. *Liang* is a weight measurement equal to 31.25 grams. *Gu* is a Na land measurement equal to 24 *dZia*.

5. According to legend, wheat and oats are the oldest known grains in the region.

6. Zhou Yinglong and others, *Yunnan tongzhi*.

7. Liu Wenzheng, *Dian zhi*.

8. *Yongbei fu zhi* was written by Chen Qidian and others during the Qing dynasty. *Liang, qian, fen*, and *li* are ancient Chinese weight measurements.

9. For an aristocratic *lignée* to be demoted to the rank of serf was an exceptional phenomenon.

CHAPTER FIVE: RELIGIONS

1. The titles of these rituals are in ancient Na; no one, not even the *daba*, is able to translate their meanings.

2. This list of rituals was obtained from the *daba* of Dapo. Other *daba* claim that there are more. But I do not know the exact number.

3. In 1989, during my third stay in the field, there were four male *daba* (three of them were over seventy, and one was fifty-four). Only one of them knew the teachings and the rituals well, without ever having formally studied with a master. In some villages, there was a person who, having attending many rituals in the past, was able to recall some of their procedures and to recite parts of prayers but unable to explain them.

4. These dates for the construction of the temples in Yongning come from governmental research on the Ninglang District conducted in 1956. They appear to be reliable, since they are backed up by the fact that in the list of Na chiefs, beginning with the seventh *tusi*, each *zhifu* has a Tibetan name listed beside his Han name. According to the genealogy of the Na *zhifu*'s family, the seventh *tusi* inherited his power on February 22, 1496. See *Naxi zu shehui lishi diaocha*.

5. Rock, *The Ancient Na-Khi Kingdom of Southwest China*, vol. 2, p. 391.

CHAPTER SIX: NEIGHBORING ETHNIC GROUPS

1. Dali was an independent kingdom (937–1253) whose capital was to the west of Yunnan. Today, the city is still called Dali.

2. Guangxi is an autonomous region in southeast China and is the equivalent of a province.

3. Population counts of the Yi are unavailable.

CHAPTER SEVEN: THE FOUNDATION OF THE NA KINSHIP SYSTEM

1. Among these sixty-five households, two had only one member: an old man abandoned by his original *lignée* and a mentally ill woman.

2. It was difficult to find anyone capable of providing complete stories on the system of representing the body. Therefore, the stories I collected sometimes seem incoherent. For example: "For his entire life, Abaodgu did not allow any human to give birth. This ban was lifted after his death." If it was only after his death that humans were able to give birth, who put the fetuses into the bellies of newborn girls? In the opposite scenario, if it is always Abaodgu who deposits the fetuses in the bellies of females, he would have to be alive today. There is a third possibility, which is that, no matter the method, once it was decided by Abaodgu, it became a rule, as is the case in a story on the subject of the visit that I will look at later.

3. This belief that bones and flesh come from the mother differentiates the Na from the Han and the Tibetans, for whom bones come from the father and flesh from the mother.

4. Murdock, *Social Structure*, p. 42.

5. I use the term *matriamony* here, to designate the belongings of a *matrilignée*, as an alternative to *patrimony*, since the *patri* in *patrimony* seems to contradict Na facts.

6. Some male chiefs are Lamaist monks.

7. *Bu sï nin* is a ritual service of offerings to the ancestors in one's *lignée*. During this ritual, a *lignée* invites a *daba* to recite its ancestors' names, going back two or three generations. Today, this practice continues only in a few remote villages.

Around New Year's Day, the Na have a custom of exchanging gifts between consanguineal *lignées*.

8. This *bugwe* is also called *tso Zi*, in reference to the hayloft on its second floor and the stable on its ground floor.

9. In the past, the back room or the lower room served as a storage space.

10. I came across only two *matrilignées* that included a +4 generation. This term is unfamiliar to most young people.

11. Murdock, *Social Structure*, p. 93.

12. *Ibid.*, pp. 93–94.

13. *Ibid.*, p. 101.

14. *Ibid.*, p. 105.

15. A *yuan* is a unit of Chinese currency.

16. The term *min dZi* is the strongest expression one can use to insult or curse someone.

17. See chapter 10 on cohabitation.

18. A lineage includes several *lignées*, see below.

19. *Mu* is a Chinese land measurement; 15 *mu* equal 1 *ha* (hectare).

20. Today, all women own traditional costumes, but only women over thirty-five or forty wear them on a daily basis. The young girls put them on during festivals or when they go into the town of Batsïgu.

21. Because the Na are very influenced by the Tibetans, the maternal uncle sometimes makes a *tchoba* (a kind of coat) for the boy, in addition to all the rest, for the puberty ritual. Before the 1960s, children younger than thirteen wore, regardless of their sex, a linen dress made by each *lignée*. However, for more than twenty years now, children have worn Han clothing. Only old people wear

traditional costumes. Young people and the middle-aged usually wear Han or Western clothing. In fact, they follow Han fashion.

CHAPTER EIGHT: THE FURTIVE VISIT

1. The Na call all dogs she-dogs, no matter what their sex. However, the Naxi from Lijiang call all dogs dogs.

2. In reassuring the young woman, my friend was saying that he would acknowledge responsibility if she became pregnant, and therefore she would not have to pay a fine. See chapter 13.

3. The central Chinese government has established criteria according to which the districts are divided into three categories: normal, poor, and extremely poor. The Ninglang District is today one of the forty-four districts in Yunnan that are considered extremely poor.

4. The villagers can be roughly divided into three age-groups: fifteen to thirty years old, thirty to forty years old, and forty years old to the end of life.

5. The word *dhu* means friend; *zï* connotes the masculine. See chapter 9.

6. In Na, *nimi go* means jealousy and jealous; *nimi* means heart, and *go* means bad or sick, so this expression literally means to have a sick heart.

7. The reference to fourteen generations ago, quite obviously, belongs to the realm of folklore. The villagers do not have a precise sense of time.

8. Everyone over forty is included in the middle-aged group, and everyone over sixty is in the old-age group.

CHAPTER NINE: THE CONSPICUOUS VISIT

1. All gifts, whether brought by a member of the *lignée* when he returns from a trip, by a friend, or by someone like myself, a researcher, are called *gwalu pinba*. When meeting a *lignée* for the first time or visiting a friend's house, the proper thing to do is bring a gift, a small part of which will be given in the ritual offering to the ancestors conducted by the female chief of the *lignée* soon after the guest's arrival. *Pinba* are called *gwalu pinba* because the offerings are always placed on the *gwa-lu*. These proprieties are signs of friendship and respect.

2. This more elaborate gift giving has become more frequent today because

the Na have attained a higher standard of living. The gifts might now include a skirt, several shirts, several jackets, a scarf, and a pair of shoes.

3. In an argument between partners in an open relationship, the woman's uncles and brothers never come to her rescue, even if they are in the house, because of the ban on sexual evocation.

CHAPTER TEN: COHABITATION

1. *Gewa* means upper village, *Muwa* means lower village.

2. By *virilocal,* I mean the cohabitation of a woman and a man in the man's house, without taking into consideration whether or not his mother is alive.

3. The number 683 comes from a count of villagers over eighteen in 1963, the age that Chinese law recognizes as the legal coming-of-age for a citizen and the one that Chinese ethnologists referred to at the time. If I were, more realistically, to include girls sixteen years old and older and boys seventeen years old and older, the number of adults would be higher.

4. The Na do not have cemeteries. After a body is cremated, they gather several pieces of the remaining bones and scatter them on a mountain slope behind the village. After some time, the pieces disappear. They do not necessarily put the ashes of a *lignée*'s deceased members in the same spot. It depends on the site chosen by the Lamaist monk for the cremation.

5. Chinese ethnologists claimed that cohabitation was a conjugal marriage and that the household with a cohabitation was a conjugal family. For example, Yan Ruxian and Song Zhaolin argued: "Like the conjugal family of other ethnic groups, the conjugal family [the household with a cohabitation] of the Naxi in Yongning can be seen as an intermediary and temporary link between group marriage and monogamous marriage. It contains, in a rudimentary way, the form of the conjugal family" (*Yongning Naxi zu de muxi zhi,* p. 267).

CHAPTER ELEVEN: THE MARRIAGE OF THE ONLY SON AS A TYPE

1. A ring of boned pork is a piece that has been sliced in circles.

2. After 1956, *daba* were no longer invited. Initially this was because of a ban imposed by the government; now it is due to a shortage of *daba*.

3. The expression *cho do tçi* means to conduct a service of offerings.

4. All in all, 71.4 percent of the cases were caused by a shortage of a member of one of the sexes.

5. I will examine other causes for marriage later.

CHAPTER TWELVE: KINSHIP IN THE *ZHIFU*'S FAMILY

1. I call the inhabitants of the *zhifu*'s residence the *zhifu*'s family, with the exception, of course, of the servants and serfs.

2. The last *zhifu*'s descendants' group includes the *lignées* listed on the *zhifu*'s genealogy that I recorded while in the field in 1988–1989 and 1992.

3. Other members of the family could inherit the position of *zhifu* if the *zhifu* died and had no sons and no brothers. I will come back to this later.

4. The numbers in parentheses refer to generation, in this case +4, and place in the birth order, in this case first.

5. Nadgo and A Zhangshen called each other brother and sister, and while they were *krwadhe*, they were not consanguineal relatives, because although A Zhangshen's father was Nadgo's mother's brother, their mothers were not consanguineal relatives.

6. The practice of calling the brother's wife *Rumi* and the sister's husband by his first name is because of the ban on sexual evocation.

7. The main Han texts I used were Song Lian, "Lijiang lu, Yongning zho," in *Dilizhi* (Geography), vol. 5 of *Yuan shi*, originally printed in 1370; Zheng Yong and Chen Wen (eds.), *Yunnan tu jin zhishu*; Zhou Jifeng, *Yunnan zhi*; Chen Qidian and others, "Yongning tuzhifu"; "Register of the Successions of tuzhifu of Yongning," I, in "Report," 1876, by Wu Yi, Tongzhi of Yongbei zhiliting; II, in "Report," 1894, by Jiang Rihong, Tongzhi of Yongbei zhiliting. See also *Naxi zu shehui lishi diaocha*. The works cited above are all in the library of Yunnan Province in Kunming, China.

The *daba*'s oral account was recorded in 1960 by Chinese ethnologists in *Yunnan Shen Ninglang Yizu zizhixian Yongning Naxizu shehui ji qi muquanzhi de diaocha paogao*, vol. I, p. 39.

8. Song Lian, *Dilizhi* (Geography), vol. 5 of *Yuan shi*, p. 1465.

9. See Chen Qidian and Liu Zao (eds.), "Yongning tuzhifu." Rock cites from this genealogy of the *zhifu* of Yongning; see "Yongbei zhiliting zhi," in *The Ancient Na-khi Kingdom of Southwest China*, vol. 2.

These reports were sent in 1876 and 1894 to the provincial government from the chiefs of Yongbei zhiliting. See *Naxi zu shehui lishi diaocha*, pp. 104–10. See also Song Lian, *Yuan shi*; Zhang Tingyu, *Ming shi*; and Zhao Erxun and others, *Qing Shigao* (The history of the Qing).

10. Kun Gang, "The Various Positions of Indigenous Chiefs," in *Da Qing huidian*, vol. 2, p. 2.

11. Li Hongzhang and others, "Tuguan chengxi," in *Da Qing huidian shili*, vol. 145, p. 2.

12. *Ibid.*, vol. 589, p. 1.

13. Kun Gang, *Da Qing huidian*, vol. 12, p. 2.

14. Li Hongzhang, *Da Qing huidian shili*, vol. 589, p. 1.

15. Wang Xianqian, *Donghua lu*, p. 12.

16. See *Naxi zu shehui lishi diaocha*, pp. 104–10.

17. A *li* is a Han measurement equal to 0.5 kilometer; 10,000 *li* means very far away.

18. Zhang Tingyu, *Ming shi*, vol. 26, p. 7982; Shen Shixing and others, *Ming huidian*, vol. 121, p. 1744.

19. Zhang Tingyu, *Ming shi*, vol. 6, p. 1752.

20. The government of the republic applied the same regulations as the Qing.

CHAPTER THIRTEEN: THE MATRIMONIAL REFORMS

1. The Han leaders who passed this legislation, as well as certain Chinese ethnologists, were not alone in judging Na customs to be morally low. Rock says: "The result of this promiscuous sexual intercourse is an enormous amount of syphilis and other venereal diseases. The moral standard of the Yung-ning is thus anything but high" (*The Ancient Na-Khi Kingdom of Southwest China*, p. 391). Ethnocentrism is a pervasive phenomenon.

2. It appears true that before the 1950s sexually transmitted diseases pre-

sented a real problem in the Yongning region. A director of the local hospital confirmed that in 1985 approximately 5 percent of the population suffered from some form of venereal disease. For the most part, they were from the older generation.

3. Zhan Chengxu, Li Jinchun, Wang Chengquan, and Liu Longchu, *Yongning Naxi zu de azhu huyin he muxi jiating*, p. 308. The local governments and Chinese ethnologists referred to the Na *matrilignée* as a family. In this chapter, the term *family* will therefore be used either in citation or to reflect their point of view.

4. *Yunnan shen Ninglang Yizu zizhixian Yongning Naxizu shehui ji qi muquanzhi de diaocha paogao*, p. 73.

5. *Adhu* means friend in the general sense of the word. During the 1960s, the Chinese ethnologists had not yet discovered the term *açia*. What is more, they contrasted long-lasting relationships with short-term relationships, and some of them even added an in-between category: a medium-long relationship. This misunderstanding was due to the fact that they did not learn the Na language. As demonstrated above, the long-lasting relationship, as a concept of classification, does not exist for the Na, for relationships between lovers can always be short or long, between *açia* as well as between *dhu zï dhu mi*.

6. In its census, the local government noticed that there were many more female adults than male adults, on average 137 females to 100 males. When it added up all of the couples, many of the women were without a partner, and the government found this situation embarrassing.

7. Mao Zedong was the leader of China from 1949 to 1976.

8. Thrown out by their receiving *lignées* and rejected by their original *lignées*, some old people were left lonely and destitute.

9. Zhou Yudong, Jiang Zhongli, and Sun Daixing, "Preliminary Research of the Matrimonial Reform of the Naxi of Yongning," p. 41.

10. With the word *wubaohu*, they are referring to homes that are made up of a single person. Within the parameters of my research, there was one case of this, an old man who did not get along with his brothers and sisters and moved into a small house on his own. He lived in wretched poverty. In fact, he was the

genitor of several people in the neighboring villages, who, of course, gave him nothing.

11. Zhou Yudong, Jiang Zhongli, and Sun Daixing, "Preliminary Research of the Matrimonial Reform of the Naxi of Yongning," pp. 42–43.

12. From 1956 to 1981, the leadership of the People's Commune of Yongning committee was entrusted to individuals from other ethnic groups. It was run by the Han for twelve years, by a Naxi for three years, by a Yi for three years, and by a Bai for three years. During this period, it was always the Han who held the position of secretary of the Communist Party cell for the entire production brigade (the base organization, the equivalent of today's village groupings). Only after 1981 were the Na of Yongning led by Na cadres.

13. Zhou Yudong, Jiang Zhongli, and Sun Daixing, *On the Socialist Reform of the Matrilineal Family of the Naxi in the People's Commune of Yongning in the District of Ninglang in the Yunnan Province*, pp. 27 and 42.

14. The Na called this matrimonial reform "the one wife and one husband campaign" (*yiqi yifu yundong*) and continue to do so today.

15. Zhou Yudong, Jiang Zhongli, and Sun Daixing, "Preliminary Research of the Matrimonial Reform of the Naxi of Yongning," p. 48.

16. The research group automatically believed that its own manner of love was the correct one, according to which love must end in marriage.

Chapter Fourteen: The Modalities of Sexual Life

1. These definition of *marriage* were proposed by Leach in *Rethinking Anthropology*.

2. *Ibid.*, pp. 107–108.

3. P. G. Rivière, "Marriage: A Reassessment," p. 60.

4. *Ibid.*, p. 62.

5. *Ibid.*, pp. 57–58.

6. *Ibid.*, p. 63.

7. *Ibid.*, p. 60.

8. *Ibid.*, p. 62.

9. *Ibid.*, p. 70.

10. *Ibid.*, p. 71.

11. *Ibid.*, p. 70.

12. *Ibid.*, p. 66.

13. Lévi-Strauss, "The Family," in *The View from Afar*, p. 46.

14. *Ibid.*, p. 54.

15. Love, as a passionate emotion, can be qualified but not quantified.

16. The manifestation of one individual's fondness for another constitutes not only a request for feelings from the other, as is often believed, but also a proposition of one's own feelings to him or her. The same is true of a positive response, which can only mean "I propose to you and ask from you the same thing" or "I want to accept your proposition and your request." From the moment the two individuals love each other, they have given each other and taken from each other their feelings. How can we imagine taking without giving oneself or giving without taking? Love can be actualized only through bilateral and reciprocal feelings between the two parties. In a couple's bond of love, each is at once the subject of his pleasurable desires and the object of these same desires in the other. To consider love Eros and Philia, as is often done in the Occident, is to deconstruct an indeconstructible whole.

CHAPTER FIFTEEN: VARIOUS TYPES OF DOMESTIC GROUPS

1. Murdock, *Social Structure*, p. 1.

2. *Ibid.*

3. *Ibid.*

4. *Ibid.*

5. Gough, "The Origin of the Family," p. 52.

6. Héritier-Augé, "La Famille," pp. 273–74.

7. Murdock, *Social Structure*, p. 22.

8. Lévi-Strauss, "The Family," p. 47.

9. *Ibid.*, p. 44.

10. *Ibid.*, p. 45.

CHAPTER SIXTEEN: CONCLUSION

1. When I returned to Yongning in July 1997, the Na administrator told me that this fine had just been abolished.

2. Radcliffe-Brown, *Structure and Function in Primitive Society*, p. 51.

3. Lévi-Strauss, preface to *A History of the Family*, pp. 2–3.

4. *Ibid.*, p. 3.

5. Lévi-Strauss, "La Famille," in *Le Regard éloigné*, pp. 79, 82, 84, 91, and 92.

6. *Ibid.*, p. 83.

Glossary

Han Terms

bankai (半开). Unit of silver money used during the first half of the twentieth century in Yunnan.

bashi (把事). Adjunct of the general administrator.

Cuan (爨). Group that dominated several ethnic groups in the east of Yunnan from the third to the sixth century.

dan (石). Chinese unit of weight; 1 *dan* equals 10 *dou* (see *dou*).

Dian (滇). Abbreviation of the name of Yunnan province.

dou (斗). Chinese unit of weight; 1 *dou* equals about 6 kilograms.

fangzhi (方) or *gaikuan* (志). Summary edited by the local governments.

fu (府). A territorial and administrative unit. I translate this term as prefecture.

gaituguiliu (改土). Campaigns led by the Ming and Qing dynasties that set out to replace the indigenous chiefs with magistrates in ethnic-minority regions.

guanren (管人). Head of jurisdiction under the *zhifu*.

Guanzhuang (官庄). The mandarin's official land or public land. This land is also called *Suiyintian* (随印田), which means the land that accompanies the mandarin's seal.

Guomindang (国民党). Nationalist political party that dominated all of China from 1911 to 1949.

Han (汉). Ethnic majority in China. The Han represent 92 percent of the population (1991 census).

493

hongzhao (红照). A deed to property issued by the Guomindang government.

houtou (伙头). Village chiefs.

ji mi zhi zhi (羁縻之制). Policy adopted by the central government regarding the non-Han ethnic groups, from 221 B.C. to A.D. 1253.

jun (郡). A territorial and administrative unit. I translate this term as prefecture.

kezhang (客长). Chiefs of villages whose inhabitants are not of Na origin.

liuguan (流官). Magistrate; a mandarin on whom the central government (until 1949) conferred a mandate and who could be transferred from one position to another. As opposed to a *tuguan* (see *tuguan*), his power was not hereditary.

lu (路). An administrative and territorial region. I translate this term as prefecture.

Minzu (民族). Ethnic group.

Mo-so (摩梭). Name used by the Han prior to 1956 to designate the Na, the Naxi, the NaRu, and the Nahing.

paishou (排首). Chief of a non-Na village.

Shen (省). Province.

shiye (师爷). Secretary.

tuguan (土官). Indigenous chief named by the central government of each dynasty and by the Guomindang government. His power was hereditary.

tusi (土司). Indigenous chief (non-Han).

xian (县). Still used today, this term is translated as district.

yi di (夷狄). Term used by the Han prior to 1949 to designate non-Han ethnic groups.

yiqi yifu (or *yifu yiqi*) *yundong* (一妻一夫运动). Monogamy campaign.

Yongning (永宁). A canton in the autonomous Yi district of Ninglang (Yunnan). The majority of the Na live here.

zhao (诏). This word literally means chief or king; it figuratively means principality or kingdom.

zhifu (知府). Title of the governor of the prefecture.

zhongjian zhuman (众建诸蛮). Policy adopted by the Ming dynasty that sought to multiply the number of indigenous chiefs in regions in which there was only one, with the goal of weakening his power.

494

zhou (州). A territorial and administrative unit, this term can be translated as district or sub-prefecture and is still in use today.

zongguan (总管). General administrator.

zonghuotou (总伙头). Chief of a village grouping; superior of the *huotou*.

Na and Other Non-Han Terms

açia. A lover who practices the furtive visit.

adhu. Friend.

A-gv. The term that Joseph Rock used to translate *ewu*, the Na word for maternal uncle.

apo. External; branch *lignée*.

baolu. Construction of a little house. This term metaphorically designates the act by which a woman separates from her original household because she does not get along with the other members of her *lignée*.

chai dZié. Putting on a skirt; the puberty ritual for girls.

chumi. Wife.

daba. Na priest.

dabu. *Lignée* chief.

dhu zï dhu mi. Male friend and female friend.

dzé hing. Intimate friend.

dzéka. Commoner.

elu. Official land or public land.

gepié sésé. Conspicuous visit.

gnao. House; founding *lignée*.

hing. People; human beings.

hinshuba. Husband.

hli dzié. Putting on pants; the puberty ritual for boys.

idi. Cooperative use of buffalo between two or more *lignées* after they have reached an agreement.

krulu. The *zhifu*'s private land.

krwadhe. The relationship between consanguineal lineages that do not have any economic ties between them.

495

lhe. Lignée; a group of consanguineal relatives living under the same roof.

min kru. Theft of sex.

moio. Intermediary (arbitrator).

mu min. Name a woman receives in relation to her partner's *lignée* when she moves into his house.

nana sésé. The furtive visit.

ong. Bone; the carrier of hereditary traits for the Na.

ong hing. Bone people; all persons descended from the same female ancestor, independent of their place of residence. We translate this term as consanguineal relative.

Pumi. An ethnic group that has members living in the Yongning region. Most of them follow the patrilineal rule of descent.

raimi (the same as *huotou* in Chinese). Chief of several villages under the regime of the Na *zhifu.*

sïpi. Head, chief, director, or president. This term is also used to designate the aristocracy.

sïzi. Lineage.

ti dzï (jï mao the). Cohabitation in which there was no organized ceremony.

ti dzï jï the. Metaphorical term that means marriage.

we. Serf.

zidu bubu. Division of the matriamony when a *lignée* separates into two parts.

zo min. Name given to a male cohabitant in relation to his partner's *lignée* when he moves into her house.

Other Terms

affine. A relative by marriage.

binary kinship. Kinship made up of social consanguinity and affinity.

cadre. An individual who works for Communist Party organizations and receives a salary from the state.

female-lineal and male-lineal rule of transmission. The rule that only allows for social status to be passed on from mother to daughter for females and from maternal uncle to nephew for males.

lignée. A group of individuals belonging to different generations who are all descendants of the same ancestor and live under the same roof.

matriamony. A *matrilignée's* possessions.

matrilignée. A group of individuals who are all descendants of the same female ancestor and who all live under the same roof. Given the absence of the matrimonial institution in Na society, *matrilignée* and other terms, such as *matrilocality, uxorilocality,* and *virilocality,* are used throughout this book without any reference to marriage, most of the time.

polyandrogyny. Modality of sexual life that allows each individual (male or female) to maintain sexual relations with several partners of the opposite sex at the same time.

unary kinship. Kinship constituted by social consanguinity only.

497

Bibliography

In Chinese

Chen Deqi. "Two Exciting Results of the Studies of the Example of the Matrilineal System: Commentary on Two Works: *Azhu Marriage and the Matrilineal Family of the Naxi in Yongning* and *The Matrilineal System of the Naxi in Yongning*." *Zhongguo shehui kexue* (Social Science in China) (Beijing), 5 (1985).

Chen Qidian and others. "Yongning tuzhifu tusi" (The indigenous *zhifu* of Yongning). In *Yongbei fu zhi* (The account of the prefecture of Yongbei). Edited by Liu Zao. Vol. 25. 1765.

Chen Qixin. "Essay on the Matrilineal Yidu of the Naxi and on the Ovachira of the Iroquois." *Minzu Yanjiu* (Ethnic Minority Studies) (Beijing), 4 (1982).

Chen Zhifang. "Commentary on the Work: The Matrilineal System of the Naxi of Yongning." *Yunnan shehui kexu* (Social Sciences in Yunnan) (Kunming), 5 (1983).

Fan Ye. "Xinan yi zhuang" (The ethnic groups of the southwest). In *Houhan shu* (The history of the late Han). Vol. 6. Collections of Shanghai Edition, 1888.

Fu Maoji. "The Matrilineal Family and the Terminology of Kinship in the Naxi of Yongning." *Ethnic Minority Studies* (Beijing), 3 (1983).

He Jiren and Jiang Zhuyi. *Naxi yu jianzhi* (The handbook of the Naxi language). Beijing: Ethnic Minorities Press, 1985.

499

Kun Gang. *Da Qing huidian* (The collections of decrees of the great Qing). Commercial Press, 1899. Lithograph.

Li Hongzhang and others. "Tuguan chengxi" (The succession of indigenous chiefs). In *Da Qing huidian shili* (The illustration of the collection of decrees of the great Qing). Commercial Press, 1887. Lithograph.

Li Jing. *Yunnan zhilue* (Monographic account of the Yunnan), from the Yuan dynasty (1279–1368).

Liu Wenzheng. *Dian zhi* (The report of the Dian), 1652, under the Ming dynasty.

Mo-so people from the autonomous district of the Yi in Ninglang in Yunnan. *The Report on the Petition to the Organization Concerned with the Central Government to Re-identify the Mo-so and Grant the Wishes of the Mo-so People to Recognize the Mo-so as a Separate Ethnic Group.* Ninglang, July 1982.

Naxi zu shehui lishi diaocha (An investigation of the society and the history of the Naxi). Kunming: Ethnic Minorities of Yunnan Press, 1983. Vols. 1 and 2. Five collections of books on the subject of ethnic minorities by the Press Committee of Yunnan.

Naxizhu jianshi (An account of the history of the Naxi). Kunming: People's Press of Yunnan, 1984.

Qiu Pu. "An Essay on Conjugal Marriage from the *Azhu* Marriage of the Naxi of Yongning." *Social Sciences in Yunnan* (Kunming), 5 (1984).

Shen Shixing and others. *Ming huidian* (The collection of Ming decrees). Reprint, Taiwan: Xinwenfeng Editions, 1973.

Sima Guang. *Zizhi tongjian* (General references for governing). Beijing: Zhonghua Press Edition, 1956.

Song Enchang. "Remnants of the Family of Group Marriage of the Naxi in Yongning," *Studies of the History of Ethnic Minority and of Peripheral Regions* (Kunming), 1 (1975).

Song Lian. *Yuan shi* (History of the Yuan). Reprint, Beijing: Zhonghua Press, 1976.

Wang Chengquan. "Essay on the Causes of the Long Existence of the *Azhu* Marriage and the Matrilineal Family under the Regime of the Feudal Lords." *Forward Thinking* (Kunming), 1 (1979).

Wang Xianqian. *Donghua lu*. Vol. 32. Jiuchao ed. Printed in Hunan, 1884.

Xie Jian. "An Essay on the *Azhu* Marriage of the Naxi of Yongning in Yunnan." *Forward Social Sciences* (Changchun), 3 (1980).

Xie Zhaozhe. *Dian lue* (The story of the Dian), printed under the Ming dynasty.

Yan Ruxian. "A Living Fossil of the Appearance and Development of the Family: Studies on the Various States of the Naxi Family in the Region of Lake Lugu." *Social Sciences in China* (Beijing), 3 (1982).

Yan Ruxian and Song Zhaolin. *Yongning Naxi zu de muxi zhi* (The matrilineal system of the Naxi of Yongning). Kunming: People of Yunnan Press, 1983.

Yanyuan gaikuan (The records of Yanyuan), printed between 1911 and 1949.

Yanyuan xianzhi (Account of the Yanyuan District), printed in the era of Daoguang (1821–1850), under the Qing dynasty.

Ye Rutong. *Yongbei zhiluting zhi* (The record books of Yongbei zhiluting). 1904.

You Zhong. *Zhongguo xinan de gudai minzu* (The ancient ethnic groups of Southwest China). Kunming: People of Yunnan Press, 1980.

Yunnan shen Ninglang Yizu zizhixian Yongning Naxizu Shehui ji qi muquanzhi de diaocha paogao (Investigative report on the society and matriarchy of the Naxi of Yongning in the autonomous district of the Yi of Ninglang in Yunnan). Kunming, vol. 1, 1963; vol. 2, 1977; vol. 3, 1964; and vol. 4, 1978. A report compiled by the investigative team of ethnic minorities in Yunnan from the Institute of Ethnic Minority Research and the Academy of Sciences of China and the Laboratory of Research on Ethnic Minorities from the Institute of Historical Research of Yunnan.

Zhan Chengxu. "The Matrilineal Family of the Naxi of Yongning." *History Monthly* (Beijing), 7 (1965).

Zhan Chengxu, Li Jinchun, Wang Chengquan, and Liu Longchu. *Yongning Naxi zu de azhu huyin he muxi jiating* (The *azhu* marriage and the matrilineal family of the Naxi of Yongning). Shanghai: People's Press of Shanghai, 1980.

Zhang Tingyu. *Ming shi* (The history of the Ming). Beijing: Zhonghua Press, 1974.

Zhao Erxun and others. *Qing Shigao* (The history of Qing). Beijing: Zhonghua Press, 1977.

Zheng Yong and Chen Wen, eds. *Yunnan tu jin zhishu* (Record books of Yunnan). Vol. 3. 1455.

Zhou Jifeng. *Yunnan zhi* (The account of Yunnan). Vol. 8. 1553.

Zhou Rucheng. "Yongning jianwen lu" (Notes on Yongning). In *Naxi zu sheshui lishi diaocha* (Investigation of the society and history of the Naxi), vol. 2. pp. 151–201. Kunming: Ethnic Minorities of Yunnan Press, 1986.

Zhou Yinglong and others. *Yunnan tongzhi* (The general report of Yunnan). Edited by Li Yuanyang. 1576. Reprint, Villa of Lingshi Longyuan, 1934.

Zhou Yudong, Jiang Zhongli, and Sun Daixing. *On the Socialist Reform of the Matrilineal Family of the Naxi in the People's Commune of Yongning in the District of Ninglang in the Yunnan Province* (Kunming). Edited by the Institute of Historical Research of Yunnan, 1977.

———. "Preliminary Research of the Matrimonial Reform of the Naxi of Yongning." *Bulletin of Studies* (Kunming). Edited by the Institute of Historical Reasearch of Yunnan 1 (1978).

In Occidental Languages

Bacot, Jacques. *Ethnographie des mo-so, leurs religions, leur langue et leur écriture.* Leiden: Brill, 1913.

Balandier, Georges. *Anthropologie politique.* Paris: PUF, 1984. Translated by A.M. Sheridan Smith as *Political Anthropology.* New York: Pantheon, 1970.

Bonin, C.E. "Les mossos." In *Les royaumes des neiges: États himalayens.* Edited by C.E. Bonin, pp. 281–96. Paris: Armand Colin, 1911.

———. "Note sur un manuscrit Mosso." *Actes Xie Congr. int. Orient* (1897): 1–10.

Burguière, André, Christian Klapisch-Zuber, Martine Segalen, and Françoise Zonabend, eds. *Histoire de la famille.* Paris: Armand Colin, 1986. Translated by Sarah Hanbury-Tenison, Rosemary Morris, and Andrew Wilson as *A History of the Family.* Cambridge, Mass.: Belknap Press of Harvard University Press, 1996.

Cai Hua. "Discussion du système de parenté mo-so (Naxi) de Yongning (Yunnan)." Master's thesis, University of Paris X, Nanterre, 1986.

————. "Une société sans père ni mari." *Géo* (July 1994): 55–74.

Chavannes, Edouard. "Documents historiques et géographiques relatifs à Li-Kiang." *T'oung Pao* 13 (1912): 565–653.

Cordier, H. "Les mo-sos: Mo sié." *T'oung Pao* 9 (December 1908): 663–88.

Cresswell, Robert, and Maurice Godelier, eds. *Outils d'enquête et d'analyse anthropologiques.* Paris: Françoise Maspero, 1976.

Dumont, Louis. *Introduction à deux théories d'anthropologie sociale.* Paris: La Haye, Mouton, 1971.

————. "Les mariages nayar comme faits indiens." *L'Homme* (Paris), 1 (1961): 11–36.

Evans-Pritchard, E.E. *Kinship and Marriage among the Nuer.* New York: Oxford University Press, 1951.

Fox, R. *Anthropologie de la parenté.* Paris: Gallimard, 1972.

Gough, Kathleen. "The Origin of the Family." In *Toward an Anthropology of Women.* Edited by Rayna R. Reiter, pp. 51–76. New York: Monthly Review Press, 1975.

Goullart, P. *Forgotten Kingdom.* London: John Murray, 1955.

Héritier, Françoise. *Les deux soeurs et leur mère.* Paris: Odile Jacob, 1994. Translated by Jeanine Herman as *Two Sisters and Their Mother.* New York: Zone Books, 1999.

————. *L'Exercice de la parenté.* Paris: Editions du Seuil, 1981.

Héritier-Augé, Françoise. "La Famille." In *Dictionnaire de l'ethnologie et de l'anthropologie,* pp. 273–75. Paris: PUF, 1991.

Hocart, A. M. "Kinship Systems." In *The Life-Giving Myth and Other Essays.* London: Methuen, 1952.

Jackson, A. *Na-Khi Religion.* The Hague: Mouton, 1979.

Leach, E. R. *Political Systems of Highland Burma: A Study of Kachin Structures.* London: London School of Economics and Political Science, 1964.

————. *Rethinking Anthropology.* London: Athlone Press, 1961.

Lévi-Strauss, Claude. *Anthropologie structurale, deux.* Paris: Plon, 1973. Translated by Monique Layton as *Structural Anthropology.* Chicago: University of Chicago Press, 1983.

————. "The Family." In Joachim Neugroschel and Phoebe Hoss. *The View from Afar*. New York: Basic, 1985.

————. "Introduction à l'oeuvre de Marcel Mauss." In *Sociologie et anthropologie*. Edited by M. Mauss. Paris: PUF, 1983. Translated by Felicity Baker as *Introduction to the Work of Marcel Mauss*. London: Routledge and Kegan Paul, 1987.

————. Preface to *Histoire de la famille*. Edited by André Burguière, Christian Klapisch-Zuber, Martine Segalen, Françoise Zonabend. Paris: Armand Colin, 1986. Translated by Sarah Hanbury-Tenison, Rosemary Morris, and Andrew Wilson as *A History of the Family*. Cambridge, Mass.: Belknap Press of Harvard University Press, 1996.

————. *Le regard éloigné*. Paris: Plon, 1983. Translated by Joachim Neugroschel and Phoebe Hoss as *The View from Afar*. New York: Basic, 1985.

————. *Les structures élémentaires de la parenté*. Paris: Mouton, 1967. Translated by James Harle Bell, John Richard von Sturmer, and Rodney Needham, editor, as *The Elementary Structures of Kinship*. Boston: Beacon, 1969.

Murdock, George Peter. *Social Structure*. New York: Free Press, 1965.

Needham, Rodney. *Rethinking Kinship and Marriage*. London: Tavistock, 1971.

Polo, Marco. *Dévisement du monde — le livre des merveilles*. Paris: Editions La Découverte, 1984.

Radcliffe-Brown, A.R. Introduction to *Systèmes familiaux et matrimoniaux en Afrique*. Edited by A.R. Radcliffe-Brown and Cyril Darryl Forde. Paris: PUF, 1953.

————. *Structure and Function in Primitive Society*, Glencoe, Ill.: Free Press, 1952.

Reshetov, A.V. "L'organisation matrilineal chez les Na-khi (Mo-so)." Moscow: Science, 1964.

Rivière, P.G. "Marriage: A Reassessment." In *Rethinking Kinship and Marriage*. Edited by Rodney Needham, pp. 57–70. London: Tavistock, 1971.

Rock, Joseph F. *The Ancient Na-khi Kingdom of Southwest China*. 2 vols. Cambridge, Mass.: Harvard University Press, 1947.

Schneider, David M., and Kathleen Gough. *Matrilineal Kinship*. Berkeley and Los Angeles: University of California Press, 1961.

Verdon, M. *Contre la culture: Fondement d'une anthropologie sociale opérationnelle*. Paris: Editions des Archives Contemporaines, 1991.

Westermarck, Edward. *The History of Human Marriage*. London: Macmillan, 1971.

Zimmermann, F. *Enquête sur la parenté*. Paris: PUF, 1993.